The Garrison State

Other Volumes in the Same Series:

The Garrison State

The Military, Government and Society in Colonial Punjab, 1849–1947

TAN TAI YONG

Sage Series in Modern Indian History-VIII

SERIES EDITORS

Bipan Chandra
Mridula Mukherjee
Aditya Mukherjee

SAGE Publications
New Delhi • Thousand Oaks • London

First published in 2005 by

Sage Publications India Pvt Ltd
B-42, Panchsheel Enclave
New Delhi 110 017

Sage Publications Inc
2455 Teller Road
Thousand Oaks, California 91320

Sage Publications Ltd
1 Oliver's Yard, 55 City Road
London EC1Y 1SP

Published by Tejeshwar Singh for Sage Publications India Pvt Ltd, typeset by S.R. Enterprises in 10/12 Palatino and printed at Chaman Enterprises, New Delhi.

Library of Congress Cataloging-in-Publication Data

Tan, Tai Yong.
    The garrison state: the military, government and society in colonial Punjab 1849–1947/Tan Tai Yong.
        p. cm—(Sage series in modern Indian history; 8)
    Includes bibliographical references and index.
    1. Punjab (India)—History—19th century. 2. Punjab (India)—History—20th century. 3. India—History—British occupation, 1765–1947. 4. Great Britain—Colonies—Administration—History—19th Century. 5. Great Britain—Colonies—Administration—History—20th century. I. Title. II. Series.

DS485.P87T36   954'.55035—dc22   2005   2004026669

ISBN: 0-7619-3336-0 (Hb)   81-7829-472-9 (India-Hb)

Sage Production Team: Ankush Saikia, Radha Dev Raj and Santosh Rawat

Contents

Series Editors' Preface

The Sage Series in Modern Indian History is intended to bring together the growing volume of historical studies that share a very broad common historiographic focus.

In the 50 years since independence from colonial rule, research and writing on modern Indian history has given rise to intense debates resulting in the emergence of different schools of thought. Prominent among them are the Cambridge School and the Subaltern School. Some of us at the Jawaharlal Nehru University, along with many colleagues in other parts of the country, have tried to promote teaching and research along somewhat different lines. We have endeavoured to steer clear of colonial stereotypes, nationalist romanticization, sectarian radicalism and a rigid and dogmatic approach. We have also discouraged the "flavour of the month" approach, which tries to ape whatever is currently fashionable.

Of course, a good historian is fully aware of contemporary trends in historical writing and of historical work being done elsewhere, and draws heavily on the comparative approach, i.e., the historical study of other societies, states and nations, and on other disciplines, especially economics, political science, sociology and social anthropology. A historian tries to understand the past and make it relevant to the present and the future. History thus also caters to the changing needs of society and social development. A historian is a creature of his or her times, yet a good historian tries to use every tool available to the historian's craft to avoid a conscious bias to get as near the truth as possible.

The approach we have tried to evolve looks sympathetically, though critically, at the Indian national liberation struggle and other popular movements such as those of labour, peasants, lower castes, tribal peoples and women. It also looks at colonialism as a structure and a system, and analyses changes in economy, society and culture in the colonial context as also in the context of independent India. It focuses on communalism and casteism as major features of modern Indian development. The volumes in the series will tend to reflect this approach as also its changing and developing features. At the broadest plane our approach is committed to the Enlightenment values of rationalism, humanism, democracy and secularism.

The series will consist of well-researched volumes with a wider scope which deal with a significant historiographical aspect even while devoting meticulous attention to detail. They will have a firm empirical grounding based on an exhaustive and rigorous examination of primary sources (including those available in archives in different parts of India and often abroad); collections of private and institutional papers; newspapers and journals (including those in Indian languages); oral testimony; pamphlet literature; and contemporary literary works. The books in this series, while sharing a broad historiographic approach, will invariably have considerable differences in analytical frameworks.

The many problems that hinder academic pursuit in developing societies—e.g., relatively poor library facilities, forcing scholars to run from library to library and city to city and yet not being able to find many of the necessary books; inadequate institutional support within universities; a paucity of research-funding organizations; a relatively underdeveloped publishing industry, and so on—have plagued historical research and writing as well. All this had made it difficult to initiate and sustain efforts at publishing a series along the lines of the Cambridge History series or the history series of some of the best US and European universities.

But the need is there because, in the absence of such an effort, a vast amount of work on Indian history being done in Delhi and other university centres in India as also in British, US, Russian, Japanese, Australian and European universities which shares a common historiographic approach remains scattered and has no "voice". Also, many fine works published by small Indian publishers never reach the libraries and bookshops in India or abroad.

We are acutely aware that one swallow does not make a summer. This series will only mark the beginning of a new attempt at presenting the efforts of scholars to evolve autonomous (but not indigenist) intellectual approaches in modern Indian history.

Bipan Chandra
Mridula Mukherjee
Aditya Mukherjee

List of Maps and Tables

Maps

Tables

List of Abbreviations

Addl	Additional
Adj. Gen.	Adjutant General
AR	Assessment Report
Cmd	Command
DCRO	Deputy Commissioner's Record Office
DSBs	District Soldiers' Boards
FR	Fortnightly Report
GoI	Government of India
GoP	Government of Punjab
Gov. Gen.	Governor General
Home (Pol)	Home (Political)
IOR	Indian Office Records
LSR	Land Settlement Report
MSS.EUR	European Manuscripts
NAI	National Archives of India
NAM	National Army Museum
Offg	Officiating
PDG	Punjab District Gazetteer
PHP(M)	Punjab Government Home (Military) Proceedings
PP	Parliamentary Papers
Pro(s)	Proceedings
Sec.	Secretary
SGPC	Shiromani Gurdwara Parbandhak Committee

Preface

One of the most distinctive features of Punjab's colonial experience was its close and sustained relationship with the military. In the aftermath of the 1857 Revolt, the established military labour market in north-central India—the mainstay of the Bengal Army—gradually gave way to an alternative, but equally established, military labour market in north-western India, centred on the old Sikh empire in the Punjab. By the 1880s, with the Great Game in vogue and the martial races doctrine dominating recruiting policies, the Punjab province became the principal recruiting ground of the Indian Army. This book examines the impact of the military in the development of colonial Punjab. Given the importance of the army as the bulwark of the British Raj in India, the task of maintaining control over the army's primary recruiting base was a matter of extreme gravity for the British imperial rulers. This study examines the processes and extent by which the province was militarized, largely due to the demands of maintaining a reliable military labour market, from the late nineteenth century onwards. By focusing on the relationship between the military and the colonial state in the Punjab, this study seeks to enhance our understanding of the nature of the colonial state and the mechanism of imperial governance and control in India. It intends also to throw light on the historical continuities in the processes of state-formation by showing how military exigency impinged upon the functioning, and ultimately shaped the character, of the colonial state and society in the Punjab, leaving a legacy which has persisted into the post-colonial states of South Asia.

This study begins with an examination of the processes that led to the opening of certain districts in the Punjab as a recruiting ground for the Indian Army during the second half of the nineteenth century. It analyses the nature of this military labour market and shows that although the recruiting ground was a restricted one, the need to maintain it, nevertheless, influenced key official decisions in the Punjab, most notably the adoption of the Land Alienation Act of 1900 and the repeal of the Colonization Bill in 1907. During the First World War, the need to mobilize and control a substantially expanded recruiting ground led to the integration of the civil administration—with its rural intermediaries—and the military command into a monolithic edifice, thereby laying the foundations of a civil-military regime in the Punjab. This integrated civil-military administration remained very much intact in postwar Punjab to facilitate the management of the problems caused by demobilization and, later, the insulation of the military districts from the political influences of the nationalist movement. The extent to which military considerations influenced the behaviour of the colonial state was emphasized during the Akali agitation between 1920 and 1925, as the government sought to contain Sikh unrest without precipitating a mutiny of Sikh regiments and a rebellion in the Sikh districts. In managing the military districts, the Punjab had traditionally relied on its rural-military allies—the province's landed elites and rural notables. Their importance as military intermediaries of the state facilitated their entrenchment in the provincial legislative councils created by post-war political reforms as well as their subsequent dominance in Punjabi politics in the form of the Punjab National Unionist Party. This was largely achieved through the support of an electoral base which was dominated—during dyarchy and provincial autonomy—by landlords, peasant-proprietors and the military classes. The civil-military regime survived the Second World War, but not before being strained almost to the breaking point by all-India issues such as the food crisis and the demand for Pakistan. The militarization of Punjabi society reached a violent denouement when the province was partitioned at Independence. Nevertheless, the civil-military oligarchy in western Punjab—comprising the military, bureaucracy and landed notables—survived the partition of the province in 1947 and went on to dominate the post-independence state of Pakistan.

Originally conceived as a doctoral dissertation for Cambridge University in the early 1990s, this book has had a long gestation period. During its formative stages, it benefited from invaluable inputs from Professor D.A. Low, my doctoral supervisor. I could not have asked for a better teacher and mentor and I remain grateful for his constant guidance and encouragement over all these years. In the past decade, I have made numerous attempts to prepare the manuscript for publication, only to be distracted time and again. I would have given up if not for the constant encouragement from a number of close friends and colleagues. I would like to express my gratitude to Gyanesh Kudaisya, Medha Kudaisya, Teow See Heng and Lily Kong for their unfailing friendship and encouragement. This book has also benefited from inputs from a number of teachers and scholars. Those who have given invaluable suggestions and comments include Seema Alavi, Imran Ali, Sanjoy Bhattacharya, Lionel Carter, Bipan Chandra, Ernest Chew, Clive Dewey, Gordon Johnson, Indivar Kamtekar, Edwin Lee, Andrew Major, Dilip Menon, Peter Reeves and Anil Sethi.

I am indebted to Bipan Chandra, Aditya Mukherjee and Mridula Mukherjee, the editors of the Sage Series in Modern Indian History, for their role in making this book possible. They not only took an interest in my work but were generous with comments and suggestions. I am grateful to Mimi Choudhury for the meticulous and expeditious care with which she has managed the editorial preparations of the manuscript.

My research has taken me to many archives and libraries, and I wish to record my appreciation towards the staff of the following libraries for their assistance and guidance: India Office Library and Records, National Army Museum, London; National Archives of India, Nehru Memorial Museum and Library, New Delhi; Civil Secretariat Records Office (Lahore Archives), Deputy Commissioner's Record Offices in Jhelum, Rawalpindi and Sargodha districts, Pakistan; Cambridge University Library and the Centre for South Asian Studies, Cambridge; Central Library, National University of Singapore and the National Archives of Singapore.

I have drawn upon material for some of the chapters from pieces that I have published earlier. Chapter four draws upon "An Imperial Home-Front: Punjab and the First World War", originally published in *The Journal of Military History* in April 2000; chapters five and six from "Maintaining the Military Districts: Civil-Military Integration and District Soldiers' Boards in the Punjab, 1919–1939" and "Assuaging the Sikhs: Government Responses to the Akali Movement, 1920–1925", published in *Modern Asian Studies* in 1994 and 1995 respectively; chapters seven and eight from "Punjab and the Making of Pakistan: The Roots of a Civil-Military State" and "Mobilization, Militarization and 'Mal-contentment': Punjab and the Second World War", published in *South Asia* in 1995 and 2002 respectively. I am grateful to the editors of these journals for their permission to draw upon these previously published materials for this book.

This book owes most to Sylvia, who has been involved in the writing of this book from conception to completion. She has been a pillar of strength and support, and the source of love and sustenance that has kept me going. It is to her and our two lovely children, Cheryl and Benjamin, that I dedicate this book.

August 2004   **Tan Tai Yong**

Introduction

Punjab's colonial experience was arguably distinctive in a number of ways. As one of the last major regions to be incorporated into the British Indian Empire, the Punjab territories, unlike the older provinces elsewhere in India, came to be governed as a "non-regulation" province under its own unique style of administration. It was a form of government that emphasized dynamic administrative flexibility over "rigid adherence to legislative regulations" and which became the basis of the paternalistic despotism that was to characterize the famed Punjab school of administration.[1] It was in the Punjab that the British experimented with and created an "new agrarian frontier" through its massive irrigation works that opened huge tracts of land in the arid western districts, leading to large scale migration to and settlement of the so-called new canal colonies.[2] And by the second half of the nineteenth century, following the extraordinary events of 1857, the Punjab became the popularly acclaimed "sword arm of the Raj", maintaining an intimate association with the military by serving as the principal recruiting ground of the Indian Army for more than half a century, from the late 1880s to the end of colonial rule in 1947. Its contribution of military manpower to the colonial armed forces during this period was unmatched by any other province in colonial India: at the turn of the nineteenth century, more than half the combatants

---

[1] See Andrew J. Major, *Return to Empire: Punjab under the Sikhs and British in the Mid-Nineteenth Century* (henceforth *Return to Empire*), New Delhi, 1996, pp. 127–33, and Clive Dewey, *Anglo-Indian Attitudes: The Mind of the Indian Civil Service*, London, 1993.

[2] See Imran Ali, *The Punjab Under Imperialism, 1885–1947* (henceforth *The Punjab Under Imperialism*), New Delhi, 1988.

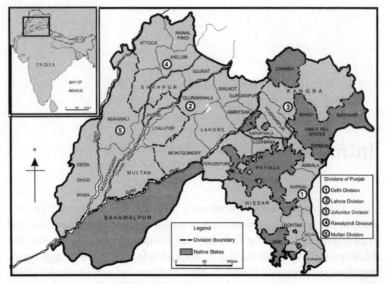

Administrative units of the Punjab
Source: *Imperial Gazetteer of India*, Vol. 20, 1908 (facing p. 394).

of the army were drawn from the province and up to the outbreak of the Second World War, the Punjabi element of the Indian Army (excluding the Gurkhas from Nepal) never fell below sixty per cent. The dominance of Punjabis in the respective arms of the army was far more significant. On the eve of the First World War, Punjabis accounted for sixty-six per cent of all cavalrymen in the Indian Army, eighty-seven per cent in the artillery and forty-five per cent in the infantry.[3] These figures indicate the highest rate of military participation ratio from a particular province ever experienced in colonial India, suggesting that the army was likely to have exerted an unusually dominant influence in the social, economic and political development of the Punjab.

It would, of course, be erroneous to suggest that the militarization of Punjabi state and society emerged essentially out of the demands of colonial rule. The military theme has always featured prominently in the region's pre-colonial history. Strategically situated at the

[3] Annual Caste Returns showing class composition of the Indian Army on 1 January 1910. IOR:L/MIL/14/226.

north-western fringe of the Indo-Gangetic plains, at the frontier
where the Indian subcontinent leads into Central Asia, the Punjab
had for centuries functioned as the "route zone, [connecting] the
areas of Peshawar and over the Hindu Kush into Afghanistan [with]
the cultural-political centres around Delhi and Agra"[4] and the gate-
way for the overland movements of traders and invaders into
India. As a frontier society that had long been the "primary arena
for military conflicts between contestants for political control of
the Indian subcontinent",[5] the Punjab has long been imbued with
a culture of violence and militarism, where internecine armed conflicts were often the order of the day. The military theme persisted
into the nineteenth century, when, after a century of turbulence
and semi-anarchy caused by warring bands battling for territorial
control in the wake of the weakening and eventual collapse of
the Mughal Empire, the Punjab was galvanized into a militarized
state under the Sikh ruler, Maharajah Ranjit Singh.[6] The Sikh
kingdom was a classic example of "a regional Indian fiscal-military
state" in which resources generated by a centralized authority
were largely devoted to maintaining its military machinery.[7] Upon
his death in 1839, however, Ranjit Singh's empire disintegrated
and the Punjab once again fell quickly into the all-familiar pattern
of disastrous internal strife. The ensuing unrest in the Punjab
prompted the British, who were concerned about the security at
the north-western borders of their Indian Empire, to annex the region after two successive military campaigns against the Sikhs in
1845 and 1848.

British rule was to have ushered in a period of Pax Britannica in
which demilitarization and a paternalistic civilian administration
would lay the foundations for the rapid and extensive economic
development of the newly-annexed province. Economic development was achieved from the second half of the nineteenth century
onwards, most spectacularly with the "development of canal irrigation, accompanied by a process of migratory settlement ... in

---

[4] Bernard S. Cohn, *India: The Social Anthropology of a Civilisation*, New Jersey,
1971, p. 25.

[5] Andrew J. Major, *Return to Empire*, p. 1.

[6] See, for example, J.S. Grewal, *The Sikhs of the Punjab*, Cambridge, 1990, pp. 99–115.

[7] D.A. Low, 'Pakistan and India: Political Legacies from the Colonial Past', in
South Asia: Journal of South Asian Studies, Special Issue, Vol. 25(2), 2003, p. 262.

the canal colonies".[8] The British were, however, less successful in their plans for a permanent demilitarization of the province. Within ten years of annexation, the mutiny of the Bengal Army and the ensuing revolt across north-central India had necessitated the re-arming of the Punjab again. By the late nineteenth century, with the north-west of India regaining strategic significance following the onset of the Great Game, the Punjab became, to all intents and purposes, the garrison province of the Raj. Not only was it home to the bulk of the soldiers of the Indian Army, resources were also generously expended for military purposes. The scale of capital invested on building a military infrastructure in the province was not replicated elsewhere in colonial India; in the 1880s the Government of India (GoI) poured billions of rupees into the Punjab for the building of strategic railways, roads and cantonment towns.[9] In the late nineteenth century, state resources, most notably land from the large tracts of newly opened canal colonies, were also diverted for military purposes.[10] The militarization of the Punjab was not without its social and political repercussions. At the end of nearly a century of British rule, the partitioning of the Punjab unleashed a violent reaction on an unprecedented scale. It might safely be asserted that the scale of violence that erupted in the Punjab, which stood in stark contrast to relatively bloodless partition of Bengal, was in no small measure the outcome of the region's long association with the military. The story did not, of course, end in 1947. The Punjab's part in the military dominance of the post-independence state of Pakistan on the one hand, and the militant ethno-nationalist struggle of the Sikhs in Indian Punjab from the 1960s on the other, attest to the persistence of the military legacy in the region.

Despite this long and pervasive entrenchment of the military, with its evident social, economic and political ramifications in the province, there are still major gaps in the understanding of the role played by the military in the development of the Punjab, particularly while under colonial rule. While the existing literature on

---

[8] Imran Ali, *The Punjab Under Imperialism*, p. 4.
[9] See Clive Dewey, 'Some Consequences of Military Expenditure in British India: The Case of the Upper Sind Sagar Doab, 1849–1947', in Clive Dewey (ed.), *Arrested Development in India: The History Dimension* (henceforth *Arrested Development in India*), New Delhi, 1988, pp. 123–42.
[10] Imran Ali, *The Punjab Under Imperialism*, pp. 110–57.

the colonial history of the Punjab readily acknowledge that imperial military requirements had weighed heavily on the political
and economic development of the province,[11] the extent and processes by which the province had become militarized from the late
nineteenth century onwards has not been sufficiently explored.
What was the nature of the relationship between the colonial army
and the government in the Punjab? To what extent were the dynamics of recruitment and military service built on the military
traditions that were already in existence in Punjabi society? What
was the nature of the military labour market—to borrow a term
from Dirk Kolff—in the province, and how was demand (for the
preferred types of military manpower) and supply (the readiness
of the chosen recruits to enlist) in that market managed? How did
the state maintain the loyalty of this crucial military base? And
ultimately, what was the nature of civil-military relations in this
unique garrison province? By focusing on the relationship between
the military and the colonial state in the Punjab, this study seeks to
enhance our understanding of the nature of the colonial state and the
mechanism of imperial governance and control in India. It intends
also to throw light on the historical continuities in the processes of
state formation by showing how military exigency impinged upon
the functioning, and ultimately shaped the character, of the colonial state and society in the Punjab, leaving a legacy which has
persisted into the post-colonial states of South Asia.

The study of the military impact on the development of the province not only enables us to obtain a better understanding of Punjab's
colonial history, but also offers an important way of enriching the
military history of South Asia. Until recently, as Clive Dewey has
lamented,[12] there has been a dearth of literature that has been able
to provide useful insights and analysis on the impact of the military factor in various aspects of South Asian historiography. As
the keystone of the British Empire, the army (or the military) in India
has certainly attracted its fair share of attention. There has clearly
been no shortage of accounts on the subject, and the evolution of

[11] See for instance, Ian Talbot, *Punjab and the Raj, 1849–1947*, New Delhi, 1988;
Imran Ali, *The Punjab Under Imperialism*, New Delhi, 1988; Clive Dewey (ed.),
Arrested Development in India.

[12] See Clive Dewey, 'The New Military History of South Asia', in IIAS (International Institute of Asian Studies), Newsletter, No. 9, 1996.

the colonial armed forces in India, their organizational structure
and operational roles are well-documented.[13] Until recently, however, the military history of colonial South Asia was dominated by
a genre of literature that has been typified on the one hand by a
"bugle and drum" approach to military history that concentrated
on regimental histories, military formations and uniforms, accounts
of campaigns and wars, and biographies, and on the other, by the
triumphalist "guts and glory preoccupation of the British imperial
school."[14] Many of these often offer interesting factual and anec-
dotal material on the institutional set-up of the military in India,
and useful insights into campaigns and wars, but little critical analysis. Beyond a history that places the military's central role in terms
of "self-contained narratives of the major military campaigns in
which Indian and British–Indian armies served"[15]—as one historian puts it—studies of the impact of the military factor in the political, social and economic history of colonial South Asia are few
and far between.

A number of crucial elements need to be addressed if the wider
impact of the military factor in the colonial history of South Asia is
to be understood. First, the part played by the military in the processes of conquest and construction of the Empire in India require
deeper analysis. The establishment of the British dominion in India
from the Battle of Plassey in 1757 to the annexation of the Punjab a
century later came on the back of a series of successful military
campaigns, fought mainly by colonial armed forces comprising of

---

[13] The extent of the very extensive literature on the military in India is evident in
S.N. Prasad's *A Survey of the Work done on the Military of India*, Calcutta, 1976. For a
bibliography of regimental histories, see R.A. Myers, 'Regimental Histories of the
Indian Army: A Bibliography', unpublished MA thesis (University of London, 1957).
A good bibliographic essay on the military in colonial India can be found in Dou-
glas M. Peers, *Between Mars and Mammon: Colonial Armies and the Garrison State in
Early Nineteenth-century India*, London, 1995, pp. 269–73.

[14] Some of the more notable books on the Indian Army in this genre include T.A.
Heathcote, *The Indian Army: The Garrison of British Imperial India, 1882–1922*, London, 1974; Boris Mollo, *The Indian Army*, Poole, 1986; Charles Chenevix-Trench, *The
Indian Army and the King's Enemies, 1900–1947*, London, 1988; Sita Ram, *From Sepoy
to Subedar*, translated by Lieutenant Colonel Norgate and edited by James Lunt,
London, 1988; Field Marshal Lord Roberts, *Forty-One Years in India. From Subaltern
to Commander-in-Chief*, London, 1897, 2 Vols.

[15] *Ibid.*, p. 268.

mainly Indian regiments led by British officers. Indeed, of the many ingenious exploits of the British during their 200-year presence in South Asia, one of the most significant, and perhaps most ironic, was the creation and establishment of a formidable Indian-based colonial army, to which was entrusted the responsibilities of holding and defending the Empire. How was the sword of conquest forged, used and maintained? That this mighty military machinery "was put together out of materials within the subcontinent"[16] perpetuated its own dilemma which was manifested most dramatically during the 1857 Mutiny of the Bengal Army. The outbreak and eventual suppression of the military mutiny that turned into a political revolt was a timely reminder that imperial supremacy and dominance in India rested primarily on military power, of which the army was the key instrument. It demonstrated, at the same time, that the colonial army was always a double-edged sword: if it served as the final arbiter of imperial order, it was also its greatest threat. This was a truism that remained right up to the final stages of British rule in India, with the army remaining the last line of defence for internal security, and an indispensable instrument of coercion against threats to the colonial state. Even at the apogee of British power in India, senior officials, civilian as well as military, constantly reminded themselves that the India they ruled had to remain, at its core, a garrison state. The Governor of Bombay best expressed that lingering sentiment when he said in 1875: "We hold India by the sword. If we cease to maintain our military ascendancy, our rule will speedily come to an end ... thus the maintenance of the highest state of efficiency of everything connected to the army becomes most binding to the British government".[17]

If it has become axiomatic that military might formed the very basis of imperial power and that the army was constantly the major consumer of state revenues and resources, it is not unreasonable to assume that the colonial state was in effect a highly militarized polity. How was this expressed in civil-military relations, and what were the impact and long-term repercussions of militarism (or militarization) on the ideological and structural bases of the colo-

[16] Robert E. Frykenberg, 'India to 1858' in Robin W. Winks (ed.), *The Oxford History of the British Empire, Volume V: Historiography,* Oxford, 1999, p. 201.

[17] Colonel J. McDonald, Secretary to Government of Bombay, Military Department, 29 June 1875, in *Parliamentary Papers* (henceforth *PP*), 1877, Vol. 62, p. 33.

nial state in India? That the military clearly persisted as a major factor in India's colonial system in the eighteenth and nineteenth century has been well established. Recent studies have suggested that from very early on, during the eighteenth century, the great conquistadors of the East India Company—Robert Clive and Warren Hastings in particular—were left in no doubt that British dominance in India was secured by armed force and that Company rule had to be predicated upon the establishment of a military-fiscal regime, in which centrally collected and controlled revenues were utilized for the maintenance of an all-powerful army. The "Clive-Hastings model of a British military-fiscal state" in India was followed in the early nineteenth century by what David Washbrook calls a "very military state", in which the army was a dominant and "highly visible" institution, where soldiers assumed civilian functions, including revenue collection, and civil disorder would often trigger a military response with military-style punishment.[18] Douglas Peers[19] has shown that during the first half of the nineteenth century, with the Company maintaining a constant state of preparedness for war in India, the colonial administration and treasury were virtually held ransom by an increasingly autonomous and demanding army and by the acceptance that British rule was ultimately underpinned by its all-powerful military force. The military-fiscal tradition was to persist into the twentieth century, but came to be adopted in large measure (and concentrated) in the Punjab, which already had its own long history of militarization, when after the events of 1857 the province was made into the military bulwark of the Raj. It was therefore Pakistan, and not India, that became the direct successor of the "military state", as D.A. Low explains, for "Pakistan's post-independence propensity towards a military-dominated state" had a clear and direct lineage that could be traced to the early military-fiscal state of Company rule through the re-entrenchment of the military in the Punjab from the late nineteenth century onwards.[20] If Low's argument holds, the story of

[18] D.A. Washbrook, 'India, 1818–1860: Two Faces of Colonialism' in Andrew Porter (ed.), *The Oxford History of the British Empire, Volume III: The Nineteenth Century*, Oxford, 1999, pp. 395–421.

[19] Douglas Peers, *Between Mars and Mammon: Colonial Armies and the Garrison State in Early Nineteenth-century India*, London, 1995.

[20] D.A. Low, 'Pakistan and India: Political Legacies from the Colonial Past', in *South Asia: Journal of South Asian Studies*, Special Issue, Vol. 25, 2, 2003, pp. 257–72.

the Punjab, indeed, provides a critical historical juncture in the pre-history of Pakistan.

While security and military concerns dominated policies and imprinted itself on state structure, it is important to note that the army did not function in isolation from the milieu in which it operated. The military organization in India, and the way in which it operated, raises important questions with broad and significant historical implications not least because it often interacted intensively with indigenous societies in which it was based.[21] The construction of strategic railways and cantonment towns effected technology transfers and generated a multiplier effect on local economies. Intelligence gathering required extensive networks and close civil-military interactions at all levels while the political economy of the militarily sensitive border regions was often shaped by military imperatives.

Perhaps the most fundamental aspect of the military's penetration into indigenous society was the enlistment of local Indian communities as sepoys for the colonial armed forces. Paradoxically, the army in India, upon which British military predominance in India rested, was not made up of European expeditionary or occupational forces; the overwhelming bulk of the soldiery was drawn from the very population that the army was ultimately expected to coerce and control. An understanding of the relationship between the colonial state and the sepoys is crucial in understanding the nature of imperial rule. The military hierarchy, as David Omissi points out, provided a "microcosm of the wider colonial order".[22] A couple of issues here warrant closer attention. The first pertains to British recruitment policies. As the colonial army was a voluntary force, indeed a mercenary one in which military enlistment and service in uniform were motivated more by material gains rather than national (or communal/caste and ethnic) pride, how did the military always ensure a constant supply of recruits for its rank

---

[21] Some studies which have attempted to tackle these issues are Stephen Cohen, *The Indian Army: Its Contributions to the Development of a Nation*, Berkeley, 1971; Imran Ali, *The Punjab Under Imperialism*; Clive Dewey, 'Some Consequences of Military Expenditure in British India, pp. 93–169; and Clive Dewey, 'The Rural Roots of Pakistani Militarism' in D.A. Low (ed.), *The Political Inheritance of Pakistan*, London, 199, pp. 255–83.

[22] David Omissi, *The Sepoy and the Raj: The Indian Army, 1860–1940*, London, 1994, p. 18.

and file, especially when the occasions warranted it? How were these recruits selected, and why did they respond to the call of military service?

A second, related issue revolves around the role of the colonial state in securing the stability of the social base of the Indian Army, and the basic assumption here is that the function of the military in India cannot be divorced from its wider social and political context. If Indian soldiers, armed and organized for fighting, ultimately posed a threat to security, how were their loyalty and reliability maintained? Clearly, the tasks of securing the reliability of the Indian Army did not merely pertain to regimental discipline and punishment; the maintenance of its social base—the soldier at his home—was equally, if not more, important, as 1857 showed. One could plausibly argue that it was in the soldiers' homes and villages, and not in the regiments, that the "loyalty" of the army was often won or lost. Similarly, the maintenance of the recruiting ground did not merely entail ensuring a constant supply of recruits. More than that, it demanded the safeguarding of the interests of the general military population—recruits, serving soldiers, pensioners and their dependents—as a whole. The tasks of maintaining the army, therefore, had to begin in the military districts, where it involved keeping the soldiers and their families contented and insulated from external political influences.

In this respect, the close analysis of military labour markets, as I have suggested above, can be instructive in providing insights into the intricate manner in which the military, state and society interacted with each other, in the process shaping economies as well as identities. In his penetrating study of the evolution of the military labour market of north-central India from the medieval period to the mid-nineteenth century, Kolff's ethno-historical study gives a good account of how the Indian north-central military market provided open avenues for employment which then broke down the barriers of ascriptive identities and blurred the distinctions between ethnic groups during the eighteenth and nineteenth centuries.[23] Similarly, David Omissi's ground-breaking study of the army from the perspective of the sepoys offers a refreshing and important dimension to the history of the military in India. By

[23] Dirk H.A. Kolff, *Naukar, Rajput and Sepoy: The Ethnohistory of the Military Labour Market in Hindustan* (hereafter *Naukar, Rajput and Sepoy*), 1450–1859, Cambridge, 1990.

looking closely at the sepoy and the reasons for his participation in the colonial armed forces, Omissi provides useful insights on the structure of military collaboration that was essential for the maintenance of the army in India.

At a broader level, therefore, this bottom-up history of military recruitment and civil-military integration in colonial Punjab offers an attempt to contribute to and enlarge the scope of the military history of South Asia. It seeks to demonstrate the extent to which military penetration and the military structure had left an imprint on colonial state and society. In the case of the Punjab, how was its fate affected by its long and intimate association with the military, and what legacies did militarization leave?

To put our discussion into context, it is first of all necessary to examine the processes that led to the opening of the Punjab as the main recruiting ground for the Indian Army. It has become commonplace to refer to the Punjab towards the end of British rule there as the "sword arm of the Raj". But how and why did the Punjab, coming late as it did to British rule, come to assume such a prominent position as the primary recruiting ground for the Indian Army? Chapter one examines the process that led to the opening of the Punjab as the principal recruiting ground for the Indian Army towards the end of the nineteenth century by showing that initial policies of demilitarization had to be reversed following the outbreak of the Great Revolt of 1857, when an alternative army had to be raised to combat the Bengal regiments which had mutinied. In the aftermath of the Revolt, the British first reconstructed their Indian Army by enlisting Punjabi recruits to balance the remnants of the Bengal Army. By the 1880s, the Punjab regiments came to be favoured over the Bengal soldiery as they were deemed more suitable to function in the north-western passes from where the perceived threat of the time—a Russian invasion—would come. Thereafter, and for the next half-century, the Punjab became the principal military bulwark of British rule in India.

Although the position of the Punjab as the main recruiting ground for the Indian Army is generally well known, much less, however, is understood about the actual nature of the military labour market in the Punjab. What was the size of this market in the Punjab, and who were recruited and from where? How was recruitment actually carried out and what motivated the so-called military classes amongst the Punjabis to take up military service with the British? How was this military labour market then provided for? Chapter two shows that despite the commonly-held belief to the contrary, the area from which recruits were drawn in the Punjab was actually a limited one. These military districts, as I call them, were carefully selected and the martial race ideology which governed military recruitment at the turn of the twentieth century had as much an element of location as of race. The exclusive recruitment strategy, coupled with the economic dimension of enlistment created a recruiting equilibrium in which demand and supply were kept in careful balance.

Punjab's involvement in the First World War brought about substantial changes in the recruiting ground, the ways in which recruitment was carried out and the state's role in it. The Punjab supplied more than sixty per cent of the manpower raised in India during the war, and all twenty-eight districts of the province were opened for recruitment. The mobilization of the province during the war consequently involved the establishment of a close and extensive nexus between the civil government and the military command. Chapter three examines the effects of the war on the recruitment process in the Punjab, and shows how the need to mobilize and control the substantially expanded recruiting base in the Punjab during the war brought about the interlinking of the civil and the military structures within the province. This was to lay the foundation for the establishment of an integrated civil-military administration in the Punjab.

The next three chapters run more or less parallel to each other and examine how developments in the Punjab between the wars perpetuated this nexus between the military and the state in the Punjab. In the immediate aftermath of the First World War, a combination of war weariness, economic hardship and political unrest in the Punjab threatened to disrupt its military districts. As these problems were of an economic, social and political nature, the Punjab government found itself compelled to cooperate closely with the military in order to manage them. The integrated civil-military administration therefore remained very much intact in post-war Punjab, and was institutionalized in the form of the District Soldiers' Boards. These unique civil-military organizations created by the state and the military to tackle post-war problems were maintained till the end of the Raj, and remained a part of the bureaucratic edifice of the Punjab throughout, effectively insulating

the military districts from the gathering momentum of the nationalist movement in the 1920s and 1930s. This theme of civil-military
integration during the inter-war period, and the institution which
facilitated it, will be examined in chapter four.

The salience of the civil-military nexus in the Punjab was also
reflected in the orientation and behaviour of the colonial state,
particularly in its responses to civil unrest that threatened to affect
the military districts. The extent to which military considerations
influenced the behaviour of the state was emphasized during the
Sikh agitation between 1920 and 1925. The Sikh unrest was rooted
in the important Sikh recruiting grounds of central Punjab, and at
its height threatened to destabilize the Sikh regiments and to erupt
into a local rebellion in the Sikh districts. Government responses
to the movement reflected its concern to contain Sikh unrest without precipitating a mutiny of Sikh regiments and a rebellion in the
Sikh districts. The Akali movement has been examined in depth in
chapter five as it shows clearly the political and military implications of a disrupted recruiting base, as well as how government
policies and orientation were affected by military considerations.

In managing the military districts the Punjab government had
traditionally relied on its rural-military allies, the province's landed
elites and rural notables. Their importance as military intermediaries of the state, especially emphasized during the First World
War, facilitated their entrenchment in the provincial Legislative
Councils created by political reforms after the war, as will be shown
in chapter six. The rural-military elites eventually dominated Punjab
politics in the form of the Punjab National Unionist Party, which
was able to remain in power through the support of its electoral
base comprising the landlords, peasant-proprietors and the military classes which constituted the overwhelming bulk of the
Punjab's electorate both during dyarchy and provincial autonomy.
Their entrenchment in the local political structure was to reinforce
civil-military integration in the province.

The special bond between the rural-military elites and the colonial state in the Punjab was severely tested during the Second World
War. When the province was mobilized in 1939, the Punjab, now
practised in the processes of civil-military cooperation, seemed
well placed to handle the challenges ahead. But, as chapter seven
shows, mobilization and militarization did not reinforce the garrison
province as it had done in the previous war. Although wartime

discontent, all-India political developments and the food crisis weakened the collaborative mechanism that had formed the bedrock of the colonial state in the Punjab, it did not disrupt the civil-military oligarchy, particularly in the western part of the province. Following Partition the western rump came to constitute the core of the new Pakistani state and became the basis of the civil-military dominance that followed.

ONE

A "Return to Arms": Colonial Punjab and the Indian Army

The identification of local collaborating groups, or indigenous allies, and their incorporation into the structures of colonial rule was an essential strategy adopted by European rulers in their subjugation and control of non-European societies. Of the different types of collaborating groups, ruling classes, landlords and merchants, the most important were those who served in the imperial armed forces, given that military power was often the underpinning factor in the creation and maintenance of imperial authority. This being the case, recruiting strategies adopted by imperial rulers, by which local military allies were identified and absorbed into the ranks of their native armies, were usually a matter of crucial importance.

The case in colonial India is a prime example. The creation of the British Indian Empire and its subsequent garrisoning was achieved largely with Indian manpower. Initially, the East India Company recruited their local soldiers, or sepoys, from available local manpower sources within the vicinity in which they first established their foothold in the subcontinent. But by the nineteenth century, as the armed forces of the East India Company grew in size and became better organized, distinct military labour markets emerged in different parts of the Empire from the Gangetic plains in the north to the Carnatic plains in the south. The three Presidency Armies, Madras, Bombay and Bengal, had, by the nineteenth century, each developed their respective sources of military manpower to which recruitment was faithfully restricted. The Madras

Army's recruiting ground included most of south India, and from there, a diversity of social and ethnic groups—Malabaris, Guntars, Rajputs, Muslims and Tamils—provided its mainstay.[1] The Bombay Army, like the Madras Army, was composed of men from a wide variety of social and religious backgrounds. But it too had its particular recruiting grounds, and by the early nineteenth century the overwhelming bulk of the Bombay Army was constituted by Hindustanis and Konkanis from the Gangetic plains.[2] The Bengal Army, unlike its two southern counterparts, was more restrictive in its choice of recruits. To start with, the militarized north Indian peasantry provided a rich source of military manpower from which officers from the Bengal Army could pick and choose what they regarded were the "handsomest and cleanest looking men" for their regiments.[3] High-caste Rajputs and Brahmins, sought after by regiments of the Bengal Army, took advantage of the economic opportunities that military service offered to dominate posts in the regiments at the expense of lower castes. As a result, regiments of the Bengal Army were filled almost entirely with high caste Rajputs and Brahmins from Rohilkhand, Oudh and Bihar by the middle of the nineteenth century.[4]

But within a period of less than fifty years, by the end of the nineteenth century, all this had changed. The old recruiting grounds of the Company had virtually ceased to be used, and in their place emerged not several, but one main recruiting ground for the British Indian Army.[5] By about 1900, slightly more than half the combatants

[1] Lieutenant Colonel Sir Wolesley Haig, 'The Armies of the East India Company' in H.H. Dodwell (ed.), *The Cambridge History of India*, Cambridge, 1932, Vol. 6, p. 158.

[2] In the early nineteenth century, Hindustanis and Konkanis accounted for over ninety per cent of the native regiments of the Bombay Army. Madan Paul Singh, *The Indian Army Under the East India Company*, Delhi, 1976, p. 156.

[3] T.A. Heathcote, *The Indian Army: The Garrison of British Imperial India, 1822–1922*, London, 1974, pp. 83–84.

[4] See Dirk Kolff, *Naukar, Rajput and Sepoy*, pp. 177–81.

[5] The term "Indian Army" came into official use following Kitchener's reorganisation in 1903 to distinguish between British officered Indian regiments and regiments of the British Army serving in India. Prior to 1903, the term "Army in India" was used to refer collectively to the Bengal, Madras and Bombay Armies and the British and European regiments garrisoned in India. For an account of the growth and development of the armed forces in colonial India, see *Army in India and Its Evolution*, Calcutta, 1924.

of the native regiments of the army in India were recruited from the region known as Greater Punjab[6] in north-western India. What had brought about this dramatic inversion in the recruiting pattern of the colonial armed forces in India, from the utilization of a wide and diverse range of recruits to an eventual concentration in the north-western region of India, principally in the newly annexed province of Punjab? To the extent that the value of local military allies were defined in the context of imperial security and strategic considerations, the composition of the local armed forces in India underwent changes as British threat perceptions shifted in the second-half of the nineteenth century, from the Mutiny and Rebellion in 1857 to the Great Game against Russia thereafter. The changes in the composition of the army in India and the consequent contraction of the recruiting grounds were the result of the re-selection by the British of their military allies in India.

This chapter will explain the gradual opening of the Punjab as the main military labour market of the army in India during the second half of the nineteenth century. This will be seen in the context of the shifting security concerns of the colonial state in the wake of the Great Revolt of 1857.

Annexation and Demilitarization

With the annexation of the Punjab by the British in 1849, a potentially rich recruiting ground in the north-west of India was laid open for the regular native infantry and cavalry regiments of the Bengal Army. Located on the strategic north-western invasion route from central Asia into India proper, the region known as the Punjab has witnessed an almost interminable series of violent military and political struggles. For at least 800 years, from the eleventh century

---

[6] At annexation, the region known as the Punjab stretched from the Afghan border to Delhi. Although Punjab proper refers to the five inter-riverine tracts between the Indus and the Sutlej, the name Punjab has been applied historically to cover a much wider area stretching from the trans-Indus frontier districts of Peshawar, Kohat, Bannu, Dera Ismail Khan and Dera Ghazi Khan to Delhi in the east. In 1901 the five frontier districts were separated from the Punjab and formed into the North-Western Frontier Province, and in 1911, Delhi was separated from the Punjab when it replaced Calcutta as the imperial capital of the Raj. O.H.K. Spate, T.A. Learmouth and B.H. Farmer, *India, Pakistan and Ceylon: The Regions*, London, reprint, 1960, p. 518.

to the end of the eighteenth century, the history of this frontier region has seen at least seventy invasions and the rise and fall of several non-Punjabi dynasties.[7] This long history of turbulence and instability, together with a demanding physical environment, has produced in the Punjab a restless frontier society prone to violence and militarism.[8] The period of Sikh rule in the Punjab had seen the transformation of the region's highly militarized and violent peasantry[9] into a veritable military labour market supplying the Sikh army of Ranjit Singh. In the first three decades of the nineteenth century the Sikh army—organized, equipped and trained along western lines—provided a major source of employment for the peasantry of the Punjab. The groups incorporated into the military were the erstwhile military followers of the Sikh confederacies, Muslim tribesmen from western Punjab, Hindu Jat peasants from the east and the Sikh peasantry of central Punjab.[10] The death of Ranjit Singh in 1839 brought about a succession crisis at the Punjab court, and in the absence of a strong successor, the Sikh army emerged as the most powerful arbiter in Punjabi politics.[11] During this period, the strength of the army increased from about 80,000 in 1839 to 123,000 in 1844.[12] Eventually, the political deterioration caused by internecine feuding and factional in-fighting, as well as the increasing menace of the Sikh army, prompted the British situated to the east of the Jumna to intervene. After the first Anglo-Sikh War in 1846, the eastern part of the Sikh kingdom, the trans-Sutlej territories of Jullunder and Hoshiarpur were annexed, and in the process, a portion of the Sikh military labour market was opened to the British. This was duly exploited by the British, who had been impressed by the fighting qualities of the Sikhs, and in 1847 two regiments of Sikh infantry, the Ferozepur and Ludhiana

---

[7] See Andrew J. Major, *Return to Empire*, pp. 1–2.

[8] *Ibid.*

[9] For an account of the militarization of the peasantry of the Punjab following the diminishing of Mughal authority in the region, see Irfan Habib, *The Agrarian System of Mughal India*, Delhi, 1963. See also Muzzafarh Alam, *Crisis of Empire in Mughal North India: Awadh and the Punjab, 1707–48*, Delhi, 1986.

[10] C.A. Bayly, *Indian Society and the Making of the British Empire*, Cambridge, 1988, p. 127.

[11] For an insightful and authoritative account of the transition from Sikh to British rule in the Punjab, see Andrew J. Major, *Return to Empire*.

[12] Fauja Singh Bajwa, *The Military System of the Sikhs*, Delhi, 1964, p. 102.

Regiments, were raised. In the same year, the famous Guides Corps of Lieutenant Harry Lumsden was formed, comprising mainly of Sikhs from the annexed region.[13] The rest of the Punjab was still dominated by the old Sikh army, but not for long. In 1849 a revolt of the Sikhs in Multan sparked off the second Anglo-Sikh War, which led eventually to the final defeat of the Sikh armies and the annexation of the entire Punjab to the British Indian Empire. Together with the acquisition of the erstwhile Sikh kingdom, the British inherited the remnants of the once all-powerful military force in the Punjab comprising some 60,000 soldiers, mostly Sikhs, who had been disbanded and thrown out of employment.

The presence of such a large force of unemployed soldiers, amidst a potentially volatile population, at the point of annexation proved a problem for Governor General Dalhousie. It was tempting to allow the Bengal Army to exploit this available source of manpower, to wean the army away from its dependence on the north-central military labour market. Furthermore, the Sikhs had been trained by Europeans, and could easily be incorporated into the Bengal Army. However, the Governor General had serious misgivings about having Punjabis, especially the Sikhs, back in arms again so soon after they had been defeated. He was anxious to pacify the newly annexed region to lay the foundation for a stable civil government that would bring about the rapid development of the province, but he was only too aware that before all that could be achieved, the Sikh population had first to be demilitarized. He took the view that the "Sikhs, a people warlike in character and long accustomed to conquest, must of necessity detest the British",[14] and as long as they were held under subjugation, they would welcome any opportunity to again wage war against the British. As he saw it, "there will never be peace in the Punjab so long as its people are allowed to maintain the means and the opportunity of making war".[15] Dalhousie was therefore determined to render the Sikhs submissive and harmless, and he sought to achieve this by depriving them of the means of resistance and facilities for war.[16]

[13] Boris Mollo, *The Indian Army*, Poole, 1981, p. 52

[14] Despatch from Governor General (Gov. Gen.) to Secret Committee, 7 April 1849, in *Papers Relating to Punjab, 1847–49, PP*, 1849, Cmd. 1071, Vol. 41, p. 700.

[15] *Ibid*.

[16] *Ibid*., p. 702.

John Lawrence, a member of the newly constituted Board of Administration, and later Chief Commissioner of the Punjab, shared his Governor General's fears. He stated

> I do not like to raise large bodies of old Sikhs.... I recollect their strong nationalities ... and how much they have to gain by our ruin.[17]

Within six weeks of annexation, backed by the presence of a strong coercive force of 50,000 soldiers of the Bengal Army, the Governor General accordingly ordered the Board of Administration to push ahead with the task of disbanding the erstwhile Sikh army. He further instructed his Commander-in-Chief, General Sir Hugh Gough, to take steps to disarm this "turbulent population while they are still disheartened and in fear of punishment".[18] A proclamation was issued to confiscate all arms; possession of gunpowder and arms of all description was made illegal, and offenders were threatened with heavy punishment. Consequently, more than 120,000 weapons of all sorts, ranging from daggers to matchlocks, were confiscated in the Punjab.[19] A general muster of Sikh soldiers was subsequently called at Lahore, where nearly 50,000 soldiers of the former Sikh army were paid off and disbanded. Military strongholds throughout the province, except those which were needed by the new British administration for military and political purposes, were dismantled.[20]

While the act of demilitarization was carried out to minimize the risk of a revolt by the disgruntled and demobilized Sikhs, it also had the effect of imposing the psychological dominance of the victors over the vanquished. Indeed, it has been pointed out that the paternalistic administration that was quickly established to govern the province had a "strong military flavour ... in both form and spirit",[21] and was a "masterly attempt" to "prolong the atmosphere of military conquest...".[22] The physical and psychological subjuga-

---

[17] R. Bosworth-Smith, *Life of John Lawrence*, London, 1883, Vol. 2, p. 53.

[18] *General Report on the Administration of the Punjab for the Years 1849–50 and 1850–51*, in *PP*, Misc. 1854, Vol. 69, p. 459.

[19] *General Report on the Administration of the Punjab, 1850–51*, p. 480.

[20] *Ibid.*

[21] Andrew J. Major, *Return to Empire*, p. 127.

[22] Eric Stokes, *English Utilitarians and India*, Oxford, 1955, p. 268.

tion of the local population may have, for the moment, been effectively administered, but Dalhousie was aware that it was politically injudicious to leave several thousands of ex-soldiers without employment. When these soldiers were sent back to their villages following the disbandment of their regiments, they found limited economic opportunities there. The situation was further exacerbated by a general fall in agricultural prices soon after annexation, giving rise to an increase in crimes and dacoity (banditry) in the Punjab countryside. To alleviate the situation Dalhousie decided, the general policy of demilitarization notwithstanding, to make use of the Sikhs and Punjabis to control the newly created northwestern frontier of the Indian empire. The annexation of the Punjab had extended the Empire's geographical and political frontier in the west to be roughly coterminous on the north-west frontier and brought the British in contact with the troublesome and warlike Pathan tribes there. The policing of this newly created 800-mile frontier, an area with a trying climate and very difficult terrain, had initially been entrusted to locally raised horse and foot levies and police battalions.[23] Aware that the annexation of the Punjab had created a new military situation, Dalhousie decided to recruit Punjabis for service at the frontier. This had two obvious advantages. On the one hand this would provide some employment for the disbanded Sikh soldiers and other Punjabis, and on the other, the irregular regiments would have soldiers who were better adapted for the terrain and climate at the frontier. In 1849 the Board of Administration was empowered to raise ten regiments of Punjabis, five of cavalry and five of infantry, to form the Punjab Irregular Frontier Force, to replace the levies and police battalions. It was originally intended that these irregular regiments, each of which would consist of four European officers, sixteen native officers and 900 native sepoys, be filled with Punjabis. As a form of control, the Board required that these regiments be constituted in the following proportion: fifty per cent Punjabis, mainly hillmen (from Kangra district) and Muslims, twenty-five per cent Sikhs and twenty-five

---

[23] Irregular regiments were occasionally raised to add to the strength of the Bengal and Bombay Armies, and were normally used for frontier duties. Irregular regiments were considerably cheaper than regiments of the line, and had only a sixth of the full number of European officers in a normal regiment. Furthermore these regiments were usually recruited from the border tribes.

per cent Hindustanis.[24] Despite these guidelines, the regiments which were eventually constituted were dominated by Hindustanis, as well as Pathans from across the Indus. Local commanders, still unsure if the Sikhs could be trusted, restricted the number of Sikhs in their regiments while attempts to fill the Punjabi quota were unsuccessful because of the unwillingness of Punjabi Muslims and Dogra Rajputs, for reasons not specified, to enlist for military service.[25]

The lid on the recruitment of Punjabis into the regular corps of the Bengal Army was officially lifted in 1851, when the army authorities in India decided that it was safe enough to authorize the recruitment of Sikhs into the Bengal Army. But they were quick to add the provision that Sikhs should not be allowed to exceed 200 per regiment, or about twenty per cent of the strength of the regiment.[26] Although this measure was welcomed by some commanders of the native infantry regiments of the Bengal Army, some of whom had boasted of enlisting "a hundred or more fine Sikhs who had fought against us in every battle in both campaigns",[27] the measure was not a popular one. Many commanding officers of the Bengal regiments were satisfied with their tried and tested soldiers and, influenced perhaps by opposition from their high caste recruits, kept the Sikhs away from their corps. Several excuses were offered for not taking the Sikhs into the Bengal regiments. Some commanders expressed unwillingness because they felt that there was "too much of the leaven of insubordination in the Sikh Army to make the sepoy ranks fitting places for the old *Khalsa*",[28] while others were worried that there were problems of mixing the Sikhs, who were notorious for their laxity in caste observances, with the high-caste Hindu sepoys from Oudh and Rohilkhand who despised the Sikhs as "untidy and dirty" and refused to associate with them. The memoirs of Sita Ram, a Rajput sepoy from Oudh who had served in the Bengal Army during the campaigns in the Punjab,

[24] Secretary (Sec.) to Governor General (Gov. Gen.) to Board of Administration, 28 May 1849 in *India Office Records* (henceforth *IOR*), Home/Miscellaneous, File 318, Vol. 761, p. 1035.

[25] *General Report on the Administration of the Punjab, 1849–51*, p. 24.

[26] Sec. to Gov. Gen. to Board of Administration, 28 May 1849.

[27] 'Army Review', in *Calcutta Review* Vol. 26, (July–December, 1856), London, 1856, p. 107.

[28] *Ibid.*

contained references to the difficulties caused by the inclusion of Sikhs soldiers into his regiment soon after the Sikh wars.[29] He mentioned that the older Hindustani sepoys regarded the Sikh soldiers as "interlopers" and did not associate with them.[30] Nevertheless, by 1851 some Sikhs and Punjabis did manage to get themselves recruited into the regular regiments of the Bengal Army serving in the Punjab. But the recommendation to include up to 200 Sikhs per regiment was largely ignored by commanders of regiments of the Bengal Army. In the 1850s, it was observed that no more than ten Sikhs were usually found in each infantry regiment of the Bengal Army.[31] Consequently, of the nearly 60,000 Sikhs that were thrown out of employment following the defeat of the Sikh Army, not more than 3,000 Sikhs could be found in the seventy-four infantry regiments of the Bengal Army by the early 1850s.[32]

For the first few years after annexation, the Punjab thus remained on the fringe of the colonial armed forces in India. A general policy of demilitarization of the province, coupled with the reluctance of the Bengal Army to look beyond its established recruiting grounds for manpower, precluded Punjabis, particularly the Sikhs, from entering the ranks of the colonial army in any significant numbers. The traditional military labour pools of Rohilkhand, Oudh and Bihar, from which the Bengal Army drew most of its soldiers, were yielding a sufficient supply of recruits. Since no changes were envisaged for the Bengal Army, now settled into its role as an occupying force in the Punjab and Sind, there was no need for the British to look for new recruiting grounds.

This state of affairs was, however, to change with the mutiny of the Bengal Army in 1857. From a military point of view, the Mutiny had a tremendous impact on the thinking of the military authorities in India, particularly with regard to the structure and role of the colonial army. It had shown the weaknesses of the prevailing military set-up in India, and the threats it posed to the security of the Raj. The 1857 uprising brought in its wake a new military arrangement in northern India, one in which the Punjab began to

[29] Sita Ram, *From Sepoy to Subedar*, James Lunt (ed.), London, 1988, p. 159.

[30] *Ibid*.

[31] Kripal Chandra Yadav, 'British Policy Towards Sikhs, 1849–57' in Harbans Singh and N.G. Barrier (eds.) *Punjab Past and Present: Essays in Honour of Ganda Singh*, Patiala, 1976, p. 191.

[32] *Calcutta Review*, Vol. 26, July–December, 1856, pp. 108–9.

play a bigger part. The following section shows how the crisis of Empire compelled the British to turn to the Punjab for military manpower, and how this was to eventually determine the form of the post-mutiny reconstruction of the Bengal Army.

The Punjab and the 1857 Rebellion

On 10 May 1857, the 11th and 20th Bengal Native Infantry Regiments and the 3rd Light Cavalry stationed at Meerut cantonment broke into mutiny, murdering their European officers and fleeing southwards to Delhi. Within twenty-four hours, news had spread of the successful capture of the old imperial capital of Delhi by the sepoys from Meerut and the proclamation of Bahadur Shah II as the Emperor of Hindustan. What followed was an almost spontaneous outburst of military uprisings and civil rebellion which quickly engulfed most of north-central India, from Delhi to northern Bihar. The conflagration, sparked off by the mutiny in Meerut, was to last for more than a year, until June 1858, when the last of the rebel strongholds in Gwalior finally fell to British troops.

The military mutiny of 1857, which quickly developed into a rebellion, highlighted the political vulnerability and military fragility of an imperial power whose authority was underpinned by a local mercenary army. The British Empire in India had been acquired by military conquests, and it was largely upon the continued possession and monopoly of military might that imperial power and authority in the subcontinent were predicated. But in India, the shortage of European manpower had compelled the imperial authorities to rely on local mercenaries for their armed forces. As a result, European troops which were stationed in the subcontinent as praetorian guards of the British Raj were perpetually, and hopelessly, outnumbered by their native counterparts (see Table 1.1). The military and political repercussions of such a military arrangement were dramatically highlighted in 1857: when the native regiments of the Bengal Army mutinied, the British found themselves almost immediately shorn of their military power in northern India; and with the loss their army, British authority in north-central India consequently ceased to exist. The events of 1857 are a familiar story by now, but it will be retold briefly here to explain how the Punjab came to feature so prominently in the post-mutiny reforms of the colonial armed forces in India.

Table 1.1
Proportion of Indian to European Troops in India, 1852–1856

	Europeans (Royal and Company Troops)	Percentage of Total	Indian Soldiers (in service with Royal Troops and Company)	Percentage of Total	Total
1852					
Bengal Army	26,089	16	139,807	84	165,896
Madras Army	11,687	18	53,714	82	65,401
Bombay Army	10,933	19	45,552	81	56,485
Total	**48,709**	**17**	**239,073**	**83**	**287,782**
1853					
Bengal Army	24,986	15	139,246	85	164,232
Madras Army	11,370	17	53,787	83	65,157
Bombay Army	10,577	19	45,312	81	55,889
Total	**46,933**	**16**	**238,345**	**84**	**285,278**
1854					
Bengal Army	26,531	19	138,674	81	165,205
Madras Army	11,172	17	53,254	83	64,426
Bombay Army	9,443	17	44,921	83	54,364
Total	**47,146**	**17**	**236,849**	**83**	**283,995**
1855					
Bengal Army	25,344	15	139,162	85	164,506
Madras Army	10,927	17	53,031	83	63,958
Bombay Army	9,822	18	44,898	82	54,720
Total	**46,093**	**16**	**237,091**	**84**	**283,184**
1856					
Bengal Army	24,594	15	137,109	85	161,703
Madras Army	10,352	16	53,201	84	65,553
Bombay Army	10,158	18	44,911	82	55,069
Total	**45,104**	**16**	**235,221**	**84**	**280,325**

Source: Derived from *Report of Commissioners, 1859*, Parliamentary Papers, Cmd. 2515, Vol. 5, p. 377.

The mutiny that started in Meerut in May 1857 had evidently dumbfounded the British and caught them unawares. This was surprising given that just before the outbreak at Meerut, there had been clear symptoms of disquiet amongst the native regiments of the Bengal Army. In 1850, the 66th Native Infantry Regiment stationed at Barrackpore, a cantonment near Calcutta, mutinied over the decision by the military authorities to withdraw compensatory allowances for services in the newly conquered territory of Punjab. Service in the remote and unfamiliar territory of the Punjab had never been popular with the sepoys from the North-Western

Province and Oudh, and in the past, Hindustani sepoys stationed in the Punjab had been compensated by extra service allowances. However, with annexation, the Punjab was no longer considered foreign territory and the extra allowance for foreign service was consequently withdrawn.[33] The Commander-in-Chief, Sir Charles Napier, had the Regiment disbanded as an example to the rest of the Army, but even he had sensed that the mutiny by the 66th was a symptom of a much more deep-seated malady that was afflicting the Bengal Army.

From the 1850s, grievances amongst the sepoys of the Bengal Army had been mounting, caused largely by growing unhappiness over service conditions. This was heightened by the General Service Act of 1856, which decreed that all sepoys, irrespective of their caste, would in future be liable for overseas service. For the high-caste recruits from north-central India this ruling was abhorrent, as the crossing of the dreaded *kala pani* or "black waters" would mean a loss of caste. Consequently, many high-caste Rajputs and Brahmins chose not to enlist, and in so doing lost a lucrative source of employment. There was also a belief amongst the high-caste Brahmin and Rajput sepoys of Benares and Oudh that their favoured position in the Bengal Army was being threatened by the intention of the British to expand their recruiting base to include a wider range of castes and regional groups. The opening of the Punjab and the permission to recruit up to 200 Sikhs per regiment, although as we have seen not fully exploited by British commanders of the Bengal Army, was perceived by the sepoys as an indication that their monopoly of military service, crucial for their economic well-being, was being threatened. These fears were compounded by grievances over the loss of foreign service in Oudh (1846) and Punjab (1849).[34] The conditions were certainly ripe for a sepoy revolt in the Bengal Army. Almost prophetically, Napier had warned, soon after he completed his term as Commander-in-Chief of the Bengal Army, that all was not well with the Bengal Army and that a mutiny could not be ruled out.

The spark that ignited the tense situation was provided by the introduction of the controversial greased cartridges for the

---

[33] Eric Stokes (C.A. Bayly ed.), *The Peasants Armed: The Indian Rebellion of 1857*, Oxford, 1986, pp. 50–54.

[34] *Ibid.*

Lee-Enfield rifles used by the sepoys. Rumours that these cartridges were to be greased with the fat of cows and pigs caused consternation amongst the Hindu and Muslim sepoys, the former because they regarded the cow as a sacred animal and the latter because they regarded the pig as an unclean animal.[35] The belief that the British were deliberately trying to pollute them in order to convert them into Christianity agitated the soldiers, and in parades the sepoys began to openly defy orders to handle these cartridges. But British commanders, believing that their sepoys were incapable of mutiny, chose to interpret their defiance as minor problems of insubordination rather than ominous warnings that the sepoys of the Bengal Army were on the verge of a mutiny. Consequently, when the mutiny erupted and spread across northern India, the British were caught disastrously off balance and could momentarily do nothing to quell the spread of the sepoy rebellion.

As the British took stock of the situation after recovering from their initial shock it became clear that their position was indeed critical. At the outbreak of the Mutiny, the only force immediately available to the British were 23,000 European troops of the Bengal Army, about half of whom were stationed in the Punjab. Reinforcements from England would take more than half-a-year to arrive, possibly too late by then to be of any good, and even if they did arrive in good time, the inhospitable climate of India in May would render most of the troops ineffective before they could be put against the mutineers.[36] The British were chary of rushing up native troops from the Madras and Bombay Armies, unsure if they too had mutinous tendencies. For the moment, therefore, the only immediate option open to the British was to regroup and consolidate the European regiments in northern India. As the bulk of these forces were stationed in the Punjab, the tasks of consolidating the British position and organizing the counter-attack against the mutinous sepoys to regain northern India therefore fell on the province, particularly on the shoulders of John Lawrence, its Chief Commissioner.

The tasks confronting John Lawrence and his fellow British officers in the Punjab were daunting. Although there had been no

---

[35] Philip Mason, *A Matter of Honour: An Account of the Indian Army, Its Officers and Men*, London, 1974, p. 225.

[36] *Ibid.*

spontaneous outbreaks of rebellion in the Punjab, the situation in the province was far from secure. The population had remained subdued, but officials believed that it was "watching developments with strained attention", very possibly waiting for the right moment to break out into open rebellion. On the north-western border, the menacing presence of hostile tribesmen presented another cause for concern. The turbulent frontier had been kept under careful watch by the Frontier Force, but if the Force were to be weakened by mutiny or desertions the situation at the frontier would become untenable. Furthermore, at the outbreak of the Mutiny there was a fairly substantial force of 36,000 armed and potentially mutinous Hindustani troops stationed in the Punjab itself, which needed overawing, and possibly overpowering.

With the available troops at hand, comprising twelve regiments of Europeans numbering 10,326 men and 13,430 Punjabi Irregulars from the Punjab Frontier Force, which had remained steadfast, Lawrence took action to prevent an insurrection from erupting from within the Punjab. He immediately set about securing strategic installations and disarming the Hindustani sepoys in the Punjab. European troops were despatched to secure Lahore with its fort and arsenal[37]; the arsenal at Ferozepur, which contained 7,000 barrels of gunpowder and a large armoury of weapons; and the strategically important forts of Phillaur and Govindgarh in central Punjab.[38] Having secured some of the key installations in the Punjab, the authorities next turned their attention to the Hindustani forces present in the Punjab. The Chief Commissioner ordered that regiments whose loyalty was suspect were to be disarmed. Consequently, prompt and firm action by local commanders and civilian officers in Amritsar, Lahore, Multan and Jhelum secured the peaceful disarming of eighteen native infantry and cavalry regiments, totalling some 13,000 men.[39] Native gunners of artillery batteries were removed from their guns, and their places taken over by volunteers from the European force.[40]

---

[37] R. Temple, Sec. to Chief Commissioner to G. Edmonstone, Sec. to Government of India (GoI), 25 May 1858, in *Mutiny Records* (Report) (henceforth *MRR*), Lahore, 1911, Vol. 8, part II, p. 331.

[38] *Ibid.*

[39] *Ibid.*, pp. 309, 317–18.

[40] *General Report on the Administration of the Punjab, 1856–58*, in *PP*, 1859, Session 1, Vol. 18, p. 485.

Not all the native regiments capitulated so easily. Several native regiments resisted the attempts to have them disarmed and mutinied before rushing to Delhi to join forces with the other mutineers. Between May and August of 1857, during the continuance of the siege in Delhi, twelve regiments of Hindustani troops mutinied in the Punjab on eight separate occasions.[41] Most of the mutineers were, however, resolutely put down by British troops; of the eight cases of mutiny, all but three were beaten and destroyed.

While Lawrence and his officers were attempting to consolidate their position in the Punjab, urgent calls came from Delhi for reinforcements. The old Mughal capital of Delhi had fallen to the mutineers on 10 May, and its recapture soon became an objective of extreme urgency, if only to achieve a symbolic victory over the mutineers and rebels. In July, a contingent from the Punjab comprising twelve European regiments, the Guides, 4th Sikhs, 1st Punjab Infantry, 1st Punjab Cavalry and two squadrons of the 2nd and 5th Punjab Cavalry were despatched to Delhi to reinforce the troops already there.[42] Despite the reinforcements, the situation in Delhi remained critical; by August, death and sickness had thinned the ranks of the British forces at Delhi, while the numbers of mutineers had been swollen by reinforcements from other parts of northern India.[43] General Arthur Wilson, commanding officer of the Delhi Field Force, wrote to the Chief Commissioner that unless reinforcements were sent from the Punjab, the troops in Delhi would not be able to hold their position, much less assault the city.[44]

The call from Delhi placed the Chief Commissioner in a quandary. Punjab was not totally free from trouble and required all its available troops to protect the frontier and to watch and guard the Hindustani troops, of whom nearly 6,000 were still armed. Some of his colleagues, notably Herbert Edwardes, had urged Lawrence to secure the Punjab first, arguing that "...[it] will serve the Empire better by holding the Punjab than by sacrificing [it] and recovering

[41] Memorandum by R. Montgomery, Judicial Commissioner, Punjab, n.d., in *MRR*, Vol. 8, part II, pp. 345–46.

[42] Temple to Edmonstone, 25 May 1858, in *MRR*, Vol. 8, part II, p. 333.

[43] *Ibid.*, p. 355.

[44] Brigadier General A. Wilson to John Lawrence, 18 July 1857, in *Mutiny Records* (Correspondence) (henceforth *MRC*), Lahore, 1911, Vol. 7, part I, pp. 230–31.

Delhi".[45] Despite such exhortations, and the continuing uncertainty of his own position in the Punjab, Lawrence decided to despatch reinforcements to Delhi. The Chief Commissioner feared that a retreat of the troops from Delhi would be disastrous for the morale of the native regiments, which in turn would have an adverse effect on the fidelity of Punjabi troops in the Punjab itself, making the hold over the Punjab impossible.[46] Unwilling to use the Hindustani regiments which had already been disarmed and confined to the barracks in the Punjab, the Chief Commissioner was compelled to turn to the Punjab itself to raise fresh forces to secure the positions of the British in the Punjab, and, at the same time, to augment the Delhi Field Force.

By the middle of 1857, when the authorities in the Punjab were convinced that the Punjabis did not sympathize with the movement in the east, calls were sent out to raise the requisite number of men to augment the Punjab Force. Between May and December of 1857, a new force of approximately 34,000 Punjabis was raised, which included eighteen new regiments of infantry, a body of 300 veteran Sikh artillerymen, re-enlisted after being disbanded in 1849, and a corps of about 1,200 low caste Sikh pioneers.[47] The nucleus of this force was formed from the Sikhs and Punjabi Muslim elements of disarmed infantry regiments of the Bengal Army, which the Punjab authorities believed would not empathize with the Hindustani mutineers.[48] In addition, irregular levies numbering 7,000 on horses and 9,000 on foot were raised to replace Punjab regiments sent to Delhi, to keep a watch on the Hindustani elements in the Punjab, and to quell disaffection wherever it might arise.[49]

In 1857, the crisis of Empire necessitated the raising of a large body of troops from the Punjab, which a few years before had been undergoing a process of gradual demilitarization. The military fervour of the Punjabis, which the British had hitherto been trying to dampen, was rekindled; Sikhs, Punjabi Muslims and Dogras, who had constituted the mainstay of the Sikh military machinery

[45] Quoted in J.W. Kaye, *History of the Sepoy War in India*, Vol. II, London, 1867, pp. 614–15.

[46] Brandreth to Edmonstone, 23 July 1857, in *MRC*, Vol. 7 (i), p. 226.

[47] Memorandum by R. Montgomery, Judicial Commissioner, Punjab, n.d., in *MRR*, Vol. 8 (ii), p. 328.

[48] Lawrence to Edmonstone, 13 May 1857, in *MRC*, Vol. 7 (i), pp. 21–22.

[49] Temple to Edmonstone, 25 May 1857, in *MRR*, Vol. 8 (ii), p. 339.

before annexation, were called back to arms, this time in defence of the Empire.

There was, nonetheless, considerable official concern about the return to arms of this potentially turbulent population. Lawrence, for example, had initially been reluctant to authorize the raising of Sikh troops, being still distrustful of them.[50] Although British rhetoric at that time spoke of the Punjabis' "splendid and noble response to the call of duty", there were no illusions that the Punjabis had responded to the British call out of a sense of loyalty.[51] The Punjab had been secured by the tough and resolute actions of the civil and military authorities; the Sikhs and Punjabi Muslims had turned to the service of the British lured mainly by the opportunity to plunder the wealth of Delhi, and hoping to have a share of the largesse when the crisis was over. Furthermore, there was the hope that the British would reopen the Punjab as a military recruiting ground, the prospects of which would provide a golden opportunity for Punjabis, especially the Sikhs, to restore their shattered fortunes. But doubts lingered in the minds of the British. The Chief Commissioner noted that when the chances of victory were slim, these mercenaries would in all probability join the enemy, and "think how he can best shift for himself".[52] It was believed that the Muslims were still imbued with fanaticism, and were secretly impatient of British rule, and that when they believed that British rule was drawing to an end they would rise and strike. Similarly, the Sikhs, it was believed, still harboured memories of their recent defeat by British forces; there were fears by the British that the present crisis would provide a good opportunity for the Sikhs to attempt to revive the *Khalsa*.[53] The Chief Commissioner accordingly decided to proceed with caution in the matter of recruiting and to enlist no more men than was absolutely necessary to hold the Punjab and to supply reinforcements to Delhi. He also made sure, in a manner reminiscent of Ranjit Singh's army some decades before, not to allow a preponderance of armed force to any one particular group of Punjabis. Consequently, the composition of the

---

[50] Captain H.R. James, Offg. Sec. to Chief Commissioner, Punjab to Sec., GoI, Foreign Dept., 17 May 1857, in *MRC*, Vol. 7 (i), p. 36.

[51] *Ibid.*, pp. 359–60.

[52] Temple to Edmonstone, 25 May 1857, in *MRR*, Vol. 8 (ii), p. 363.

[53] Captain H.R. James, to Sec., GoI, Foreign Dept., 17 May 1857, in *MRC*, Vol. 7 (i), p. 35.

new force came to be a mixed one, comprising Sikhs from the central Punjab, various tribes of Muslims from the western Punjab (which had little in common except religion), Pathan and Baluch tribes from the frontier, hillmen and Punjabi Hindus.[54]

The raising of a Punjab Force, and its subsequent despatch to Delhi, in addition to meeting British manpower needs at a crucial moment, provided the British with an important tactical advantage: it reduced the threat of an internal uprising by Punjabis by drawing in potentially dangerous elements and sending them out of the Punjab. During the Mutiny, there were disturbing signs that some elements in the Punjab were using the crisis to revive old factional disputes,[55] and some of the rival tribes were preparing to reassert their interests should British rule collapse under the present crisis. Towards the end of May 1857, it was rumoured that clan heads in the Bar tracts of Shahpur district in the western Punjab had met secretly to pledge themselves to a common cause of action, should the locally cantoned sepoys rise in mutiny.[56] There was also evidence of similar developments taking place amongst the tribes of the Jhelum district.[57] There, recruitment to the Punjab Force provided an outlet for the restless tribes to channel their energy. As it turned out, the raising of a levy of horsemen from Jhelum gave employment to the local spare hands, whose absence for duties elsewhere kept the district relatively quiet.[58] In Shahpur district, the dominant and influential chieftains of the Tiwana tribes were encouraged to raise 1,000 horsemen for the levies. Many of those who joined the levies were the headmen of villages, often related to the chieftain, and their presence on the side of the British "afforded an excellent guarantee for the good behaviour of those who remained at home".[59] But, at the same time, local officials expressed "great relief" when these horsemen departed for service elsewhere.[60]

---

[54] *General Report on the Administration of the Punjab for the Years 1856–58*, p. 487.

[55] Thornton to Montgomery, 23 February 1858, in *MRR*, Vol. 8 (i), pp. 315–16.

[56] *Ibid.*, p. 395.

[57] W.S. Talbot, *Punjab District Gazetteer, Jhelum*, (hereafter, *PDG*, followed by district) 1904, Lahore, 1904, Vol. 26, p. 71.

[58] Report by R. Montgomery, Judl. Comm., Punjab, n.d., in *MRR*, Vol. 8 (ii), p. 246.

[59] Ouseley to Thornton, 25 February 1858, in *MRR*, Vol. 8 (i), pp. 396–97.

[60] *Ibid.*

The Mutiny of 1857 thus saw the recruitment of large numbers of Punjabis into the British armed forces in India. This was a complete reversal of the policy of demilitarization which had been faithfully pursued by the Punjab Board of Administration since annexation. Within barely six months in 1857, eighteen new regiments of infantry, comprising more than 34,000 men, were raised in the Punjab. In addition to the 14,000 irregular levies which were raised for services within the Punjab, a total of almost 50,000 Punjabis were put under arms, marking a significant increase in the number of Punjabis in the Bengal Army from what it had been in 1851.[61] Punjabis who came to the side of the British during the crisis were rewarded by employment in the colonial army, and, for many of them, it promised a return to an association with the military in India.

Yet, in 1858, continued employment for Punjabis in the regiments of the Army in India was by no means inevitable. We have seen that, despite being forced by circumstances to depend on Punjabi troops, British authorities were still quite unsure of their reliability. While it was quite clear that the Sikhs and Punjabi Muslims would have no sympathies for the *purbiya* high-caste Hindus, there were signs, whilst the crisis lasted, of unrest generated by the belief that the end of British rule might just be occurring. British officials, reflecting after the crisis, felt that the Punjab would have risen against them had the defeat of the mutineers at Delhi been delayed.[62] It was clear that caution still governed the authorities' decision to recruit Punjabis into the ranks of the army. It was not simply a case of providing military employment to the Punjabis as a reward for good and loyal services; rather, the questions persisted: what should be done with the Punjabi regiments that had been called to arms during the Mutiny? Should they be disarmed now that the crisis was over, or was it safe enough, at this stage, to include large numbers of Punjabis in the colonial army? If so, what numbers of Punjabis could safely be recruited into the army, and how would the recruitment of Punjabis serve the interests of the colonial army, and ultimately of British rule in India?

---

[61] *Return of Actual Strength of Queen's and East India Company's Forces in the Three Presidencies and the Punjab, 1859*, in *PP*, 1859, Session 2, (64), Vol. 23, p. 491.

[62] *General Report on the Administration of the Punjab, 1856–58*, in *PP*, 1859, Session 238, Vol. 18, pp. 495–99.

Post-Mutiny Army Reforms

In July 1858, a Commission was appointed under the chairman-
ship of Major General Jonathan Peel, Secretary of State for War, to
study the lessons of the Mutiny and to consider and recommend
ways of enhancing the security and viability of the armed forces in
India.[63] The Commission received testimonies and evidence from
several senior civil servants and military men, all of whom had
had long experiences with the native army in India. On the question of the forces required for the garrison of the Indian Empire,
almost all the witnesses agreed that it was inconceivable for the
British Indian Empire to be held solely with British or European
troops. Not only was European manpower scarce, but the cost of
raising and maintaining an all-European colonial army in India
was prohibitive.[64] Some witnesses suggested that, since the native
troops had shown themselves untrustworthy, they should be replaced by mercenaries from outside India, like the Africans, Malays
and Chinese.[65] This measure was, however, strongly opposed by
John Lawrence, who argued that[66]

> ... there was no necessity of bringing in Muhomedan, Hindoo
> and Buddhist foreigners from other tropical countries ... every

[63] The Commission, which came to be known as the Peel Commission after its
Chairman, included the Duke of Cambridge, General Officer Commanding the British Army, Lord E.H. Stanley, Commissioner for Affairs of India, General G.
Tweeddale, Colonel of the 30th Foot Regiment, Viscount Melville, Colonel of the
100th Foot Regiment, Sir G.A. Wetherall, Adjutant General, British Army, Major
General P. Montgomery, Colonel Will Burton, Colonel Thomas Tait, and Major
General Hancock. *Report of the Commissioners Appointed to Inquire into the Organization
of the Indian Army; together with Minutes of Evidence and Appendix* in *PP*, Cmd. 2515,
1859, Session 1, Vol. 5, p. 11.

[64] It was estimated that the cost of maintaining one infantry regiment of British
troops was around 573,343 rupees per annum, more than double the cost of maintaining a native regiment, which was estimated at Rs 277,612. See Minute by J.P.
Grant, President, Council of India in Council, 4 June 1858, in *Report of Commissioners.* Cmd. 2515, p. 411.

[65] See, for example, the testimony of Colonel C.B. Becher of the Bengal Army, in
ibid., pp. 69–70.

[66] Evidence of the Punjab Committee as cited in 'Precis of Answers Received in
India,' by Lieutenant Colonel H.M. Durand, August 1858, Appendix 71. *Ibid.*,
p. 534.

foreign coloured soldier that you bring into India displaces an Indian soldier, a soldier by caste and profession, who will take to no other livelihood. What would the advocates of foreign mercenaries propose to do with these displaced military classes? No statesman can ignore them. The wise policy is to feed, use, and control them.

Unable to rely totally on a European army, and unwilling to recruit mercenaries from outside India, the Commission accepted that there was no alternative but to continue to rely on native troops for the garrisoning of the subcontinent. Safeguards, however, had to be introduced to make this overwhelmingly native army "safe and viable". The Commission recommended several measures: an increase in the number of European troops stationed in India; the ratio of native troops should not bear a greater proportion to the Europeans in the Cavalry and Infantry than two to one for the Bengal Army, and three to one for the Bombay and Madras Armies; artillery and arsenals should be monopolized in the hands of European forces.[67]

Central to the issue of safeguards in the armed forces was the question of the future composition of the native army. The ease with which the Mutiny had spread through the Bengal Army was attributed to the fact that most of the regiments had been composed of men from the same caste and region, who shared the same affiliations. Most of the witnesses agreed that the reconstructed Bengal Army should be composed of different "nationalities and castes", but there was little agreement on the types of soldiers and the proportion of the different "nationalities and castes" which the army should recruit in future. Some argued that having a wide range of recruits for the army was the safest policy, and that recruitment should be opened to all sections of society, with no one excluded on account of caste.[68] There were several who disagreed with this open policy, arguing that certain groups should be excluded from the ranks of the native army. Lieutenant Colonel Mayhew, Adjutant General of the Bengal Army argued, for example, that the events of 1857 had shown that Brahmins could not be

[67] *Report of Commissioners*, Cmd. 2515, p. 14.
[68] See for example the testimony of Major General C.B. Low, a retired officer of the Madras Army, but who had served principally in the Bengal. *Ibid.*, p. 53.

trusted and recommended that they be excluded from any future recruitment;[69] Sir George Clerk of Bombay, on the other hand, thought that "we should be most guarded and watchful with the Sikhs", while Major General Hearsey felt that "there was no more dangerous man than a religious Mahomedan".[70] With such contradictory evidence, all that the Commission was eventually able to recommend was "that the Native Army should be composed of different nationalities and castes, and as a general rule mixed promiscuously through each regiment".[71] It did not, however, specify in detail which "nationalities and castes" were to be recruited, or excluded.

The Commission's recommendation that a wide variety of castes be recruited to the native army shattered the monopoly of the Bengal Army by high caste Brahmins and Rajputs of north-central India, but it offered no guidelines as to who should be recruited in their place. The post-Mutiny Bengal Army was consequently reconstructed from the establishments still in force in 1858, but its underlying organizational principle was influenced by the strategy of "divide and rule" advocated by John Lawrence, Neville Chamberlain and Herbert Edwardes, the three members of the Punjab Committee formed to advise the Peel Commission. The recommendations of the Punjab Committee were based on the logic of making the army safe by the counterpoise of natives against natives. The rationale behind their recommendations was summed up thus:[72]

> To preserve that distinctiveness which is so valuable, and which while it lasts makes the Muhomedan of one country despise, fear, or dislike the Muhomedan of another, corps should in future be provincial, and adhere to geographical limits within which differences and rivalries are strongly marked. Let all races, Hindu and Muhomedan, of one province be enlisted in one regiment, and no others, and having thus created distinctive regiments, let us keep them so against the hour of need by confining the

[69] Testimony of Lieutenant Colonel Mayhew. *Ibid.*, Cmd. 2515, p. 538.

[70] Testimonies of Sir George Clerk, Governor of Bombay, and Major General Hearsey. *Ibid.*, p. 78.

[71] *Ibid.*, p. 14 .

[72] Punjab Committee recommendations quoted in 'Precis of Replies to Questions Having Reference to the Native Infantry of the Bengal Army' by Lieutenant Colonel H.M. Durand, 4 September 1848, in Appendix 71. *Ibid.*, p. 540.

circle of their ordinary service to the limits of their own province, and only marching them on emergency into other parts of the Empire, with which they will then be found to have little sympathy. By the system thus indicated, two great evils are avoided; firstly, that community of feeling throughout the native army, and that mischievous political activity and intrigue which results from association with other races and travel in other Indian provinces, and secondly, that thorough discontent and alienation from the service which has undoubtedly sprung up since extended conquest has carried our Hindustani soldiers so far from their homes in India proper.

The political object of the policy was clear enough: the native army in India should be organized on a principle of "divide and rule" to prevent it from galvanizing into a unified force capable of threatening British interests again. This policy reflected the concerns of the military authority at the time: the post-Mutiny Indian Army was there to uphold the Raj, and not just for the defence of India. Internal security was, therefore, to be the underlying factor governing the way in which the armed forces in India were to be organized. The "divide and rule" policy was to take place at all levels of the army. At the all-India level, it was taken to mean that the three presidency armies should remain segregated, and totally unconnected by common interests and sympathies, so that they could function as checks upon each other. The desire to preserve three distinct regional armies explains why, despite the fact that the Bengal Army had all but ceased to exist following the mutiny of more than eighty per cent of its regiments, the military authorities chose to have it reconstructed instead of abolishing it altogether.

The policy of the Punjab Committee also meant that within each army, there was to be localization of recruitment and service. This meant that regiments would now be raised strictly within the confines of the area in which they were expected to serve. Making regiments serve in peace time in their own country had two distinct advantages. First, military service nearer home was understandably more popular with the sepoy than service at a distance and in a climate to which he was unaccustomed. One of the major grievances of the Bengal sepoys which contributed to the eventual uprising in 1857 was their reluctance to serve outside their presidency. Having to leave their homes for extended periods of time, to garrisons far off and unfamiliar places was something they could not tolerate, and these duties often led to serious discontent amongst the sepoys.[73] By localization, the remnants of the Hindustani portion of the Bengal Army would no longer be expected to serve in the Punjab and at the frontier. This necessarily meant that regiments would have to be raised for the garrisoning of the province and the north-western frontier in the Punjab.

As a result of this policy, Punjabis, who had been called to arms during the Mutiny, found their permanent places in the ranks of the infantry and cavalry regiments of the Bengal Army which were stationed in the Punjab and its north-west frontier. Consequently, by 1861, the old Bengal Army was reconstituted into practically two separate bodies: one comprising the old elements of the high-caste Hindus from north-central India, but significantly reduced in strength, consisting of the remnants of the Bengal Army that had remained loyal during the Mutiny, and mixed with men of low caste; and the other created out of the regiments and levies of the Punjab Force which had been raised to put down the mutinous Bengal Army.[74] By 1862, a third distinct component—the Gurkhas—had been added to the Bengal Army. By 1870, of the forty-nine infantry regiments of the Bengal Army, the Gurkha and hill troops constituted four regiments. Mixed regiments of Sikhs and Punjabi Muslims, most of them raised in 1857–58, accounted for sixteen regiments, and the rest were the remnants of the Bengal Army, most of them of a mixed nature.[75] To preserve the distinctiveness of these regiments, the Governor General ordered that these regiments specially recruited from one class should continue to confine recruitment entirely to that class, and that no alteration to the constitution of the regiments should take place.[76] With these changes,

[73] Extract from 'Historical Account of the Rise and Progress of the Bengal Native Infantry, from its formation in 1757 to 1796', by Captain Williams, of the Invalid Establishment of the Bengal Army, n.d., in *PP*, 1877, Vol. 62. p. 370

[74] *Further Papers Respecting Proposed Changes in India's Army System, 1893–94* in *PP*, 1892–94, Vol. 63, p. 4.

[75] 'Notes on the Native Army of Bengal, with its Present Material and Organization, as Compared with the Past', by C.H. Brownlow, September 1875, Appendix T in Despatch from Adj. Gen., Army Headquarters to Secretary to the GoI, in *PP*, 1877, Vol. 62. p. 226. (See Table 1.2).

[76] Lieutenant Colonel H.W. Norman, Secretary to GoI, Military Dept. to Offg. Adj. Gen. of Army of India, 25 November 1862, in *Correspondences Relating to the Composition of the Army. Ibid.*, p. 392.

thirty-five per cent of the Bengal Army was recruited strictly from the Punjab proper by 1870.[77]

Table 1.2
Races and Castes Recruited to the various Corps of the Indian Army, 1858

	Light Artillery	Regular Infantry	Infantry–Irregular Infantry	Regular Cavalry	Artillery Irregular	Sappers and Miners	Total
Christians	–	25	486	20	41	–	572
Muslims	552	624	3,590	1,853	3,831	2	10,450
Brahmins	77	344	6,205	1,532	350	18	8,508
Rajputs	88	231	6,404	2,911	549	179	10,183
Other Hindus	445	35	4,326	3,821	181	10	8,808
Sikhs	–	–	135	3,504	833	–	4,472
Punjabis	–	–	192	15,286	2,401	495	18,374
Hindustanis	–	–	–	896	1,219	38	2,153
Nepalis	–	–	–	358	19	–	377
Hazara Tribes	–	–	–	23	–	–	23
Afghans	–	–	–	32	105	–	137
Gurkhas	–	–	590	271	29	–	890
Hillmen	–	–	–	3,677	2	–	3,679
Others	–	–	–	2,507	–	–	2,507

Source: Extracted from Lieutenant Colonel W. Mayhew, Adj-Gen, Bengal Army, 13 April 1858, Cmd. 2515, 1859, p. 537.

The second, and perhaps more important, rationale for localization was to keep troops of different "nationalities" apart, to preserve natural "race" antagonisms.[78] In the post-bellum Bengal Army, the Punjab, already furnishing a large part of the army to fill up the gap in the Bengal Army created by the revolt, provided a convenient counterpoise against the Hindustani elements remaining in the Army. Sikhs, Punjabi Muslims and Pathans, with their age-old antipathy to the *purbiyas*,[79] would provide a useful balance in the strength of the Bengal Army, an advantage which would be lost if they were allowed to develop an *esprit de corp* by mixing freely.

[77] *Ibid.*, p. 489.

[78] From GoI to Secretary of State for India, 2 November 1892, Papers respecting Changes in the Indian Army System, 1893–94, Vol. 63. p. 254.

[79] The term *purbiya*, which literally means "easterner", was derived from the Persian word "Purab", meaning east. The Punjabis and British officers serving in the Punjab often used the term to refer, in a pejorative sense, to the Hindustani sepoys from the north-central plains of India.

The Punjab was indeed custom-made to play the role of counter-weight to the Hindustanis within the Bengal Army. There was a certain amount of historical hostility between the Punjabis and the *purbiyas* reinforced as it were by differences in religion, race and language. Furthermore, by localization of recruitment and services, these two components could be set physically apart so that their mutual antagonisms could be preserved. The army was further able to exploit the heterogeneous nature of Punjabi society, riven by caste, tribal and religious differences, to make it difficult for the Punjab component to fuse into a united hostile bloc against the British. Sikhs could be used against Muslim tribesmen and vice versa, and the Pathans could be used against both of them. It was with this in mind that the Punjab regiments in the 1860s and 1870s were formed entirely on the "class company" system, which meant that each company of a regiment should comprise a different race or caste, one of Sikhs, one of Punjabi Muslims, one of Pathans, etc. A typical Punjab regiment would therefore comprise one company of Sikhs, two companies of Pathans and one company of Hindu Jats, maintaining a crude ratio of one Sikh to every two Punjabi Muslims.[80] The army authorities, when recruiting in the Punjab, made the added safeguard that neither Sikhs nor Punjabi Muslims should be allowed to exceed one-half the complement of the regiment.[81]

Changes were thus made to the constitution of the Bengal Army after the Mutiny in a deliberate attempt to prevent the northern native army from being dominated by a single bloc of soldiers. Punjabis were recruited not so much to replace but *to balance* the Hindustani component of the army, with the Gurkhas included as a further safeguard. It would be erroneous to say at this stage that the Indian Army had been "Punjabicised". As late as 1875, out of a total Bengal Army strength of 44,690, sepoys from the Punjab accounted for only 12,558; Punjabis hardly featured in the Madras Army, and only 4,542 of them were serving in the Bombay Army.[82] Military authorities continued to be cautious about expanding recruitment in the Punjab because of uneasiness in the military circles that just as easily as the Punjabis had come to the aid of the British

---

[80] Precis of Returns, August 1858, in *Report of Commissioners*, Cmd. 2515, p. 23.

[81] *Correspondences on the Organization of the Army, 1870*, in *PP*, 1877, Vol. 62, p. 392.

[82] *Caste Returns for the Armies of Bengal, Madras and Bombay Presidencies, 1875*, IOR:L/MIL/14/216.

during the Mutiny, they could, once they had a monopoly of force, foment another mutiny themselves.[83] The number of Punjabis recruited was thus restricted to the limit which was deemed necessary and practicable for the division of the strength of the army, and although officers were still keen to enlist more Sikhs into their regiments, the military authorities laid down that no changes should be made to the balance of the army which might prejudice its safety.[84]

Up to 1885, the views of the Punjab Committee held sway and the army was maintained strictly on principles that looked toward internal security. During this period, no material changes were made to the recruiting balance. Although Punjabis came to be recruited in fairly significant numbers into the Bengal Army, care was taken not to allow too many of them into it. By the early 1880s, however, a long series of frontier troubles culminating in the Russian scare led to a new thinking about the colonial army. The army had to be reoriented from its sole purpose of maintaining internal security to meeting the challenge of an external danger. This resulted in a restructuring of the army, the lifting of restrictions on recruitment of Punjabis, and ultimately paved the way for Punjab's eventual domination of the colonial army.

"Martial Races" Class Regiments and the Punjab

In 1880, soon after the Second Afghan War,[85] the state of the colonial army once again came under official review. British India's

---

[83] *Report of Commissioners*, Cmd. 2515, pp. 179–81.

[84] Minute by Major General H.W. Norman on 'The Organization of the Native Army in India' 11 October 1875, in *PP*, 1877, Vol. 62, p. 509.

[85] Aghanistan and Britain fought their first war in 1848, after which the pro-British Dost Muhammad Khan was installed as the Amir in Kabul. But after his death in 1863, Anglo-Afghan relations began deteriorating, as the new Amir seemed more disposed to lean towards Russia. In 1878, after failing to reach an exclusive alliance with Kabul, Lord Lytton decided to adopt a forward policy by extending the Indian border beyond Peshawar. This precipitated a war against Afghanistan which broke out on 20 November 1878. The British successfully concluded the war in February 1879, but soon after an uprising broke out in Kabul where the British envoy, Sir Louis Cavagnari, was murdered. The uprising was quickly squashed by General Roberts, and a British puppet, Yakub Khan, was subsequently installed as the new Amir of Afghanistan. For an account of the two Anglo-Afghan wars, see Anthony Verrier, *Francis Younghusband and the Great Game*, London, 1991.

uneasy relationship with its western neighbour Afghanistan was now complicated by suspicions of Russian intentions to extend their imperialist designs into India.[86] The prospects of Indian regiments having to fight against a formidable European enemy provided the impetus for a rethinking of the existing state of the local component of the colonial army and how it would fare when faced with such an enemy. In the aftermath of 1857 and up to the 1880s, although the army in India had been involved in campaigns against Afghan troops across the frontier, its function was regarded primarily as an internal one—as the guardian of imperial order within the Empire. But by the late nineteenth century, threat perceptions by the army authorities had undergone a change. The British military authorities in India became obsessed with the "Great Game" with Russia, and were no longer content to maintain the army in India merely as an internal policing force. With the army now more likely to function as a protection force against foreign attack, the military authorities in India began to talk of the need to improve the fighting efficiency of the army in India.

The most prominent military voice during this period belonged to Lord Roberts, Commander-in-Chief of the Bengal Army.[87] Roberts had extensive experience of military operations across the northwestern frontier, having commanded the Punjab Frontier Force, the Afghan Field Force during 1878–79, and later made his name with his famous march from Kabul to Kandahar in 1880.[88] In a series of letters and notes compiled during his term as Commander-in-Chief of the Bengal Army from 1885 to 1893, Roberts asserted that the efficiency of the native army could only be improved by

---

[86] There are several good accounts of the historical background leading to the nineteenth century "Great Game" between Britain and Russia. See, for example, M.S. Anderson, *Britain's Discovery of Russia, 1553–1815*, London, 1958; J.H. Gleason, *The Genesis of Russophobia in Great Britain*, Cambridge, Mass., 1950; E. Ingram, *The Beginning of the Great Game in Asia, 1834–1838*, Oxford, 1979; Malcolm Yapp, *Strategies of British India, Iran and Afghanistan*, Oxford, 1980.

[87] Although the official designation of Lord Roberts was that of Commander-in-Chief of the Bengal Army, the appointment carried with it supervisory authority over the Madras and Bombay Army. This effectively made him Commander-in-Chief of the entire Army in India.

[88] General Lord Frederick Roberts, "Bobs Bahadur" as he was known to the men under his command, was commander of the Madras Army from 1880, and the Bengal Army from 1885–93. See Roberts, *Forty One Years in India: From Subaltern to Commander-in-Chief*, London, 1897.

recruiting the best fighting materials that could be found in India.[89] He argued that the prevailing practice of recruiting different classes of soldiers[90] just for the sake of keeping a check on each other was outdated. British India, he added, was faced with a pressing threat from the north-west, and the potential foe, unlike any other the Indian Army had faced before, was a powerful European one—the so-called "Russian Bear". There was a need, therefore, to organize the army in such a way as to enable the government to put in field troops that were composed of the best fighting materials.[91] By the 1880s, Roberts, and indeed most of his fellow officers in India, had no doubts where these warlike classes could be found.[92] He announced:

> I have no hesitation myself in stating that except Gurkhas, Dogras, Sikhs, the pick of Punjabi Muhammadans, Hindustanis of the Jat and Ranghur castes, and certain classes of Pathans, there are no native soldiers in our service whom we could venture with safety to place in the field against the Russians.[93]

The notion that certain social groups or "races" in India, namely the Sikhs, Punjabis, Pathans and Gurkhas, were inherently better warriors than others was based upon the belief, popular amongst British soldiers in the nineteenth century, that in India "certain clans and classes can bear arms; the others have not the physical courage necessary for the warrior".[94] The belief that "martial" qualities were

[89] Roberts, 'On the Necessity of Increasing the Efficiency of the Native Army', 25 September 1886, in *Minutes and Notes &c, January-December 1889*, Vol. 6, pp. 153–54, National Army Museum (henceforth NAM).

[90] The term "class" as used by the army authorities in colonial India refers to social groups based on religion and caste rather than in the strict sense to describe social grouping by economic status.

[91] Roberts, 'On the Improvement of the Fighting Efficiency of the Native Army, and the Recruiting and Organization of the Bombay Army', 20 May 1891, in *Minutes and Notes &c, January-April 1893*, Vol. 6, part (ii), pp. 889–90, NAM.

[92] In 1884, Sir Edwin Collen noted that "if the Commanding Officers of the Native Army were polled and their views accepted, the whole army would be composed of Sikhs, Pathans, and Gurkhas". *Recruiting in India*. IOR:L/MIL/17/5/2152.

[93] Roberts, 'On the Necessity For Improving the Fighting Qualities of the Native Army', 8 February 1890, in *Minutes and Notes &c, January-April 1893*, Vol. 6, part (ii), p. 544, NAM.

[94] See G.A. MacMunn, *Armies of India*, London, 1911, p. 129.

inherent in an individual belonging to a particular group eventually developed into a racist recruiting doctrine known as the "martial race theory".[95] The ideology of the "martial race" was, in a way, a reflection of wider British perceptions of Indian society. The British saw that the Indian caste system, with its emphasis on the division and specialization of labour, necessarily implied that some people made better soldiers than others; the existence of the *kshatriya* or warrior caste as traditional arms bearers indicated that the distinction between warlike groups and non-martials was indeed indigenous to India.[96] Lieutenant General George MacMunn, one of the most persuasive proponents of the martial race theory, argued that tradesmen, artificers and goldsmiths could never make good soldiers, for they had all come under the "ancient grooming of the Vaisha.... and had never worn a sword by their side".[97] It was highly plausible that the British "martial race" theory had been influenced by Indian self-images, but the selection of a "martial race" was certainly not based merely on the social hierarchy of traditional Indian society. How else would one account for the identification of groups such as Gurkhas, Sikhs, Punjabi Muslims, Jats, Ranghurs and Pathans as "martial races", while high-caste Brahmans and Rajputs from the south and east were regarded as "non-martials"? Furthermore, why were most of the "martial classes" concentrated in north-western India, particularly in the Punjab? Clearly, a different selection process, quite apart from the Indian caste system, was actually at work.

To a large extent, British estimates of the respective military value of different castes and races were the result of their own military experiences in India. The army's most recent military experiences had been confined to the north: the two Anglo-Sikh wars, frontier skirmishes against the trans-Indus border tribes and the 1857 Mutiny. In all these, the army had the opportunity to observe, at first hand, how their soldiers, particularly the border Pathans, Punjabi Muslims, Sikhs and Gurkhas had performed militarily. The case

---

[95] For a discussion on the martial race theory see David Omissi, 'Martial Races: Ethnicity and Security in Colonial India, 1858–1939', in *War and Society*, Vol. 9, No. 1 (May 1991), pp. 1–26, and Omissi, *The Sepoy and the Raj: The Indian Army, 1860–1940*, London, 1994, pp. 10–43.

[96] Mason, *A Matter of Honour*, p. 349.

[97] Lieutenant General George MacMunn, *The Martial Races of India*, London, 1933, pp. 2–4.

of the Sikhs was typical. Despite having defeated the Sikhs twice in the middle of the nineteenth century, British commanders were full of admiration for the bravery of Sikh soldiers.[98] Even Dalhousie, who deeply distrusted the Sikhs just after the annexation of the Punjab, was ready to admit that they were a warlike people who were ready to take up arms at a moment's notice. The deeply embedded military ethos of the Khalsa Sikhs and military efficiency of Ranjit Singh's army, trained and equipped in European fashion, had long since led the British to regard the Sikhs as a martial people.[99] This admiration was later reinforced by the support given by the Sikhs during the 1857 Rebellion, when many Sikh soldiers fought alongside British soldiers in the vanguard of the final assault on Delhi.

The same was true of the Muslim tribes from the Salt Range tract of western Punjab. In their military campaigns against the Sikh forces in 1848–49, the British had enlisted the military services of Muslim chieftains from the districts of Rawalpindi and Jhelum, in the area known as the Salt Range tract. Many of these warlike tribes had exercised political control in their respective ancestral tracts until the Sikhs subjugated and reduced them to destitution. When offered the opportunity, they were, therefore, more than prepared to rally to the banner of the British and exact their revenge on the Sikhs. The head of the prominent Gakkhar tribe in Rawalpindi, Raja Muhhammud Khan, for instance, joined Nicholson in 1848 and fought in Hazara and Multan alongside the British in 1849.[100] As a reward for their services, members of this tribe had been enlisted into the Indian Army since annexation, serving mainly in the Punjab Frontier Force. In 1857, the Gakkhars once again proved their steadfastness and many of them did excellent service by providing men for the Delhi Field Force while raising local levies to maintain order in their respective localities. Since then members of these tribes, most prominently the Gakkhars, Janjuas, Awans and Rajput Tiwanas, classified broadly by the military authorities as Punjabi Muslims, were regularly recruited for

[98] See, for example, the testimony of General Thackwell, a British commander who fought in the Second Anglo-Sikh War, in E.J. Thackwell, *Narrative of the Second Sikh War, 1848–49*, London, 1851, p. 213.

[99] Fauja Singh Bajwa, *The Military System of the Sikhs*, Delhi, 1964.

[100] Lepel Griffin et. al., *Chiefs and Families of Note in the Punjab*, Lahore, rev. edn., 1907, pp. 218–19.

cavalry regiments of the Bengal Army and the Punjab Frontier Force. Besides being impressed with their track record, the British saw in them, with their traditional and historical enmity against the Sikhs, an effective counterpoise against the latter in the army.[101]

The perceptions of the British were, therefore, important determining criteria in the definition and selection of a "martial race". Familiarity and fondness of the men under their charge entered into the judgement and observations of influential officers and commanders. In the 1880s, the northern races enjoyed more prominence than their southern counterparts because the former's military qualities had caught the attention of British officers whose opinions generally carried weight in military circles. The better officers of the colonial army tended to gravitate towards the northwest, where there was constant campaigning and from where career advancement was more pronounced, while the other presidency armies would normally end up with the rejected and disaffected second-class officers.[102] As a result, senior posts in the army were dominated by those whose experiences were limited to the Punjab section of the Bengal Army. Consequently, officers like Roberts, whose authority extended to the Madras and Bombay Armies, tended to take greater interest in the northern races with whom they were better acquainted; they were convinced that India's fighting army, as far as a great campaign beyond the northwestern frontier was concerned, must be composed mainly of the Sikhs, Punjabis and Pathans.[103] They pointed out that the northern races under their command were physically more robust, and particularly suited to military service in the frontier. Not only were they thought to be better adapted to the rigours of the climate and terrain than their eastern and southern counterparts,[104] they were seen to be more adept at the kinds of warfare that were fought at

[101] Roberts, 'On the Necessity of Improving the Fighting Qualities of the Native Army', 8 February 1890, in *Minutes and Notes &c, January–April 1893*, Vol. 6, part (ii), p. 545.

[102] Adj. Gen. to Military Dept., 3 April 1875, Cmd. 1698 (1877) Vol. 62. Stephen P. Cohen, *The Indian Army: Its Contribution to the Development of a Nation*, Berkeley, 1971, p. 47.

[103] Government of India to Sec. of State, India, 2 November 1892, *Accounts and Papers, 1893–94*, Vol. 63, p. 259.

[104] Memorandum by W.R. Mansfield, Commander-in-Chief, India, 'On the Localization of the Native Regiments', 15 March 1870, in *Correspondences on the Organization of the Native Army*, in *PP*, 1877, Cmd. 1698, Vol. 62, p. 367.

the frontier.[105] These perceptions were soon translated into policies as Hindustani elements of the Punjab Frontier Force were finally eliminated in 1883 on the ground that their health was not up
to the rigorous climatic demands which the Punjabis were capable
of withstanding.[106]

These perceptions were not without their basis. The "martial
race" theory became popular in the late nineteenth century, some
two decades after the Punjabis had been partially entrenched in
the ranks of the Bengal Army. With the army's adherence to the
principles of localization of recruitment and services, military action, which was limited almost invariably to the north-western frontier, became the strict preserve of the Punjabi regiments serving
there. Inevitably, the Punjab regiments were conditioned by the
active and unremitting service of the past twenty to thirty years in
a rugged terrain. Under such conditions, it was natural for the
northern regiments to develop a higher level of efficiency and spirit.

Regiments garrisoned in the east and south, on the other hand,
saw little or no action, with their regimental lives revolving around
drill, cantonment duties and the maintenance of cantonment lines.
The prospect of spending an entire military career in the drudgery
of cantonment duties had a negative effect on the image of military service. Recruiting officers in the Bombay Army complained,
for instance, that it was difficult to obtain quality soldiers when it
was believed that the Bombay sepoy was more often employed as
a labourer than as a soldier. High-caste Rajputs, for whom military service had been regarded as a traditional vocation as indicative of their social status, considered manual labour derogatory,
and were often discouraged from enlisting by the knowledge that
extensive line building or repairing had been of late occupying the
native infantry regiments in nearly every cantonment.[107] It was a similar situation in Madras. In 1871 Sir Frederick Haines, Commander-

---

[105] This has been convincingly argued by Clive Dewey in his paper, 'The Rise of
the Martial Castes' presented at a seminar at the Council of Historical Research in
London in 1989.

[106] Colonel J.W. Mcqueen, Sec. to Government of Punjab (GoP) to Chesney, Sec.
to GoI, Military Department, 5 October 1883, Punjab Government Home (Military)
Proceedings [henceforth PHP(M)], 'A', February 1884, Lahore Archives, Lahore,
Pakistan.

[107] *Confidential Report on Recruiting*, Adj. Gen., Bombay Army, 20 October 1894,
p. 7, NAM.

in-Chief of the Madras Army, lamented that his officers and men were "falling into the delusion that they had nothing but police duties to perform",[108] with the result that only second rate recruits were attracted to the army. A vicious cycle subsequently developed. The admission of poorer and probably less motivated recruits only served to reinforce the prejudices of British officers against the southern sepoy; eventually, as fewer were recruited because they were thought poorly of, fewer actually regarded the army as a viable career. This phenomenon was not unique to Madras. Philip Mason, who served as Deputy Commissioner in the highly recruited hill district of Garhwal in the United Provinces observed that in areas where recruitment was intensive, getting a place in the army was a "common ambition and a laudable goal; but where opportunities diminished, men would forget to think of life in the army".[109]

The army's preferences for the so-called "martial races" brought about a gradual geographic shift northwards in its recruitment pattern. When Roberts became Commander-in-Chief of the Bengal Army in 1885, he began to put into practice what he had advocated. In September 1886, he proposed that all "unwarlike" portions of the armies of all the three presidencies be replaced by men drawn from the "martial" races.[110] By the end of the nineteenth century, the idea of filling the colonial army with the most suitable fighting material was no longer a matter of personal choices of respective commanders-in-chief; it became a full-blown recruiting doctrine which the military and the state in colonial India faithfully adhered to for the next fifty years.

Recruiting came to be guided by a series of manuals and handbooks, which contained detailed evaluations of the military potential of various classes of recruits. Couched as ethnological and anthropological studies, these handbooks were often nothing more than observations based on colonial stereotypes and racism that imbibed an extreme form of cultural and environmental determinism. These handbooks justified their choice recruits by attributing

[108] T.A. Heathcote, *Indian Army*, pp. 91–92.

[109] Philip Mason, *A Shaft of Sunlight: Memories of A Varied Life*, London, 1978, pp. 130–31.

[110] Government of India, *Short Report on the Important Questions dealt with during the Tenure of Command of the Army in India by General Lord Roberts, 1885–1893*, Simla, 1893, p. 147. IOR:L/MIL/17/5/1613.

to them inherent qualities such as masculinity, fidelity, bravery and loyalty. These "martial races" were closely identified, down to the relevant sub-castes and places from which they were to be found. For example, the recruiting manual for the Sikhs indicated that the best Sikh soldiers were to be found in the Manjha region of central Punjab, the heartland of the Jat Sikh peasantry, while those from the urban areas and the eastern districts were deemed less than ideal because their purity had been diminished by physical distance from the fount of their martial qualities. Guided by these handbooks, the military authorities subsequently implemented a system of recruiting in which specific social and ethnic groups, deemed to possess martial qualities, were identified and recruitment was to be intensified in areas where these groups were to be found.[111] In 1891, territorial recruiting depots were established and district recruiting officers who would be responsible for recruiting a particular class were appointed. These depots came to be located in the following areas where the "martial races" were concentrated: Peshawar for Pathans, Rawalpindi for Punjabi Muslims, Amritsar for Sikhs, Jullunder for Dogras, Delhi for Jats and Lucknow for Hindu castes east of the Jumna.[112] This form of recruitment was to remain the main system of recruiting by the colonial army until 1917. This new system meant that recruiting was now given a territorial focus, and this focus was shifting irrevocably towards the Punjab.

By the 1890s, the role of the armed forces in India had undergone a reappraisal. In the 1860s and 1870s, the army was kept mainly as an internal security force, and "divide and rule" was the underlying policy governing its organization. But towards the end of Robert's tenure as Commander-in-Chief of the army in India, defence of Empire was the role which the army was expected to perform. This meant that the army in India had to be reorganized accordingly and that "divide and rule" was no longer thought to be a cardinal organizational principle.[113] First, priority was to be given to acquiring the right materials for the army. Consequently,

---

[111] *Questions dealt with during the Tenure of Lord Roberts, 1885–1895*, p. 152.

[112] Lieutenant General H. Hudson, *Recruiting in India before and during the War of 1914–1918*, (henceforth *Recruiting in India*) Army Headquarters in India, October 1919, p. 14. IOR:L/MIL/17/5/2152.

[113] During his tenure as Commander-in-Chief, Roberts began a process of galvanizing the three presidency armies into a unified armed force, but the process was only completed during Lord Kitchener's tenure as Commander-in-Chief of the Indian Army.

from 1890 onwards Sikhs, Punjabi Muslims, Dogras, Jats, Pathans and Gurkhas were the main classes recruited into the Indian Army; their recruitment gradually intensified as heavy reductions were made in the Madras Army. In 1891, in the place of Telugus, Ahirs, Gujjars and others who were considered "non-martial", more battalions of Punjabis and Gurkhas were raised. The following year, the active part of the Madras Army which garrisoned Burma was reconstituted into six battalions of northerners, comprising thirteen companies of Sikhs, twenty of Punjabi Muslims, two of Jats, and eight of Gurkhas and hillmen. These changes were not limited to the Madras Army; in 1891 four Hindustani regiments of the Bengal Army were replaced by Punjabi Muslims drawn from Rawalpindi Division, a Dogra regiment and a Garhwal regiment, and orders were issued for the elimination of thirty companies of "other Hindus" including Gujjars and Ahirs. The composition of non-Punjabi regiments in the Bengal Army was subsequently to be confined to Muslims, Brahmins, Rajputs, Jats, Bundelas and the hillmen from Garhwal. In the Bombay Army, similar changes were made by expanding the number of Baluchis and Punjabis into the cavalry.[114]

Roberts further proposed that regiments be reorganized from mixed to mono-regiments, arguing that regiments comprising a homogeneous "martial class" would be more efficient that mixed regiments.[115] Consequently, as recruitment came to be concentrated on a handful of select "martial classes", class company regiments gradually gave way to class regiments in which the entire regiment consisted of a single class.

Roberts' policies of concentrating recruitment on a few select groups of northern races and reintroducing the single class regiments were diametrically opposed to the tenet laid down by the Peel Commission that "the native army should be composed of different nationalities and castes ... mixed promiscuously through each regiment". Warnings had been sounded against allowing, "one tribe, such as the Sikhs, [to] be armed in such comparative numbers as to become in themselves a source of danger",[116] in 1892 the

---

[114] Record of Kitchener's Administration of the Army in India, pp. 300–301. IOR:L/MIL/17/4/1617.

[115] *Questions dealt with during the Tenure of Lord Roberts*, L/MIL/17/5/1613.

[116] Testimony by Sir J.P. Grant, 4 June 1858, Cmd. 2515, 1859, Vol. 5; see also Military Dept., 15 September 1885, 'On the Increase and Organization of the Army in India' Files 6 and 8–10, Vol. 5, Military Collection 120, p. 10. IOR:L/MIL/7/5460.

Secretary of State for India, Viscount Cross, saw it necessary to caution Roberts "to be careful when selecting the best fighting material, to enlist only those who were likely to remain faithful ... [and] to equalize the proportion of each race".[117] To the detractors of his policy, Roberts replied that it was ultimately a question of priorities: having a large number of northern fighting men in the colonial army entailed a risk, but the "greatest risk of all is to be without an army which will fight".[118] Nevertheless, due to some official reservations, Roberts' proposal of converting all regiments of the Indian Army to mono-regiments was never fully executed, and the army retained a mixture of mono and mixed regiments.

Like Roberts, Lord Kitchener, who became Commander-in-Chief of the Indian Army in 1903, believed that it was more crucial, at a time when the Empire was still very much under the threat of a possible Russian invasion, to organize the army on principles of fighting efficiency rather than security. He perceived that the main danger threatening British India in 1905 was the menacing advance of Russia towards India's north-western frontier. He was convinced that, despite Russia's recent defeat in the Russo-Japanese War, the Russian army was still intact and formidable, and that Russian designs on Central Asia and the British Indian Empire had not been forgotten. As far as Kitchener was concerned, the need to strengthen India's defence, especially at its north-western frontier, was now more urgent than ever.[119] Accordingly, he continued Robert's work of weeding out the non-martial elements from the army, and replacing them with the "martial classes" of north India. Fourteen Madras regiments were reconstituted into nine Punjabi and five Gurkha regiments, and at the turn of the century, Sikhs and Punjabi Muslims recruits gradually replaced the old classes of soldiers from Rohilkhand and Oudh.[120]

During his tenure as Commander-in-Chief, Kitchener saw the completion of the process, which had begun in 1895, of the

[117] Quoted in *Recruiting in India*, October 1919, p. 3. IOR:L/MIL/17/5/2152.
[118] Roberts to Alfred Lyall, 28 July 1890, in *Correspondence with England while Commander-in-Chief, India, 3 January–8 March 1890*, Vol. 9, p. 55, NAM.
[119] 'Note on the Military Policy in India', by Lord Kitchener, 19 July 1905 (Simla, 1905), pp. 5–7, in Roberts Papers, NAM:7101-23-170.
[120] Record of Kitchener's Administration of the Army of India, 1901–1909, p. 312. IOR:L/MIL/17/5/1617.

amalgamation of the three separate presidency armies into a single Indian Army. The unified Indian Army of 1895 was initially divided into four regional commands: the Punjab (including the Punjab Frontier Force), Bengal, Madras and Bombay. In 1903, Kitchener reorganized it into formations which were expected to operate during a war. It was divided into a field force of about 152,000 men organized into five divisions and three brigades, and an internal security force of 80,000. These reforms confirmed Punjab's status as the most important province to the military establishment in India. Not only was it strategically crucial as the ideal staging and supply base for operations across the north-western frontier, but the Punjab was, by 1900, supplying more than half the combatants of the entire Indian Army.[121] Although the Russian threat dissipated with the Anglo-Russian Convention of 1907 the military importance of the Punjab remained undiminished. It maintained a close relationship with the military as the main recruiting ground for the army, a relationship which was to last until the British departed from India in 1947.

In this chapter, we have seen that the opening of the Punjab for recruitment and its subsequent development as the major recruiting ground for the colonial army in India was the direct result of the changes made in the Indian Army from 1858 to about 1900. As I have pointed out, changes were made in the Indian Army in response to the requirements of the imperial state, and the colonial administration carefully and consciously developed the army in the way that could best serve their imperial interests. The form and content of the Indian Army was, therefore, closely related to British perceptions of the threat to their security in India.

After the 1857 Mutiny, the main function of the Indian Army was limited to the maintenance of internal security; the military authority's chief concern was to keep the army safe and to prevent a repeat of 1857. To achieve this, the strength of the army was divided and different components of the armed forces used as checks and balances on each other. At the all-India level, the segregation of the three Presidency Armies was maintained; and within the

---

[121] In 1900, Punjabi Muslims, including the Hazara tribes, Sikhs, Punjabi Hindus and Hindus from the cis-Jumna territories around Delhi accounted for about 75,000 out of a total Indian Army strength of 141,000. *Annual Caste Returns, 1900.* IOR:L/MIL/14/224.

Bengal Army, a Punjabi contingent was introduced as a counter-poise to the Hindustani elements. Consequently, Punjabi troops, which were raised as an ad hoc measure to quell the Mutiny, became a permanent feature in the Bengal Army after 1858.

In the third quarter of the nineteenth century, military thinking in India underwent a change and the Indian Army was accordingly restructured. The new enemies were the Russians and their allies, the Afghans, on the north-western frontier. After the end of the Crimean War (1854–56), the Russians had sought to extend their political influence eastwards by securing the favours of the Shah of Persia and the Amir of Afghanistan through trade and investment. The British in India tried to develop closer ties with Afghanistan in the 1870s, but met with little success. In an attempt to check the power of the British, the Amir of Afghanistan decided to get closer to the Russians. As the main function of the colonial army shifted from internal security of the Raj to its protection against foreign attack, the British put more emphasis on increasing the fighting capabilities of the army. "Safety" had to give way to efficiency, so recruitment came to be concentrated on a few select groups who were perceived to be better equipped for fighting the enemy across the north-west frontier. This recruitment policy was eventually couched in the "martial race" ideology.

The Punjab became militarily important because of its continued relevance to the successive phases of army reforms. Punjabis first showed their military value with their vital intervention on the side of the British during the 1857 Mutiny. In the post-Mutiny reforms, Punjab regiments formed an essential component in the execution of the policy of "divide and rule" in the army, and by the end of the century, the Punjab had assumed an unrivalled position as the home of the "martial classes". By the end of the nineteenth century, the Punjab had, to all intents and purposes, become the main military labour market of the Indian Army.

TWO

Recruiting in the Punjab: "Martial Races" and the Military Districts

By the end of the nineteenth century, the Punjab had replaced north-central India, Bombay and Madras as the main recruiting ground for the Indian Army, supplying more than half the combatants for the entire force (see Tables 2.1 and 2.2). This need not suggest, however, that the entire province had been opened as the main recruiting ground for the army in India by the turn of the century. Rather, the military labour market in the Punjab—the numbers and types of soldiers who were recruited and the localities from which they were drawn—was an extremely limited one; in 1900, out of a total male population of 11,255,986, just over 50,000 were in direct military service.[1] In 1897, when the military authorities had virtually ceased recruiting from elsewhere but the north, the total annual intake of Punjabi recruits in the Indian Army was estimated at no more than 4,500.[2] This restriction was imposed essentially by the "martial class" doctrine, which was already at its most influential stage by the turn of the niinteenth century. Within the Punjab only the selected group of martial classes, mainly Sikhs, Punjabi Muslims and, to a lesser extent, Dogras and Hindu Jats, were eligible for recruitment. All other groups and classes of

[1] See H.A. Rose, *Census of India: Report of Punjab, 1901*, Vol. 17, Simla, 1902; and *Annual Caste Returns of the Indian Army, 1900*. IOR:L/MIL/14/224.

[2] 'Recruiting in the Native Army', Sec. to GoP, 13 January 1899 in PHP(M) 'B', pros. 82.

Punjabis that did not fall in the categories designated as martial classes were automatically excluded.

Table 2.1
Number of Indian Infantry Units

Year	Gurkhas	North-central	North-west (Punjab and NWFP)	Bombay	Madras
1862	5	26	28	20	40
1885	13	20	31	26	32
1892	15	15	34	26	25
1914	20	15	57	18	11

Source: Extracted from *Recruiting in India before and during the War of 1914–1918*, Army Headquarters, India, 1919, IOR: L/MIL/17/5/2515, p. 7

Table 2.2
Recruitment of Punjabis, 1858–1910

Year	Number of Punjabis in the Army	Percentage of Punjabis in the Army	Percentage Increase on 1858
1858	22,790	32.7	
1880	38,538	27	+ 69
1890	44,940	30	+ 97
1900	65,820	50.6	+ 188
1910	93,295	53.7	+ 309

Source: Extracted from *Annual Caste Returns of the Native Army, 1880–1910*, IOR: L/MIL/17/4/221, 223, 224, 226.

Very specific sub-divisions went into the definition of a "martial class" and many regiments narrowed their selection to include only recruits from particular sub-castes, clans, tribes and localities. The cases of the Sikhs and the Punjabi Muslims are instructive in this respect. Although the Sikhs were generally regarded as a "martial class", and by the 1880s constituted a significant portion of the infantry regiments of the Indian Army, their numbers in service, as a proportion of their population in the Punjab, was not strikingly high. Recruitment handbooks produced by Army Headquarters for officers recruiting for and commanding Sikh regiments spelt out who were considered suitable recruits: only Sikhs belonging to the dominant peasant Jat caste and adhering to the *Khalsa* creed were deemed ideal recruits and should be targeted for Sikh regiments. These recruiting manuals advised that

... in judging the values of tribes which supplied converts to Sikhism in the time of Guru Gobind Singh, who in fact formed the Singh people, ... those tribes who, though they now supply converts to Sikhism, did not do so then, cannot be considered (or it is inadvisable to consider) as true Sikhs.[3]

The choice of the *Khalsa* Jat Sikh was perhaps understandable, given the British belief that the socially dominant and militaristic Jat peasantry found in the heart of Punjab was naturally good material for the army, while Sikhs imbued with the martial values of the *Khalsa* would possess the right types of military virtues necessary for a soldier. Sikhism had, after all, been militarized by the influx of numerous Jat peasants into the faith in the seventeenth century.[4] But the prejudice did not end there. In addition to stressing the importance of being of the "right social and religious type", these handbooks revealed an astonishing adherence to elements of environmental determinism by articulating that the value of Sikh recruits and the characteristics they were likely to show depended more upon the district they came from rather than on the caste or clan to which they belonged. Some districts were to be avoided for recruiting purposes because "they were too far east to be desirable, the characteristic of the people more of the Hindustani type ... and that Sikhism [in the eastern districts] had been diluted by Hinduism".[5] The manuals to recruiting officers described the Jat Sikhs from central Punjab as "hardy, strong, and full of hard work ... and the best quality Sikhs for military purposes....[while] Sikhs from the sub-montane tract, including the districts of Hoshiarpur, Ambala, Gurdaspur, Sialkot and Gujrat, were considered poor types, and not suitable for enlistment".[6] Consequently, in the whole of the Punjab, the recruitment of Sikhs was virtually limited to the Manjha area of central Punjab, and over ninety per cent of Sikhs recruited

---

[3] Captain R.W. Falcon, *Handbook on Sikhs for Use of Regimental Officers* (henceforth *Handbook*), Allahabad, 1896, p. 65. Captain Falcon served in the 4th Sikh Infantry Regiment in the Punjab Frontier Force, and later as district recruiting officer in the Sikh districts.

[4] See H. Mcleod, *Evolution of the Sikh Community: Five Essays*, Delhi, 1975, pp. 9–12.

[5] R.W. Falcon, *Handbook*, pp. 71–72, 102. These views were reinforced by A.H. Bingley, *Handbook on the Sikhs*, Simla, 1899.

[6] Major A.E. Barstow, *Recruiting Handbooks for the India Army: Sikhs* (henceforth *Sikhs*), Calcutta, 1898, pp. 70–72, and Appendix 1, p. 200.

were listed as Jat Sikhs. Amritsar district, at the heart of the Manjha tract, supplied more than a third of all Sikhs recruited in the Punjab,[7] and practically every regiment which had a Sikh company contained men enlisted from this district.

The only other noticeable group of Sikhs recruited for the Indian Army in addition to Jat Sikhs were the low-caste Mazhabi Sikhs. Mazhabis were originally *Churas*, a sweeper caste, who had been converted to Sikhism after three of their kind snatched the quartered body of Tegh Bahadur, the Sikh's ninth Guru, from a Muslim crowd in Delhi and brought it back to his son, Gobind Singh. As a reward, the sweepers were admitted to the *Khalsa* and granted the title of Mazhabi (faithful). Maharaja Ranjit Singh patronized them and recruited them into his army, but due to objections from high-caste Sikhs, they were formed into separate companies which were attached to regular battalions. Mazhabis traditionally served as pioneers, infantrymen who were trained for the construction of roads, canals and bridges, but who, unlike ordinary labourers, could defend themselves when attacked. After the defeat of the Sikh army, Mazhabis lost their access to military service but during the 1857 Mutiny they were raised again as a pioneer regiment. Since then the Mazhabis, whose population was concentrated in Ludhiana district, became a permanent feature of the Indian Army. Although initial classified as rural menials by the British, access to military service and the award of colony land grants in the canal colonies had contributed to their general social elevation in the rural hierarchy. In 1911, the Mazhabis were officially accorded the status of an agricultural caste in Gujranwala and Lyallpur.[8]

Recruitment of Punjabi Muslims was similarly restricted in the Punjab. As with the Sikhs, the expansive rhetoric surrounding the "martial class" theory concealed the fact that at the end of the nineteenth century, the total number of Muslims recruited from the region between the Indus and the Sutlej in western Punjab formed only about ten per cent (about 14,000) of the Indian Army.[9] This rather low demand for Punjabi Muslim recruits meant that regimental recruiters could afford to be very selective in their choice of recruits. A recruiting officer pointed out that in calculating the numbers of

---

[7] H.D. Craik, *PDG, Amritsar, 1914* (Lahore, 1914), Vol. 20A, p. 162.

[8] Imran Ali, *Punjab Under Imperialism*, p. 112.

[9] *Annual Caste Returns, 1900*, IOR: L/MIL/14/224.

each tribe available who were likely to enlist, experience showed that two per cent of the total male population was the outside limit. The standard of requirement was deliberately set high: the recruit had to be between sixteen and nineteen years in age, with a minimum height requirement of five feet eight inches, and a chest measurement of thirty-four inches. If he fulfilled these requirements, he was then subjected to a stringent medical examination.[10] Those who eventually passed through this rigorous selection process constituted but a small section of the population. The Settlement Officer for Jhelum district noted that in 1880, out of a total district Muslim population of 522,840, only 926 were in receipt of military pay.[11] The population figures, unfortunately, did not include data on sex and age, but if it is assumed that men of military age constituted about twenty-five per cent of the population of the district, then one can see that less than one per cent of the male population of military age was actually involved in military service.

But the choice of Muslims was not merely one of physical suitability. As in the case of the Sikhs, recruiting authorities showed a clear bias in favour of the dominant landowning tribes of the region, and recruitment of Punjabi Muslims was limited to those who belonged to tribes of high social standing or reputation—the "blood proud" and once politically dominant aristocracy of the tract. Consequently, socially dominant Muslim tribes such as the Gakkhars, Janjuas and Awans, and a few Rajput tribes, concentrated in the Rawalpindi and Jhelum districts in the northern Salt Range tract in the Punjab, accounted for more than ninety per cent of Punjabi Muslim recruits.[12]

Recruitment in the Punjab was, therefore, based not only on class, but on locality as well. Military service was consequently restricted strictly to certain groups from more or less fixed areas: Jat Sikhs from Amritsar and Lahore, and to a lesser extent Hoshiarpur and

---

[10] W.S. Talbot, *PDG, Jhelum, 1904*, p. 253.

[11] R.G. Thompson, *Land Settlements Report*, (henceforth *LSR*) *Jhelum District, 1874–80* (Lahore, 1883), pp. 40–41, 78–79. IOR:V/27/314/542–43. This figure may not be totally accurate as by 1880, especially in the wake of the Afghan war, Jhelum was one of the major recruiting grounds for the Punjab regiments. However, it may be noted that only a very small percentage of the population of the district was directly involved in military service.

[12] Lieutenant Colonel J.M. Wikeley, *Punjabi Mussalmans*, Calcutta, 1915, p.125. IOR:L/MIL/17/5/2166.

Ludhiana, and the aristocratic Muslim tribes from the Salt Range tract, mainly in the districts of Jhelum and Rawalpindi. In addition, a small proportion of Hindu and Muslim Jats from the southeastern districts of Rohtak and Hissar and Dogras from Kangra district made up the entire military labour market of the Punjab.[13]

There were two main reasons why recruitment was so localized in the Punjab: one was military and the other political. The military rationale was straightforward enough: recruiting in the Punjab was localized largely as a result of the organization of companies and regiments along class lines. Class companies or regiments contained recruits belonging to the same class, drawn mainly from the same locality. When recruiting for the regiments, it was important for the recruiting officer to draw from the same sources that had supplied the regiment in the first place. Hence, if the regiment was a class regiment formed entirely of Jat Sikhs from the Tarn Taran tehsil of Amritsar district, the recruiting officer would recruit only Jat Sikhs from the same locality for the regiment. From the point of view of regimental efficiency, getting the right type of recruits for the regiments was important: there was a need to preserve the clan purity of the regiment or the company because the solidarity and morale of the regiment often hinged on the shared values and traditions of the men who made up the regiment. Many of the tribes and castes were very conscious of their social status and would not serve with those whom they considered their social inferiors. For example, the socially dominant Gakkhars would readily enlist in single class regiments or mixed regiments, but they would not serve in a company with other Punjabi Muslims, unless their ranks in the company were made commensurate with their social position in the district.[14] Similarly, the Janjuas, who in the western Punjab tribal hierarchy ranked as high as the Gakkhars, were very particular as to the company in which they would serve, and would not enlist readily into a company which was not commanded by a Gakkhar, a Janjua or a person from some tribe of equal standing.[15] In a way, therefore, the social structure of the village was often replicated in the company or the regiment, and usually, the authority of the subedar major within the regiment was reinforced by his position as a village elder.

[13] *Annual Caste Returns*, 1900.
[14] PDG, *Jhelum*, 1904, p. 254.
[15] *Ibid*.

Localization had a political purpose too. As suggested earlier, recruiting in the Punjab in the immediate aftermath of the Mutiny was governed by an overriding strategy of "divide and rule", a strategy not dissimilar to that adopted by Ranjit Singh for his army. Although the Sikhs formed the largest single group within the *Khalsa* army, the Maharaja wisely recruited Muslims, Afghans, Pathans, Hindustanis, Dogras and Europeans to ensure that no single group monopolized the army.[16] In a sense, the British virtually decided to take over the recruiting practices of the former Sikh army and recruited from the Punjab different groups separated by religious, caste, ethnic and geographical differences, and then kept them apart in different regiments or companies within each regiment so that each could be utilized as a counterpoise against the other.

Although in the last decades of the nineteenth century concern for the security of the army in India was superseded by the desire to improve its fighting efficiency, the policy of John Lawrence had not been totally jettisoned. In the Punjab, the recruitment practices of the 1860s, based on "divide and rule", persisted. But in order to make "divide and rule" effective, the choice of recruits was critical. Groups had to be selected which possessed traditional and historical animosities and whose value or culture system still reflected these cleavages. In other words, recruiting was carried out in such a manner as to reproduce, within the Punjab contingent, the historical cleavages that existed within their society. The class basis of recruitment and organization and the careful nurturing of class tradition helped reinforce caste and class compartmentalization. *Khalsa* Jat Sikhs with their historical animosity towards Muslims dating back to the period of Mughal persecution were the ideal counterpoise against the Muslims. Similarly, it was expected that the aristocratic Muslim tribes of the Salt Range tract, who had been reduced to destitution during the reign of the Sikhs, would not hesitate to turn against the Sikhs, should the occasion arise. Little wonder, therefore, that the army authorities should insist that the tenets of the Sikh religion be strictly observed by Sikhs soldiers in the Indian Army, and took such care in observing the tribal standings of the aristocratic Muslim tribes of western Punjab. While the army in India, with its European-style organizational structure, uniforms, weapons systems and tactical doctrines, was in many ways

---

[16] C.A. Bayly, *Indian Society and the Making of the British Empire*, p. 127.

a modern Anglo-Indian institution, its effect on society, especially where recruitment was concerned, was to reinforce and perpetuate the old order of rural Punjab.

The localized pattern of recruiting in the Punjab was reflected in a system of recruitment that limited the army's contact to the very classes and districts in which it was recruiting. In 1891, in accordance with the recommendations of Roberts, regional depots were established, each under a district recruiting officer responsible for recruiting a particular class of recruits.[17] Under this system, district depots were set up in the Punjab in Rawalpindi, Amritsar and Delhi for the recruitment of Punjabi Muslims, Sikhs and Jats respectively. Thus, Punjabi Muslims would be recruited only in the Rawalpindi depot, and since most of the Punjabi Muslims were recruited from that area, from the districts of Jhelum, Attock and Rawalpindi, the depot was ideally suited to tap the material there. Similarly, the Amritsar depot would only recruit Jat Sikhs from the Manjha area, while the Delhi depot was responsible for obtaining Hindu Jat recruits from the nearby Rohtak and Hissar districts, as well as from the districts of the western United Provinces. This was an extremely localized system for it meant that the classes were only recruited from confined areas. For instance, a Jat Sikh living in Rawalpindi would have very little opportunity of being recruited as he would be deterred by the need to travel all the way to the Amritsar depot at his own expense for the necessary medical examination and other recruitment procedures. This system suited the requirements of a small peacetime army. It made no provisions at all, however, for expansion, should the need arise. Its shortcomings were highlighted by the outbreak of the First World War, as shall be discussed in chapter three.

The class system of recruiting revolved around the district recruiting officer who, by being in charge of the recruiting depot, served as an indispensable link between the recruiting base and the regiments. He possessed an intimate knowledge of his locality and of the class of recruits for which he was responsible.[18] How then did the recruiting officer facilitate the process of recruitment under the class recruiting system? For example, if the 13th Lancers,

[17] Hudson, *Recruiting in India*, p. 14. IOR:L/MIL/17/5/2152.

[18] Army Headquarters, India, *Development of Manpower in India and its Utilization for Imperial Purposes, April 1919*, p. 4. IOR:L/MIL/17/5/2398.

a cavalry regiment composed entirely of Punjabi Muslims, found themselves at the end of the season short of twenty men, the commanding officer would inform the recruiting officer in Rawalpindi that he wanted twenty recruits for his regiment and that they would have to be Gakkhars or Awans from a particular village. The recruiting officer would despatch a recruiting party, led by a native officer or a non-commissioned officer, to the village where the men were to be recruited from. The recruitment party usually comprised of men who belonged to that part of the country; their familiarity and local influence enabled them to obtain recruits of the required class. Before recruits were taken to regimental depots, their caste and sub-castes had to be verified by the village headmen. This process was sometimes supplemented by a more informal system which relied on kinship and village networks of serving soldiers. Indian soldiers on returning from furlough from their villages would bring back with them kinsmen and relatives for their regiments. Here the onus for obtaining the right recruit, and thus preserving the clan purity of the regiment or the company, would fall on the native officer himself.

The Economics of Military Service

So far we have seen recruitment merely as a one-way process by which the imperial rulers identified and selected their military collaborators by incorporating them into the armed forces. But to understand fully the relationship between the army and the military districts in the Punjab, there is a need to look at the other side and to ask why the "martial classes" chose the British. In other words, why were the Sikhs, Muslims, Jats and Dogras prepared to take up military service so readily when it was offered to them? The Indian Army was after all a voluntary army, and no recruit who did not wish to join the army could be coerced, at least in times of peace, into enlistment. To account for their preference of the "martial classes", the military authorities would point to the cultural propensity of certain groups for military service, and declare that these "martial classes" had traditionally been sword bearers and service in the Indian Army was merely their response to the calling of their profession. If this were simply the case, the army would have no reason to run short of their desired recruits. But this was certainly not the case in the 1880s and 1890s, when the military authorities constantly complained that they were running short of their favoured recruits.[19]

In considering motivations for military service, the cultural propensity of certain social groups, such as the Rajput tribes and militarized Jat peasantry, to readily pursue a vocation in arms should not be dismissed. In traditional societies where military service was regarded less as a professional career option than an assertion of social identity, self-image and status were often powerful factors explaining the desire to bear arms. The desire of these groups to upkeep a warrior tradition may suggest that military service was a natural act; but this should not, however, disguise the fact that there were equally important material factors that motivated enlistment. Economic necessities and opportunities were often fundamental "push factors" for most recruits seeking enlistment into the army. Interestingly, behind the official rhetoric about the favoured "martial races", there was no delusion amongst the military authorities that the army in India was essentially an alien and mercenary one which served the state "when all is said and done, for the monthly wage, the other pecuniary wages and the pension".[20]

Service in the military was generally attractive because of the certain and regular pay it promised. In the late nineteenth century, a soldier in the Indian Army was paid seven rupees a month and enjoyed other perks, such as foreign service *batta* (bonus), good conduct pay and free travel on railways. However, military pay *per se* does not fully explain the preference for military service. In the Punjab, the essential fact was that there was a prominent nexus between the economic conditions of the military districts and the preparedness of the so-called military classes to enlist in the army. During one of his tours of the villages in the Punjab in 1929, Malcolm Darling asked the people whether they joined the army due to *shauq* (keenness) or *bhuq* (hunger). Most of them replied *bhuq* first and then *shauq*.[21] The ebb and flow of recruits from the

[19] Despatch, GoI, Military Dept. to Secretary of State for India, 14 August 1887, in *Extracts from Correspondences on the Subject of Increase of Army in India*, 16 September 1887, in *PP*, 1887, Vol. 62, pp. 38–40.

[20] Note by E.H.H. Collen, 3 November 1900, in *Punjab Revenue and Agricultural Proceeding 'A'*, March 1902. IOR:P/5842.

[21] Malcolm L. Darling, *Rusticus Loquitur, or the Old Light and The New in The Punjab Villages*, London, 1930, p. 30.

military districts, therefore, depended largely on the economic conditions of their respective districts and the relative profitability of military service over other economic activities. Given the diversity of Punjab's peasant society, the full extent of the nexus between economic conditions and enlistment can only be uncovered by local studies at the tehsil and village levels across the Punjab.[22] To obtain a general picture, we shall examine the connections between economic pressure and enlistment into the army by looking at the importance of military earnings in the internal economies of three military districts in the three main recruiting regions of the Indian Army, which represent a cross-section of Punjabi peasant society: Jhelum district in the Salt Range tract from where the bulk of the Punjabi Muslims were recruited; Amritsar district in the Manjha region of central Punjab, home of the Jat Sikhs; and the southeastern district of Rohtak, from where Hindu Jats were recruited.

Punjabi Muslims from the Salt Range Tract

General poverty and agricultural insecurity were features of the *barani* or rain-fed lands in the district of Jhelum. The district formed part of the Salt Range tract, dominated by a terrain so craggy and physically broken that it was described as "a confused medley of hillock and hollow".[23] The uneven terrain, inferior quality soil (with large deposits of rock salts) and scarce and uncertain rainfall rendered cultivation in the region near impossible. The limited agricultural activities in the area were at the mercy of rainfall as irrigation of any form was almost entirely absent. In 1883, only parts of the Pind Dadan Khan tehsil within the entire Jhelum district had the benefit of two small inundation canals, and accounted for less than three per cent of the total area of the district (about 27,000 acres)

[22] The magnitude and complexity of the task is shown in Clive Dewey's pioneering work on the economic connections between military service and peasant society in the Punjab. See, for example, Clive Dewey 'Some Consequences of Military Expenditure in British India: The Case of Upper Sind Sagar Doab, 1844–1947', pp. 93–169, and some of his unpublished seminar and conference papers, namely, 'The Army as Safety Net: Military Service and Peasant Stratification in British Punjab', and 'The Rise of the Martial Castes: Changes in the Composition of the Indian Army, 1878–1914'.

[23] Malcolm L. Darling, *The Punjab Peasant in Prosperity and Debt*, London, 1936, p. 74.

under artificial irrigation.[24] As a consequence, less than one-third of the total area in this tehsil was considered cultivable. Scanty rainfall made cultivation extremely precarious, and when the rains failed, the cultivating population was driven to hardship.

Not only were existing conditions poor, but the potential for agricultural growth in this district was, by the late nineteenth century, virtually non-existent. Between 1863 and 1883, during which the First Regular and Second Land Settlements were carried out respectively, Jhelum district experienced significant agricultural and economic growth. By then, it had reached its maximum agricultural output and, by the time of the Third Settlement in 1901, there was hardly any increase in the agricultural output of the district. In 1901, the Land Settlement Officer observed that "in respect of agriculture, the District has nearly reached the end of its tether".[25] Under such conditions, the major Muslim tribes of the districts— the Awans, Rajput Janjuas and Gakkhars—often found it necessary to turn to military service for their economic survival.

The conditions in the Khuddhar assessment circle in the eastern part of the Jhelum district, where the Gakkhars held several villages, were typical of the general condition of the Salt Range tract. Sixty-four per cent of the terrain, covered by forests and broken by ravines and water courses, made the better part of the circle impossible to cultivate and of little use for cattle grazing.[26] Consequently, only thirty-six per cent of the tehsil could be put under the plough.[27]

Where tilling was possible, agricultural output remained precarious due to uncertain rainfall and was not sufficient to sustain a proper livelihood. Of the twelve recorded harvests between 1892 and 1898, only six were considered as having given good yields; the rest were barely sufficient to keep the villages in subsistence.[28] The Gakkhar tribe, which formed the proprietary body in this depressed tract, found themselves perpetually in debt. Their limited

[24] W.S. Talbot, *LSR, Jhelum, 1895–1901* (Lahore, 1902). IOR:V/27/314/544.

[25] R.G. Thompson, *LSR, Jhelum, 1874–80*; W.S. Talbot, *LSR, Jhelum, 1895–1901*, p. 4.

[26] W.S. Talbot, Assessment Report (henceforth *AR*), Jhelum tehsil, 1900, in Punjab Revenue and Agriculture (Revenue) Proceedings (henceforth PRAP), April 1900. p. 12. IOR:P/5890.

[27] *Ibid.*, p. 24.

[28] *Ibid.*, p. 7.

earnings from agriculture made it difficult for them to maintain their *sahu* (gentle) lifestyles of hawks, horses and servants. Economic alternatives were limited. They were reluctant to take to the plough as agricultural tenants, nor were they prepared to engage in trade and manual labour, regarding such activities as demeaning to their aristocratic standing in the region of the Salt Range.[29]

The Gakkhars, therefore, responded enthusiastically when the Indian Army began recruiting Punjabi Muslims on a large scale, especially during the second Afghan War from 1878 to 1880. It may be noted here that cultural propensity played a part—military service was not new to the locally dominant Gakkhars; they had been a part of almost every army that had marched across the Indus in the past centuries.[30] Regarding themselves as the dominant aristocratic tribe of the region, the Gakkhars found military service in the Indian Army compatible with their high social status in the region. Consequently, military earnings, through pay and pensions, constituted the main source of their extraneous income. In 1901, it was reported that proprietors in the Jhelum tehsil earned over 500,000 rupees in military pay and pensions, almost three times what they had to pay in land revenue, which was fixed in 1901 at Rs 185,772.[31] The importance of military earnings amongst the Gakkhars can be seen most clearly in Domeli and Lahri, two Gakkhar villages in the Khuddar assessment circle in Jhelum district. In 1901 in these two villages, 1,179 peasant proprietors were in military service and received an annual aggregate pay of 190,675 rupees, in addition to 17,347 rupees received annually in military pensions. The land revenue for the Khuddar circle in 1901 was only 49,084 rupees.[32]

Similar dynamics to economic conscription could also be found working amongst the Awan tribe in the same district. The Awans, unlike the "blood-proud" Gakkhars, were more amenable to agricultural work and were more predisposed to stay in farms than to take to military service. Awans have been described as "good and hardworking cultivators" and the "backbone of cultivation" in the tract, and where they did not own lands they could be found cultivating

[29] D. Ibbetson, *Report on the Census of Punjab, 1881*, Calcutta, 1902, Vol. 1, p. 241.
[30] J.M. Wikeley, *Punjabi Mussalmans*. IOR:L/MIL/17/5/2166.
[31] See *LSR, Jhelum, 1901*, p. 24.
[32] *LSR, Jhelum District, 1901*, p. 4.

as tenants.[33] In the Tallagang tehsil, where they were mostly concentrated, the Awans tilled over ninety per cent of the cultivated land.[34] Although the Awans were industrious enough to make good embankments on their plots to make the most of scanty rainfall, the coarse and sandy soil of the land, coupled with very poor rainfall, rendered it impossible for the Awan cultivators to grow good crops. Tallagang tehsil, for instance, received the least rainfall, and the soil was too poor to be capable of yielding heavy crops.[35] Returns from agriculture were, as a consequence, extremely precarious. Economic shortage was, therefore, a chronic problem in the area and although the Awans were prepared to invest much effort on their lands they had difficulty keeping out of debt. As with the Gakkhars, the Awans welcomed the opportunity to enlist in the Indian Army.

In the Salt Range tract, economic depression was a powerful "push" factor for men from the select military districts to enlist in the army. Military service offered an "escape route from the ecological impasse"[36] and many family incomes were dependent on military earnings. In these districts, it was indeed rare to find a family without a member in the Indian army. M.S. Leigh, the Settlement Officer of Shahpur district, a district in western Punjab which was a fairly popular recruiting ground for Punjabi Muslims, wrote in 1917:[37] "... the peasants will have to take military service in increasing numbers if they wish to maintain their standard of living".

The economic dependence on the state for military service was, therefore, one of the main reasons why the tribes of the Salt Range tract so readily provided recruits for the army. Military service accordingly became an exclusive opportunity that was guarded jealously by those who enjoyed that privilege. Nevertheless, when harvests were good, there was less motivation to enlist, and men from agricultural tribes like the Awans would rather work the fields than join the army. Thus, if a good farming season was to coincide with military needs, this could cause problems for the military

[33] W.S. Talbot, *AR*, Tallagang Tehsil, 1898, in PRAP, November 1899, IOR:P/5609, p. 25. Tallagang tehsil was transferred to Attock district in 1904.

[34] *LSR, Jhelum District, 1874–80*, p. 2.

[35] *AR, Tallagang Tehsil, 1898*, p. 27.

[36] Clive Dewey, 'Some Consequences of the Military Expenditure in British India: The Case of the Upper Sind Sagar Doab, 1849–1947', p. 96.

[37] M.S. Leigh, *LSR, Shahpur District, 1911–1917*, Lahore, 1918, p. 3.

authorities. But because the Salt Range tract was a perennially disadvantaged area, such incidents were rare, and Punjabi Muslims constituted a fairly consistent and reliable source of recruits for the Indian army. The same, however, could not be said of the south-east Punjab and central Punjab.

Jats from South-east Punjab

The frequency of famines in the south-eastern districts of the Punjab—"at least once or twice in a generation"—made recourse to military service an essential insurance against poverty and starvation. Indeed, during such economically difficult times the villages that were targeted by army recruiters regarded access to military service as a prized privilege. The region's most important district for recruiting purposes was Rohtak, which supplied just under half of the total number of Hindu Jat recruits in 1897–98 and 1898–99.[38] The canal irrigated parts of the district were agriculturally productive and prosperous as most of the district was blessed with fertile soil which, with a little labour and sufficient moisture, could easily yield a heavy crop. However, in the un-irrigated parts of the district, with inadequate and uncertain rainfall, harvests were chronically insecure. Precarious rainfall had made these parts of the district particularly prone to famines: between 1860 and 1906, the district was hit by seven major famines, caused mainly by the failure of the rains.[39] In a report of the famine of 1877–78, the conditions of the villages were thus described:[40]

> With a very limited amount of moisture, the soil of this country is extremely prolific, all, however, depends on the rainfall. When the rain fails, all is lost, and the soil becomes hard as iron. The feature of absolute drought and failure is a remarkable one in these parts. Every considerable town and village can point to

[38] The figures were 202 out of 579 and 222 out of 476, respectively. The next most important source of recruits for the Punjab was Hissar, which supplied 37 and 39 recruits respectively for the two years in question. 'Report on the Recruiting Operations in Delhi District, 1899–1900', in PHP(M) 'B', February 1901.

[39] E. Joseph, *PDG, Rohtak, 1910* (Lahore, 1911), Vol. 3A, pp. 145–51.

[40] W.C.Purser and A.C. Fanshawe, *LSR, Rohtak District, 1873–79*, (Lahore, 1880), p. 45. IOR:V/27/314/616–17.

its former site or sites, prior to which such and such a famine or drought had depopulated the country, and these occurrences appear to serve as eras in the popular record of the past.

Men were less tempted to enter into military service from the canal irrigated tracts of the district, with their great demand for agricultural labour and the good returns they promised.[41] Military service was, however, extremely popular with the Jats from the unirrigated parts of the district, and for them, army pay and pension were regarded as a sort of "famine insurance policy". The Jats of Rohtak tended to enter the army to ensure a regular income which was not certain from land and cattle, and to enable them to survive their frequent losses of cattle.[42] The tradition of military service among the Hindu Jats of eastern Punjab was, therefore, built around an economic necessity—to avoid starvation during times of famine. Jats from the district, therefore, regarded enlistment as an economic "safety-net" and many of them were prepared to flock to the colours whenever the opportunity arose. As with the Salt Range tract, income from military pay and pension in this district was found to be very significant; in 1910 it was estimated that annual pay and pensions from military sources amounted to no less than 16,000,000 rupees, more than the 1,186,020 rupees which the district had to pay as land revenue.[43]

Because the Jats from Rohtak district regarded military service as nothing more than a reliable source of income, very few of them would stay in the army for long. The turnover of Jats in the army was very regular; the Jat was as ready to leave military service as he was to enlist, and he would seldom serve on in the ranks until a pension became due. A great majority of Jats preferred to take their discharge after a few years of service, or to pass into the reserve to exploit the opportunities outside the regiment during the better seasons, with the safety-net of a reservist salary. Conversely, during a famine, with food scarce and expensive, Jat recruits chose to remain within the comfortable confines of the cantonment, where they would be assured of food and employment. The result was

---

[41] *PDG, Rohtak, 1910,* p. 167.

[42] E. Joseph, *LSR, Rohtak District, 1905–1910* (Lahore, 1910), p. 23. IOR:V/27/314/618.

[43] *Ibid.*, p. 1

that the supply of Jats in the army was neither significant nor consistent as many of them would only turn to military service when there were very definite gains to be made from enlistment.[44]

Sikhs from Central Punjab

Economic conditions in the fertile plains of central Punjab were much better than the Salt Range tract and the south-eastern districts. With its flat terrain and fertile soil, the region was ideal for extensive and productive cultivation. Furthermore, the region was well watered by an extensive canal irrigation system, originally built by the Mughals in the eighteenth century and later improved by the British, making it less vulnerable than south-eastern Punjab, for example, to the effects of prolonged droughts.[45] Over two-thirds of the entire cultivated area in the district was irrigated.[46] These favourable conditions made the Manjha region the most heavily cultivated area in the Punjab. In Amritsar district, for example, more than seventy-five per cent of the district as a whole was under cultivation, and in Tarn Taran, the district's most populous tehsil, over eighty-five per cent of the land was under the plough.[47]

Extensive cultivation, however, brought with it inherent problems: heavy pressures on the soil and fragmentation of agricultural land. The Manjha tract was one of the most densely populated in the Punjab; in 1901 Amritsar, its main district, had a population density of 640 persons per square mile.[48] In its two southern tehsils of Amritsar and Tarn Taran, the incidence of population per square mile of agricultural land was 724 and 731 respectively, leaving virtually no room for further expansion.[49] Agricultural land was a very valuable commodity in the district; the demand for land was high and competition for it keen. Consequently, the average size

[44] E. Joseph, *LSR, Rohtak, 1905–1910*, p. 167.

[45] H.D. Craik, *LSR, Amritsar District, 1910–1914* (Lahore 1914), p. 2. IOR:V/27/314/461.

[46] In Amritsar tehsil 60.3 per cent of land was irrigated; in Tarn Taran tehsil, 65.5 per cent; and in Ajnala tehsil, eighty per cent. See H.D. Craik, *PDG, Amritsar, 1914* (Lahore, 1914), Vol. 20A, p. 59.

[47] *Ibid.*, p. 12.

[48] *PDG, Amritsar, 1914*, Vol. 20B, pp. 12–13.

[49] *PDG, Amritsar, 1914*, Vol. 20A, p. 24.

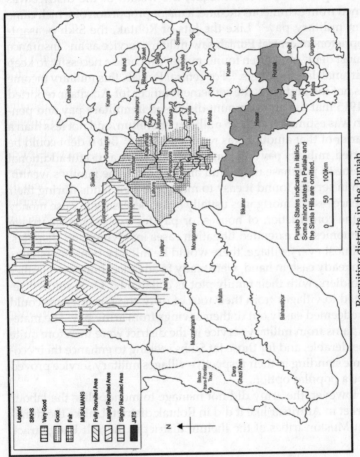

Recruiting districts in the Punjab

Source: Indian Army Recruiting Manuals, Punjab

of land held by a peasant-proprietor in Amritsar district was only four-and-a-half acres.

Although income from agriculture brought about a standard of living in the Manjha region that was higher than that in the less advantaged areas of the Punjab, the wealth of the district was earned from extraneous income, a major proportion of which came from military pay.[50] Like the Jats of Rohtak, the Sikh peasant-proprietors of central Punjab saw military service as an "insurance against debt", and often found military income a necessity to keep their small landholdings.[51] For central Punjab, this military income was not insignificant; the settlement officer for Amritsar reported in 1915 that the gross amount disbursed in military pay and pension was estimated at Rs 25 million per annum, and not less than a quarter of that amount was remitted home.[52] But if debt could be averted, military pay and pension would serve as useful additional income to purchase more land and to add to the family's wealth. Men in service found it easy to mortgage their lands during their absence—such mortgages usually being necessary to raise money for the construction of houses, or pay for extravagant marriage ceremonies, or extended litigation cases involving land disputes. In almost every village, there would be military pensioners who, with ready cash in hand, were ready to advance money to families of soldiers, with their family plot as collateral.[53] Once soldiers returned to villages from their tour of duty, these mortgages could be redeemed easily out of their savings from army pay. The material gains from military service in the district were therefore quite considerable, and for those Jat Sikhs seeking to enhance their economic standing in their respective villages military service proved to be a popular option.

However, the army did not manage to monopolize the labour market in Amritsar like it did in Rohtak district. Unlike the dominant Muslim tribes of the Jhelum district in the Salt Range tract,

---

[50] Large remittances were also made by émigré Sikhs from Canada, Australia, South Africa and elsewhere where they were engaged in commerce or in the service of private firms. Much money also flowed from Sikh colonists settled in various Punjab colony lands.

[51] Richard Fox, *Lions of the Punjab: Culture in the Making* (henceforth *Lions of the Punjab*), New Delhi, 1990, p. 46.

[52] *LSR, Amritsar, 1910–1914*, p. 3.

[53] A.E. Barstow, *Sikhs*, p. 121.

the Jat Sikhs were less averse to taking on other types of employment to supplement their income from the land. At the turn of the nineteenth century, Jat Sikhs were migrating out of the Punjab in large numbers in search of employment in different parts of the world. Many went as far afield as Canada and America, while others travelled east to Thailand, Malaya and the Straits Settlements to seek employment in the local police and security forces.[54] Resources generated from overseas remittances added to the wealth of the region, and the Sikh peasant was so adept at availing himself to these alternative employment opportunities outside the land that over time "petty cultivation, military service and overseas wage labour ... formed an ensemble, each part of which bolstered the other".[55] At the end of the nineteenth century, recruiters were complaining that they were having difficulties in enlisting Jat Sikhs from the district; the pay offered by the army was evidently insufficient to attract the desired types of recruits, who were showing greater interest in joining more lucrative services outside India.[56] By the 1890s, to maintain the Sikh element in the Army, the recruiting authorities had found it necessary to raise companies from outside the Jat Sikh community. Consequently, members from the smaller and socially less dominant Sikh castes like the Labanas, Kambohs and Mahtams, were recruited into the Army.[57]

There was thus a close link between economic necessity and military service amongst the Punjabi Muslims from Jhelum district, the Hindu Jats from Rohtak district, and the Jat Sikhs from Amritsar district. But these military classes sought enlistment in the Indian Army for different economic reasons. The aristocratic tribes of Punjabi Muslims of north-western India saw military service as a viable and acceptable vocation which was necessary for their economic well-being, especially in a land where agricultural yields were very limited. The Hindu Jats saw army employment

---

[54] For the migration patterns and economic patterns of the Sikhs into South-east Asia, see Kernial Singh Sandhu, *Indians in Malaya: Some Aspects of Their Immigration and Settlement, 1786–1957*, Cambridge, 1969.

[55] Richard Fox, *Lions of the Punjab*, p. 44.

[56] Reports from Commanding Officers of 22nd and 24th Native Infantry Regiments (both Sikh regiments) in Lumsden to Secretary of State, India, 30 June 1875, in *PP*, 1877, Vol. 62, p. 21.

[57] *Record of Kitchener's Administration of the Army in India, 1902–1909*, Simla, 1909, p. 302. IOR:L/MIL/17/5/1617.

as a safety-net against famine, while the Sikhs saw it as a means of earning more money to supplement their incomes. In most cases, economic benefits from military service were quite compelling incentives for the desired recruits to enlist, but as we have seen, in some cases, particularly in central Punjab and south-east Punjab, the army had to compete with other economic lures for the services of recruits. The willingness to enlist, and indeed the overall "loyalty" of the military labour market in the Punjab had to be bought. But, as military pay and pensions were sometimes insufficient in themselves to procure the services of these military allies, the colonial state found that it often had to resort to other means of encouragement. The army had sometimes to provide a compelling "pull" factor to encourage recruitment. The case in the Punjab was illuminating: in a manner and on a scale not replicated anywhere else in India, the state in the Punjab also made generous use of its landed resources for the purpose of strengthening its bonds with its military districts.[58]

Land and Loyalty

As early as the 1870s, before the major canal colonies were opened, land grants and leases of wasteland had been distributed by the British in the Punjab for those who had served in the military campaign in 1857 and the Afghan wars. In addition, reward grants, usually around 500 acres a grant, were awarded each year to selected military officers. After 1890, when the canal colonies were opened, the volume of land grants awarded to the military increased dramatically. Large tracts in these newly opened canal-irrigated wastelands were reserved for allotment as *Fauji* grants to soldier-settlers, pensioners, and ex-soldiers.[59] The bulk of the military grantees were settled in the four large canal colonies: the Chenab, Jhelum, Lower Bari Doab and Nili Bar. The magnitude of the entire exercise was phenomenal: in the canal colonies as a whole, the total amount of land allotted to military grantees was almost in the region of half-a-million acres.[60]

[58] For a comprehensive study of the link between the military and land in the Punjab, see Imran Ali, *The Punjab Under Imperialism*.

[59] *Ibid.*, pp. 110–20.

[60] *Ibid.*, p. 115.

The use of landed resources for military purposes was not a new phenomenon in the Punjab; under the Mughals and the Sikhs, land had been generously distributed to generals and military allies to secure their loyalty. Land rewards were particularly relevant in traditional Punjabi society where ownership of land was tantamount to political power, and the acquisition of land was important for elevating or maintaining social status. In the tradition of an indigenous ruler, the British imperial authority returned to the feudal system of endowing land to the military classes in return for their valuable supportive role to the governing authority.

The use of land as a form of military reward was aimed not only at strengthening the appeal of military service, but also ensuring the loyalty of the military classes to the state. One of the conditions laid down in the terms of the *Fauji* grants stated explicitly that:

> Tenants shall be bound to be and to remain at all times of loyal behaviour, and to render active support to government and its officers in times of trouble or disorder ... and if local government is of opinion that the tenant has committed a breach of this condition, it may resume the tenancy [of the land].[61]

Ex-soldiers were eligible for grants only after completing twenty-one years of service, and grants were made on conditions of continued loyalty.[62] Grantees were usually chosen by the recommendations of their regimental commanders, and their military record was usually the sole criterion for eligibility for land grants. The promise of land was, therefore, a great incentive for prolonged and loyal military service.

The desire to utilize land ownership to secure loyalty to the Raj extended beyond the dispensation of newly opened canal-colony lands to the soldiering classes. More importantly, the military and the colonial state in the Punjab had to ensure that the mainstay of its recruiting base—the landed tribes and peasant proprietors—would not fall into penurious circumstances as a result of land alienation. In a rural hierarchy where social status was closely associated with land, soldiers who were also landowners not only

---

[61] F.C. Wace, *Punjab Colonization Manual*, Lahore, 1936, p. 93.
[62] Adj. Gen. in India to Revenue Sec., 1 October 1901, in PRAP (General), November 1901, No. 67. IOR:P/5283.

gave military service a good image, but would also become good agents of the state. It was not surprising that the Punjab government was particularly sensitive to the conditions of its military districts, and at the heart of its desire to maintain a contented rural population lay the fear of a rural-military revolt in the home ground of the Indian army.

Nowhere was this seen more clearly than in the government's response to growing peasant indebtedness and land alienation in the province in the last two decades of the nineteenth century. Briefly, it was the economic prosperity of the Punjab, brought about by political stability and the standardization of revenue collection introduced by British rule, that created the problem of peasant indebtedness, and consequently an alarming increase in the alienation of land from peasant proprietors to urban moneylenders. With the increased profitability of agricultural output, land became a valuable commodity and peasants began to use it as collateral to obtain credit from urban moneylenders. When debts or mortgages could not be repaid, agricultural land fell into the hands of the moneylenders, who were able to use the judiciary machinery introduced by the British to recover their dues. Gradually, as more and more peasants fell into debt, the volume of land alienation from the peasants to urban moneylenders increased. This development alarmed several district officers, some of whom had advocated as early as the 1860s that legislation be passed to curb this alienation. A great debate ensued between the paternalists in the Punjab, who argued that the naive peasants had to be protected against the cunning moneylenders, and the believers in laissez faire, who argued that the government should not interfere with the free market economy. The debate has been studied in full detail elsewhere,[63] and it need not be repeated here. But it will suffice to say that the argument that further alienation would inevitably hurt the interests of the military classes, whose loyalty the state could not afford to compromise, was incontrovertible. The political imperative of state intervention to curb further alienation through legislation was

[63] For a full scale discussion of the debates between these groups, see Clive Dewey 'The Official Mind and the Problem of Agrarian Indebtedness, 1870–1910' (unpublished Ph.D. dissertation, Cambridge University, 1973); see also P.H.M. Van den Dungen, *The Punjab Tradition*, London, 1974, and N.G. Barrier, *The Punjab Land Alienation Bill of 1900*, Durham, 1966.

forcefully put across by Lieutenant General Charles Rivaz, when he introduced the Punjab Alienation of Land Bill to the Imperial Legislative Council on 27 September 1899. He stated:[64]

> The Punjab is preeminently a land of yeoman and peasant pro-
> prietors, and the expropriation by moneylenders of these sturdy
> landowners, men who furnish the flower of the Army in India,
> and who look forward amidst all hardships and glories to a mili-
> tary career, to spend the declining years on their ancestral acres,
> had been progressing.... The sole and entire object of the mea-
> sure is to arrest ... an ever increasing political danger.

Eventually, the government decided in 1900 to take the drastic step of passing the Land Alienation Act, which prohibited the trans- fer of land to non-agricultural classes. The Act was a piece of leg- islation motivated in part by the government's paternal attitude towards the illiterate peasantry, but its main raison d'etre was to deflect the possibility of agrarian unrest, which, if it engulfed the military districts, could pose a serious political threat in the Punjab, and thus to the Indian Army and utlimately to the Raj itself.

Agrarian unrest, which the government feared so much, erupted in 1907, and its military implications became evident immediately.[65] The immediate cause of the agrarian unrest in 1907 was the pro- posed amendment of the 1893 Punjab Colonization of Land Act, affecting the Chenab colony. The colony had been settled by care- fully selected grantees who, in turn for occupancy rights, were to ensure that they paid their revenue and observed their contractual obligations. The latter made it mandatory for them to live on their land, ensure proper sanitation and cleanliness, and to cut wood only from designated areas. Initially, the scheme worked wonderfully and the Chenab colony seemed to be a model farm created out of cooperation between the peasants and the government. Before long, however, things had begun to turn awry. First, the government had run out of choice land and the irrigation department, which was responsible for the distribution of land, began distributing

[64] Rivaz's Speech in the Imperial Legislative Council, 27 September 1899, quoted in Dewey, 'The Official Mind and the Problem of Agrarian Indebtedness', p. 216.

[65] The following is based on the narrative in N.G. Barrier, 'Punjab Disturbances of 1907: Government Responses', *Modern Asian Studies (MAS)*, 1967 (1), pp. 353–83.

Turban

relatively inferior land. This sparked off a series of complaints from the new colonists. Furthermore, landholding became increasingly fragmented, as colonists sub-divided their plots of land among their sons. Gradually too, colonists began flouting regulations by evading residency and sanitary requirements. The threat to confiscate land grants proved ineffective, and the government resorted to introducing a system of fines. However, much to the chagrin of the government, colonists began contesting the imposition of fines in civil courts, and frequently won their cases against the canal authorities.

Determined to put an end to the deterioration of conditions in the colony, the Punjab government decided in 1906 to pass an amendment bill to the original Punjab Colonization of Land Act. This Bill, provisions of which were to be made retroactive, contained several unpopular measures. It forbade the transfer of property at will, permitting only strict primogeniture; it also legalized the hated fine system, which the colonists believed provided for extortion and bribery by junior officials. Furthermore, recourse to the judiciary in disputes concerning fines was barred as civil courts were excluded from interference with executive orders concerning the colony. The Bill aggrieved a large portion of the rural population and, coming as it did so soon after the widespread destruction of crops in 1905 and 1906 by boll worms, provoked the colonists into open agitation. The agitation which began in the Chenab colony soon spread to central Punjab, the original home of many of the colonists, and the unfortunate decision of the government to announce, at about the same time, a twenty-five to fifty per cent increase in the water rates of the Bari Doab Canal fanned the unrest among the local Jat Sikh peasantry.

The cause of the peasants was soon taken up by urban politicians; Lajpat Rai, a Punjabi Arya Samaj leader, and Ajit Singh, a revolutionary Jat leader, soon assumed the leadership of the agitation. The agitation now took on political overtones, as Ajit Singh appealed to the martial traditions of the Sikhs and called on "the brave soldiers of the Khalsa ... [to] give up the British service ... and expel the English from the land".[66] The protesters made use of emotive slogans like *Pagri Sambhal Jatta* (Jats, Watch your Turban!) to stir up the Jat peasantry.

---

[66] Rajiv Kapur, *Sikh Separatism: The Politics of Faith*, London, 1987, pp. 49–50.

The Punjab government initially chose to ignore the cause of the agitation, blaming it on the machinations of the revolutionaries and urban politicians. The Lieutenant Governor, Denzil Ibbetson, tried to convince the central government that the peasantry was inherently loyal, and had only been led astray by the urban professional "fomenters of unrest". He obtained sanction from Delhi to adopt a series of repressive measures: public meetings were prohibited in certain districts and dispersed by force in others; newspapers supporting the agitation were sued for sedition; and the agitation's prominent leaders, Lajpat Rai and Ajit Singh, were deported to Burma.

Despite such measures, the unrest carried on unabated, with riots breaking out in Amritsar, Lahore and Rawalpindi. The unrest was centred on the Manjha region, the army's main recruiting ground for Jat Sikhs. Before long, there were indications that agitation had spread to the army. Reports were received of Sikh sepoys endeavouring to spread sedition within their regiments,[67] and there was talk of an imminent revolt.[68] The effects of this unrest on the army caused consternation in the Viceroy's Executive Council, particularly with the Commander-in-Chief, Lord Kitchener, and C.H. Scott, the Military Member. Kitchener was particularly alarmed that the unrest might affect the Sikh regiments and eventually destabilize the entire army. His concern was compounded by persistent rumours that a military revolt would break out on 10 May 1907, the fiftieth anniversary of the Mutiny.

Although Ibbetson and his colleagues in the Punjab government believed that the unrest had nothing to do with the amendment Bill and was determined to force it through, the Viceroy, Lord Minto, was beginning to have his doubts. He was urged by Kitchener, who, after conducting his own investigation, had come to the conclusion that the root cause of the disaffection amongst the soldiers from central Punjab was the unpopular Colonization Bill, to veto the offending bill. Kitchener was convinced that repression would

---

[67] See Note for Foreign Office, 'Endeavours of Sikh Sepoys to spread sedition', 26 June 1907, GoI, Home (Political) 'A' Pro(s). 113, August 1907. National Archives of India (NAI).

[68] These warnings were contained in the Weekly Reports of the Director of Criminal Intelligence to the Government of the Punjab on the Political Situation in October, 1907. GoI, Home (Pol.) 'B' October 1907, NAI.

not alleviate the disaffection unsettling the military districts in central Punjab. Eventually, Minto decided to heed the advice of his Commander-in-Chief, and vetoed the bill. "The appearance of surrender to agitation", as he later explained, was "far less dangerous than to insist upon enforcing the unfortunate legislation proposed upon a warlike and loyal section of the Indian community".[69] The decision of the Viceroy was clearly based on the conviction that the Punjab must remain loyal at all costs, if only because the army, and by implication the Raj, depended upon it.

Conclusion

By the end of the nineteenth century, it was commonplace to regard colonial Punjab as the "sword arm of the Raj" or "nursery of the martial races", denoting the extent to which the army in India had come to depend on the province for its recruits. Significant though the Punjab might have been for the army in India, the military labour market in the province, as this chapter has shown, was not a huge one. Recruitment in the Punjab was extremely restricted, even within those groups designated as "martial classes". Only selected groups within specific localities, which have been termed "military districts", had access to military service. The military was able to secure the loyalty of their sepoys because the right to military service, which conferred tangible economic rewards and other state benefits such as land grants, was guarded jealously by the exclusive few who had the privilege of being labelled a "martial class". Within those military districts, a full-fledged military labour market was at work, and the interaction with the military was intense. In the Punjab, it was no coincidence that the "martial classes" coincided with the dominant landholding elements of rural Punjab. The grafting of the army's regiments onto the social base of Punjab's rural order demonstrated a masterful appreciation by the military and the state in colonial Punjab that the essence of a reliable and stable military lay in a contented peasantry.

The military labour market functioned well when the demand and supply of military manpower were kept in steady equilibrium. In the decades following the Afghan wars, the army in India fought

---

[69] Quoted in N.G. Barrier, 'Punjab Disturbances of 1907', p. 376.

no major wars, and was kept mainly on garrison duties. The relatively small size of a peacetime army did not tax the exclusive military labour market in the Punjab. But this was to undergo a dramatic change when the First World War broke out in 1914.

THREE

Garrison Province at Work:
Punjab and the First World War

Although not directly involved in, and physically far removed from the battlefields of, the First World War, India's contribution to that war was not insignificant. From September 1914 to November 1918, India's material and financial contribution amounted to an equivalent of £479 million[1] and approximately one-and-a-half million men from the Indian army—both combatants and non-combatants—fought in the battlefields of Europe, the Middle East and Africa.[2] Out of a total of 683,149 combatant troops recruited in India between August 1914 and November 1918, 349,688—about sixty per cent—came from the Punjab.[3] The material and monetary contributions from the province were no less significant: the total amount of money raised through war investments and donations aggregated 92,118,664 rupees, roughly equivalent to £700,000 in 1918.[4] This tremendous output from the Punjab was the result of the mobilization of the entire province, a process which started modestly in 1915 and gathered momentum towards a peak at the end of 1918. During the war, the Punjab was converted into a virtual

---

[1] For the economic aspects of the war, see Krishnan G. Saini, 'The Economic Aspects of India's Participation in the First World War' in Dewitt C. Ellinwood and S.D. Pradhan, *India and World War One*, Delhi, 1978.

[2] *India's Contribution to the Great War*, published by the Authority of the Government in India, Calcutta, 1923, pp. 72–73. IOR:V/27/281/32.

[3] *India's Contribution to the Great War*, Appendix C, p. 275. IOR:V/27/281/32.

[4] M.S. Leigh, *The Punjab and the War*, Lahore, 1922, pp. 64–81.

"home front",[5] with the state firmly oriented towards supporting the war effort.

This chapter aims to show how military requirements generated by the war, particularly in the mobilization of military manpower, affected the existing structure of the colonial state in the Punjab. The demands of war brought about a change in the administration of the province, and by 1917, the whole administrative structure of the province was converted into a formidable and monolithic recruiting machinery, utilized mainly for the purpose of supplying military manpower for the Indian Army.[6] The extent to which the civil administrative machinery was used for military purposes in the Punjab was unique, and throughout the war no other provincial government in India followed Punjab's example.[7] A major feature of civil-military integration in the Punjab during the war was the involvement of the state's rural intermediaries as military contractors. All forms of local influence in the province, from minor officials to the landed aristocracy and gentry class, were mobilized by the government to stimulate recruitment to the army. Although the rural intermediaries in the Punjab had on occasions functioned as military contractors in the past, the scale of their involvement during the war was unprecedented. By coming to the assistance of the state during the war, the social and political positions of these collaborators were significantly strengthened, which enabled them to emerge, in post-war Punjab, as an entrenched rural-military elite.

The Early Phase: 1914–1915

When the war broke out, no one in the Punjab, and indeed India, had anticipated that the Indian Army would be fully involved in what was then considered a European war. In 1914 the GoI had intimated to the Home Government that in the eventuality of a war in Europe, India could offer a maximum force of two divisions

[5] The phrase "home front" was used by M.S. Leigh in his compilation of the various contributions made by the Punjab during the war. *Ibid.*, p. 30.

[6] Michael O'Dwyer, *India As I Knew It*, London, 1925, pp. 214–19.

[7] The Government of India had envisaged that if the war went beyond June 1919, civil administrations all over India would have to follow Punjab's example and assume a more prominent part in the mobilization process. This was, however, never realised as hostilities were terminated before 1919. *Ibid.*, p. 200.

of infantry and one cavalry brigade;[8] anything beyond that would weaken the Indian Army, and could jeopardize India's own security. On the eve of the war the fighting force of the Indian army, consisting of nine divisions with a total strength of approximately 150,000 soldiers, was organized for the purposes of maintaining internal security and keeping a watch on India's north-west frontier. It had the capability for engaging in limited military operations outside India, as it had done on various occasions during the past fifty years, serving as the Empire's "fire brigade" in China, Africa, Hong Kong and Malaya[9], but its size and organizational structure were clearly not geared for fighting a major war outside India.[10] Nevertheless, in September 1914, in response to urgent requests from the War Office in London, the Government of India despatched two divisions of infantry—the Meerut and Lahore Divisions—to reinforce the British Expeditionary Force in France. At about the same time, a mixed force was despatched from India to East Africa to protect Zanzibar and the Mombasa–Nairobi railway line from German designs. In November 1914, Turkey entered the war against Britain. As British troops were concentrated in Europe, the task of holding on to the strategically crucial Persian oilfields and the Suez Canal was entrusted to the Indian Army.[11] Consequently, two more divisions from India were hurriedly despatched to Mesopotamia and Egypt. By June 1915, more than 80,000 combatants had been sent abroad from India to France, Mesopotamia, Egypt and East Africa, well in excess of the maximum envisaged by the military authorities before the war.

To bolster the rapidly dwindling regiments in the wake of the outflow of men to the various war fronts, the Army Department in India decided to increase the establishment of the infantry and cavalry regiments of the Indian Army. Consequently, soon after the first divisions were despatched to France, it sanctioned the increase

---

[8] *India's Contribution to the War*, p. 22. IOR: V/27/281/32.

[9] The Indian Army was used in most foreign military engagements of the Empire, with the exception of the Anglo-Boer War, 1899–1902. See Byron Farwell, *Armies of the Raj: From the Mutiny to Independence, 1858–1947*, London, 1986, p. 191; Boris Mollo, *The Indian Army*, Poole, 1981, pp. 108–11.

[10] Policy stated in Army in India Committee, quoted in *India's Contribution to the War Effort*, p. 72, IOR:V/27/281/32.

[11] For a discussion on British strategy in the Middle East, see David French, 'The Dardanelles, Mecca, Kut: Prestige as a Factor in the British Eastern Strategy, 1914–1916' in *War and Society*, Vol. 5, 1, (May 1987), pp. 45–61.

in the strengths of native infantry regiments from 912 to 1,000 men, and of cavalry from 625 to 700 men.[12] In May 1915, the Army Department authorized the emergency formation of an additional twenty companies, with an establishment of 114 men each.[13]

The ranks of the Indian expeditionary forces which went into combat in France and Mesopotamia were rapidly depleted by casualties. In France, both the Ferozepur and Jullundur Brigades of the Lahore Division lost more than half their men—killed, wounded or missing—within the first few weeks of arriving at the battle-front.[14] The first two Indian regiments in France to engage the German onslaught were the 57th Rifles and the 129th Baluchis. They were in the trenches from 23 to 30 October 1914, and during that time lost a total of 290 and 235 men respectively. The average strengths of the two regiments had been about 750 men.[15] At the second battle of Ypres, when poison gas was used for the first time, in a single night in April 1915 the Lahore Division lost 3,889 men, more than thirty per cent of its total strength.[16] A Sikh sepoy who was at the scene of the battle recounted the event to a friend serving in Kohat (in present-day Pakistan), telling him that "the Lahore Division was attacked and destroyed ... [and] there were only 900 men left in the whole division".[17] The situation was similar in the Middle East. In a series of fierce battles against the Turkish army in Ctesiphon, near Baghdad, the Indian regiments suffered heavy losses; this was followed by a spate of reverses in battles at Gallipolli and Kut-e-Amara, which took a heavy toll on the Indian troops.[18] Consequently, to make up for the rapidly depleting strengths of the regiments engaged in battle, urgent calls were sent to India for more men.

[12] Minute by Military Department, Government of India, dated 9 September 1914, in India Office Military Collections No. 425, File 11. IOR: L/MIL/7/17164.

[13] See enclosure to Despatch No. 51 (Army) dated 20 May 1915 in *ibid*.

[14] Leigh, *The Punjab and the War*, p. 199.

[15] James Willcocks, *With the Indians in France*, London, 1920, p. 44.

[16] Leigh, *The Punjab and the War*, p. 206.

[17] Letter from a Sikh sepoy in a hospital in Brighton to a sepoy of the 55th Rifles in Kohat, in *Reports of the Censor of Indian Mails in France* (henceforth *Censor*), Vol. 1, part III, fo. 377, IOR:L/MIL/5/825. The sepoy could not have known the actual extent of the damage and could have been exaggerating to his friend. But the letter did give an indication of how the losses suffered at the trenches were viewed by those involved.

[18] The story of the Indian Army's involvement in the various warfronts is taken up in Charles Chenevix Trench, *The Indian Army and the King's Enemies, 1901–1947*, London, 1988, pp. 31–90.

The increase in the establishment of the infantry and cavalry regiments in India, coupled with a need to make heavy drafts to keep up the strengths of the regiments already at the war fronts, led to a sharp rise in the demand for military manpower from India. The focus of recruitment fell, inevitably, on the Punjab. That the Punjab should bear the brunt in meeting the demands for manpower was the result of the "class system" of recruitment which was standard recruiting practice in the Indian Army since the late nineteenth century. The increase in the establishment of the existing infantry and cavalry regiments meant that recruiting had to be stepped up in the existing recruiting depots, and in the established military districts in the Punjab. Furthermore, most of the regiments engaged in the fighting were composed of Punjabi troops: of the sixty-nine Indian regiments despatched to the war fronts since the beginning of the war, forty-one were either wholly or partly composed of Punjabis.[19] These class regiments or class companies when depleted had to be replenished by soldiers belonging to the same class, and regimental recruiters were compelled to go back to the same villages in the Punjab to look for replacements for their regiments. Recruitment in the military districts was thus intensified to keep up the strengths of the units already in Europe and the Middle East. In the last four months of 1914, of the 28,000 new recruits enlisted from India, 14,000 came from the Punjab; by July 1915, out of 78,232 soldiers recruited in India, 37,591 were Muslims, Sikhs and Jats from the Punjab.[20] Rather like Europe during the first months of the war, the initial response of the Punjab to early recruitment drives was characterized by enthusiasm. Recruits, perhaps under the impression that they were being enlisted for a limited expedition to another part of the Empire, volunteered eagerly, enticed by the promise of economic benefits, and possibly lured by the prospects of travel to a foreign land. Furthermore, from late 1914, the prices of staple food and produce, especially wheat and sugar, increased dramatically, and this provided an economic "push" factor for enlistment. Consequently, the Punjab responded remarkably

[19] Leigh, *The Punjab and the War*, pp. 198–280.

[20] 'Numbers Recruited by Class, from 1 August to 30 November 1918' App. 7, in Recruiting in India. IOR:L/MIL/17/5/2152. The figures given cannot be taken to be wholly accurate. Different accounts and official records give varying sets of figures. These discrepancies may be due to the decentralised manner in which recruiting data are gathered, and other inconsistencies in data collection.

well in the first few months of the war where recruiting was concerned, and no difficulties were reported by recruiting officers in obtaining the required manpower. But as the war wore on, and the demands for military manpower kept increasing, recruiting officers in the Punjab started to encounter difficulties in finding men who were willing to enlist.

The main problem lay in the system of recruiting that was being practised in the Punjab.[21] The most serious drawback of the existing system was that its infrastructure was constructed around the principle of class recruiting. It was suitable in the past when recruitment was limited and kept within the exclusive bounds of certain villages in the Punjab. But when the demands generated by the war necessitated an expansion of the recruiting base, the system proved deficient. The recruiting depots, from where the recruiting officers operated, were too few and far apart, and only the villages and tehsils which had traditionally supplied men to the army had their links with the military; outside these areas, institutional facilities to tap manpower resources were virtually nonexistent. This proved to be a serious matter when the catchment area for recruiting had to be expanded to increase the available sources of manpower. For example, Sikhs from Rawalpindi who wished to be recruited could not do so in the Rawalpindi depot, which was responsible solely for recruiting Muslims. They would have to be taken, or travel on their own account, a considerable distance to the Sikh recruiting depot in Amritsar. This usually entailed too many difficulties and uncertainties for young peasants who had rarely travelled beyond the boundaries of their own villages. If, moreover, after having made his way to the depot a recruit was found unfit, he would have had to make his way back to his village without any compensation from the army. The inconvenience and expenses which had to be incurred were sufficient to deter many prospective recruits from enlisting. Furthermore, the time taken for them to travel all that distance could well lead them to develop cold feet and withdraw.[22] Recruitment in Karnal district

[21] Both the class recruiting system, instituted by Lord Roberts in 1892, and the more informal system of direct recruitment, whereby serving soldiers would bring to their regiments relatives from their villages who were keen on military service, have been discussed in detail in chapter two.

[22] GHQ, *Development of Manpower, and its Utilization For Imperial Purposes*, pp. 3–4. IOR: L/MIL/17/5/2398.

was typical of the problem. When the war broke out, only 270 men from the district were in the army because, prior to the war, the minor agricultural tribes and clans from the district—the Rors, Gujars and Kambohs—were not particularly sought after by the military. In the first two years of the war, the district hardly yielded any additional manpower simply because the facilities for recruiting were totally absent from it. But in 1918, under the new recruiting system (which will be discussed), the district yielded more than 3,000 men in a period of less than six months.[23]

On the other hand, output from the established military districts had not been optimized because of the competition that had developed amongst rival regiments trying to secure the necessary men for their rank and file. Lieutenant Colonel D.G. Rule, an officer who was on recruiting duties in Amritsar district in November 1914, noted that there were forty-one recruiting parties, outside his own, which were simultaneously searching for recruits in the district.[24] The competition for particular classes of recruits by various regiments, as they stepped up their recruiting activities, often led to rivalry, friction and wastage on the recruiting ground. The zealousness for securing recruits was generated partly by the dire need for men and partly by the knowledge amongst regimental recruiters that their chances for promotion depended on the number of recruits they could produce. A father wrote to his son, a sepoy at the front, informing him that he had tried to enlist ten recruits for his son's regiment in the hope that it would secure the latter's promotion.[25] Often, in their zealousness to acquire their

[23] *Record of War Services in Karnal District*, compiled by Tek Chand, Deputy Commissioner, Karnal District (Lahore 1920), p. 4. IOR:Pos. 5547.

[24] Diary of Lieutenant Colonel D.G. Rule, entry dated 16 November 1914, in Papers of Lieutenant Colonel D.G. Rule, Centre for South Asian Studies (SAS), Cambridge.

[25] Letter to Sepoy Guljehan Khan at the front from his father in the Punjab, dated 5 May 1915, in *Censor*, Vol. 1, part III, fo. 452. IOR:L/MIL/5/825.

A note on the mail: Soon after Indian troops were sent abroad from India to Europe, a censor's officer was set up at Boulougne in France, to censor letters to and from Indian troops. The object was to prevent seditious materials from reaching Indian troops in Europe, and information from abroad from reaching home, which might be militarily sensitive or which might produce unintended results in India. Incoming and outgoing letters were thus examined by a censor officer, who wrote a weekly report to Army Headquarters in Delhi. Each report gave a summary and commentary of the tone and contents of the letters, and was accompanied by some

quota of recruits, regimental recruiting parties would discourage prospective recruits from joining the other regiments. They would scare off potential recruits by attributing faults to rival units. This usually generated confusion and scepticism amongst the young men in the countryside, with the result that many of them were frightened off, rather than encouraged to enlist, by the recruiting parties. An adjutant in a regiment enlisting Muslims from Gurgaon district in 1914 complained that his regiment was robbed of a rich crop of recruits owing to the rivalry of a recruiter from another regiment.[26] This confusion could not easily be resolved when the recruiting process remained solely a military affair, organized by the recruiting officer at the depot who was in charge of a particular class of recruits and carried out by regimental recruiting parties operating in the villages. Each regimental recruiting party was only interested in acquiring recruits from the right classes for their regiment, and the recruiting officer at the depot merely endorsed the process by certifying the new recruits to be socially and physically fit for enlistment. There was little coordination between the different regimental recruiting parties when they carried out recruiting activities in the military districts, and the civil administration did not have much of a part to play in the whole process. Furthermore, as their areas of operations did not correspond with the administrative units of the province, there was little interaction between the recruiting officers and the district officers.

In addition to the structural problems created by the class recruiting system, another obstacle in the way of increasing the supply of men in the province was the sense of apprehension that was felt by people after receiving news from the war front. News of the military disasters in Europe and Mesopotamia had induced a much more critical attitude amongst the population towards the war. By the middle of 1915, the initial enthusiasm for recruiting amongst the local population began to give way to reluctance, especially after the experiences of those who had fought in the western front

---

excerpts. Most of the excerpts quoted in this chapter were translated and reproduced in typescript and attached to the officer's report. It is, therefore, impossible to tell if the letters were actually allowed to be forwarded, and if they were, what sort of information had been deleted.

[26] *Record of War Work in Gurgaon District*, compiled by the Deputy Commissioner, Gurgaon District (Poona, 1923), p. 8. IOR:Pos. 5540.

were made known to them through letters sent from the front. Soon
after their arrival in Marseilles, the Indian soldiers were sent to the
front, and in October they had their first experience of full-fledged
war at the battles of Ypres and Neuve Chapelle. The ferocity of the
battles was something which the Indian soldiers had never experienced before; in their letters sent home from the western front, almost all spoke of the tremendous scale on which the war was fought
and of the extensive losses that the Indian regiments were suffering. A letter from a Jat sepoy, writing from his hospital bed in
Brighton to a member of his village, carried the typical impressions that the war had on the Indian soldiers:

> Here the war is very severe, corpses lie upon corpses, and riv-
> ers of blood flow. When an attack is made, parapets are made of
> dead bodies, then soldiers shoot and do not take heed of others
> ... in the regiment we have lost six hundred killed, two hundred
> rendered unfit, and three hundred wounded.[27]

That the war had such an impact on the soldiers and resulted in
such heavy casualties was hardly surprising. The war in Europe
was a major departure from the military experience the Indian soldier had been used to: little fighting, not much hardship, and plenty
of rewards and gratuities to earn. Except for the occasional skir-
mish against frontier tribesmen, Indian soldiers had hardly had
any battle experiences for the past half century. Although the Indian
Army had been sent overseas before 1914 for limited imperial campaigns and policing duties, it had not been involved in actual warfare.[28] In tactics and weaponry, the Indian soldier was far behind
his European counterpart; Indian regiments were not armed with
machine guns, and their firearms consisted of obsolete British
rifles.[29] Therefore, while the Indian soldier was found to be hardy

[27] From Ude Ram, 6th Jats, Kitchener's Indian Hospital to Ranj Lal, zamindar,
village Nardana, Rohtak, April 1915, in *Censor*, Vol. 1, part II, fo. 305. IOR:L/MIL/5/825.

[28] The Indian Army's battle experiences prior to the War had been limited almost exclusively to frontier skirmishes. See *Returns of wars and military operations on
or beyond the borders of British India in which the Government of India has been engaged
since 1849*, 20 January 1900, in *PP*, 1900, Vol. 58, pp. 784–881. In the two major wars
in which Britain was involved—the Crimean War and the Anglo-Boer War—Indian
troops were never used, as both were considered "white man's wars".

[29] Mollo, *The Indian Army*, p. 139.

on the mountain passes of the frontier, he was hardly prepared for the trench warfare of the western front, which was characterized by heavy firepower, immense attrition and exhaustion. Several soldiers writing home from the war fronts told of the horrors of the war, and exhorted their friends and relatives not to enlist into the army, and to "feign sickness or make excuses" to avoid enlistment should the recruiting officer visit their villages.[30] A letter from a Punjabi Muslim to a friend in the Punjab was indicative of the mood that was then prevalent amongst most of the soldiers who had been sent to the front.

> For God's sake, don't come, don't come, don't come to this war in Europe. Write and tell me if you and your regiment are coming or not. I am in a state of great anxiety, and tell my brother Muhammud Yakub Khan for God's sake not to enlist. If you have any relatives, my advice is do not let them enlist. I write so much to you because I am a pay havildar and read the letters to the double company commander. Otherwise, there is a strict order on writing such a subject. Cannons, machine guns, and bombs are going day and night, just like the rains of the month of *shrawan* (July to August). Those who have escaped so far are like the few grains cooked in the pot. That is the case with us. In my company there are only about ten men. In the regiment there are about two hundred.[31]

The mood of these letters seemed to create a sense of unease amongst prospective recruits who had begun to doubt if the advantages promised by military service would be worth the immense sacrifices that it now entailed.[32] Furthermore, some of the letters accused the British of racial discrimination—of sparing their own while callously sending Indian troops to the slaughter in the trenches. All these impressions, further reinforced by the tales of

---

[30] Letter from Sardar Singh, Lady Hardinge Hospital, Brockenhurst to Raghbir Singh, tehsil Palompra, Kangra District, Punjab, May 1915, in *Censor*, Vol. 1, part III, fo. 392. IOR:L/MIL/5/825.

[31] Letter from Havildar Abdul Rahman, 59 Scinde Rifles, 8th Company, to Naik Rajwali Khan, 31st Punjabis at Fort Sandeman, 20 May 1915, in *Censors*, Vol. 1, part III, fo.394. IOR:L/MIL/5/825.

[32] Report of the Chief Censor, Boulogne, 29 May 1915 in *Censor*, Vol. 1, part III, fo. 394. IOR:L/MIL/5/825.

the sick and wounded who had returned to the Punjab, contributed to an increasing reluctance among the local population to
enlist. In Amritsar district, for example, it was noted that wives
and mothers went to extraordinary lengths to prevent their men
from being enlisted, mainly out of fear for their safety.[33] There was
little the military authorities could do, short of coercion, to overcome this growing aversion to enlist.

By 1916 it was thus found that existing recruiting arrangements
in the province were wholly inadequate to meet the "wastage of a
prolonged war and the demands of an army largely expanded and
actively engaged in military action in [Europe and the Middle
East]".[34] In the Punjab the demand for military manpower showed
no signs of receding: in the first year of the war, 13,490 men were
required from the Punjab; in the following year, the number of
recruits required shot up to 45,776.[35] These demands were met each
time only after strenuous efforts. It was now evident to the military authorities that the existing recruiting system was buckling
under the strain. If the province was to further fulfil war obligations without army recruiters having to resort to coercion and force,
the recruiting system would have to be supported by the civil administration. Only with the assistance of the civil administration,
with its infrastructural means to reach new pools of recruits, as
well as local influence to prise reluctant recruits from their villages, could the army hope to achieve the necessary increase in the
number of recruits from the Punjab.

Civil-Military Cooperation

By the middle of 1915, the demand for manpower had reached
crisis proportions. For the past few months, the Punjab had supplied
over 40,000 men, an eightfold increase from the average peacetime
yearly demand of men from the province. Yet, the demand for manpower was showing no signs of abating. This prompted a review

[33] Lieutenant Colonel D.G. Rule, Recruiting Officer in Amritsar district, mentioned cases of women who would trail recruiting parties for several miles, pa-
tiently awaiting opportunities to lure away recently acquired recruits. Diary, D.G.
Rule, 24 November 1914, Rule Papers, SAS, Cambridge.

[34] Note by L. French, Additional Secretary Sec to GoP, 26 March 1918, in PHP(M)
'B', March 1919, Lahore Archives, Lahore, Pakistan.

[35] *Recruiting in India, 1919*, Appendix 9, p. 67.

of the recruitment system in the Punjab. In August 1915, a soldier-bureaucrat, Lieutenant Colonel Sir Frank Popham-Young, Commissioner of Rawalpindi Division, suggested that the recruitment process could be improved by closer cooperation between the military and the civil administration in the province. He pointed out that recruiting operations in the Punjab were severely hampered by a "want of coordination between the civil and military officers",[36] and stressed that there was a need to bring about a closer link between the civil and military authorities in the province in order to stimulate and facilitate a greater output of manpower from the province. To this end, he suggested appointing an officer from the provincial civil service to act as a district civil recruiting officer to work in concert with the class recruiting officer. The district officer would assist in the recruiting process by coordinating the activities of different recruiting parties in his district, offer advice on local conditions, provide the necessary facilities, and, if necessary, bring some of his influence to bear on the local population to generate enthusiasm for enlistment.[37]

Following Popham-Young's proposals, some cautious tinkering was done with the recruiting system in the Punjab. Additional British recruiting officers and pensioned Indian Viceroy Commissioned Officers (VCOs) were appointed to strengthen the recruiting staff operating in the military districts, and to serve as outside arbitrators who could stay out of recruitment quota conflicts. To facilitate the intensification of recruiting activities, sub-offices, linked to the existing recruiting depots, were opened in three districts, namely, Jhelum, Ludhiana and Sialkot, and a number of tehsildars from the military districts were officially appointed by the Punjab government to serve as district liaison officers to the recruiting officers. Officers on recruiting duties were to communicate their tour programmes to the civil officers in the districts they proposed to visit and to make a point of calling on these officers whenever the opportunities arose. All recruiting parties were instructed to bring in suitable recruits of any martial class, irrespective of the particular class for which they themselves were recruiting at that time.[38]

[36] 'Note on Recruiting' by Lieutenant Colonel Popham-Young, 24 August 1915, in PHP(M) 'B', 1914, Vol.1. Lahore Archives.

[37] *Ibid.*

[38] David Brief, 'The Punjab and Recruitment to the Indian Army, 1846–1918' (M.Litt thesis, Oxford University, 1978), pp. 127–38.

These modifications were made in an attempt to overcome some of the inherent weaknesses of the existing recruiting system. They failed, however, to improve the efficiency of the system and did not succeed in bringing about the desired expansion in the volume of recruitment.

The main problem with the system was that recruiting was still confined to the existing military districts; and although operations had been intensified by the increase in the size of the recruiting staff in each of these districts, the army was still limiting recruitment activities to its traditional catchment area, which, by 1916, was already showing signs of drying up. More importantly, the recruiting process was carried out in a decentralized and poorly coordinated manner, with the civil administration still largely excluded from the actual recruiting operations. Although some minor civilian officers had been appointed to assist the recruiting officers, it was found that recruiting operations in the villages were still hampered by the absence of effective coordination between the recruiting officers and the local district officers. District officers complained that they were frequently ignored by recruiting officers operating in their villages. In instances where recruiting parties did seek the help of the district administration, the situation was not any better. Several recruiting parties would arrive at the same village without prior notice to demand immediate assistance from the local officials. Tehsildars and sub-inspectors often found themselves thrown into confusion, having to attend to several different demands at the same time. Consequently, despite a substantial increase in the recruiting staff at the various recruiting depots, the province was still hard-pressed put to meet the demands of the war.[39] By 1916, it became clear that the task of mobilizing the manpower of the province could no longer be left to the limited means of the military alone; if the province was to sustain, if not increase, its supply of soldiers to the army, the civil administrative had to assume a more conspicuous role.

The call for greater involvement of the civil administration in the recruiting process was made in April 1916 by the newly appointed Viceroy of India, Lord Chelmsford. He pressed the view

[39] 'Notes on Recruiting Methods Employed in the Punjab' by L. French, Additional Secretary to GoP, 4 June 1918 in GoI, Home (Pol.) 'B', February 1920, File no. 373, NAI.

that if the Indian Empire as a whole was to bear an adequate share in the war the whole machinery and influence of the civil government must be utilized to strengthen the organization engaged in raising manpower.[40] The Viceroy's call was welcomed by the Lieutenant Governor of the Punjab, Sir Michael O'Dwyer. For two years since the beginning of the war O'Dwyer had asserted the necessity for the provincial government to play a more significant role in the mobilization of the province for the war effort. A committed paternalist in the true tradition of the "Punjab school of administration", O'Dwyer believed that no efforts should be spared for the successful execution of the war. He declared that he would not flinch from removing "every obstacle to the successful prosecution of the war".[41] The Punjab, he argued, had enjoyed peace and prosperity brought by British rule and now in the Empire's hour of need the province should return the benefits in full.

O'Dwyer was a civil service officer from a strictly civilian background,[42] yet he appreciated the importance for his government of being more involved with the military. This, he felt, was important for the security not only of the army, but of his province also. In a lengthy memorandum, submitted to the Viceroy in September 1916 at the latter's request, O'Dwyer stressed the importance of the civil government in the Punjab being "intimately acquainted with the temper and conduct of the troops" in the Indian Army, half of which was raised in the Punjab.[43] He complained that the tendency of Army Headquarters in India to adopt a "policy of extreme secrecy" in cases of mutiny and sedition in the regiments would expose the civil government to the "risk of having at any time to deal with hidden and unknown danger".[44] The absence of inter-communication between

[40] Michael O'Dwyer, *India As I Knew It,* p. 218.

[41] *Ibid.,* p. 214.

[42] The son of an Irish landowner, O'Dwyer joined the Indian Civil Service in 1882, and began his service in Shahpur district in the Punjab. From 1901 to 1908, he served as Revenue Commissioner in the newly formed North-Western Frontier Province. In December 1912, he was appointed Lieutenant Governor of the Punjab, an appointment he held until 1919. See his autobiography, *India As I Knew It.* For an assessment of his governorship of the Punjab, see J.M. Burns, 'Sir Michael O'Dwyer and the Polarization of Punjab Politics (unpublished thesis for Diploma in History, Cambridge University).

[43] Memorandum by Sir Michael O'Dwyer, 6 September 1916, encl. in Chelmsford to Chamberlain, 11 October 1916, Chelmsford Papers, no. 2. IOR:MSS.EUR.E.264/2.

[44] *Ibid.*

the Punjab government and the army in such matters, he argued, would not only handicap the civil administration, but would adversely affect the military machinery as well.

The danger which O'Dwyer was afraid might afflict the army and its recruiting base in the Punjab was highlighted by the *Ghadr* rebellion of 1914–15, a revolutionary movement centred on the returned Sikh émigrés of central Punjab. The *Ghadr* episode has been recounted fully in many accounts,[45] and I shall only give a brief narrative of the events and how the problem was dealt with by the government. The *Ghadr* party was organized by a small group of revolutionaries from Delhi and Punjab in exile in North America. The party's ideology was a syncretic brand of revolutionary nationalism, with its ultimate aim the violent overthrow of the British government in India. Its prime mover was Har Dayal, a Punjabi who planned to use his home province as the base for his revolutionary activities; his America-based newspaper, the *Ghadr*, was the vehicle through which he sought to spread his revolutionary ideas amongst the Punjabis, at home and abroad. The initial target group of the *Ghadr*ites appeared to be the Sikh soldiers and the peasantry, the two main bulwarks of British colonial rule in the Punjab. The party concentrated its attention in particular on Sikh regiments in the Indian Army and prospective Sikh recruits. Through contacts made with sepoys while the latter were on furlough, *Ghadr* agents were believed to have created revolutionary cells within some Sikh regiments[46] and intelligence officers estimated that more than fifty per cent of the active *Ghadr*ites were ex-soldiers of the Indian Army.[47] Soon after the outbreak of war, the party attempted to start a rebellion in Punjab, believing, not incorrectly,

---

[45] See, for example, *Report of Committee Appointed to Investigate Revolutionary Conspiracies in India* in *PP*, 1919, Cmd. 9190, Vol. 8, pp. 482–90. F.C. Isemonger and J.S. Slattery, *An Account of the Ghadr Conspiracy, 1913–1915*, (henceforth *Ghadr Conspiracy*) Lahore, 1919; Harish K. Puri, *The Ghadr Movement: Ideology, Organization and Strategy*, Amritsar, 1983; Mark Jurgensmeyer, 'The Ghadr Conspiracy' in *Sikh Studies: Comparative Perspectives in Changing Tradition*, Berkeley, 1979; Max Harcourt, 'Revolutionary Networks in Northern Indian Politics 1907–1935: A Case Study of the Terrorist Movement in Delhi, Punjab, the UP, and the Adjacent Princely States' (unpublished Ph.D. dissertation, Sussex University, 1972).

[46] Harcourt, 'Revolutionary Networks in Northern India', p. 179.

[47] See Amrita Cheema, 'Punjab Politics, 1919–1923' (unpublished D.Phil. Dissertation, Oxford University, 1987), p. 85.

that the time was ripe as the province would have been stripped of all troops, especially the British regiments which had been despatched to the western front. It also felt that it had done the necessary preparatory groundwork; small groups of *Ghadr*ites had infiltrated into the Punjab and were operating extensively in the Sikh districts of Amritsar, Ludhiana, Jullundur Ferozepur and Gurdaspur, where they mingled with the local population during festival celebrations and fairs to spread their ideas. The government had been aware that some Sikh companies of the 25th and 26th Punjabis, stationed at Jhelum and Ferozepur cantonments respectively, had been infiltrated by *Ghadr* agents while serving in Hong Kong.[48] Having thus prepared the ground, the *Ghadr*s planned to spark off an instantaneous and widespread rebellion in the Punjab through a series of disturbances, dacoities and murders carried out by agents who would slip into the Punjab disguised as returned émigrés.

The GoI was first alerted to the potential political threat of the returned Sikh émigrés by the *Komagata Maru* incident. In May 1914 the *Komagata Maru*, a ship chartered by a Punjabi entrepreneur, set sail for Canada from India with about 300 hopeful Punjab emigrants. The voyage was an attempt to evade Canadian legislation which prohibited Indians from entering Canada who did not come directly from India. However, on arrival, the Canadian authorities refused admission to the immigrants on the grounds—under another Canadian law used to limit the number of Indian immigrants to the country—that they did not possess enough ready cash. After much heated argument the *Komagata Maru* was, with its passengers, sent back to India. On the return voyage, many of the disgruntled Sikhs came under the influence of *Ghadr* agents and, in the mood they were in, were soon spoiling for a fight. When the ship arrived at Calcutta the authorities, hoping to avoid trouble, tried to force the Sikhs into special trains to be taken back to the Punjab. The Sikhs refused to comply with the order and a riot broke out. The police opened fire on the rioters, killing eighteen men and wounding twenty-five others. More than two hundred other Sikhs were subsequently despatched to the Punjab, where they were interned.[49]

---

[48] Memo of O'Dywer, 11 October 1916.

[49] For an account of the *Komagata Maru* incident, see Sohan Singh Josh, *Tragedy of Komagata Maru*, New Delhi, 1975.

To stem the infiltration of revolutionary agents into the country, the GoI passed the Ingress into India Ordinance in 1914, a law which enabled the government to screen returned emigrants before they were let into India. Those suspected of revolutionary affiliations were instantly detained at the port of arrival; those whose demeanour was in doubt were despatched back to their villages in special trains to be kept under local internment or probation.[50] Despite the Ordinance, some revolutionaries managed to slip through the net and made their way undetected to the Punjab. From October 1914 to September 1915, *Ghadr* agents went into an intensified phase of propaganda and sedition activities, followed by a series of explosions, murders, gang robberies and bomb attacks in the Punjab. The attempted rebellion by the *Ghadrs,* which threatened to destabilize the Punjab at this rather critical moment ultimately drove O'Dwyer to the conclusion that greater cooperation had to be established between the civil and military authorities in the Punjab if the province was to continue being militarily viable as a major recruiting ground for the Indian Army.[51]

But what was perhaps most crucial to the Punjab at this crucial juncture, argued O'Dywer, was that the civil and military authorities should work closely together to enable the province to maximize its output of manpower. He asserted that without the support of the civil government and its officers working through their local collaborators, the military authorities would never succeed in effectively mobilizing the Punjab for its manpower. The existing recruitment machinery was failing at every level and was unable to cope with the pressures put upon it. Some of the fault, he argued, lay in the fact that the recruiting officers were too inexperienced to handle the job. This was further aggravated by the cumbersome administrative procedures which were involved once recruits reached a recruiting officer. If the military was allowed to continue with its present mode of operation, not only would the flow of men cease, but the political repercussions might be considerable. O'Dwyer argued that the only way in which the province could be exploited to its maximum capacity was by recruiting to be done by districts, in which recruiting officers would take all classes belonging to the district in their charge. In order to

[50] Isemonger and Slattery, *Ghadr Conspiracy*, p. 80.
[51] O'Dwyer, *India As I Knew It*, p. 200.

strengthen the operational capacity of the recruiting officer, the civil administration would be fully incorporated into the recruiting process.[52] Local officers, either civil service officers or retired Indian military officers, working in association with the deputy commissioner, would greatly facilitate the working of the recruiting machinery. They would provide an effective means of dealing with local obstruction to recruiting, and would encourage recruitment by serving as a connecting link between the recruit's home and the regiment. Furthermore, so he argued, such an officer from his intimate knowledge of local conditions would be able to advise recruiting parties on details such as the demeanour and attitude to be adopted when visiting the various tracts which had not hitherto figured as a recruiting ground for the army. Cooperation with the civil authorities could also open new ground for the military authorities, who seemed to be prevented by military tradition in attempting to widen their recruitment to new sources within the Punjab.[53] In December 1916, in what would seem to have been a consequence of O'Dwyer's recommendations, the old system of class recruiting was finally replaced by a new system, first introduced in the Punjab, and later extended to the United Provinces and the rest of India.[54]

The new system removed the inconsistencies of the existing one by concentrating all recruiting operations in the office of the Adjutant General in Delhi. To give mobilization the official sanction and support of the GoI, a Central Recruiting Board was constituted in Delhi. The Board was presided over by the Finance Member of the Viceroy's Council, Sir William Meyer, and comprised two other civilian members of the Viceroy's Council, the Adjutant General, the Secretary of the Army Department, two Indian princes and the Lieutenant Governor of the Punjab. Its basic responsibility was to study the overall demand for manpower from India, and fix a quota for each province to fulfil.[55]

But it was in the Punjab that the main recommendations of O'Dwyer, namely the coordination of all recruiting agencies within a particular area, and the intimate association of civil and military

[52] Memo by O'Dywer, 11 October 1916.
[53] *Ibid.*
[54] Hudson, *Recruiting in India,* p. 23. IOR:L/MIL/17/5/2152.
[55] Development of Manpower in India, April 1918. IOR:L/MIL/17/5/2398.

officers in the recruiting process, were effected.[56] Under the new recruiting system, known as the "territorial system", recruiting areas were redrawn to correspond with the administrative divisions of the province. Each of the newly constituted recruiting areas was put in the charge of a divisional recruiting officer, whose office was strengthened by an expanded staff. In each district, which under the new system constituted a basic recruiting unit, a district recruiting officer, normally an English-speaking Indian civil officer nominated by the district administration, was appointed to function as the civilian link to the military recruiting staff. The activities of the district recruiting officer were in turn supervised and coordinated by the divisional recruiting officer, who dealt with all the recruits sent to him, had them medically examined, enlisted those passed as fit and despatched them to their respective regiments.[57] The divisional recruiting officer was made responsible for the recruitment of all classes within the civil division in which he was operating and his office was the ultimate stage a prospective recruit had to pass through before joining the regiment.[58]

The most important improvement in the revised system was the integration of the military function of recruiting into the civil administrative structure, thus providing the framework for the civil administration to assume direct control of recruiting operations in the province. This afforded the army a very important advantage: the civil administration, unlike the army, had a structural framework which was province-wide and which reached into every level of society. This meant that groups of Punjabis who had hitherto been excluded under the old class system of recruiting could now be reached and recruited into the army.[59]

After the institution of the new system, recruiting operations assumed a province-wide nature and all twenty-eight districts of the province were duly exploited, although in varying degrees, for their available manpower. By the end of 1917 more than twenty-two "new" classes of Punjabis found military service opened to them for the first time. Under the new system, the entire line of the civil hierarchy from the Lieutenant Governor in Lahore to the village

[56] Note by L. French, Addl. Sec. to GoP, 26 March 1918, in PHP(M) 'B' March 1919.
[57] *Development of Manpower in India*, April 1918, p. 5. IOR:L/MIL/17/5/2398.
[58] *Ibid.*
[59] General A. Walters to French, 16 December 1916, PHP(M) pro. no. 9, File 2, 1914.

lambardars was utilized for the purpose of mobilization. Mirroring the provincial administrative set-up the new territorial recruiting system in the Punjab now functioned as an integrated multi-tiered structure.

In June 1917, soon after the Central Recruiting Board was appointed in Delhi, a Provincial Recruitment Board was set up in Punjab's capital, Lahore, to assume direct control of a province-wide recruiting campaign. O'Dwyer sat at the helm of the Board which included the financial commissioner, commissioners of the divisions of the province, district recruiting officers and a number of tribal chiefs and landed elites from the province, including Sardar Bahadur Gujjan Singh of Ludhiana, Khan Bahadur Malik Muhammad Amir Khan of Shamasabad, Rai Bahadur Chaudhri Lal Chand of Rohtak, Khan Bahadur Sayid Mehdi Shah of Gojra, Major Malik Sir Umar Hayat Khan Tiwana of Kalra, Sardar Raghbir Singh Sindhawalia of Raja Sansi, Amritsar, all of them leading notables in their respective localities.[60] The composition of the Board reflected O'Dwyer's determination to exploit all means available to him to mobilize the province for the war effort.

In the Punjab the ultimate responsibility and direction of the recruiting campaign rested with the Provincial Recruitment Board. After receiving its recruiting quota from the Central Recruiting Board in Delhi, it in turn decided how the load should be shared amongst the districts of the province and subsequently fixed the recruitment quota for the various districts in the province. The onus for meeting the quota then fell on the local district officials. To publicize the recruiting campaign, and to emphasize the determination of the government to achieve its given quota of military manpower, the Lieutenant Governor himself made regular tours of the districts and held regular recruiting *darbars* where he would personally reward those who had contributed to the recruiting effort.[61] To goad communities and districts to increase the yield of their available manpower, the Board collected and published monthly

[60] Lieutenant Governor's proceedings in Home/Military Department, 26 March 1918 in PHP(M) 'B', March 1919, pros. 866, 1919.

[61] The efforts of the various districts and the rewards that they received were recorded in their *War Histories,* compiled by their respective deputy commissioners or their subordinates after the war. The whole collection of these *Histories,* with the exception of Jhelum district, have been microfilmed and are now available at the India Office Library in London. See IOR: POS 5540, 5545 and 5547.

recruitment statistics with the object of stimulating recruitment through inter-district and inter-tribal rivalry.[62]

While the Board at Lahore directed the province-wide campaign, recruiting activities at the district level revolved around the deputy commissioners, who coordinated all such activities in their respective districts. The responsibilities for getting the required number of men were placed squarely on the shoulders of the local officials, and every level of district officialdom, from the tehsildars to the village headman, was enlisted for the mobilization campaign.[63] At a Recruiting Board meeting in July 1917, it was decided that the land revenue rules should be amended to make recruiting part of the duties of the village revenue officials. The entire revenue administration of the district was thus mobilized. The tehsildar, a provincial civil service officer, the zaildar beneath him, who was usually selected and appointed by the deputy commissioner from amongst the leading landholders of the zail, the sufed poshes, who assisted the zaildar in the basic duties of revenue administration, and the lambardars, the village headmen, were all expected to put recruiting at the top of their priorities.[64] Deputy commissioners supervised closely the work of their local minor officials. Some commissioners and deputy commissioners fixed recruiting quotas for each zaildar and sufed posh to fill periodically; in Ludhiana district, for example, zaildars and lambardars were expected to produce two recruits per month, while sufed poshes needed to produce one per month.[65] Deputy commissioners saw that their subordinates knew what was expected of them, and ensured that they kept up their recruiting efforts. Local officials were then left to their own devices to induce the villagers to enlist for military service.

[62] 'Notes on Recruiting Methods Employed in the Punjab', GoI, Home (Pol.), 1920, February, No. 373, NAI.

[63] The district in the Punjab was divided into sub-units known as tehsils. Each district had between three to five tehsils, and each of these were under the charge of a tehsildar, who was usually an Indian official. The tehsil was further divided into zails, headed by a zaildar. Each zail would consist of a group of villages, and the lambardar or village headman, usually a person who was the most influential man in the village, assisted in the collection of revenue, and had semi-official status.

[64] Minutes of the Punjab Recruiting Board Meeting, 14 July 1917, in PHP(M), Case No. 9, Vol. 6. LA.

[65] *War History of Ludhiana District*, compiled by Sheikh Munir Husain, Extra Assistant Commissioner, (Lahore 1921), p. 16. IOR:POS 5540.

The decision to involve these lower echelon Indian officials and semi-officials was designed to enlist local influence to stimulate the recruitment process. Many of these lower echelon posts were filled by "the natural leaders" of rural society who were co-opted into the administrative structure by the British. The best example was the zaildar, a government appointee in charge of a group of villages formed into an administrative unit known as the zail. He was usually appointed from amongst the leading men of the tribe or locality, and the social authority which he already possessed was reinforced by his official authority as a representative of the government. As a result, the zaildar exercised tremendous authority amongst villagers, many of whom looked to him for patronage and assistance.[66] The zaildar was therefore able to use "threats and blandishments [which he alone possessed in his specific locality] to induce men under his influence to promise to enlist".[67] By using their local influence, these intermediaries of the state were not only able to force reluctant recruits to come forward for enlistment, but could ensure that resentment against enlistment was contained, and would not develop into social unrest.

Unlike the army, the civil government had the means to apply pressure on local officials to take their recruiting tasks seriously. For their part local officials tended to respond better to the dictates of the civil than the military authorities, knowing that they had more to gain or lose from the former. It was made known that for future appointments for posts such as honorary magistrates and district sub-registrars, the recruiting services of the prospective candidates would be taken into account.[68] The Deputy Commissioner of Ludhiana openly made known that vacant posts in his district would be awarded to those who produced the greatest number of recruits.[69] The emphasis placed upon their recruitment efforts was such that local revenue officials knew that they worked under the threat of dismissal if their efforts did not live up to what was required of them. They were reminded that the main reason

[66] David Gilmartin, *Islam and Empire*, p. 21.

[67] Popham-Young to French, 22 July 1918, PHP(M), pro. 733 of 1918.

[68] Minutes of Provincial Recruiting Board Meeting, Punjab, 14 July 1917, in File U/XIV/316, Deputy Commissioner's Record Office (henceforth DCRO), Jhelum district, Pakistan.

[69] Note by Sheikh Asghar Ali, deputy commissioner, Ludhiana district, 31 October 1916, PHP(M) 'B', File 19, proc. 72, 1916.

for "their enjoying emoluments and land grants from the government was their claim that they were men of real influence in the countryside", on whom the government could rely in times of need. The government now required them to justify the retention of their posts through their recruiting efforts.[70] Even hereditary lambardars were threatened with future dispossession if they failed in their recruiting duties. A zaildar from the Punjab wrote that he had been given a month by his deputy commissioner to furnish his quota of recruits or he would be dismissed from his zaildarship and lambardarship.[71] To put pressure on local officials, registers showing monthly recruiting records were kept in villages and zails, and monthly meetings were held at which the results of the previous month's recruiting were publicly announced with appropriate commendation for good work and condemnation for bad work. In Ludhiana district, four zaildars and two sufed poshes were dismissed for "laziness and lack of interest in recruiting".[72]

Local leaders, official and non-official, not only functioned as individual recruiting agents but, under the aegis of the deputy commissioner, organized themselves into various associations, known variously as war committees, war leagues or war associations to coordinate the process of mobilization and fund raising in their respective districts. In Ludhiana district, for example, a committee was started to obtain recruits from the Muslim Rajputs, Jats and Gujar tribes from the district. The members of the committee were to remain in constant touch with the recruiting officer for these classes and had to inform him from time to time when there was a number of recruits prepared for enlistment at any place, or if there was a chance of success by visiting a particular village or villages.[73] In Rohtak, the inspector of the district cooperative bank, an influential Jat, took the lead in forming ten local committees, staffed entirely by local notables, mainly retired Indian officers, and located at various important centres in the districts to generate recruits. The value of such committees soon became apparent, prompting the Deputy Commissioner in Rohtak to open a formal

[70] Hallifax to French, 'Note on Recruiting', 4 November 1916, in File U/XIV/195A, DCRO, Jhelum.

[71] Letter from a Punjabi zaildar to a friend, 11 December 1917 in *Censors*, Vol. 3, Pt. III, fo. 806. IOR:L/MIL/5/827.

[72] *War History of Ludhiana District*, p. 17. IOR:POS 5540.

[73] *Ibid.*, p. 13.

recruiting office to guide these local committees to coordinate their efforts.[74]

Such committees served also as an important link between the district administration and the local population, particularly crucial in a situation where the province was being hard pressed by the war effort. During the war, it was imperative that the administration kept a finger on the pulse of the population; local grievances, if not spotted and rectified early, could lead to widespread discontent, which could prove harmful to a province crucial to the war effort. These committees, therefore, served an important function by enabling the district officer to keep in touch with the mood at the local level and at the same time to deal expeditiously with localized grievances before they were allowed to ferment into deeper-seated resentments. To take the example of Rohtak again: district officers received complaints from several soldiers and their families that they were not receiving prompt attention from the authorities in the matter of domestic disputes. The deputy commissioner responded to these complaints by revamping the war committees into *Fauji panchayats,* whose main function was to deal with petitions received from absent soldiers promptly. A special secretariat was established within the district office to deal specially with the work of the *Fauji* panchayats. Furthermore, the panchayats were put under the direct charge of the district treasury office, giving it the ability to deal with matters regarding pay and pension instantly.[75] By 1918 the panchayats in Rohtak had dealt with 14,774 cases involving pension claims, verification rolls and distribution of relief money to families of soldiers who were injured or killed in battle.[76]

Through these committees, the Punjab government was able to assume some of the functions of the army by taking a direct interest in the welfare of the soldiers. In Ludhiana district for example, prominent Sikhs served in war committees to assist in the recruiting of Sikhs and, at the same time, to look after the household affairs of soldiers when they were away on field service.[77] In Attock,

---

[74] *War History of Rohtak District,* compiled by S.H. Harcourt, Deputy Commissioner, Rohtak district, (Delhi, n.d.), pp. 14–15. IOR:POS 5547.

[75] *Ibid.,* pp. 17–20.

[76] *Ibid.,* p. 41

[77] This included the protection of the rights of the absent soldier in litigation cases involving his land, settlement of marriage arrangements and the prevention of abduction of wives. See *War History, Ludhiana District,* p. 14.

the District War League, with its branches in all the tehsils in the district, gave cash and other forms of rewards to parents whose sons were fighting in the war.[78] Through such welfare activities, the government sought to ensure that mobilization in the province would in no way be jeopardized by any perceived insensitivity to the needs of the soldiers. This would also serve to deflect any sedition aimed at undermining the willingness of Punjabis to enlist in the Indian Army. By working through agencies like the panchayats in Rohtak and the Sikh committees in Ludhiana, several complicated problems like family differences, disputes about property and inheritance, and delicate questions regarding betrothals and marriages, which were likely to affect the morale of the soldier, were settled quickly and effectively, thereby giving little cause for discontent. Men who were to leave for the war fronts were assured that in their absence their interests would be well taken care of by men of acknowledged position and influence in the neighbourhood.

In addition to the use of local influence and welfare schemes the Punjab government, during the war, offered a whole range of rewards to induce recruitment. It put at the disposal of the Commander-in-Chief of the Indian Army 180,000 acres of valuable canal irrigated lands for later allotment to Indian officers and men who had served with special distinction during the war. A further 15,000 acres were set aside for reward grants to those who gave most effective help in raising recruits.[79] Monetary rewards were given to individuals for bringing in recruits, and village communities that had good records, for example by contributing more than half their male population during the war, were awarded with generous remissions of land revenue.[80] In the middle of 1917, in a desperate measure to raise even more men from the province, the government offered a bonus of fifty rupees to every recruit upon enrolment. The economic advantages of such a scheme, accruing both to those who were prepared to enlist and to their families, were powerful incentives for enlistment.[81]

[78] M.S.D. Butler, *Record of War Services of Attock District, 1914–1919*, Lahore, 1921, p. 11. IOR:POS 5545.

[79] O'Dwyer, *India As I Knew It*, p. 221.

[80] See Table 3.1 and various *War Histories* for details.

[81] 'Note on Recruiting Methods Employed in the Punjab', GoI, Home/Pol. 'B', 1920, February, No. 373, NAI.

Table 3.1
Rewards Distributed in the Punjab during the First World War

District	Titles	Sword of Honour	Jagirs (Rupees)	Land Grants (in Squares)*
Hissar	13	–	1,500	52
Rohtak	14	7	1,500	72
Gurgaon	4	6	1,000	44
Karnal	6	2	–	76
Ambala	12	3	–	139
Kangra	2	4	500	85
Hoshiarpur	8	2	1,250	106
Jullundur	19	2	750	92
Ludhiana	14	9	2,250	113
Ferozepur	10	5	1,000	100
Lahore	39	3	1,000	101
Amritsar	17	–	750	176
Gurdaspur	5	2	–	147
Sialkot	4	–	250	83
Gujranwala	6	1	1,000	115
Gujrat	5	3	250	72
Shahpur	16	11	200	191
Jhelum	17	6	500	157
Rawalpindi	18	6	1,750	118
Attock	7	7	1,500	171
Mianwali	4	1	500	97
Montgomery	1	–	–	30
Lyallpur	10	2	750	15
Jhang	3	–	–	17
Multan	9	2	500	78
Muzzafargarh	3	–	500	101
Dera Ghazi Khan	10	1	–	207

Note: * one square = 27.7 acres.
Source: M.S. Leigh, *Punjab and the War*, pp. 140–74.

The apparent willingness of the Punjab government to reward those who would rally to its call prompted communities to respond eagerly, with the hope that by doing so they would be beneficiaries of future government patronage. In Rohtak district for example, prominent Jat leaders took it upon themselves to push the recruiting campaign in their community so that they would have good grounds to petition the government to increase the employment of Jats in the provincial service.[82] Their efforts eventually paid off. In

[82] *War History of Rohtak District*, pp. 7–8; p. 26, and Appendices. IOR:POS 5547.

1915, during the Lieutenant Governor's visit to Rohtak, he was presented with a petition from the Jat community for an increase in their representation in the provincial service. The request was immediately granted by the Lieutenant Governor, who issued a circular urging all heads of departments to increase the number of Jats in their respective departments.[83] The government's decision to erect war tablets in villages in recognition of their good efforts during the war was welcomed by several villages which saw in the tablets a claim for receiving further rewards from the government in preference over their neighbours.[84] During a reassessment for land revenue carried out in the districts during the war, the war services of the rural population seemed to be a deciding factor in the amount of assessment and the terms to be fixed.[85] Individual soldiers too were made aware that loyal service to the *sircar* during the war would earn them favours from the government. After 1916 (when the civil government began to take an active part in the recruiting campaign) several soldiers writing from the front in Europe urged their families to assist the war in all means possible. A Sikh sepoy, serving in France, encouraged his father to send all his brothers to the deputy commissioner to be enlisted, reminding him that they would reap their "rewards from the government"[86] if they rendered help on such an occasion. Similarly, brothers and sons fighting in the front were urged to remain "true to their salt", and to discharge their duties faithfully.[87]

The direct assumption by the Punjab government of the military responsibilities of recruiting and of soldiers' welfare from the end of 1916 was, by most measures, a great success. Besides possessing the organizational framework which could reach every corner of the province, and into all levels of Punjabi society, the civil authorities possessed a range of inducements and threats to encourage reluctant villagers to enlist, something quite beyond the powers of the military authorities. The results achieved as a consequence

---

[83] *Ibid.*, pp. 7–8.

[84] Minutes of Proceedings of the Provincial Recruiting Board, Punjab, 22 November 1918, in File U/XIV/195A, DCRO, Jhelum district.

[85] O'Dwyer, *India As I Knew It*, p. 212.

[86] From Hazura Singh, 38th Central India Horse, France, to his father, Risaldar Inder Singh, pensioner, Lahore, 8 January 1917, in *Censors*, Vol. 3, part I, fo. 50. IOR:L/MIL/5/827.

[87] To Ahmed Khan, 34th Poona Horse, France, from his mother in Jhelum, Punjab, 10 November 1916, in *Censors*, Vol. 3, Pt. I, fo. 46. IOR:L/MIL/5/827.

of civil-military integration in the Punjab were impressive. From 1917 onwards, the Punjab consistently yielded its quota of men; the traditional military districts continued to yield a high number of combatants, and in the districts which hitherto had had no tradition of service in the army, recruits were being found without any apparent difficulties. By the beginning of 1918 almost 200,000 men had been recruited from the Punjab, one-and-a-half times the size of the entire pre-war Indian Army.

Mobilizing the Rural Notables

When O'Dwyer mobilized his administration to generate military manpower from the Punjab, he was intent on utilizing all means of influence available to him to achieve his goals. When the Punjab Recruiting Board was formed in Lahore in 1917, O'Dwyer deliberately incorporated a number of landed elites from the province—"the territorial aristocracy and ... landed gentry"[88]—to serve on it. By doing so, he was acknowledging the potential of the province's landed elites as military contractors and sought to encourage them to exert their influence to generate manpower in the province. In fact, the rural elites came to constitute an important component of the wartime civil-military regime in the Punjab.

O'Dwyer's faith in the ability of the rural notables, comprising the big landlords and tribal chieftains of western Punjab as well as the religious and clan leaders of central and eastern Punjab, to assist in the recruiting process, mainly as independent military contractors, was not without grounds. In September 1916, Army Headquarters in Delhi informed the Punjab government that the province was required to supply 3,500 mule and camel drivers for service in Mesopotamia.[89] The Army Department had decided to place the main burden on the Punjab because the western and south-western parts of the province had traditionally supplied the bulk of animal transport for the army, and also because it believed that "Punjabis were more prepared to take up service overseas".[90] This demand could not have come at a less opportune time. In April 1916 officers

<hr/>

[88] O'Dwyer, *India as I Knew It*, p. 227.
[89] Proceedings of the Lieutenant Governor of the Punjab in Home/Military Department, November 1916, in GoI, Army Department, Note 92 of 1920, NAI.
[90] *Ibid.*

from the western districts which had continuously supplied muleteers and sarwans (camel drivers) since the beginning of the war
reported that their respective districts had almost reached their
limits where available manpower was concerned.[91] O'Dwyer decided that the most effective way by which his administration could
assist in raising manpower during the present emergency was to
engage the assistance of the landed elites to use their local influence to persuade their tribal followers to enlist themselves. The
Punjab government subsequently appointed four prominent men
from the province, Malik Khuda Baksh Khan Tiwana, Sheikh Najja-
ud-Din, Khan Sahib Muhammud Zafar Khan and Lala Ram Chand,
and gave them the task of raising the required numbers by working through the agencies of large landlords, zaildars and influential gentlemen. In a little more than a fortnight, they managed to
raise about 8,500 camel and mule drivers, more than double the
original target.[92]

In addition to their functions as military contractors, local elites
were instrumental in propping up an administration weakened
by the departure for the war of several British officials and soldiers. From 1915 onwards, several district posts usually held by
the British, such as the posts of deputy commissioners, magistrates,
sub-registrars and inspectors of police, were assumed by local notables. In such capacities, they were not only able to assist in the
recruiting process but helped overcome tensions and troubles related to political sedition, general unrest and disturbances related
to pressures created by the war. Sikh elites, for instance, played a
major part in helping the British stem the spread of the *Ghadr* movement in the Sikh districts. On 27 February 1915, leading Sikh gentlemen gathered in Lahore to form a non-official advisory committee
to help the government overcome the *Ghadr* threat. Sikh religious
leaders publicly declared that the Sikh *Ghadr*ites were apostates,
and leading Sikh politicians from organizations like the Chief
Khalsa Dewan and Singh Sabhas issued manifestos "repudiating
the revolutionary activities of the returned emigrants".[93] In Sikh

---

[91] Report on the Political Situation in the Punjab, for period ending 15 April 1916,
in GoI, Home/Political 'D', 1916. (henceforth Fortnightly Reports, followed by date).

[92] *Ibid.*

[93] Proceedings of a meeting held at Government House, Lahore, on 27 February
1915. Sunder Singh Majithia's Papers, Nehru Memorial Museum and Library, Subject File No. 40.

majority districts, local Sikh leaders formed jigars (committees), utilizing their influence to isolate returned emigrants with suspected connections to the revolutionaries. These committees provided the deputy commissioners with information which supplemented reports from the police and advised officials on releases from internment and other restrictions applied to returned Sikh émigrés.[94] In Ludhiana, potentially the most troublesome district because it was made the distribution centre of all returned emigrants, and a centre of revolutionary activities, a Sikh committee was formed in March 1915 comprising seventeen prominent Sikh members of the district.[95] The committee subsequently made a public declaration denouncing the *Ghadr*ites, and later published and circulated a manifesto in April 1915 condemning their activities. By late 1915 the *Ghadr* movement had ceased to pose a threat to the Punjab government. Its dismal failure could be attributed to several reasons: poor leadership and organization, effective government surveillance, lack of popular support and, not least, the crucial support which the government enjoyed from the local elites who were fully integrated into the war effort and anxious to show their loyalty to the government.[96] Perhaps the greatest disadvantage which faced the *Ghadr* conspiracy was that the conditions, at least in the central districts of Punjab where they were most active, were not conducive for a revolution or rebellion against the government. The *Ghadr*s had hoped to capitalize on the weakness of the administration at the ground level caused by preoccupation with the war, and had hoped that the attendant wartime social and economic disruption would create conditions that were ripe for rebellion. Unfortunately for the *Ghadr*s both sets of circumstances were absent. The early years of the war did not cause severe economic hardship or social dislocation in the Punjab and the economic assistance and rewards handed out by the state militated against any hardship which might come about from military service. And while British presence was indeed thin on the ground, the gap was made up by the local elites.

[94] O'Dwyer, *India As I Knew It*, p. 205.

[95] Amongst them were Sardar Bahadur Sardar Gajjan Singh, OBE, Ludhiana, Sardar Bahadur Sardar Dal Singh, Sardar Bahadur Bhai Arjan Singh, OBE, Bagarian, Subedar Major Uttam Singh. See *War History of Ludhiana*, p. 10.

[96] *Ibid.*, p. 52.

The mobilization of the rural elites as military contractors was not a new phenomenon in the Punjab. The military value of the rural gentry class had been evident to the British from their earliest involvement in the Punjab. During the Anglo-Sikh wars, several chieftain families from the Punjab had provided military assistance to the British. One such example was Malik Fateh Sher Khan from Shahpur district, who provided 400 horsemen to Colonel Herbert Edwardes during the Sikh rebellion in Multan in 1848.[97] During the 1857 Rebellion, several Sikh and Muslim chieftains in the Punjab responded quickly to John Lawrence's call for soldiers by raising their own armed men and mounted levies to fill the ranks of the moveable column to Delhi.[98] The lessons of their timely and decisive intervention in 1857 were not lost on the British; in the aftermath of the Rebellion, the Punjab government decided to revive the region's natural aristocracy "as the great bulwark of the state".[99] The province's old aristocracy, which was slowly dissolving under John Lawrence's pro-peasants policies, was given a new lease of life. Their social and economic positions were accordingly strengthened by generous land grants and jagirs, while their local influences were enhanced when the British incorporated them as intermediaries in the administrative set-up in rural Punjab, particularly through the zaildari system. Furthermore, members of the rural gentry class were given direct appointments into the Indian Army as viceroy commissioned officers, and were appointed to civilian posts such as honorary magistrates and sub-registrars in the district administration.[100]

The Mitha Tiwanas of Shahpur district were typical of this class of rural notables on which the British relied for political and military support. The Tiwanas had had a long involvement with the British, dating back to the 1840s. Malik Sahib Khan Bahadur, a leading member of the clan, obtained a grant of nearly 9,000 acres of

[97] One such example was Malik Fateh Sher Khan from Shahpur district, who provided 400 horses to help the British quell the Multan rebellion in 1848. See L. Griffin *et. al.*, *Chiefs and Families of Note in the Punjab*, Lahore 1910, Vol. II, p. 179.

[98] Andrew J. Major, 'The Punjab Chieftains and the Transition from Sikh to British rule' in D.A. Low (ed.), *The Political Inheritance of Pakistan*, London 1991, p. 75.

[99] See Ian Talbot, *The British and the Punjab*, p. 49; D. Page, *Prelude to Partition: The Indian Muslims and the Imperial System of Control, 1920–1932*, Delhi, 1982, pp. 49–50, and Andrew J. Major, 'The Punjab Chieftains'.

[100] Major, 'The Punjab Chieftains', pp. 76–77.

land in Kalra and a life jagir of Rs 1,200 from the British for his loyal services during the Rebellion. He subsequently built a private canal to irrigate his land, and had since turned it into a huge and valuable estate. The control of both land and water gave his family immense political and economic influence over their tenants. Malik Sahib Khan died in 1879 when his son, Umar Hayat Khan, was still a minor. His estate was administered by the Court of Wards until Umar Hayat was old enough to inherit it, an indication of British intentions to preserve the position of the family. In 1903 Umar Hayat Khan was made an honorary lieutenant in the 18th Tiwana Lancers, a regiment formed almost exclusively by men of the Tiwana tribe in Shahpur. In January 1906, he was appointed to the Punjab Legislative Council, to which he was reappointed two years later for a further term. In 1910 he was nominated to serve in the Viceroy's Legislative Council. In the district bureaucracy, Umar Hayat Khan held the concurrent appointments of zaildar and honorary magistrate.[101]

The tribal landlords of western Punjab were particularly well suited to play the part of military contractors for the British government. They exercised considerable influence in their respective localities by virtue of their ownership and control of scarce resources such as land, water and credit, and through the domination of local biraderi (kinship) networks. These were effective means by which tenants and kinsmen could be goaded into enlisting. For example, the Nawab Khuda Baksh Tiwana, a kinsman of Umar Hayat Tiwana and leader of a prominent landowning family in Shahpur district, offered a twenty-five rupee bonus and undertook to remit water rates to any of his tenants who would enlist.[102] At the outbreak of the war, he offered his services to the British together with 500 men from his locality.[103] His successful mobilization of muleteers and sarwans—which has just been referred to—was in no small measure due to the substantial influences which he yielded in his home district. Like his relation, Umar Hayat Tiwana played an active part in the war effort too. He volunteered for active service and was sent with the first Indian contingent to France. After

---

[101] For a full family history of the Tiwanas, see L. Griffin, *Chiefs and Families of Note in the Punjab*, 1910 edn., Vol. II, pp. 168–93.

[102] *War Services of Shahpur District*, p. 75.

[103] *Ibid.*

serving there for fifteen months, he was posted to Mesopotamia, on special duty connected with propaganda amongst Muslim troops.[104] Umar Hayat was later promoted to the honorary rank of Major, and served as an honorary recruiting officer in his home district of Shahpur. From his own estate at Kalra, he managed to get more than 200 men enlisted during the war.[105] The list of landed notables from western Punjab who offered assistance to the state during the war was a long one, and it was hardly surprising that the western districts of Rawalpindi division produced the highest number of soldiers throughout the war.[106]

The success of the mobilization campaign in the western districts of the Punjab owed much to the participation of the pirs who were sajjada nashins (custodians of shrines and the tombs of saints) in the recruitment campaign.[107] Descendants of Sufi saints who had established themselves in western Punjab in the eleventh century, pirs were believed to possess religious power and spiritual charisma inherited from their ancestors. This provided the basis of their considerable religious influence among the tribal Muslim population of the western Punjab. Their spiritual influence was further reinforced by the pir-muridi tie where a disciple, the muridi, took an oath of allegiance to his pir to achieve access to the latter's spiritual charisma. Consequently, several of these pirs were leaders of sizeable followings, in some cases as large as 200,000, and exercised substantial political influence in the area around their shrines. When the province was annexed, the British recognized the political importance of these religious leaders and incorporated them as rural intermediaries. Several pirs, as a result, served as local officials and were awarded land grants in the canal colonies under the Landed Gentry Scheme, making many of them influential landed magnates in western Punjab.[108] During the war, several pirs and sajjada nashins enjoined their followers to serve the British cause. A prominent example was Pir Ghulam Abbas of

religious leaders

[104] *Ibid.*, p. 78.

[105] This may not appear to be a very substantial figure for a period of four years, but if taken in proportion to the number of able-bodied men employed in his estate would represent a significant number. *Ibid.*, pp. 78–79.

[106] See Table 3.2.

[107] Leigh, *The Punjab and the War*, p. 115.

[108] See Talbot, *The British and the Punjab*, pp. 50–51.

Makhad, from Attock district, who personally enrolled 4,000 of his followers into the army.[109]

Table 3.2
District Recruitment Figures, Punjab, August 1914–November 1918

District	Number of Enlistees during the War
Rawalpindi	31,291
Jhelum	27,743
Rohtak	22,144
Gujrat	22,071
Amritsar	21,988
Gurgaon	18,867
Ferozepur	18,809
Hoshiarpur	18,651
Ludhiana	18,067
Hissar	15,561
Gurdaspur	15,385
Attock	14,815
Kangra	14,731
Shahpur	14,040
Jullundur	13,973
Sialkot	13,376
Gujranwala	12,618
Lahore	10,054
Ambala	8,341
Karnal	6,553
Lyallpur	6,507
Multan	4,636
Mianwali	4,242
Montgomery	2,813
Muzzafargarh	2,018
Simla	1,934
Dera Ghazi Khan	1,012
Jhang	946

Source: M.S. Leigh, *Punjab and the War*, pp. 59–60.

In the Sikh majority districts of central Punjab, few landed gentry families could be found which enjoyed the same degree of political influence as the landed magnates of western Punjab. Nevertheless, the state was able to enlist the support of a handful of families, like the Ramgharias, Sindhanwalias, Ahluwahlias, Majithias,

[109] *War History, Attock District.* IOR:POS 5545.

Bagarians and Bedis, who occupied positions of some standing within the Sikh community by virtue of being descendants of the former Sikh aristocracy. Some of these families, in addition to their social authority, exercised religious influence over the Sikh community. The most notable example was Bhai Arjan Singh Bagarian of Ludhiana, who possessed great spiritual influence amongst the Sikhs of Malwa, and Bhai Khem Singh Bedi of Rawalpindi, a direct descendent of Guru Nanak. Although the latter was a resident of Rawalpindi district, he exercised considerable influence over some sections of the Sikh community in Amritsar and Lahore. Bhai Arjan Singh made extensive tours of the Malwa districts of Ludhiana and Ferozepur to encourage Sikhs to join the army.[110] These families proved such a boon to the recruiting process that one recruiting officer lamented that Jullunder, with its "lack of born leaders whose influence [would] extend far beyond their village or zails" was not able to match its neighbouring districts, Ludhiana, Ferozepur and Amritsar, in getting recruits.[111]

Although an "old established aristocracy" was largely absent in southeast Punjab, the heartland of the peasant proprietors, the region did not lag far behind western and central Punjab in generating military manpower. This was due mainly to the efforts of the leading zamindars of the dominant Jat caste who took it upon themselves to encourage the enlistment of Jats into the army. Most notable amongst them were Chhottu Ram and Lal Chand, both of whom played leading roles in the enlistment of Jats during the war. Their contributions elevated them to the status of rural elite, and with the assistance of subsequent official patronage these individuals, particularly Chhottu Ram, were given considerable political influence within the Jat community in south-east Punjab.

When O'Dwyer and his government turned to the rural notables to enlist their support in the mobilization campaign, the latter saw in it an opportunity to further entrench their positions in the province and almost without exception responded with alacrity and scrambled to furnish men and material for the war effort. They knew that the rewards for active cooperation would be substantial. The government had held out promises of generous land grants in the canal colonies, known as the Landed Gentry Grants, for notable

[110] Leigh, *The Punjab and the War*, p. 117.
[111] *War History of Jullunder District*, p. 12. IOR:POS 5540.

families who played an active role in recruiting.[112] In addition, individuals who contributed to the war effort were handsomely rewarded with titles, swords of honour, recruiting badges and jagirs, and other forms of rewards. For his efforts, Khuda Baksh Tiwana was knighted and awarded 415 acres of land under the Landed Gentry Grants.[113] Bhai Khem Singh Bedi was similarly knighted, awarded a seat in the provincial darbar, a jagir worth 1,000 rupees and 125 acres of prime land. Chhottu Ram was awarded the title of Rai Sahib and given 100 acres of land in the canal colony at Montgomery for his assistance in the war efforts.[114]

More importantly, these rural elites knew that those who provided "good and loyal service to the government during the war"[115] would have their names entered into the officially compiled *Chiefs and Families of Note in the Punjab*. This was a regularly updated list of local elites whom the government regarded as "noteworthy", and an entry into this Who's Who of the politically important in the Punjab was essential for the continued enjoyment of official favours and patronage.

Not unexpectedly, therefore, the rural elites who contributed during the war came to have their positions in the province firmly entrenched. Before the war, the significance of these elites lay mainly in their political functions, as the state's rural intermediaries. During the war, they had demonstrated another dimension of their importance to the colonial state in the Punjab—that of intercessors and contractors in the all-important military districts of the province. Accordingly, they now constituted a rural-military elite, whose importance to the state, and hence their position in the provincial polity, had been much enhanced.

The utilization of the rural-military elites and the policy of recruiting through the civil administration could not, however, ensure a limitless supply of men from the province. Their shortcomings were most evident during the last stages of the war. The province, by 1918, had been severely exhausted by the war. The weariness caused by the war was further compounded by the outbreak, in late 1917,

---

[112] The bulk of the Landed Gentry Grants were allotted during and just after the First World War. See Imran Ali, *The Punjab Under Imperialism*, p. 78.

[113] *War Services of Shahpur District*, p. 74. IOR:POS 5545.

[114] *War History, Rohtak District*, p. 28.

[115] O'Dwyer to Chelmsford, 20 October 1916, in Chelmsford Papers, No. 17. IOR: MSS.EUR.E.264/17.

of two serious epidemics. Heavy rains in the autumn of 1917 brought
a widespread epidemic of malaria in the province. The death toll
was high, and the disease afflicted many men of military age, ren-
dering them unfit for military service.[116] Then no sooner had the
malaria epidemic subsided than an outbreak of plague swept across
parts of the province which claimed many lives, and diminished
the number of young men available for military service. Even
O'Dwyer, who believed that no effort should be spared for the successful prosecution of the war, felt that the province had outdone
itself for the time being. Disease and the unrelenting demand for
cannon fodder from the warfronts had drained the province of most
of its available manpower.[117] By February 1918, despite the full
commitment of the civil and military authorities to the task of raising more manpower, the Punjab seemed to have reached its limit.
The commissioner of Rawalpindi, the division with the highest
recruiting figure in the country, reported that the strain had become too intense, and that signs of tension had begun to appear.[118]

But the demand for recruits continued unabated, and as it did
became more desperate. Rewards and incentives could no longer
induce recruits to come forward in sufficient numbers from war-
weary villages and, as a consequence, pressures used took on some
quite draconian forms. In south-west Punjab, recruits were being
bought and sold for huge sums of money, or press-ganged by subordinate officials into enlisting.[119] In Multan, villagers had to sub-
scribe to a fund for the purchase of recruits from other villages if
none of them wished to be compelled into enlisting.[120] A villager
from Shahpur district complained that the security provisions of
the Indian Penal Code were used by a local magistrate to summon
him and other men to Nowshera, where they were then forcibly
enlisted into the army.[121] In Rohtak district and certain other areas

---

[116] Leigh, *The Punjab and the War*, p. 11.

[117] Fortnightly Report, Punjab (henceforth FR), 28 February 1918.

[118] *Ibid.*

[119] Leigh, *The Punjab and the War*, p. 43.

[120] *War Services of Multan District, 1914–1918*, Lahore, 1921, p. 23. IOR:POS 5540.

[121] *Censors*, Vol. 3, Pt. III, fo. 811. IOR:L/MIL/5/827. Another popular device
was to force men of supposedly bad character to either enlist or furnish security
under Section 109 or 110 of the Indian Penal Code to be of good behaviour. See Report
of the Committee appointed by the Punjab Sub-Committee of the Indian National
Congress, 20 February 1921, in *Punjab Disturbances, 1919–1920*, Delhi, 1976, p. 21.

local recruiters adopted a method known as "sitting *dharna*", in which they would show up at a village and insist they be fed and housed until recruits were produced.[122]

The pressure on the local population soon produced some adverse reactions. Recruiting-related violence erupted in several villages in Multan, Muzzafargarh, Shahpur and Jhelum. One such incident involved the Awans from the village of Mardwal in Shahpur. There the Awans bound themselves to an oath to repudiate enlistment into the army and tried to persuade the neighbouring villages to follow their example. When an inspector of the police tried to arrest the ringleader, the inspector was forcibly retained by the villagers, who threatened to murder him unless he left them alone. The situation was, however, contained by the intervention of the deputy commissioner, together with the leading men of the villages. Not only were they able to defuse the situation, the local leaders even managed to secure more than a hundred men from the village for the army.[123] A similar incident took place in Lakk, a village inhabited mainly by pastoralists. A disorderly resistance to enlistment by some villagers turned into a riot when police arrived to maintain order.[124] The situation, which ended with several wounded and killed, would have had a disastrous effect on the surrounding villages had it not been for the intervention of the leading men of the neighbourhood, who were quick to show their disapproval of the behaviour of the villagers. In the absence of dominant elites amongst the pastoral tribes who could control their unruly behaviour, the Tiwana maliks, whose estates acted as a buffer between the pastoralists and the settled peasants of the Jhelum valley, supplied contingents of mounted men to prevent the trouble from spreading.[125]

Fearing that the situation might become untenable, O'Dwyer appealed to the Adjutant General to suspend recruiting in the Punjab for a period of ten weeks from 1 April 1918 to allow the recruiters and the recruited a much needed respite.[126] The request was initially acceded to, but in April 1918, in the wake of a major

---

[122] Minutes of the Proceedings of the Provincial Recruiting Board, 7 February 1918, in File U/XIV/212, DCRO, Jhelum District.

[123] *War Services of Shahpur District*, p. 9. IOR:POS 5545.

[124] *Ibid.*, p. 10.

[125] *Ibid.*

[126] FR, 31 March 1918.

German offensive in France, the military authorities were forced to rescind the order to suspend recruitment and renewed its call for fresh recruits from India. Under the circumstances, the GoI promised to raise half-a-million recruits in the coming year from June 1918. Of this number, the Punjab was to supply 180,000 combatants and 20,000 non-combatants.

The quota fixed for the Punjab put the provincial government under tremendous pressure. It represented a twenty-five per cent increase over the provincial quota of the previous year, which had only been achieved after a tremendous recruitment drive by the state. Believing the Punjab to be at the end of its tether as far as voluntary recruiting was concerned, the Punjab government considered the possibility of introducing conscription. Several deputy commissioners had already expressed their concern that the government was "riding the voluntary horse to a standstill";[127] and at a meeting of the Provincial Recruiting Board held on 8 June 1918 to discuss the need for conscription in the province, most deputy commissioners felt that the introduction of some form of compulsion, through the passing of an enlistment ordinance, was the only way of ensuring that there was an adequate response from the more "backward" areas, where recruiting was concerned.[128] The Commissioner of Rawalpindi, Lieutenant Colonel Popham-Young, was convinced that it would make a good "scare tactic": "the passing of an act or ordinance will make it apparent to everyone that we definitely intend to raise an army of 200,000 in the Punjab during the current year, and that if voluntaryism fails, compulsion will be applied without delay".[129] He cautioned, however, that such pressure might produce "mischievous results", but added that, ultimately, it would be a question of balancing risks, "the risk of the German menace against the risk of internal disturbances".[130] His reservation was echoed by the deputy commissioner of Mianwali district, who pointed out that such pressure "would [prove] effective for

[127] FR, 15 May 1918.

[128] Minutes of Meeting of Provincial Recruiting Board, 8 June 1918, D/O W79 in File U/XIV/204, DCRO, Jhelum.

[129] Note on Recruiting by Lieutenant Colonel Popham-Young, Commissioner, Rawalpindi, in File U/XIV/195A, DCRO, Jhelum district.

[130] Minutes of Proceedings of the Sub-Committee of the Provincial Recruiting Board appointed to consider a Bill for the provision of compulsory service in the Punjab, in GoI, Home (Pol.) 'B' 1920, February. No. 373, NAI.

the immediate purpose of recruiting, but it will leave a legacy of distrust and resentment behind it".[131] Despite these reservations, it was unanimously agreed that some compulsion was imperative at this stage if the province was to meet its obligations. Consequently, a draft bill prepared by the Provincial Recruiting Board was submitted to the Viceroy for consideration.

The Central Recruiting Board in Delhi, advising the Viceroy in matters connected with recruiting, however rejected the proposal to introduce conscription in the Punjab. The Board's greatest reservation was that compulsion in recruiting would produce grave political consequences; it might give rise to widespread disturbances and unrest which, at this critical juncture, was to be avoided at all cost.[132] Although compulsion was proposed only for the Punjab, the general hostility to the idea of conscription could well spread beyond the province. Rumours of conscription had already resulted in unrest in Bombay, and in the states of Hyderabad, Kholapur, Alwar and Janpur.[133] The Board consequently informed the Punjab government that conscription was politically unacceptable, and instead, it would welcome "proposals relevant to a large increase of recruitment on a voluntary basis".[134]

Unable to force through the necessary increased recruitment through conscription, the Punjab government turned once again to its local collaborators. Several rural notables were given additional powers by being appointed as assistant recruiting officers, posts usually reserved for British officers, with the legal authority to enlist directly without having to go through the British recruiting officers. Umar Hayat Khan Tiwana of Shahpur district, Sikander Hayat Khan of the Wah family in Attock and Rai Bahadur Subedar Pal Singh of Gujranwala were appointed as honorary recruiting officers in their respective districts in September 1918; two months later, two more notables, Malik Sardar Khan of Rawalpindi and Honourary Captain Ajab Khan of Attock, were added to the list of rural notables serving as assistant recruiting officers.[135] In the six

[131] Letter no. 28–C, from Deputy Commissioner, Mianwali, to Addl Sec., Punjab Government, 29 May 1918, in File U/XIV/195A, DCRO, Jhelum District.

[132] *Development of Manpower in India, and Its Utilization For Imperial Purposes*, April 1918, published by General Headquarters, India, p. 6. IOR:L/MIL/17/5/2398.

[133] *Ibid.*, p. 7.

[134] Note by Popham-Young, File U/XIV/195A, DCRO, Jhelum district.

[135] See PHP(M), September 1918, 'B' procs: 167, 251, 255; and November 1918, procs.134. LA.

months from April to October in 1918, through a mixture of coercion, pressure and inducements propagated by the rural elites, and possibly because men were trying to escape the miserable conditions in parts of the province that had been ravaged by the outbreak of plague, malaria and influenza, the Punjab government was able to raise 77,728 men.[136] But just as the situation was reaching its critical stage towards the end of 1918, the First World War came to an end. For the authorities in the Punjab, it came as a great relief as the simmering combination of recruiting pressures, disease and general war weariness which had been threatening to erupt into widespread unrest, or even rebellion, in the Punjab villages had been averted.

During the war the rural notables played a significant part in bolstering the state structure and generating recruits for the war. Their roles were acknowledged by O'Dwyer who wrote that "the success [in recruiting] in the Punjab was due mainly to the district officials and rural gentry ... the latter class have shown they are invaluable to the administration in the Punjab".[137] It was to have an impact on government perception in the Punjab and resulted in its determination to maintain their position in the province at all cost. That the position of the rural notables in the Punjab did not deteriorate like that of their counterparts in the United Provinces, the landed taluqdars, could perhaps be attributed to their indispensability to the functioning of the Punjab as the military bulwark of the Raj.

Conclusion

During the First World War, the Punjab became a virtual "home front" for the British war effort, supplying the majority of manpower for the Indian Army, which fought in all major theatres of the war—in Europe, Africa and the Middle East. For four-and-a-half years, the entire province was subjected to an unrelenting demand for military manpower; by the end of the war, one in every twenty-six adult males in the Punjab had been mobilized.[138] This

---

[136] See Fortnightly Reports for the Punjab, April to September 1918.

[137] O'Dwyer to Chelmsford, 26 October 1916, in Chelmsford Papers, No. 17. IOR: MSS. EUR. E.264/17.

[138] Leigh, *Punjab and the War*, p. 41.

had not been achieved easily; during the final months of the war, there were outbreaks of isolated cases of violent resistance to recruiting activities, confirmation that parts of the province had been strained almost to breaking point. In addition to war stresses, the state had to cope with a period of political unrest generated by the short-lived *Ghadr* rebellion. Yet, despite all these, the colonial state in the Punjab seemed to have emerged in 1919 very much intact, and not weakened in any way.

That the state had remained resilient despite the pressures of war was due, in no small measure, to its successful management of the mobilization process. This was achieved, first, by the integration of the functions of the civil and military authorities in the province. From 1916 to 1919, the civil and military structures in the province, which had hitherto functioned quite independently of each other, coalesced into a formidable machinery dedicated to generating cannon fodder for the war.

Second, the state, once it assumed a direct role in the mobilization campaign, in a manner similar to the 1857 Rebellion, enlisted the support of its local collaborators—the minor officials, men of local influence, the aristocracy and landed gentry elites—to stimulate recruitment in their respective areas of influence. These rural intermediaries not only had the means to impel reluctant men to come forward for enlistment, but were able to do so, in most cases, without eliciting violent reactions from the local population. That the administration had to rely on local influence to generate recruitment indicated that although the British had built an efficient administrative structure in the Punjab, the state was still unable to penetrate the indigenous social structure, beyond its upper crusts. Here was an indication perhaps of another case of "limited Raj".

Third, the offer of generous rewards by the state to those who assisted in the war effort militated against the tensions created by war colonialism. Civil government was able to motivate a response from the population in a way which the army, if it had been left to its own devices, could not have, by dangling titles, land grants and other patronage if they played their parts well.

Although the state seemed to have emerged relatively unscathed by the war, it is not to say that the Punjab had been totally unaffected by its involvement in the war. Two discernible developments did emerge from the war. The process of mobilization brought about an unusually close association between the military and the provincial

civil administration, laying the foundations of a militarized bureaucracy in colonial Punjab. From 1916 to 1919 the Punjab "home
front" was in effect governed by a military bureaucracy, whose
administrative/military tentacles reached into every level of society and the economy. The direct assumption of a military function
by the Punjab government, and its intrusion into society on behalf
of the military during the war, was to mark the beginning of a
quasi-military state in the Punjab. As we shall see in chapter four,
civil-military integration persisted after the war, when the government continued to work closely with the army authorities in
the Punjab to maintain the military districts, amidst a background
of social and economic problems created by demobilization and
political change. Civil-military integration was to remain a distinctive characteristic of Punjabi political life, and was inherited
by one of its successor states, Pakistan.

The second development which came out of the war was the
emergence in the Punjab of a potent and influential rural-military
lobby. The rural elites had demonstrated their indispensability to
the state, militarily and politically, during the war; and as a result
almost all of them had their positions strengthened by the acquisition of landed rewards, titles and appointments in the civil and
military service. More importantly, however, their roles in the war
gave them an increased importance, which they were not slow to
use to influence the state, securing official favour and patronage
for themselves and their followers, the rural-military classes, at
the expense of others. These elites subsequently constituted themselves into a potent rural-military lobby in the post-war politics of
the Punjab.

Four

Maintaining the Military Districts: Civil-Military Integration and District Soldiers' Boards

The termination of hostilities in Europe and in the other the-atres of war by the end of 1918 gave a much needed respite to the civil and military officers of the Punjab. Towards the end of 1918 the province had been strained almost to the breaking point by the relentless demand for cannon fodder generated by the war. Fortu-nately for the colonial state, a total breakdown was averted as the cessation of hostilities in Europe removed the pressures of recruit-ing on the already war-weary rural population. The respite, how-ever, proved to be short-lived. By 1919, the rural-military districts of the Punjab were again threatened by disruption, this time not by recruiting pressures, but by problems caused by a deteriorating economy and political unrest.

Economic conditions in the Punjab at the end of the war were chaotic. In 1919, as a result of war-time controls and the suspen-sion of trade due to damage to the transportation infrastructure, the province was hit by a severe scarcity of essential commodities. Inadequate monsoon rains caused an exceptionally bad autumn harvest in the same year, further straining the already depleted food stocks and causing a dramatic increase in prices of agricul-tural produce. Wheat was forty-seven per cent more expensive in 1919 than in 1914; European cloth 175 per cent more expensive; Indian cloth 100 per cent more expensive; and sugar sixty-five per cent more expensive.[1] Economic hardship created by conditions at the end of the war coincided with a worldwide pandemic of influenza, which, in the Punjab alone, claimed nearly a quarter of a million lives.[2]

The general demobilization of the armed forces following the Armistice in Europe brought back into these hardship-stricken villages thousands of soldiers returning from the warfront. Probably aware of the adverse conditions which prevailed in their villages, many of the discharged soldiers had no wish to be sent home so soon after the war. Many were disgruntled by what they saw as indecent haste on the part of the military authorities in terminating their services. Discharged soldiers further protested that they had been badly treated and not given their due when released from their regiments, and that the relief that had been promised to them had not been distributed punctually and adequately.[3] Under such conditions, a tide of resentment swept through the ranks of soldiers who were sent home to face near certain economic adversity. Much of this resentment was directed against the government, which the affected soldiers alleged was interested only in enlisting men in times of need, and curtly discharging them when they were no longer needed.[4] This sense of disappointment was further compounded amongst those who had failed to obtain the rewards promised by the government during its recruiting campaigns.[5] The most glaring of these unfulfilled promises were those concerning land grants. These had been the most sought after of the "prizes" which the soldiers had expected from the government after the war. Upon their return from the fronts, war veterans inundated

---

[1] *Report of Committee Appointed to Investigate the Disturbances in the Punjab, 1920* (Hunter's Commission: Disorders Enquiry Committee, Report and Evidence), (henceforth Report of Hunter's Commission), in *PP*, 1920. Cmd. 681. Vol. 14.

[2] Report of Hunter's Commission.

[3] The General Officer Commanding Lahore Divisional Area reported claims of bad treatment by soldiers on demobilization; some even reported that they were deprived of their kits and clothes and ordered to clear the cantonments or they would be handed over to the police. GoI, Home (Pol.) 'B', February 1920, File No. 373. A list of grievances of demobilised soldiers was submitted by Umar Hayat Khan to the Punjab Soldiers' Board on 7 June 1919, PHP(M) 'B', June 1920, pro. 72.

[4] Note by Major H.S.L. Wolley, Divisional Recruiting Officer, Jullunder Division, to Adj. Gen., 17 June 1919, in PHP(M) 'B', File 127B, June 1920.

[5] A list of grievances of demobilised soldiers was submitted by Umar Hayat Khan to the Punjab Soldiers' Board on 7 June 1919, PHP(M) 'B', pro. 72, June 1920.

the government with applications for grants of land which they felt they had earned by their sacrifices for the *sircar*.[6] The Punjab government was, however, unable to cope with the demand, as land available in the Punjab canal colonies for such rewards was limited. Consequently, many of the applicants had to be turned away empty-handed. These promises, real or alleged, which the government had made but could not redeem, tarnished the image of the *sircar* and, as one historian has pointed out, "the issue of land which had been intended as a political advantage now backfired, as it created a sense of resentment amongst those who remained ungratified".[7] Not surprisingly, therefore, disaffection was rife amongst the demobilized troops after they returned empty-handed to an economically depressed Punjab countryside.[8]

To the Punjab authorities, the implications of demobilization were clear enough: thousands of "discharged soldiers, full of complaints and grievances",[9] were returning to a Punjab facing a host of economic problems. This discontented section of the population, which blamed the government for all its economic hardships and troubles, constituted a fertile ground for political unrest.[10] The government's fears of rural Punjab erupting into political agitation were heightened by political disturbances which broke out in five major cities in the province in early 1919. Almost immediately after the war, anti-government unrest and riots, sparked by Gandhi's satyagraha in protest against the introduction of the repressive Rowlatt Act, and provoked by urban demonstrations against the introduction of an urban income tax, had broken out in the five major district towns of Amritsar, Lahore, Gujranwala, Gujrat and Lyallpur.[11] Martial law was immediately imposed in the disturbed areas to contain the unrest which threatened to spread

[6] See Imran Ali, The *Punjab Under Imperialism*, p. 117.

[7] *Ibid.*

[8] Weekly Report on the political and economic situation in India, GoI to Sec. of State, India, 8 February 1921. IOR: L/PJ/6/1726.

[9] Sir C.R. Cleveland, Director of Central Intelligence, GoI, to H.D. Craik, 25 April 1919, GoI, Home (Pol.), File 47, May 1919. NAI.

[10] Major H.S.L. Wolley to Major C.W. Gwynne, Deputy Secretary, GoI, Home Dept., 12 February 1919, PHP(M) 'B', pro. 418, March 1919.

[11] For an analysis of the disorder which erupted in Lahore in 1919, see R. Kumar, 'The Rowlatt Satyagraha in Lahore' in R. Kumar (ed.), *Essays on Gandhian Politics: The Rowlatt Satyagraha of 1919*, Oxford, 1971, pp. 236–97.

to the rest of the province. The unrest was initially limited to the five cities with the rest of the Punjab relatively unaffected, but the indiscriminate killing of over three hundred people and the injuring of thousands by troops at Jallianwalla Bagh in Amritsar in April 1919 brought anti-government sentiments to a boil, and threatened to spill into the critical military districts of the Punjab.[12] The Jallianwalla Bagh massacre had already had an impact on some in the Indian troops of the Indian Army. Reports received by the intelligence bureau after the massacre cited several incidents of Indian soldiers refusing to fire on crowds as well as individual cases of insubordination and disobedience amongst Sikh and Muslim soldiers in the Punjab.[13]

Wary that economic adversity, coupled with political unrest, could instigate a reaction in the military districts, the Punjab government immediately addressed itself to the problems related to demobilization. A few months back, in January 1919, a Punjab Soldiers' Board had been established in Lahore. Like the Punjab Recruiting Board—set up in 1916 to assist the war effort[14]—the Punjab Soldiers' Board was essentially a civil-military organization which incorporated both senior civil and military officers in the Punjab, as well as the leading notables from the military districts. It was presided over by the Lieutenant Governor himself and its key members included the Chief Secretary, Secretary of the Revenue and Agriculture Department, the Home Secretary, Divisional Recruiting Officers, Divisional Commissioners, the Inspector General of Police and representatives of the military classes.[15]

[12] For a general narrative and analysis of the 1919 disturbances, see V.N. Datta, *1919 Disturbances*, Ludhiana, 1969; and V.N. Datta (ed.), *New light on the Punjab disturbances in 1919*, Vol. 6 and 7 of Disorders Inquiry Committee Evidence, Simla, 1975.

[13] Summary of reports concerning feelings among troops and of incidents indicating unrest among them, GoI, Home (Pol.) 'B', File 373, February 1920.

[14] In view of the close connection between the army and the Punjab, which had been widely extended during the war, the Lieutenant Governor decided to maintain the Recruiting Board on a permanent basis, with the reduction of the civilian element in the composition of the Board being the only change contemplated. L. French, Offg. Chief Sec. to Punjab Govt. to Adj. Gen. in India, 7 January 1919, in PHP(M) 'B', pros. 95–98, March 1919.

[15] Some of the representatives of the military classes included Umar Hayat Khan Tiwana, Sikander Hayat Khan, Syed Mehdi Shah of Gojra, Sardar Ragbhir Singh Sindhanwalia and Chhottu Ram. See Minutes of Meeting of Punjab Soldiers' Board, 11 September 1920, PHP(M) 'B', File 41, 1921.

In a manner similar to the set-up during the war, the Punjab Soldiers' Board was institutionalized as a provincial branch of the Indian Soldiers' Board, which had been established in Delhi in 1919. The latter had been constituted to advise the GoI in matters relating to the resettlement to civil life of demobilized Indian soldiers after the end of the war.[16] Briefly, its functions included finding employment for soldiers released from colours, distributing rewards, providing monetary assistance to relieve distress among dependents of soldiers killed or incapacitated in the war, and safeguarding the interests of serving and discharged soldiers and their dependents.[17] As with its wartime predecessor, the Central Recruiting Board, the Indian Soldiers' Board brought together both the civil and military authorities of India.[18] The Indian Soldiers' Board was, however, established only as an "advisory body" with "deliberative functions"; the real executive role was delegated to the provincial boards.[19]

In May 1919, as an immediate attempt to ameliorate the problems faced by discharged soldiers on returning to their villages, the Punjab Soldiers' Board instructed British recruiting officers operating in the districts to act as liaison officers between the soldiers and the civil and military authorities, particularly in the districts of the Punjab where the problem was most acute. These officers were directed to meet with discharged soldiers, listen to their grievances, and give advice and assistance where possible, especially in matters

[16] The function of the Indian Soldiers' Board was to duplicate the Ministry of Reconstruction set up in England in 1917, where the minister's responsibility was "to consider and advise upon the problems which may arise out of the present war and may have to be dealt with on its termination, and for the purposes aforesaid to initiate and conduct such enquiries, prepare such schemes and make such recommendations as he thinks fit". Quoted in *A Brief Account of the Work of the Indian Soldiers' Board*, Delhi, 1930, IOR: L/MIL/17/5/2317, p. 1.

[17] *Ibid.*

[18] The Indian Soldiers' Board, as constituted in 1919, was presided by the Law Member of the Viceroy's Council, Sir George Lowndes, and its members included the Lieutenant Governor of Punjab, the Revenue and Finance Member of the Viceroy's Council, R.A. Mant, the Adjutant General of the Indian Army, Secretary of the Government of India in the Army Department, A.H. Bingley, Financial Advisor in the Military Finance Department, Sir G.B.H. Fell, and the Maharajahs of Gwalior, Bikaner and Patiala. See GoI, *ibid.*

[19] In 1920, besides the Punjab, provincial boards were established in all other provinces except Bengal.

concerning the settlement of pay and relief allowances.[20] Demobilized soldiers were advised upon their discharge from the units to consult these officers if they encountered any sort of difficulties on returning home. Their complaints and petitions would then be relayed by these liaison officers to the relevant authorities. The names and addresses of these liaison officers were recorded on the discharge certificates of demobilized soldiers so that the latter would know where and to whom to turn in case of problems and complaints. The liaison officers, for their part, were informed in advance by the depots from where soldiers were being discharged about the numbers of men who were being demobilized from their districts.[21]

This arrangement had two immediate benefits. First, the liaison officer, being a recruiting officer, was familiar with the district and its population, particularly its class of soldiers, and was in the best position to advise soldiers and forward their cases to the attention of the proper authorities, whether civil or military. This procedure not only ensured that soldiers could easily be reached by the relevant authorities, but it also saved the civil authorities a considerable amount of work. The officer's work was further facilitated by the linkages which he had already established with the civil administration during the war. Second, the appointment of these liaison officers gave soldiers and ex-soldiers confidence in approaching the authorities with their problems, assuring them that "the officers of the government were wholly accessible to them".[22] It was noted that Indian soldiers had little faith in the ability of the civil administration to deal with their needs. Indeed, there was a general aversion among soldiers to deal with subordinate civil officials, many of whom were believed to be unsympathetic, corrupt and inefficient. The availability of a British army officer in uniform who was prepared to listen sympathetically to the grievances of soldiers or ex-soldiers made them feel that every endeavour was being

---

[20] The scheme was originally suggested by the Divisional Recruiting Officer of Jullunder to the Adj. Gen. in India in November 1918 (correspondence no. 2044, dated 29 November 1918), and was endorsed by the Indian Soldiers' Board in February 1919. See Major C.W. Gwynne, Secretary, Indian Soldiers' Board to the Punjab Soldiers' Board, 12 February 1919, in PHP(M) 'B', pros. 359–60, March 1919.

[21] C.W. Gwynne to Punjab Soldiers' Board, 12 February 1919.

[22] Minutes of 10th Meeting of the Indian Soldiers' Board, 30 April 1919, in PHP(M) 'B', pro. 406, May 1919.

made to have their complaints redressed, and did much to allay discontent in the military districts.[23] The appointment of a military recruiting officer performing a civil function in the district was indicative of the fact that civil-military integration in the Punjab remained a salient feature of the military districts after the war.

In addition to establishing contacts with recently discharged soldiers, liaison officers were given the added responsibility of touring military districts to address the problems faced by the dependents of soldiers. In the Punjab this particular measure was very important, more so when severe shortages of foodstuffs and high prices in the districts were causing acute distress, especially amongst the widows and dependents of soldiers. Although many of them were already drawing pensions, it was observed that the amount they were receiving was hardly adequate, especially in the context of rising inflation. There were concerns that widows who were in receipt of small pensions were especially hard hit and had difficulties maintaining themselves and their dependents on the meagre pensions which they were receiving from the army. Similarly affected were the dependents of soldiers who had died during the war without acquiring pension rights on behalf of their wives and mothers.[24] On the recommendations of the Punjab government, the Indian Soldiers' Board agreed to sanction the payment of a temporary allowance of five rupees a year to the widows of Indian soldiers who were from the Punjab.[25] District liaison officers brought the attention of these needy cases to district officials who, after investigating the individual cases, would distribute relief in cases thought to be genuine. The identification of needy cases and the quick disbursement of financial relief were instrumental in appeasing the population in the military districts who were living under the heavy strain of inflation.

It seemed that through the efforts of the liaison officers and government assistance in cases of hardship, a general crisis was averted

[23] Note by Major H.S.L. Wolley, Divisional Recruiting Officer, Jullunder Division, 17 June 1919 in PHP(M) 'B', File 127B, June 1920.

[24] Sir C.R. Cleveland, Director of Central Intelligence, to H.D. Craik, Deputy Secretary, GoI, Home Dept., 25 April 1919, in GoI, Home (Pol.), File 47, May 1919. NAI.

[25] This was to be paid out of a sum of 200,000 rupees placed at the disposal of the Punjab Government by the Indian Soldiers' Board. It is interesting to note that the Punjab was the only province in India to be awarded with money for this purpose. See Press communique issued by Indian Soldiers' Board, 18 March 1919, in GoI, Home (Pol.), File 47, May 1919. NAI.

and the Punjab countryside in general and the military districts in particular remained relatively calm despite the adverse conditions that existed in 1919. But the political danger had not yet passed. In 1920 Indian Muslims began protesting against the peace terms imposed by Britain and her allies on the Caliphate of Turkey. The Khilafat Movement gathered momentum and soon found support from Gandhi. In August 1920 the Khilafat Central Committee and the All India Congress Committee jointly announced the launch of a nationwide non-cooperation movement for the purposes of rectifying the Khilafat "wrongs", redressing the Punjab grievances,[26] and the establishment of *swaraj*.[27] The Khilafat non-cooperation movement once again heightened political excitement in the Punjab, especially as it coincided with the Sikh agitation for the reform of their gurdwaras, which, by 1920, had taken on a radical turn.[28]

The Punjab government was extremely concerned regarding the impact of the non-cooperation movement and the Akali agitation on the military districts. Government officials in the Punjab were particularly anxious that political agitators had chosen to adopt indirect and insidious methods such as sending itinerant preachers to villages in the military districts to influence the relatives and friends of the soldiers.[29] Political activists were already energetically exploiting the difficult economic conditions in the Punjab to spread their "seditious" message to ex-soldiers and their families, so that the latter could influence soldiers when they went home. Reports were received by the GoI that soldiers were also approached by anti-government agitators while they were at home on leave, or when they travelled in trains.[30] Religious appeals and sanctions

[26] This was the protest against the findings of the Hunter Commission on the Jallianwala massacre which the Congress regarded as a "whitewash" of the dreadful deed. The GoI disavowed Dwyer's use of force, but the disciplinary action which was meted out—early retirement—was not regarded as being strong enough.
[27] For a fuller account of the Khilafat movement see Gail Minault, *The Khilafat Movement: Religious Symbolism and Political Mobilization in India*, Delhi, 1982.
[28] The Akali movement, being one of the most serious threats encountered by the Punjab government, will be given fuller treatment in chapter five.
[29] Harkishen Kaul, Deputy Commissioner, Jullunder District to V. Connolly, Home Sec., Punjab Govt., 12 October 1921 in PHP(M) 'B', File 10, 1922.
[30] See Captain F.H. Malyon to Captain A.C. Blunden, 27 May 1920; Note by C.W. Jacob, CGS, 29 May 1920; and H. McPherson, Offg. Sec. to GoI, Home Dept., to all provincial governments and administration, 12 January 1920, all in GoI, Home (Pol.) 'B', pro. 72, January 1920. NAI.

were essential components of such political propaganda. While Congress and Akali agitators sought to win over the allegiance of the Sikh peasants and soldiers, Khilafat propaganda called upon Muslim soldiers to quit military service as their continued association with the British was deemed to be un-Islamic and religiously unlawful.[31] In village gatherings Punjabi Muslim and Pathan soldiers were reviled by *maulvis* for fighting against their Muslim brethren, the Turks.[32] An intercepted letter from a Muslim soldier to the Central Khilafat Committee revealed plans for the employment of paid preachers and propagandists, particularly in the recruiting districts of the Punjab to spread the Khilafat movement and to "undermine the loyalty of the army by getting at the soldiers when they were home on leave".[33] Although the army authorities had been aware of such activities, there was effectively very little they could do to prevent their soldiers from coming under the influence of these agitators. The military, by itself, simply did not have the machinery to counter the activities of the political agents who had chosen to operate in the soldiers' home villages.[34] Both the Army Headquarters and the GoI were aware that in order to effectively combat the influence of political activists, both civil and military authorities in the province had to work in close cooperation with each other, as they had during the Great War.

The GoI consequently exhorted provincial governments to assist the military by vigilantly seeking out agitators attempting to tamper with the "loyalty" of the troops, and to expedite their prosecution in the courts.[35] The importance of closer cooperation between civil and military authorities in the provinces for tackling the problem of sedition in the army was also emphasized by the Esher Committee, which was charged with the responsibility of reviewing

[31] The call was issued at a Khilafat Conference in Karachi in July 1921. Weekly Report, 8 July 1921, Punjab, IOR: L/P&J/6/1726. See also telegram from R. Mitra, Sec. District Congress Committee, Etawah to *The Zemindar* (Lahore) in Deputy Commissioner, Lahore to Commissioner, Lahore Division, 27 September 1921 in PHP(M) 'B', File 10, 1922.

[32] Weekly Report, 7 April 1920, Punjab. IOR: L/P&J/6/1556.

[33] Weekly Report, 11 June 1920, Punjab. IOR: L/P&J/6/1556.

[34] Note by C.W. Jacob, 7 June 1920, GoI, Home (Pol.), pro. 72, June 1920. NAI.

[35] H. McPherson, Sec. to GoI, Home Dept., to all Local Govts and Admin., 12 June 1920, GoI Home (Pol.), June 1920, pro. 72. NAI.

the position of the post-war army in India in 1920.[36] One of the key recommendations of the committee was that military and civil authorities in the provinces should keep each other regularly updated on matters affecting the military districts and the regiments.[37]

The call for closer ties between the civil and military authorities at the provincial level was strongly supported by the Punjab government, which had been pressing for greater civil-military cooperation since 1916. During the war, O'Dwyer had utilized the rural administrative structure for the purpose of reaching into the countryside and opening up new areas of military recruitment. In the immediate post-war period, such linkages needed to be strengthened as the Punjab government sought to tackle the problems created by demobilization. In January 1920, while giving evidence to the Esher Committee, L. French, the Chief Secretary to the Punjab Government, echoing the concerns of O'Dwyer in 1916, remarked that while the Punjab government had been sending its confidential fortnightly reports on the political situation to Army Headquarters, his civil administration had not been kept regularly informed by the military authorities of developments in the army.[38] He suggested that Army Headquarters should compile a periodic report dealing with the internal situation in the army which should be sent to the civil government. Such a report should include information concerning regiments stationed in, or recruited partially or wholly from the province concerned. He further suggested that the report should also include information on events of a political nature as these affected the army, or concerning cases involving breach of discipline.[39] He emphasized that this information could be of great value to the civil government in dealing with cases of disaffection in the military districts. For example, the dismissal or discharge of an officer or a group of men could have political repercussions, especially if the persons involved exercised some influence in their locality.[40]

---

[36] Report of Committee appointed by the Secretary of State to enquire into the Administration and Organization of the Army in India (Esher Committee), 1920, in *PP*, 1919–20, Cmd. 943, Vol. 14.

[37] Esher Committee, 1920, pp. 36–37.

[38] Minutes of Meeting, Army in India Committee, 23 January 1920. IOR:L/MIL/17/5/1761.

[39] *Ibid.*

[40] Minutes of Meeting, Army in India Committee, 23 January 1920. IOR:L/MIL/17/5/1761.

In 1920, following such representations, both the civil and military authorities in the Punjab embarked on a coordinated counter-propaganda programme aimed specifically at the province's military districts. Publicity associations composed of retired Indian Army officers were established to carry out propaganda amongst the military classes.[41] Regiments were also urged to conduct propaganda within the barracks and to "build up a useful class of men who, when they get back to their homes, would have a healthy influence on their fellow villagers".[42] Indian Army officers followed deputy commissioners and civil publicity officials on tours to the districts as "propagandist lecturers".[43] The Punjab Publicity Committee, set up in 1919 specifically for combating anti-Rowlatt propaganda,[44] produced and distributed a series of pamphlets and articles to counter anti-government propaganda amongst different sections of the population.[45] Rural notables were also closely associated in the counter-propaganda campaign. For instance, at the height of the Khilafat movement, influential *maulvis* were instructed by deputy commissioners to issue *fatwas* (religious injunctions) to the effect that service in the army was permissible for Muslims.[46]

The main agencies in the districts and villages around which the civil-military counter-propaganda campaign pivoted were the branch organizations of the Punjab Soldiers' Board, known as the

---

[41] Sheikh Asghar Ali, Addl Sec. to the Punjab Govt. to all Commissioners and Deputy Commissioners in the Punjab, 3 November 1920 in PHP(M) 'B', pro. 132B, December 1920.

[42] A.C. Blunden to Sir William S. Marris, 23 June 1919, Home (Pol.), pros. 76, January 1920.

[43] There were three such officers operating in the Punjab in 1920: Risaldar Major Harnam Singh, whose lecturing activities were confined to the Lahore Division; Khan Bahadur Zafar Muhhamud Khan, an Extra Assistant Commissioner, who worked in the Rawalpindi Division; and Risaldar Major Prem Singh, who was employed as a propagandist lecturer in the Ambala Division. Sheikh Asghar Ali to all Commissioners and Deputy Commissioners, 3 November 1920, PHP(M), pros. 132B, December 1920.

[44] Sheikh Asghar Ali to W.S. Marris, 26 July 1919, PHP(M) 'B', pros. 89–95B, August 1919.

[45] An Urdu pamphlet, dealing with the Khilafat question, was published and distributed to the Muslim population, while another, published in Gurumukhi, dealing with the benefits of British rule to the Sikhs, was circulated among them. PHP(M) 'B', pro. 132B, December 1920.

[46] A.C. Blunden to Sir William S. Marris 18 December 1921, Home (Pol.), 1922, File 669/1922. NAI.

District Soldiers Boards (henceforth DSBs). Originally set up to carry out the directives of the Punjab Soldiers' Board in the districts, these organizations were also used during 1920 for the purpose of carrying out propaganda amongst retired soldiers and the military classes.[47] They provided the centres through which published material was distributed among the local population; they were also responsible for publicizing and organizing local "darbars" at which civil officers and military lecturers could address the rural population, listen to their complaints and redress grievances.[48] By coordinating the activities of the civil and military publicity agencies in the districts, these institutions demonstrated how civil-military cooperation could be successfully carried out in the military districts. However, it was in their functions as welfare organizations for the military classes that the DSBs demonstrated the full extent of the civil-military integration of local administration which now occurred in the Punjab.

Punjab's District Soldiers' Boards

As branches of the Punjab Soldiers' Board, DSBs performed the same loosely-defined function of their parent body; namely, to advise on questions affecting Indian soldiers after they had left their colours.[49] Their activities in the districts were, however, manifold. They included improving relations between the soldiers and the civilian population; assisting the district administration in dealing with matters connected with soldiers, ex-soldiers and their families; looking after the welfare of ex-soldiers and their families; and protecting the interests of serving soldiers absent on duties away from home.[50] To carry out these functions, the organizational structure of the DSBs had to reach out to the soldier in his home, and had to incorporate both the civil and military functions at the district level. Thus, each DSB had a central executive committee, comprising a president, vice-president, secretary and representatives of each tehsil in the district. Invariably, the DSB was presided over

---

[47] J.P. Thompson, Chief Sec., Punjab Govt., to all Commissioners and Deputy Commissioners, 25 August 1920, in PHP(M) 'B', pros. 132B, December 1920.

[48] *Ibid.*

[49] Minutes of proceedings of Punjab Soldiers' Board, May 1915, PHP(M) 'C', File 418, 1926.

[50] *Ibid.*

by the deputy commissioner of the district. All DSBs had a military vice-president, usually the British divisional or district recruiting officer based in the district who served as the main link between the district administration and the military command, and who officiated for the deputy commissioner whenever the latter was not available for his duties towards the Board. The post of secretary of the Board was usually filled by a local notable, normally a Viceroy Commissioned Officer (VCO), a pensioned Indian officer, or a civil officer—either a tehsildar or a zaildar—of the district administration. Tehsil representatives were usually active or pensioned Indian officers residing in that particular locality.[51] In this way, the DSBs were representative of both the civil and military elements who wielded local authority at the district level.

All DSBs had a network of zail committees in their respective zails, each of which had its own president and further sub-committees. The size of these zail committees varied from one to three members according to the size of the zail. The primary function of the zail committees, and their sub-committees, was to extend the DSB organization to the village level so that it could acquaint itself with the circumstances of individual ex-soldiers in their homes. As the "feelers" of the DSBs, zail sub-committees were accordingly expected to bring to the notice of the central executive committees any matters requiring their attention. A typical example of the composition and organizational structure of the DSBs in the Punjab is provided by the Hoshiarpur DSB. Here, the Board was presided over by the Deputy Commissioner of Hoshiarpur and the members of its executive committee included the Jullunder Divisional Recruiting Officer, a senior sub-judge, tehsildars of the four tehsils of the district, an Indian district recruiting officer, a sub-registrar, four Indian officers holding the honorary British rank of captain, and five VCOs above the rank of subedar. Attached to the DSB were thirty-nine sub-committees representing all the zails in the district. Almost all the members of the sub-committees were serving or pensioned Indian officers.[52] The organizational structure of

[51] See pamphlet produced by General Staff, Indian Army, entitled 'Notes for Assistance of Members of District Soldiers' Boards and Officers Touring in Recruiting Areas', Simla, 1935, PHP(M) 'B', File 127, 1935.

[52] Deputy Commissioner, Hoshiarpur District, to the Commissioner, Jullunder Division, 9 October 1920, in PHP(M) 'B', File 30, 1922. See Table 4.1 (overleaf) for DSBs in the Punjab.

a typical DSB thus ensured that both the civil and military officers were easily accessible to soldiers and their families in the villages, while the membership of the DSBs provided the strongest evidence of a high degree of civil and military integration in the rural administration of the Punjab.

Table 4.1
Organizations Subordinate to the Punjab Soldiers' Board

District	Organization (s)
Ambala	1. DSB, Ambala
	2. Ambala Ex-Indian officers' Association
Amritsar	Amritsar District Zail Committees
Attock	DSB, Attock
Ferozepur	DSB, Ferozepur
Gujranwala	DSB, Gujranwala
Gurdaspur	DSB, Gurdaspur
Gurgaon	1. DSB, Gurgaon
	2. Gurgaon Ex-Indian Officers' Association
Gujrat	DSB, Gujrat
Hissar	DSB, Hissar
Hoshiarpur	1. DSB, Hoshiarpur
	2. Hoshiarpur and Jullunder Doab Ex-Indian Officers' Association
Jhelum	1. DSB, Jhelum
	2. Jhelum Ex-Indian Officers' Association
Jullunder	1. DSB, Jullunder
	2. See Hoshiarpur
Kangra	1. DSB, Kangra
	2. Zail Commitees (53)
Karnal	1. DSB, Karnal
	2. Karnal Ex-Indian Officers' Association
Lahore	DSB, Lahore
Ludhiana	DSB, Ludiana
Lyallpur	DSB, Lyallpur
Mianwali	DSB, Mianwali
Rawalpindi	DSB, Rawalpindi
Rohtak	1. DSB, Rohtak
	2. Rohtak Ex-Indian Officers' Association
Shahpur	1. DSB, Sargodha
	2. Sargodha Ex-Indian Officers' Association
Sheikhpura	1. DSB, Shiekhpura
	2. Mazbhi Singh Association
Sialkot	1. DSB, Sialkot
	2. Sialkot Ex-Indian Officers' Association

Source: Punjab Government, Home/Military Proceedings 'B', 1922, File 15.

In the first few years of their existence, the DSBs functioned primarily as welfare organizations, catering to the welfare needs of soldiers, ex-soldiers and their dependents. The structure of the DSBs and the civil-military nexus that they provided were crucial for the fulfilment of the range of welfare responsibilities assumed by them, which included, inter alia, disbursing relief allowances for families in economic hardship, distributing awards (such as *jangi inams*, money allowances usually given to a soldier in lieu of a land grant), securing employment for ex-soldiers, arranging for wounded soldiers to be treated in government hospitals, and generally providing means by which government and military policies and schemes could be publicized and explained to soldiers, and, at the same time, soldiers could turn to the DSBs to air their grievances and seek redress, where necessary.

One of the main functions of the DSBs in the early stages of their existence was to assist demobilized soldiers or families of deceased soldiers in making claims for financial relief from the civil or military authorities. Prior to the establishment of the DSBs, an ex-soldier or a dependent wishing to seek financial help from the state had to undergo a lengthy and cumbersome process of applying through the deputy commissioner's office, or through his unit. This often entailed a good many difficulties, especially for those who lived in villages far removed from the district offices or regimental headquarters. Furthermore, pensioners, especially ex-Indian officers, often complained that they were being poorly treated by civil officers, who were not only "disrespectful", but could not be trusted to treat their claims fairly.[53] Consequently, the disbursement of financial aid to ex-soldiers could be delayed and inadequate and could often generate resentment, and give cause for criticism of the *sircar*.[54] DSBs were, therefore, entrusted with the responsibility of ensuring that the process of obtaining relief by the ex-soldier and his family was expedited. In the case of an application by a soldier for relief grants, for example, the application would be investigated by an Indian officer from the applicant's local zail. The officer then reported his findings to the

[53] Cf. p. 111.
[54] Minutes of Meeting of Punjab Soldiers' Board, 28 April 1921, in PHP(M), File no. 171, 'B', November 1921.

zail committee, which would then send its report to the tehsildar for verification. After the necessary enquiries and confirmation of details, the case of the applicant would be put before the Board, which would decide whether to recommend the soldier for relief. Once a grant was approved, the amount would be paid out personally by the deputy commissioner or the secretary of the DSB. In cases where disputes occurred, tehsildars would attempt to settle the matter on the spot or, failing that, report the facts to the deputy commissioner for a final decision. While this may sound like being a protracted procedure, the entire process adopted by the DSB had the advantage of skirting the cumbersome, and sometimes acrimonious, approach involving the entire structure of the civil hierarchy, while giving the ex-soldier the reassuring impression that his claims had the constant attention of not only the civil authorities, but of the military authorities as well.

Another important function undertaken by the DSBs in the first few years after the war was to assist wounded and incapacitated soldiers in receiving free treatment from government hospitals. The aim of the scheme was to help crippled soldiers regain, albeit to a limited extent, the use of their disabled limbs, and then to receive instruction in suitable trades by which their means of livelihood could be secured.[55] While the government had all along been keen to implement such a scheme, it found that the response had been poor because many people in need of such treatment were unaware of the scheme's availability. DSBs were, therefore, ordered to publicize in vernacular pamphlets the availability of specialized institutes and orthopaedic hospitals in the vicinity; in Dehra Dun, for example, where crippled soldiers could avail themselves of treatment and training, and obtain free replacement of artificial limbs, boots, and other medical appliances where necessary. DSBs then arranged for a soldier wishing to take advantage of these facilities to be housed, fed and transported to the hospital free of charge.[56] In Lahore, a special school was set up and run by the Punjab Soldiers' Board for the purpose of teaching disabled and

---

[55] L. French, Sec. to Punjab Govt. to all Deputy Commissioners in the Punjab and political agents in the Phulkian States and Bhawalpur Agency, 2 April 1919, PHP(M) 'B', March 1920, pros. 138–39.

[56] Lieutenant Colonel F.G. Moore, Sec., Indian Soldiers' Boards to Addl Sec., Punjab Government, 17 November 1919 in PHP(M) 'B', File 13, 1921.

blind ex-soldiers useful trades to enable them to earn a livelihood for themselves.[57]

A major preoccupation of the DSBs after the war was in helping ex-soldiers find civil employment upon their discharge from the army. With post-war demobilization, thousands of soldiers found themselves back in the villages without employment after a short period of service with the army. The percentage of soldiers technically out of work in the Punjab was very small, owing to the fact that the majority of soldiers belonged to the agricultural classes, and could easily slip back into the farms after their discharge from the army. However, for many such soldiers, especially peasant-proprietors with small plots of land, their discharge from the army removed a steady source of income which was much needed to augment the meagre agricultural earnings from their small holdings. The most badly affected were the "short service" pensioners, soldiers enlisted only for the duration of the war, who, upon leaving the army, found that their pension of about six rupees a month was insufficient for them to support their families.[58] In addition to these, there were low-caste *kamins* (farm labourers) who had been enlisted in large numbers to meet the manpower demands during the war, and were discharged in their thousands almost immediately after the war. Having tasted life as soldiers, and having fought alongside their social and caste superiors in the trenches, these kamins were not pleased at having to return to their former positions as village serfs; many had hoped to remain in the army, but failing that, preferred industrial to agricultural employment. Although it was unlikely that rural Punjab would experience the sort of social and political upheavals that usually accompanied urban mass unemployment, the Punjab government was nevertheless concerned about the potentially disruptive effects of demobilized soldiers who failed to secure proper employment.[59] Unable to re-enlist them into the army, which had almost immediately after the

---

[57] L. French, Addl Sec. to Punjab Govt. to all Deputy Commissioners in the Punjab and political agents in the Phulkian States and Bawahalpur Agency, 2 April 1919, PHP(M) 'B', pros. 138–79, March 1920.

[58] This problem was not limited to the immediate post-war period, but was a perennial complaint amongst the soldier population throughout the 1920s and 1930s. See Tour Reports of Officers in Punjab in 1930, GoI, Home (Pol.), 265/30. NAI.

[59] See minutes of the proceedings of the meeting of Punjab Soldiers' Board, 6 November 1920, in PHP(M) 'B', File 41, January 1921.

war been significantly reduced to its peacetime establishment, the government found that it was necessary, and indeed politically essential, to assist ex-soldiers to acquire employment in other services, outside the army.[60]

In late 1919 the Punjab Soldiers' Board accordingly constituted an employment sub-committee to address the problems related to unemployment amongst ex-soldiers. Upon its recommendation, the Punjab government issued orders to all heads of departments, divisional commissioners and deputy commissioners to give ex-soldiers who had served in the war preferential employment in certain posts in their respective administrations, and they were asked in particular to provide the Board and the divisional recruiting officers with a list of appointments suitable for ex-soldiers in their departments.[61]

Lists of vacancies suitable for ex-soldiers were thus produced. Most vacancies were for non-skilled personnel like chowkidars, peons, chaprasis, office orderlies, etc., in government departments and district administration offices, and security guards, gatesmen, pointsmen, ticket collectors, chaprasis, peons and porters in railway services.[62] Conspicuously absent in these vacancy lists was police employment. Although ex-soldiers could be easily re-employed as policemen, the Punjab government was not enthusiastic about employing them in that capacity, especially those still attached to reserve battalions. There was concern that any threat of war necessitating the calling up of reservists to the army might coincide with internal disturbances, when the police would not be in a position to spare them.[63]

Contacts between discharged soldiers who needed work in the districts and the departments offering employment were provided by officers of the DSBs. Registers of discharged men in their districts

---

[60] Tour Report, Lyallpur District, 23 February 1930, GoI, Home (Pol.), 265/30. NAI.

[61] Proceedings of the meeting of the Punjab Soldiers' Board held on 7 May 1925, PHP(M) 'C', File 418, 1926.

[62] The pay which ex-soldiers could get in civil employment was comparable to the salary they drew as soldiers. A gatesmen, Class 1, in the railway would get Rs 14 - 1 - 17 per mensem; chowkidars, class A, Rs 15 - 1-19; Pointsmen, Class 2, Rs 15 - 1 - 19; Porters, Class A, Rs 15 - 1 - 19. F.A. Hadow, Agent, N.W. Railway to Home Sec., Punjab Govt., 20 August 1921, PHP(M) 'B', pros. 28–30, June 1922.

[63] PHP(M) 'B', File 14, 1928.

who needed employment were maintained and regularly updated by the committees.[64] Recruiting officers or representatives of the Board, upon receiving information concerning employment from the Punjab Soldiers' Board, would disseminate it to the people concerned in their districts. If an ex-soldier sought employment within his district, he could apply to his district recruiting officer or directly to the secretary of the DSB of his district. After a preliminary interview, where the eligibility of the soldier was ascertained, the DSB would arrange for the prospective candidate to meet with his prospective employers. Would-be employers wishing to obtain the services of ex-soldiers were encouraged to approach the DSBs directly to consult their registers and obtain necessary information to help them locate the personnel they required.[65]

To open up the scope of civil employment for ex-soldiers and, at the same time, to ease the pressure on government departments obliged to employ ex-soldiers, the Punjab Soldiers' Board sought the cooperation of organizations such as the Punjab Chamber of Commerce and the Punjab Trades Association to help ex-soldiers in obtaining employment in the commercial sector.[66] This, however, did not prove to be very successful. It was reported that ex-soldiers found work in commercial firms derogatory, as it did not carry the same social prestige or *izzat* which an official appointment, no matter how minor, carried. Ex-soldiers given employment in private companies were found to have accepted their employment grudgingly, and were reported to have displayed poor attitude in these new occupations. The failure to appreciate commercial employment, coupled with the lack of technical training amongst the discharged soldiers, consequently hindered the attempts by the Punjab Trades Association to find civil employment for ex-soldiers.[67]

The lack of technical training among ex-soldiers, almost all of whom had been unskilled farm hands prior to their enlistment into the army, was a major hindrance in their attempts to secure civil employment. For example, although the Punjab Soldiers' Board was informed by the Railway Department of a number of

[64] Major C.W. Gwynne to Sec., Punjab Soldiers' Board, 9 May 1919, PHP(M) 'B', pros. 490–491, May 1919.

[65] *Ibid.*

[66] Punjab Trades Association to Addl Sec., Punjab Govt., 2 June 1919, in PHP(M) 'B', May 1919, pros. 237.

[67] Punjab Trades Association to Addl Sec., Punjab Govt., 2 June 1919.

vacancies in its mechanical department, the Board was unable to recommend ex-soldiers as most of them lacked the necessary technical qualifications for such jobs.[68]

Several ex-soldiers, however, did possess some basic educational qualifications, especially VCOs, who had been required to pass a basic examination for promotion. To enable these ex-soldiers to make optimal use of their qualifications, the Punjab Soldiers' Board, in conjunction with the School of Public Instruction and Central Training in Lahore, proposed in late 1919 to train ex-soldiers who had some basic education[69] as schoolmasters of village primary schools. The scheme was approved by the Punjab Government, and in April 1920 a teachers' training school was opened in Gujar Khan tehsil in Rawalpindi district to train ex-soldiers as village school teachers. The scheme was widely publicized by the DSBs in the military districts and candidates selected by the respective DSBs were given a year's training, after which, if successful, they were awarded teaching qualifications in the form of vernacular examination certificates, and offered teaching posts in schools near their homes.[70] The scheme was generally regarded as a success as it provided ex-soldiers with a fairly well-paid and respectable occupation, which was usually near their homes. At the same time, it also served to meet the shortage of primary school teachers following the spread of education in the province.[71] Following upon the success

---

[68] F.A. Hadow, Agent, N.W. Railway to J.P. Thompson, Chief Sec. to Punjab Govt., 20 August 1921, PHP(M) 'B', File 74, 1922.

[69] "The minimum qualification as set by the principal of the Central Training College in Lahore for a prospective candidate wishing to be trained as a school teacher must be a second class regimental certificate, i.e. the minimum educational standard required in the army for promotion to the daffadar or havildar rank." Press communique from V. Connolly, Home Sec., GoP, 28 June 1921, in PHP(M) 'B', File 46, 1922.

[70] Memo by H.A. Smith, Deputy Commissioner, Rawalpindi District, 1 September 1921, in PHP(M) 'B', pros. 32, File 46 April 1922.

[71] It was reported that out of the first batch of trainees, twenty passed the course in 1922 and were performing satisfactorily in the schools they were posted to. New teachers began with a salary of twenty rupees, an income which was an important supplement to the military pension they were drawing, and many of them had found employment near their homes to be a very satisfactory arrangement. See note on the subject of training of discharged soldiers as school masters by G. Anderson, Director of Public Instruction, Punjab, 23 November 1921, PHP(M) 'B', pros. 56–9, File 34, 1922.

of the first teachers' training school, it was proposed that another school, similar in scope and objective to the first, should be established in the military district of Jhelum. This scheme, however, did not take off due to a deficiency of funds and a dearth of ex-soldiers with the required qualifications.[72]

In some ways it may seem odd that the welfare activities of the DSBs in the immediate post-bellum years were geared almost exclusively towards the ex-soldier population since the reliability of the Indian army, obviously, depended principally on recruits and serving soldiers, and not on pensioners. Yet, the state's rationale for paying such attention to the ex-soldier population was well calculated. Although these pensioners were no longer in active service in the army, their influence in the military districts could not be underestimated. First, these ex-soldiers, with their military training, could form a potentially troublesome force if they should decide to oppose the government. The Akali Sikhs provided the best demonstration of this (as we shall see in chapter five). Furthermore, many of these ex-soldiers had relatives and friends among serving soldiers whom they could easily influence. If an ex-soldier found that military service with the *sircar* did not guarantee economic protection, he could easily become a disruptive influence in his village. However, if pensioners and veterans could be won over to the side of the government, they would form an important stabilizing factor in the military district. The GoI and Army Headquarters believed, therefore, that unless the immediate grievances of these ex-soldiers, caused by post-war conditions, were quickly alleviated, a discontented lot of ex-soldiers could rapidly become openly hostile against the government.

The DSBs did, nevertheless, serve the interests of serving soldiers as well, and one of their most important roles was to function as a link of communication between the soldier on service away from his home and his family in his village. It was found that soldiers who had been away from home for long periods of time usually showed signs of restlessness, caused mainly by uneasiness about possible problems at home, which usually had to do with the moneylender's claims, family relations and land disputes. To alleviate the anxieties of soldiers while they were serving away from their home

[72] *Ibid.*

districts, and to maintain their morale, the Indian Soldiers' Board felt that it was necessary for a permanent organization to be established in recruiting areas so that special attention could be given to the soldier's family and home while he was away on duty.[73]

After some consideration, it was felt that the best possible link between the soldier and his home would be a district organization which, if formed in the different recruiting districts where soldiers' homes were situated, would be able to connect the soldiers' families with the various regimental units. This task was given to the DSBs which began to function as channels of communication between soldiers serving outside their districts and their families in the villages. A nexus was established between the DSBs and the regimental training battalion, where the records of soldiers serving in the active battalions of the regiment were kept, so as to enable news of soldiers to be transmitted to their family and vice versa.[74] Thus, a soldier's wife who had no news from her husband and had no idea where his battalion was serving could get in touch with the DSB closest to her home, which could determine his whereabouts by getting in touch with the training battalion of his regiment.

Once this means of communication was established, the soldier on duty away from his home could, through the DSB, ensure that his affairs at home were taken care of. For instance, a soldier from a unit posted outside the Punjab wishing to have some matters settled in his village could write to the deputy commissioner, through the officer commanding his battalion. If the soldier in question was unable to obtain leave to look after the affair himself, the deputy commissioner would send the case to the DSB of the soldier's district to be investigated by the zail committee in the zail where the soldier resided. After investigating the case, the zail member would send his findings to the DSB, which would then refer the matter to the tehsildar, magistrate, or superintendent of police concerned for the necessary action. Through this arrangement, soldiers were not only assured that their interests were being taken care of, but also that their affairs received the due consideration of officials in the district.

[73] Minutes of Proceedings of the Meeting of the Punjab Soldiers' Board, 11 September 1920, PHP(M) 'B', File 41, 1921.
[74] *Ibid.*

In the first few years following the First World War, a whole network of DSBs was established in the rural districts of the Punjab, and they played a vital part in the government's efforts to alleviate unfavourable economic conditions which affected demobilized soldiers and their families in many parts of rural Punjab. In some districts, existing alongside these DSBs were separate organizations formed by ex-Indian officers themselves to look after the welfare of retired men, officers, soldiers and their families.[75] The whole range of welfare schemes and other functions performed by the Punjab Soldiers' Board and its subsidiaries, the DSBs, were achieved essentially through the close and constant cooperation between the civil government and the military authorities. By providing the medium—in the form of DSBs—by which the grievances and frustrations of the pensioner, soldier and their families could be brought to the attention of the authorities, a much needed safety-valve was created in the Punjab. The impact this created amongst the military classes was far-reaching: by performing their functions as dispensers of "prizes" from the government and as agencies protecting the welfare of serving and retired soldiers and their families, the soldiers' boards were visible manifestations of a caring and accessible *sircar*. Ex-soldiers who had their cases heard by touring officers of DSBs went away with the feeling that they had every opportunity to vent their grievances and that their interests were being cared for.[76] The government's benevolent and paternalistic attitude towards its military classes had the effect of engendering within the rural-military districts a dependence on the *sircar* for their continued well-being, thus providing, within the military districts of the Punjab, the very basis for the continued "loyalty" of the military classes.

[75] In districts where these two bodies existed, they were usually merged into a single district soldiers' board to coordinate their activities and make them more efficient. Where only ex-Indian officers' associations existed, they were renamed as soldiers' boards and prominent civilians were invited to join. D.J. Boyd, Sec., Home Dept., GoP, to all Deputy Commissioners, Punjab, 24 September 1923, File U/IX/40, Deputy Commissioner's Record Office (DCRO), Rawalpindi District, Rawalpindi, Punjab, Pakistan.

[76] Report of Tour of Attock and Hoshiarpur District by Major Teague and Captain Broadway, January 1936, PHP(M) 'B', File no. 186, 1936.

Districts Soldiers' Boards as Mechanisms of State Control

From what was originally conceived as welfare organizations for war veterans, DSBs had developed into important local institutions protecting the interests of the military classes. However, by the second half of the 1920s, it seemed that with conditions in the Punjab having returned to normality, DSBs had outlived the purpose for which they had been originally established and, in their routine functions of investigating claims, distributing rewards, verifying recruitment rolls, etc., that they were merely duplicating the work of the civil bureaucracy in the districts. But, although the conditions which the DSBs were created to tackle in the first place—economic disruption caused by demobilization—had more or less been dealt with by the mid-1920s, the DSBs had, by then, come to assume quite a new importance in the military districts. While their functions as welfare organizations were considerable, DSBs in due course took on the vital role of the state's control mechanism in the rural-military districts of the Punjab. Through the DSBs, civil and military authorities in the Punjab were able to penetrate into the recruiting districts, whereby they could constantly maintain a watchful presence in the military villages.

The DSBs by their very nature were especially well-suited to perform this role. First, through their numerous sub-committees and zail committees, they possessed an establishment network that could reach soldiers in every corner of the district.[77] In Amritsar district, for example, the DSB had forty-three zail sub-committees, covering almost every part of the district where there were families with military connections.[78] This meant that no village was too far or too remote from the "surveillance" of the DSB. Second, DSBs maintained regularly updated records containing detailed information on soldiers, ex-soldiers and even deceased persons as well as their dependents in their respective district offices.[79] These records enabled members of the board and, if necessary, the authorities to keep a close watch on individual soldiers and their activities. Third,

[77] Tour Report, Ferozepur District, 31 August 1930, GoI, Home (Pol.), 112/31. NAI.
[78] Report of Tour carried out by Captain C.G. Wilson, 10/15th Punjab Regiment, in Lahore and Amritsar Districts, January 1937, in PHP(M) 'B', File no. 143, 1937.
[79] Minutes of Quarterly Meeting of Rawalpindi DSB, 22 December 1926, PHP(M) 'C', File no.12, 1927.

DSBs were constituted by representatives of the civil and military hierarchy as well as by men of local influence in the districts. Committees were thus filled by individuals well-connected with the civil administrative structure as well as the military command who were familiar with local conditions. As during the mobilization during the war, these local officials were the agents through which the authority of the state was extended to the local population. As members of the DSB, in addition to performing their welfare functions, pensioned and serving Indian officers were obliged to keep a vigilant watch on their fellow soldiers and ex-soldiers in their respective villages.

The DSBs were, therefore, well-poised to function as intermediaries of the combined civil and military authorities in the Punjab in the military districts.[80] To maintain a high profile in the districts and to keep a close contact with the soldier population, regular tours were conducted by members of the DSBs and specially appointed inspector-agents, such as retired army officers, honorary magistrates, zaildars and sufed poshes, particularly in areas where the military classes were concentrated. There were two purposes here. First, they were conducted with the intention of ascertaining the needs of serving and retired soldiers and their dependents and offering them assistance, where necessary. For instance, during these tours, officers distributed leaflets and publicized information regarding educational opportunities available for children of ex-soldiers, jobs, etc., and, in the case of a lawsuit against an absent soldier who had no one to defend his interests, would arrange for legal advice to be provided. Such regular visits and contacts enabled the DSBs to acquaint themselves with the circumstances and conditions of ex-soldiers in their particular villages or zails, and provided a ready forum where ex-soldiers could express their grievances and frustrations.[81]

Such tours, at the same time, enabled the military command and the district administration to be kept informed of developments which were likely to affect the troops, such as the spread of political propaganda, attempts by agitators to excite disaffection amongst the military classes, or likely ill-feelings between troops and the local

---

[80] Major C.W. Gwynne, Secretary, Indian Soldiers' Board to all secretaries, Provincial Soldiers' Boards, 12 February 1919, PHP(M) 'B', pros. 359, March 1919.
[81] See for example the functioning of the Sargodha and Mianwali DSBs in Tour Reports, Sargodha and Mianwali, August 1930, GoI, Home (Pol.), 112/31. NAI.

population, and find ways of dealing with them.[82] Through the DSBs the deputy commissioners of Kangra, Jullunder, Ferozepur, Hoshiarpur and Ludhiana districts, for example, held periodic conferences with the district military authorities to apprise each other of the internal security situation in their respective districts.[83] During such meetings, information was frequently exchanged between the recruiting officers and other members about recruitment of particular classes of recruits and, occasionally, also about political issues.[84]

As we have seen earlier, the close contact which the DSBs maintained with the villages enabled them to be used as centres for disseminating counter-propaganda against the Congress and other anti-government organizations. Members of the DSBs kept a careful vigil on attempts by individuals to "undermine the loyalty" of ex-soldiers or soldiers on leave or furlough, and carefully monitored soldiers and ex-soldiers to see if they had been attending Congress meetings or had participated in any other "seditious" activities.[85] Conferences and assemblies of retired soldiers and pensioned officers were regularly organized by DSBs in military villages to counter anti-government propaganda and, at the same time, to remind them that their continued eligibility for land grants, jagirs, assignments of land revenues, special pensions and other rewards depended not only upon their passive loyal behaviour, but more importantly, on their willingness to come out in active support of the state in times of trouble or disorder.[86] If they failed to take an active part in helping the government suppress sedition in their respective villages, they would be liable to have their pensions forfeited.[87]

---

[82] This exchange of information between the army and the local authorities of the districts from where the soldiers were recruited had in fact been recommended by the Esher Committee in 1920. See Esher Committee Report, p. 37.

[83] Consolidated Circular from Home Sec., GoP, H.M. Cowan, 10 December 1922, in PHP(M) 'B', File no. 32, March 1922.

[84] Rai Bahadur Pandit Hari Kishen Kaul, Commissioner, Jullunder Division to J. Wilson-Johnston, Home Sec., GoP, 13 February 1922, in PHP(M) 'B', File no. 32, March 1922.

[85] Major A.F.R. Lumby, Sec., Indian Soldiers' Board to all local governments and administrations, 4 June 1930, File U/XIV/134, DCRO, Rawalpindi.

[86] R.A. Mant, Sec., Revenue and Agriculture Dept., GoI to all local governments and administrations, 22 February 1918, GoI, Home (Pol.), 1924/403. NAI.

[87] Major Lumby to all local governments and administrations, 4 June 1930, Rawalpindi DCRO, File U/XIV/134, Rawalpindi.

Although the structural organization of DSBs facilitated government penetration deep into the military districts, the viability of these institutions as control mechanisms depended to a great extent on the support of the local elites. In districts where landlords and tribal and aristocratic chiefs were present, such as in the western districts of the province, DSBs which had the support of these elements tended to be very effective. But in the Sikh districts of central Punjab, where there was a general absence of landed elite to provide the required leadership, the DSBs were relatively weaker as institutions of control. This would explain why, during the years 1922–24, when the Akalis gained influence in the Sikh countryside through their claim to religious leadership, the loyalist elements were effectively marginalized, and the DSBs failed to contain the spread of anti-government sentiments in the Sikh districts.[88]

By the second half of the 1920s, however, DSBs had become a ubiquitous feature of rural Punjab, and had become very much a part of its administrative structure. Already by 1927 there were twenty-six DSBs functioning in the Punjab, supported by hundreds of affiliated sub-district organizations. Through the DSBs civil-military integration was institutionalized in the military districts of the Punjab, enabling both civil and military officers to maintain a constant guard against disaffection in the military districts. The DSBs thus occupied a unique position in the military districts as special institutions through which the government was presented to the military classes as a benevolent civil and military *sircar*.

This link between the authorities and the military districts was particularly important towards the end of the 1920s, with the onset of deteriorating economic conditions in the Punjab due to a slump in prices caused by the Great Depression of 1929. The prices of agricultural produce, particularly of wheat and cotton, two of the most important crops in the Punjab, fell by more than fifty per cent between 1928 and 1929.[89] This dramatic drop brought about a severe economic crisis for the cultivators of the Punjab, especially those who were dependent on agricultural earnings for their living. The

---

[88] This will be discussed in chapter five on the Akali movement.

[89] Prices began falling in 1929 and continued to fall during the winter and spring of 1929–30. In the middle of May 1929, wheat was priced at Rs 3-2-6 per maund, and by July 1930, this had fallen to Rs 1-6-6. See *Punjab Administrative Report (PAR), 1930–31* (Lahore, 1932), p. 9.

areas most adversely affected were the central districts of Sheikhpura, Lahore and Amritsar, and the eastern districts of Ludhiana, Ambala, Hissar and Rohtak, districts dominated by small landholders and poor tenant cultivators. The cultivators' plight was not merely one of income loss, but of growing indebtedness as well. Despite the loss of income caused by the fall in prices, the cultivators had to continue paying land revenue and water rates, which between 1927 and 1929 had not been lowered in conjunction with the economic crisis.[90] Unable to make a living from their land, and forced to pay rent in cash and kind to the landlords and the revenue due to the state, the cultivators were soon driven to desperation.

The effects of the agrarian crisis on the military districts were soon evident. On 7 January 1929 a *jatha* of over 800 disaffected ex-soldiers, mainly ex-servicemen from Sheikhpura district who had recently been discharged from the army without pension or land, decided to march to the provincial capital to demonstrate their discontent and to pressurize the government into redressing their grievances.[91] The leader of the *jatha*, Anup Singh, was an ex-rissaldar in the Indian Army. He had, until 1926, been one of the beneficiaries of the state, having held responsible positions both in the Indian Army and in the provincial police department.[92] In 1926 Anup Singh fell out with the government and began openly criticizing the provincial authorities, culminating in the march to Lahore in January 1929. The government decided to meet with Anup Singh and representatives of the jatha, and instructed them to submit descriptive rolls of the demonstrators, with each individual stating his grievances. These cases were then communicated

---

[90] Brij Narain, *India in Crisis*, Allahabad, 1934, p. 2.

[91] FR, 15 January 1929. IOR:L/P&J/12/22.

[92] In 1921 Anup Singh presided over a local darbar to honour the visit of the Prince of Wales. The darbar, an assembly of four thousand soldiers and ex-soldiers, subsequently formed the basis of the local soldiers' association, a loyalist association which Anup Singh helped to establish. Upon his retirement from the army, Anup Singh was appointed to a senior position in the police department in the North-West Frontier Province. Things began to turn sour for him after a few months, however, and he was forced to resign and his properties forfeited. Thereafter the disillusioned Anup Singh went on a personal campaign to spread discontent amongst the soldiers and ex-soldiers in Lahore, Hoshiarpur, Jullunder, Ludhiana, Gurdaspur and Ferozepur, where he spoke to soldiers about the uncaring Raj and openly urged them to support the Congress. *Ibid.*

to the deputy commissioners of the districts concerned for investigation.[93] The government finally received 354 applications, which were duly sent to the deputy commissioners and the DSBs of the concerned districts to be investigated.[94] Despite this concession, Anup Singh remained obdurate; he continued organizing propaganda amongst ex-soldiers in several districts, calling on ex-soldiers to form local *jathas* and force the government to accede to their demands for land grants. Some of these gatherings were reported to be causing considerable restlessness amongst ex-soldiers.[95] To dampen Anup Singh's popularity amongst the ex-soldier population, loyal soldiers in Amritsar and Lyallpur denounced Anup Singh's activities in instigating disobedience amongst ex-soldiers in the Punjab on the ground that such behaviour lowered their *izzat*. Simultaneously, British officers toured the affected villages and explained to ex-soldiers that the government was fully prepared to consider and assist genuine cases of hardship if they were represented through the proper channels, namely, through the DSBs. Further, they warned that ex-soldiers who persisted in following the confrontational methods of Anup Singh would be arrested and prosecuted, and that their pensions, land revenue remissions and other civil privileges would be forfeited. Government action, including the arrest of Anup Singh in December 1929, ended the protest gatherings, and by 1930, the protest movement started by Anup Singh had, to all intents and purposes, dissipated.

Adverse economic conditions had, at the same time, however, given rise to a mushrooming of political organizations committed to improving the plight of the poor peasants. Of these, the most prominent were the Naujawan Bharat Sabha and the Kirti Kisan Party. The Naujawan Bharat Sabha, whose membership was confined mainly to students from the Lahore colleges, was an avowedly anti-British revolutionary party which aimed to organize labourers and peasants for the establishment of an independent

---

[93] According to the above fortnightly report, these rolls were collected for the purposes of allowing the authorities to investigate individual cases of grievances of the protesters. However, it also suggests that the government wanted to know the names of the demonstrators, for the purpose of perhaps keeping a watch on their future activities.

[94] FR, 30 January 1929.

[95] FR, 15 December 1929.

socialist republic of India.[96] The Kirti Kisan Party formed in April
1928 was a communist and revolutionary party whose objective
was to "liberate the working classes from bourgeois and capitalis-
tic ideology".[97] It drew support from former *Ghadr*ites and Akali
Sikhs and it sought to organize the Sikh cultivators of the districts
of central Punjab on issues of payment of taxes and land revenue.
In April 1930 the Hissar Kisan Sabha branch in particular headed
a campaign against the payment of rent in kind to the local landlords. Some others followed, and in one instance in a Lahore village, the campaign erupted in disorder, and the police had to be
employed in order to restore the authority of the government. Similar events took place in Amritsar and Sheikhpura districts, where
numerous arrests were made to suppress the agitation against the
payment of revenue.[98] Thus in the Punjab, in the autumn of 1929,
with bad seasons, a marked drop in the price of grain, financial
stringency and discontentment over certain taxes, the military districts, particularly those in central and eastern Punjab, were already
vulnerable to a concerted anti-government campaign, which was to
come before long in the form of the Civil Disobedience campaign.

The Military Districts and
the Civil Disobedience Movement

Although a Congress provincial committee had been formed in
the Punjab in the 1890s, support in the province for this nationalist
organization had always been extremely limited. The mainstay of
its support was limited to the Hindu commercial classes—the
Khatris, Banias and Aroras—and low-caste village menials.[99] It was
never able to gain popularity in the Punjab because of its image as the
political vehicle of the urban classes, the traditional antagonists of
the agricultural classes of the province. Nevertheless, on the eve of
the launching of the Civil Disobedience campaign, Congress work-
ers in the Punjab were confident that conditions, at least in central

[96] Bhagwan Josh, *Communist Movement in the Punjab, 1926 to 1947*, Delhi, 1979,
pp. 79–90.

[97] *Ibid.*, p. 94.

[98] *Ibid*, p. 106.

[99] Gerald A. Heeger, 'Growth of the Congress Movement in the Punjab, 1920–40'
in *Journal of Asian Studies (JAS)*, Vol. 32 (1), November 1972, p. 40.

and eastern Punjab, were ripe for an anti-government campaign. In preparation for an extended campaign to mobilize rural Punjab, the Punjab Provincial Congress Committee thus appointed in 1929 a special committee to strengthen the Congress organization in the Punjab by enlarging the pool of volunteers in the province. To meet its target of enrolment, set at 52,000 by 1930, the provincial committee went on a recruitment drive, and held regular meetings to encourage enlistment.[100] To prepare for the political training of these volunteers, a special committee was set up to enrol 2,000 volunteers, and to start a training camp at Lahore. The camp was to instruct a selected number of men from the districts who, on completion of their training, would return to their various headquarters and train their own local volunteers, whose main function was to organize local Congress organizations in the villages.[101] To stir up interest in the nationalist cause amongst the rural population, deputations, comprising prominent members of the local Congress committees, were despatched to tour the countryside. Prominent Congress leaders, most notably Jawaharlal Nehru and Gandhi, visited Lahore on a few occasions to help generate interest amongst the local population. During their political rallies, the Congressmen attempted to play up local grievances and thus drew on the economic distress in the countryside. To the ex-soldiers' community, Congress speakers referred constantly to the distress caused by unemployment,[102] while to landowning zamindars they emphasized the difficulties caused by the slump in agricultural prices and the extravagant demand for land revenue and taxes.

Despite these attempts at thorough preparation, the Congress Civil Disobedience of 1930–32 had only a marginal effect on the Punjab in general.[103] At the height of the movement in 1930 and 1931, the urban areas were the most affected where defiance of authority took the form of regular meetings with their anti-government speeches, flag hoistings and the boycott of foreign cloth and liquor.[104] However, in the rural areas, the response to the Civil Disobedience

[100] FR, 15 July 1929.

[101] *Ibid.*

[102] FR, 15 March 1929.

[103] If the number of arrests and convictions related to Civil Disobedience are to be taken as some index of the popularity of the movement, one could see that the movement in the Punjab was not as popular as in the other provinces. See Table 4.2 (overleaf).

[104] D.R. Grover, *Civil Disobedience in the Punjab*, Delhi, 1987.

campaign was significantly less marked. Between 1930 and 1932 there was no reported breakdown of law and order in rural Punjab, except in the east, where, as will be discussed, Congress propaganda met with some success owing to adverse economic conditions. Throughout the Congress campaign land revenue came in normally and, in spite of the numerous cases of economic difficulties among zamindars, there were no attempts to resist payment of land revenue or taxes,[105] except in a few villages and even there the boycott was rather short-lived.[106]

Table 4.2
Convictions for Civil Disobedience, 1932–1933

Province	Total Convictions from January 1932 to April 1933	Total Population (1931 Census)	Convicted Numbers As Percentage of Population
North-west Frontier Province	6,053	2,425,076	0.00250
Delhi	1,048	636,246	0.00165
Coorg	269	163,327	0.00165
Bombay	14,101	21,930,601 (incl. Aden)	0.00064
Ajmer-Merwara	298	560,292	0.00053
Bihar and Orissa	14,903	37,677,576	0.00040
United Provinces	14,659	48,408,763	0.00030
Bengal	12,791	50,114,002	0.00026
Central Provinces	4,014	15,507,723	0.00026
Assam	1,271	8,622,251	0.00015
Punjab	1,774	23,580,852	0.00008
Madras	3,490	46,740,107	0.00007

Source: Judith M. Brown, *Gandhi and Civil Disobedience. The Mahatma in Indian Politics, 1928–34,* Cambridge, 1977, pp. 284–85.

If the Congress generally failed to create an impact in rural Punjab, its failure to penetrate the military districts was even more marked. Exceptions apart, not many reports came in of the movement having a widespread effect on the military classes as they had during the Akali agitation from 1922 to 1924. Recruitment amongst the military classes was, in most cases, unaffected by the movement, and there were no reported cases of defiance to authority

[105] FR, 15 February 1931.
[106] FR, 31 May 1930.

amongst the soldiers in regiments. In contrast to what had happened when the Akali movement was at its height, regimental officers touring the military districts in 1930–31 gained the impression that the latter were, for much the most part, generally quiescent throughout the campaign.[107]

To understand the effect, or the lack of it, which the Civil Disobedience movement had on the military districts, it would be illuminating to examine four of the main recruiting districts; Jhelum, Kangra, Amritsar and Rohtak, and reasons can be found as to why the Congress was unable to penetrate these critical bases of the Indian Army.

According to the report of the recruiting officer touring Jhelum district in the summer of 1930, this key military district, which had a very high concentration of ex-soldiers, seemed practically unaffected by Congress propaganda.[108] The Congress appeared to have no influence in the villages, and its only support was derived from "the vocal well-educated minority", whereas the military classes in the district "appeared loyal and generally satisfied".[109] A major factor accounting for the lack of interest in the Congress movement was the communal divide. In this overwhelmingly Muslim rural district, the Congress was regarded with suspicion, being seen mainly as a Hindu bania organization.[110] Many among those interviewed by the touring officer felt that the activities of the Congress were likely to be detrimental to their political interests, and several leading gentlemen and Indian officers of the district expressed a lingering resentment at being used by the Congress as scapegoats during the Khilafat non-cooperation movement in 1921.[111] The general indifference of the Punjabi Muslims to the Civil Disobedience movement was best attested to by the low incidence of prosecutions for political offences, not only in Jhelum district but in the other Muslim districts of western Punjab. (See Table 4.3 overleaf).

[107] Concerned about the possibility that the military classes might be affected by the Civil Disobedience movement, a number of British officers were despatched to the military districts in 1930–31 to assess the impact of the movement there. These reports can be found in GoI, Home (Pol.), Files 265/1930 and 112/1931. NAI.

[108] Captain H.B. Harrison, 'Report of Tour of Jhelum District', 11 September 1930, in GoI, Home (Pol.), File 265/1930. NAI.

[109] Report of Tour of Jhelum District, 11 September 1930.

[110] *Ibid.*, cf. 'Report of Tour of Rawalpindi District', 31 May 1930 in GoI, Home (Pol.), File 265/1930; see also Judith Brown, *Gandhi and Civil Disobedience*, p. 145.

[111] *Ibid.*

Table 4.3
Number of Prosecutions for Political Offences during Civil Disobedience Movement in the Punjab

District	1931	1932	1933	Total
Lahore	78	888	89	1,055
Amritsar	216	332	239	787
Lyallpur	24	153	25	202
Hissar	23	134	–	157
Sialkot	14	123	6	143
Jhang	41	53	2	96
Rohtak	26	56	1	83
Hoshiarpur	1	66	4	71
Ambala	16	48	1	65
Karnal	11	51	–	62
Ferozepur	29	29	3	61
Ludhiana	41	20	–	61
Jullundur	11	43	6	60
Montgomery	2	47	3	52
Gurgaon	47	–	–	47
Gujranwala	4	36	–	40
Rawalpindi	5	25	4	34
Attock	30	–	–	30
Kangra	8	8	–	16
Gurdaspur	11	3	–	14
Jhelum	12	–	–	12
Shahpur	–	12	1	12
Multan	9	2	–	11
Sheikhpura	–	7	4	11

Source: Compiled from Fortnightly Reports, Punjab, 1931–1933, IOR: L/P&J/12/33, 44, 55.

Apart from the apathy of the Muslims towards the Congress, Jhelum district was particularly resistant to the political influence of the Congress because of the considerable economic dependence of the district on military service. As was typical of the Salt Range tract, where climate and terrain restricted the expansion of agricultural opportunities, the local population depended on the army to absorb the surplus male population which the land could not support, thereby preventing a situation in the district comparable to the perennial economic problems of the north-western frontier.[112] Military service had not only ensured survival, but a certain level

[112] *Ibid.*

of prosperity as well. Villages which contributed manpower during the war were given remission of land revenue to an aggregate of 150,000 rupees per annum for a term of ten years. Families and individuals also enjoyed remissions or assignments of land revenue, ranging from ten rupees to 250 rupees a year for life. Furthermore, in recognition of its significant contribution during the war, the current land revenue settlement for the entire district was extended for another thirty years.[113] During a horseback tour of rural Punjab in 1930, Malcolm Darling noted that "the general prosperity of the soldiers and their families [in the region] was one of the most striking features of the Punjab landscape".[114]

The district had benefited immensely, moreover, from the "multiplier effect" of heavy military expenditure by the British in the Salt Range tract.[115] The military's capital input had generated wealth and economic opportunities, not only for the soldiers, but for the general population as well. At the same time economic opportunities for ex-soldiers were considerably enhanced while improved communication networks, particularly in the form of new railway lines, marked a significant improvement in the livelihood of the people. It was hardly surprising, therefore, that the district remained impervious to any anti-government ideas from outside. The military classes had developed such a dependence on the government for their economic and social well-being that they were loathe to upset the status quo, unless this was to work in their interests.

This is not to suggest that the military classes of the Jhelum district were entirely free of economic problems. There were thousands of short service pensioners in the district whose limited pension of six to ten rupees a month was insufficient to support their families. As cultivable land in the district was scarce, many of these ex-soldiers had little or no agricultural earnings on which to fall back on. Military service had contributed significantly to alleviating the problem, but mass mobilization during the First World War had indicated that there were still thousands in the district who needed

---

[113] J.M. Jones to William Vincent, 26 May 1919, in GoI, Home (Pol.), File no. 37, July 1919. NAI.

[114] Malcolm Darling, *Wisdom and Waste in the Punjab Villages*, London, 1934, p. 23.

[115] See Clive Dewey, 'Some consequences of the military expenditure in British India: The case of Upper Sind Sagar Doab, 1849–1947' in Dewey (ed.), *Arrested Development*, pp. 93–169.

employment. But in the district, this economic difficulty only served to strengthen the dependence of the military classes on the government, not weaken it. With unemployment rife, and many still desperate for military service, the military classes in Jhelum were more prepared to turn to their DSB rather than to the Congress agitator.

In the district of Kangra, particularly amongst the heavily recruited Dogra Rajputs, the anti-government agitation gained no real sway either.[116] Like the inhabitants of Jhelum district, the Rajput Dogras of Kangra district chose to steer clear of Congress activities largely because of their dependence on the government for their economic well-being, mainly through military service. This attitude was perhaps best summed up by the recruiting officer who toured Kangra district, home of the Dogra Rajputs, in January 1931:

> Their traditions as a fighting race, hereditary calling in military service, preoccupation as small landholders, comparative inaccessibility of their terrain, difficulties of communication, and until recently, lack of education, all combined to give the Dogra Rajputs a simple outlook. Their faith is pinned to the British government, which has provided an outlet for profitable employment of the surplus which land cannot support, and which has ensured the stability necessary for the remainder to carry out their avocations in peace ... to put the matter on the lowest plane, a class in which practically every homestead had some connection with the military and government service and which is fully aware of which side their bread is buttered.[117]

Bad conditions, however—fall in agricultural prices, financial stringency, discontentment with taxes—had generated some unhappiness amongst the local population. Particularly prone to Congress propaganda were the urban traders, professional classes and farm labourers.[118] But it was reported that in Hamipur tehsil, an important recruiting centre, Congress propaganda was having some effect on sections of the military classes, particularly those

---

[116] Captain E.R.M Hall, 'Report of Tour of Kangra District', 14 January 1931, GoI, Home (Pol.), 112/31.

[117] Tour Report, Kangra District, 14 January 1931, GoI, Home (Pol.), 112/31.

[118] *Ibid.*

who were disappointed at not being able to serve for a longer term in the army.[119] In such cases, the government depended on the DSBs and other loyalist organizations to conduct counter-propaganda measures against the Congress. One such organization was the Lambragoan Peace League of Kangra district. Formed and headed by the Maharajah of Lambragoan, Colonel Sri Jai Chand, it held regular meetings in the district, kept in touch with commanders of Dogra regiments and acted as a deterrent to any anti-government activity. Likewise in Palampur tehsil, an Aman Sabha was formed under the leadership of a pensioned havildar, Tarlok Singh, who, with the assistance of other influential persons in the locality, went about rebutting rumours and preventing the spread of propaganda.[120]

Between 1930 and 1932, Amritsar district, the hotbed of the Akali movement, remained surprisingly calm. Congress propaganda created little impact here, and the touring officer noted that "there [was] no Congress worth its name outside Amritsar city ... there were no tangible signs of anything of this nature ... in the villages .... and in villages where there were substantial numbers of soldiers, the mood was generally calm, and loyal".[121] In some of these villages, protests were staged by Congress activists, but the touring officer dismissed these protests as activities staged by "small Hindu boys" with little serious implications. No instances of boycotting of soldiers' families, as had taken place during the Akali movement, were brought to his notice.[122] Throughout the Civil Disobedience movement, the responses of the Sikhs had at best been circumspect. The main Sikh political organization, the Akali Dal, was reluctant to call on the Sikhs to support the movement, having fallen out with the Congress leadership over the issue of the inclusion of Sikh colours in the Congress flag, while the Sikh activists belonging to the Naujawan Bharat Sabha and Kirti Kisan Party had been rounded up and jailed for participating in the movement.[123]

[119] Captain G.E. Tinney, 'Tour of Kangra District', August 1930, in GoI, Home (Pol.), File 265/1930. NAI.

[120] Tour of Kangra District, 14 January 1921, GoI, Home (Pol.), 112/31.

[121] Captain H.R. Jackman, 'Report of Tour in Amritsar District', February 1931, GoI, Home (Pol.), 112/31. NAI.

[122] *Ibid.*

[123] Tour Report, Amritsar District, February 1931, GoI, Home (Pol.), 112/31. See also Judith Brown, *Gandhi and Civil Disobedience*, pp. 146, 301; and K.L. Gulati, *Akalis Past and Present*, New Delhi, 1974, pp. 52–56.

In the Sikh districts, loyalist organizations and the DSBs had been mounting a concerted counter-propaganda campaign in every corner of the district, through its various tehsil and zail publicity committees, to check Congress propaganda at every level.

Nevertheless, during the officer's tour of Amritsar a whole range of causes of discontent were brought to his attention. Ex-soldiers complained of a shortage of land in the district, which had catapulted land prices beyond their reach. Agricultural earnings had at the same time plummeted due to the Depression and the consequential low prices of agricultural produce. Furthermore, a lack of employment opportunities was causing much financial difficulties for pensioners. That ex-soldiers were prepared to air all these grievances to the touring officer, with the hope of getting them redressed, was testimony to the fact that the military classes had developed a dependence on the government and would turn to it, rather than the Congress, to alleviate their plight. The touring officer was of the opinion that the pensioners would not take any part in the Congress movement, even though some of them might privately sympathize with it, for fear of losing their pensions. Serving men also realized that they would have everything to lose and nothing to gain by joining the Congress movement.[124]

It was only in the eastern districts of the Punjab that Congress propaganda succeeded in creating restlessness among the peasant-proprietors. Rohtak district, for example, was particularly susceptible to Congress propaganda because of the near famine conditions caused by the slump in agricultural prices, shortage of rains for four consecutive years and attacks on crops by locusts. There and in the adjoining Karnal district, it was reported that the Congress agitation in the rural areas had been more successful and there had been some attempts to set up a parallel government;[125] alternative "deputy commissioners" and "thanedars" were reported to have been appointed by the Congress in some *thanas* (police stations). To boost its popularity and influence in the villages, local Congress organizations had, moreover, begun conducting enquiries into the conditions of the cultivators.[126]

[124] 'Tour Report', Amritsar, February 1931.
[125] FR, 15 April 1931.
[126] FRs, 15 May 1931 and 31 May 1931.

The adverse economic conditions in the district in 1930 and 1931 served to strengthen considerably the appeal of Congress propaganda, even amongst military personnel. In the districts, Congress attempts to cause disaffection amongst the war-service soldiers were reported to have met with some success;[127] and several military pensioners and serving personnel from the district were reported to be amongst the active sympathizers of the Congress.[128] The extent of disobedience in some villages was such that the deputy commissioner of Rohtak felt compelled to instruct recruiting officers to stop enlisting Jats from those villages for the army.[129]

Ex-soldiers most susceptible to Congress propaganda were those who had been discharged without pensions, land grants or employment.[130] In Rohtak district, there were thousands of such short-service pensioners—soldiers who had been recruited during the war and discharged almost immediately after without an adequate pension—who were badly affected by the shortage of food, and unemployment. These ex-soldiers complained that their interests had not been looked after by the *sircar*, and that promises of land grants and preferential treatment in civil employment had not been kept. The plight of many of them had been worsened by the fact that their regiments, which they could sometimes turn to for assistance, had been disbanded. Ordinarily, the Rohtak DSB would have adopted measures to placate these disaffected pensioners, but the magnitude of the problem in the district, with large un-irrigated areas devastated by the slump in prices and famine, and thousands of men desperate for assistance and employment, made it difficult for the DSB to cope.

The onus of opposing the Congress influence among the military classes consequently fell on the local elites of the district, most notably Chhottu Ram, leader of the districts Jats. Chhottu Ram

---

[127] Captain T.S. Emery, 'Report of Tour of Rohtak, Hissar and Karnal Districts, February 1930', in GoI, Home (Pol.), File 265/1930. NAI.

[128] Prem Chowdhry, 'Social Support Base and Electoral Politics: The Congress in Colonial South-east Punjab' in *MAS*, Vol. 25(4) 1991, p. 815.

[129] *Ibid*.

[130] During the war thousands of men from the Punjab were enlisted to fight in the European and Eastern fronts. Most of them served only for the duration of the war and were considered "Short Service" men. With the exception of those in receipt of Wounded and Invalid Pensions, "Short Service" men did not qualify for pensions after their discharge from the army.

realized that continued recalcitrance and anti-government postur-
ing would eventually prove detrimental to the position of the Jats
in the Punjab. The Jats were a favoured military class, whose interests the government had traditionally sought to protect through
its agrarian policies. If the Jats lost their status as a military class as
a result of the government's decision to stop recruiting them, their
economic position would be eroded further still. Consequently in
1931, he gave wide publicity to the suspension of pensions of army
personnel who had shown any sympathy to Congress activities,
so as to remind the Hindu Jat community forcefully that it depended on British support, through military service and favourable
agricultural policies, for its economic well-being, and that this special treatment would be threatened by any sympathizing with the
activities of the Congress. In the following year he gathered a group
of leading landowners, ex-soldiers and lawyers at his own initiative to issue a joint resolution calling on all zamindars and retired
military officers "not only to keep aloof from any politically subver-
sive political movement such as civil disobedience or non-payment
of taxes, but to actually fight against it",[131] and in so doing he
emphasized to the Jats the vital importance of preserving their military connections, as military service was central to their economic
interests, and called on them not to waste their time in such "un-
manly" occupations as weaving and spinning, the Gandhian symbol of the nationalist movement.[132]

The efforts of Chhottu Ram were to a large extent helped by the
government decision in May 1931 to authorize the remissions of
land revenue and water rates to the amount of Rs 109 million rupees.[133] This was done in an attempt to alleviate the hardship then
prevailing in the region, but it also had the effect of demonstrating
to the people of the district that, in the final resort, it was the government and not the Congress which had the ability to ease their
plight. This particular concession by the government served, therefore, to undermine the economic basis of Congress propaganda in
the affected villages.[134] By the end of 1931 the Civil Disobedience
movement was petering out in the Punjab. Activities such as the

---

[131] Chowdhry, *Chhottu Ram*, pp. 154–55.
[132] *Ibid.*
[133] FR, 31 May 1931.
[134] *Ibid.*

picketing and boycott of foreign cloth and liquor were on the wane, and Congress meetings were often too poorly attended to generate any excitement. There had been some unsettling anti-government campaigns during the movement, like the attempts by the Congress to set up a parallel system of government in the districts of south-east Punjab, but these incidents were exceptions, and had not survived.[135]

The general failure of the Congress to create an impression in the military districts of the Punjab could be attributed to the fact that the majority of villages in these districts possessed large numbers of pensioners who depended on the government for their pensions and welfare generally, and had too much at stake in the existing order to wish it to be overthrown.[136] Even amongst those who had not obtained pensions or welfare assistance believed that, ultimately, it was the *sircar*, and not with Congress, which would be able to alleviate their plight. Economic hardship amongst ex-soldiers, although it did create difficulties and resentment which could overspill into hostilities, could at the same time deepen dependence on the government, especially when the ex-soldiers knew that the Congress was clearly not in a position to solve any of their problems. This mentality of dependence was cultivated by the proliferation of DSBs and affiliated organizations which had since the termination of the First World War in 1919 been playing an active part in protecting and furthering the interests of the military classes in the Punjab. The activities of the soldiers' boards in the first few years after the war had made a demonstrable impression on the soldier population, showing that there was a channel for them to express their grievances to the Raj, and more importantly, to get redress. Thus soldiers, who continually turned to the government for preferential treatment in obtaining civil employment, receiving grants of relief and adjustments of pensions during times of famines, could scarcely be won over by Congress vilification of the British government.

The continued existence of these boards and committees formed a ready channel for representation for the ex-soldiers' communities; they not only showed themselves capable of representing the interests of the ex-soldier population, but also reflected their feelings

---

[135] *PAR, 1931–32* (Lahore, 1933), p. 4.

[136] Tour Report of Jhelum District, 11 September 1930, GoI, Home (Pol.), 265/30.

and actively assisted individuals in adjusting their personal claims. They were even capable of "righting injuries" in matters of distribution of irrigation from the canals, which was a constant source of discontent among the rural-military classes.[137] The faith of the ex-soldiers in these organizations became so complete that it was generally believed that they could get easier access to the deputy commissioners through these agencies than through the civil officers.[138] The DSBs were, therefore, constantly inundated with complaints and petitions concerning pension claims, employment, land grants, etc. With the DSBs in his neighbourhood, the soldier knew that his interests would be looked after and there was little incentive for him to turn to agitation.

District Soldiers' Boards in the 1930s

Throughout the 1930s the DSBs continued to feature prominently in the military districts of the Punjab. Their value as the sole channel of communication between the military classes in the districts on the one hand, and the state and the military command on the other, was acknowledged by the Indian Soldiers' Board, which decided to strengthen these organizations by providing them with the necessary paid staff, accommodation and equipment.[139] The popularity of these institutions in the military districts is reflected in the large-scale problem-solving the DSBs undertook. In 1936 the DSBs throughout the Punjab investigated a total of 739 pension cases, 2,630 cases dealing with applications for relief, found civil employment for 452 ex-soldiers, investigated 209 cases of domestic affairs, verified 4,400 rolls of prospective recruits and dealt with a total of 3,244 miscellaneous cases.[140]

The DSBs' continued relevance in the military districts was due not only to their function as the link between the military classes and the state, but also to their image as dispensers of "prizes" and

---

[137] See Tour Report, Amritsar District, 19 February 1931, GoI, Home (Pol.), 112/31.

[138] Tour Report of Amritsar, 19 February 1931, GoI Home (Pol.), 112/31.

[139] 'Report on Workings of Indian Soldiers' Board, year ending March 1933'. IOR:L/MIL/5/2318.

[140] 'Annual Report on the Workings of the Punjab Soldiers' Board and Organizations subordinate thereto for the year 1936.' PHP(M) 'B', File no. 76, 1937. For a comparison of the activities carried out by DSBs in the 1930s, see Table 4.4.

Table 4.4
Activities of the Punjab Soldiers' Board, 1936

Type of Activities	Number of Cases in 1936
Investigation of pension cases	1,634
Medals distributed	837
Investigation of relief cases	2,285
Scholarships	685
Applications for grant/land	88
Investigation of cases concerning domestic affairs	164
Verification of rolls and recruits	5,449
Miscellaneous cases investigated	791
Investigation of cases of arrears of pay	68
Application for arms licences	83

Source: Extracted from *Annual Report of the Working of the Punjab Soldiers' Board and the Organizations subordinated thereto, 1936*, Punjab Government, Home/ Military 'B' Proceedings, no. 76, 1937.

favours. Serving soldiers and pensioners believed that the *sircar* had unlimited land and money at its disposal, which would eventually be given to those who remained loyal.[141] Consequently, officers on tour and DSBs were flooded with requests by pensioners and discharged men, particularly for land.[142] This expectation of "prizes" was perhaps the main reason behind Punjab's enthusiastic contribution during the Second World War, with men volunteering their services with the hope that the government would reward their loyalty as it had done in the last war.

Conclusion

The vital importance of the Indian Army as the guardian of the imperial order in India was never more evident than during the inter-war years. The period from 1919 to the outbreak of the Second World War in 1939 was a testing time for the British Raj; state authority was being challenged by a mounting nationalist movement, and public order was frequently disrupted by civil disobedience campaigns, as well as recurrent outbreaks of communal

[141] See for example 'Report of Tour of Sargodha and Mianwali Districts', 25 May 1930, in GoI, Home (Pol.), 265/1930. NAI.
[142] Annual Report of the Working of the Punjab Soldiers' Board and its subordinate organizations for 1936. PHP(M) 'B', 1937, pro. 76.

violence. In maintaining public order the colonial state had always been prepared to rely on that ultimate guarantee of its authority and power—the Indian Army.[143] However, in frequent discussions of the deployment of the military in "aid of civil power", the continued loyalty of the bulk of the army, the Indian soldiers and officers, was never questioned, and seemed to be taken for granted.[144] Yet, both the GoI and Army Headquarters were well aware that the "loyalty" of the army could never be guaranteed, and that it was conditional upon a stable and pacified recruiting base; if that base were to be "subverted", then the Indian Army, or portions of it, would not only cease to be of use as an instrument of state power, but could ultimately pose a threat to the Raj itself.[145]

The task of insulating the army from external influences was not an easy one; it was not simply a question of hermetically sealing the barracks and the cantonments from external political influences. Within cantonments and regimental lines, strict discipline and punishment, and close contact between British officers and Indian soldiers could, to some extent, prevent nationalist propaganda from infiltrating into the regiments. However, the soldier was most vulnerable to "pernicious persuasions" when he was away from his regiment, on leave at home, where he was open to "bazaar rumours", nationalist newspapers and the influence of political agitators ready to exploit his fears and his grievances over issues which concerned him directly, such as his pay, pension, land, family and religion.

The onus of maintaining the "loyalty" of the army, therefore, lay not so much on British regimental officers as on local governments and district officers, for it was in the recruiting districts and the homes of the soldiers that the "loyalty" of the army was often won or lost. In other words, the protection of the army against "disloyal" influences

[143] For discussions on official thinking concerning the role of the Indian Army in defending and holding the British Empire in India, see Anthony Clayton, *The British Empire as Superpower*, London, 1986, pp. 32–38; and Major General C.W. Gwynne, *Imperial Policing*, London, 1939.

[144] See, for example, discussions by Chatfield's Committee in its Report, 1939. IOR:L/MIL/5/886.

[145] See, for example, note by Sir William S. Marris, Sec., GoI, Home Dept., 19 December 1919, GoI, Home (Pol.), 'B', pro. 76, January 1920. In a sense, this was indicative of the continued influence of the 1857 Rebellion upon official thinking in colonial India.

had to begin at the Indian soldier's home, where he had to be kept contented to ensure that he would not harbour grievances which could make him susceptible to political persuasions. The reliability of the Indian Army depended ultimately, therefore, on the maintenance of its recruiting districts and this, in turn, was dependent upon the close cooperation, indeed integration, of the civil and military authorities in the military districts.

The Punjab has always been the critical area where the battle for the loyalty of the Indian Army was to be waged, and it was home to about two-thirds of the combatants of the army during the inter-war years, and a substantial number of ex-servicemen. By 1927, if Gurkhas were excluded from the Indian Army, Punjabis accounted for sixty per cent of the total strength of the Indian Army. British officials recognized that the Punjab was a province of key military importance, and as long as it, and especially the military districts, remained loyal and pacified, the British could rely on the army, and "could face with confidence any situation that might arise in the other provinces".[146] This chapter has argued that the maintenance of the military districts in the Punjab was mainly achieved through the merging of the civil and military authorities in the province, particularly through the post-war institution of the DSBs. These Boards were initially established as a post-war administrative expedient to assist in the resettlement of soldiers returning from the war front, but remained a vital part in the bureaucratic edifice of rural Punjab till the end of the Raj, representing the interests of the military classes. The DSBs were not unique to the Punjab. Economic adversity was a basic problem affecting most demobilized soldiers throughout post-war India, and similar boards were set up in other recruiting grounds in India. However in the Punjab, where the post-bellum problem was amplified by the sheer numbers involved, the operations of the DSBs were far more pronounced and extensive than anywhere else in India. As the Punjab had the largest number of soldiers returning after the war, and as it remained the province with the highest concentration of soldiers during the inter-war years, the degree to which the civil-military nexus was established was more prominent in the

---

[146] See Sir Henry Craik to M.H. Brabourne, 10 September 1938 in Linlithgow's Papers, IOR:MSS.EUR.F.125/87; and Sir Malcolm Hailey to Sir Frederick Hirtzel, 13 November 1924 in Hailey's Papers, IOR:MSS.EUR.E.220/6c.

province than anywhere else in India, to the extent that in the Punjab it developed into an institutionalized part of the district administrative machinery.[147] Soldiers' boards functioned essentially as institutions of control and communications by which the government established its links with the important military classes.[148] Through these structures, the image of a caring *sircar* was projected downwards into the district and sub-district levels; and in their multitude of functions, as welfare organizations, communication channels and mechanisms of state control, these soldiers' boards functioned as a *cordon sanitaire* around the military districts, keeping out "unsavoury influences" from tampering with the loyalty of the soldier population. The "unshakeable loyalty" of the army amidst a context of increasing political unrest during the inter-war period, and the readiness and ability of the Punjab to play such a significant part in Britain's war effort from 1940 to 1945 were a vindication of the success of civil-military integration in the local administration of the Punjab.

Through these boards, which were associated with the interests of the military classes, the *sircar* in the military districts of the Punjab assumed a dual civil and military image. The government in the Punjab came to be identified as a quasi-military state which was committed to preserving the interests of the military classes. This had an important socializing effect on the military districts, as the military classes came to accept government by a militarized bureaucracy, or by the military itself, as the norm rather than an aberration. This could perhaps explain the readiness of the people in western Punjab, and subsequently Pakistan, to accept the dominance of the military-bureaucracy in their political system.

[147] It would indeed be instructive if research could be carried out in these other provinces to determine the extent to which the civil government had to work with the military in dealing with the problems created by demobilisation.

[148] The roles and functions of District Soldiers' Boards could be compared to the Courts of Wards in nineteenth century Bengal. For a study of the latter, see Anand Yang, 'An Institutional Shelter: The Courts of Wards in late 19th century Bihar', in *MAS*, Vol. 13(2) 1974, pp. 247–64.

FIVE

Managing the "Martials":
Control and Concessions

In 1920, Sikhs in the Punjab started a campaign aimed at freeing their principal gurdwaras (temples) from the control of their hereditary managers. The campaign quickly gathered momentum and, within a few months, developed into a non-violent struggle between the Sikh community and the Punjab authorities. Unlike the rather short-lived "1919 Disturbances" and the Khilafat movement in the Punjab, the Sikh agitation, which came to be known as the Akali movement, did not cease until 1925 and threatened rural stability in central Punjab. The Akali movement was not limited to small groups of disaffected Sikhs, returned emigrants or Congress sympathizers; at its height in 1922, the movement encompassed the bulk of central Punjab's Jat Sikh peasantry. The problem posed by the agitation did not merely pertain to the maintenance of law and order in the Sikh countryside; it had significant military dimensions as well. First, the Jat Sikh community constituted an important source of combatant recruits for the Indian Army. This meant that the abiding allegiance of the Sikh community to the Raj was a matter of considerable importance, and their estrangement, especially that of the Jat Sikh peasantry, would adversely affect the Sikh regiments of the Indian Army. Second, the unrest was rooted in one of the most militarized sections of Punjabi society— the Sikh peasantry. The Sikh community's martial traditions, fostered by their history, religious doctrines and culture, had been kept alive during British rule by the recruitment policies of the

Indian Army, where, in 1920, one in every fourteen adult Sikh males in the Punjab was in service.[1] This made the community a particularly potent danger if provoked into open rebellion against the authorities. Although the agitation did not eventually amount to a mutiny, the Akali unrest could be said to have constituted the most sustained and widespread case of military dissent in British Punjab. The threat posed by unrest in the heartland of the Sikh population was not lost on the colonial state; in February 1922, at the height of the agitation, V.W. Smith, a police superintendent of the Punjab Criminal Intelligence Department, noted:

> The Akali movement is likely to be a cause of much greater concern and anxiety than the civil disobedience campaign instituted by Mr Gandhi.... Gandhi's propaganda makes its appeal to the urban classes, which lack both stamina and physical courage to oppose successfully even small bodies of police; the Akali campaign is essentially a rural movement, and its followers are men of fine physique with a national history of which the martial characteristics have been purposely kept alive both by the government and the Sikhs themselves.[2]

The Akali movement has been studied in terms of indigenous resistance to the imperial embrace or as a defining moment, a watershed, in the evolution of Sikh political consciousness.[3] In these accounts, the nature of the official response has been relegated to a secondary position, often portrayed as the rigid reactions of a cumbersome monolithic colonial state. However, a careful analysis of the Akali movement and the manner in which it was contained is important in three respects. First, it should be noted that the response of the Punjab government to what the authorities termed

---

[1] See Census of India, 1921, Vol. 15–16, *Report of the Punjab*, and *Annual Returns of Caste Composition of the Indian Army, 1920–21*. IOR:L/MIL/14/230.

[2] 'The Akali Dal and the Shiromani Gurdwara Parbandhak Committee, 1921–1922', a secret memorandum by V.W. Smith, Superintendent of Police (Political), Criminal Intelligence Department, Punjab Govt., GoI, Home (Pol.), File no. 459/II of 1922, NAI. (Henceforth referred to as 'Akali Dal and SGPC').

[3] See Mohinder Singh, *The Akali Movement*, Delhi, 1974; Rajiv Kapur, *Sikh Separatism: The Politics of Faith*, London, 1988. The Akali movement is also the subject of Richard Fox's *Lions of the Punjab: Culture in the Making*, New Delhi, 1987.

the "Sikh problem"[4] was not so much a simple case of containing local anti-British resistance; it was determined by two underlying military concerns: to prevent a rebellion of the Sikh community against the government, and to reassert control over the military districts of the central Punjab. The task facing the Punjab government during the Akali movement was complicated by the fact that the disaffection among the Sikhs was not motivated by material deprivation. If it were simply that, the crisis would have been avoided by the timely dispensation of rewards and implementation of welfare schemes. The disaffection which spurred the movement had deep religious-cultural roots, involving issues of identity and community. Such causes of discontent could not be dealt with by mere suppression. The implementation of military repression and martial law, as had been done in the 1919 Disturbances, would not have served the cause of the military and the state in the Punjab. Rather, official response to the Akali movement required close civil-military collusion with a dexterous combination of control and concessions, aimed at the assuagement of the Sikh peasantry, and in turn the maintenance of the military districts of central Punjab.

Second, the episode highlighted the importance of the civil-military nexus in the major recruiting ground of the Indian Army. The Akali episode was a stark reminder to the British that the "loyalty" of the Indian Army could not be taken for granted, but was conditional upon a pacified recruiting ground. As disturbances in the military districts of the Punjab had both civil and military implications, the line between the military and civil in the Punjab became increasing blurred. The government, therefore, found its behaviour, response and policy influenced by the need not only to maintain law and order, but also to preserve the quiescence of the military districts as well.

Finally, a study of official responses to the Akali movement would reveal that the colonial state, far from being an inept and inflexible administrative machine, often displayed a remarkable degree of adroitness when tackling political crises.[5] This chapter

---

[4] See for example John Maynard, 'The Sikh Problem in the Punjab, 1920–23', in *The Contemporary Review*, September 1923, Vol. 124, July–December 1923, pp. 292–303.
☆ [5] See for example D.A. Low 'The Government of India and the First Non-Cooperation Movement, 1920–1922' in *Journal of Asian Studies (JAS)*, Vol. 25 (2), 1966, pp. 241–59.

will show that the course and outcome of the agitation were, to a large extent, determined by the nature of official responses. One could wonder, for instance, as to what would have been the outcome of the 1919 Disturbances in the Punjab if the government had, instead of implementing martial law, adopted a more conciliatory approach in dealing with the unrest. The dexterity of the colonial state in dealing with the Akali movement offered a glimpse perhaps of the secret of its continued success in governing the Empire amidst mounting political pressures in the final decades of the Raj.

Growth of a Movement

The roots of the Akali movement can be traced to the late nineteenth century, when Sikh reformists attempted to generate a resurgence of cultural and religious awareness within the Sikh community, mainly in response to increasing Christian missionary activities in the Punjab. Underlying the flurry of cultural and literary activities spearheaded by the Singh Sabhas (Sikh reformist societies) in the Punjab was the desire to define the true identity of the Sikhs. Throughout the evolution of the Sikh community, the question of what constituted a Sikh had posed a perennial problem, as the dividing line between Sikhism and Hinduism had never been clearly defined.[6] When Guru Gobind Singh instituted the Khalsa in 1699, he was in effect attempting to give the Sikhs an independent identity by galvanizing a disparate community into a distinct religious-military brotherhood. Gobind Singh required Sikhs to make a firm commitment to the faith by going through a baptismal ritual known as the *pahul,* and to wear five external symbols to differentiate them

---

[6] The Sikh religion had its origins in the teachings of Guru Nanak during the first decades of the sixteenth century. The teachings of Nanak preached a way of life based on simple egalitarianism and strict monotheism, both of which represented a fundamental rejection of the stratification of Hindu society imposed by the caste system, and Hindu practices of idolatry and worship of diverse deities. Nanak's teachings were basically moral and philosophical, and he did not, in his lifetime, institute conventions which effectively separated his followers, who were called Sikhs, from the Hindus. For a summary and discussion of doctrinal and religious debates surrounding the definition of the Sikh identity , see W.H. McLeod, *The Sikhs: History, Religion, and Society* , New York, 1989. See also McLeod, *The Evolution of the Sikh Community*, New Delhi, 1975, pp. 5–6.

from non-Sikhs.[7] Those Sikhs who were initiated into the Khalsa were known as *keshdhari* Sikhs, literally Sikhs with uncut hair *(kesh)*, which was one of the external symbols required of a Khalsa Sikh, and they were henceforth regarded as orthodox Sikhs. Not all Sikhs agreed to accept Gobind Singh's decree, and those who chose not to be baptized into the Khalsa brotherhood but who still followed the teachings of the Sikh Gurus preceding Gobind Singh were subsequently called *sahajdhari* Sikhs, or "slow converters". There was in fact little to differentiate the *sahajdhari* Sikhs from the Hindus; the distinction between them had "always been more of a philosophical belief than visible difference".[8] However, even within the Khalsa community the links with Hinduism had not been totally severed for many *keshdhari* Sikhs continued, by tradition, to observe Hindu practices and caste observations. Even at the height of Khalsa power in the Punjab, Sikh rulers continued to observe Hindu rituals and traditions in addition to Sikh religious practices. A British observer of the Sikh religion recorded in 1845 that "*keshdhari* Sikhs worshipped the *Granth Sahib* [the holy book of the Sikhs] with ceremonies akin to the ritualistic worship of Hindu gods and goddesses, observed pollution inhibitions towards converts from the outcastes of Hindu hierarchy, and consulted astrologers and the mystics".[9] Therefore, despite the constitution of the Khalsa, the differentiation between Sikhism and Hinduism remained blurred, and there was little to separate purely Sikh practices from those of the Hindus.

Following the demise of Sikh rule in the Punjab, the Khalsa Sikhs, feeling a sense of loss and disorientation after their political and military defeat by the British, began shedding the outward signs of their faith and reverting to Hinduism. Governor General Dalhousie, who made two visits to the Punjab after its annexation, commented on the decline of the *keshdhari* Sikhs: "The Sikhs are gradually relapsing into Hindooism, and even when they continue Sikhs, they are yearly Hindoofied more and more".[10] Sir Richard

---

[7] The five symbols that all Khalsa Sikhs were enjoined to wear were: *kesh* (uncut hair), *kanga* (a comb), *kara* (a steel bangle), *kirpan* (a sword) and *kachcha* (a type of breeches).

[8] Kapur, *Sikh Separatism*, p. 7.

[9] Major R. Leech, 'Notes on the religion of the Sikhs and other sects inhabiting the Punjab', December 1845, quoted in Kapur, *Sikh Seperatism*, p. 7.

[10] J.G.A. Baird (ed.), *Private Letters of the Marquess of Dalhousie*, Edinburgh, 1911, p. 69.

Temple, writing as secretary to the Punjab government in 1853, concurred. He noted:

> The Sikh faith and ecclesiastical polity is rapidly going where the Sikh political ascendency has already gone.... The Sikhs of Nanak, a comparative small body of peaceful habit and old family will perhaps cling to the faith of their fathers, but the Sikhs of Govind, who are of more recent origin, who are more specifically styled the Singhs or Lions, and who embraced the faith as being the religion of warfare and conquests, no longer regard the Khalsa now that the prestige has departed from it. These men joined in thousands, and they now depart in equal numbers. They join the ranks of Hinduism whence they originally came, and they bring up their children as Hindus.[11]

The slide into Hinduism was, however, arrested by the recruitment of Sikhs into the Indian Army after the 1857 Rebellion. In the Rebellion's aftermath, the British realized that it was politically expedient to promote a distinct Sikh Khalsa tradition, as part of an overall strategy to create ethnic and racial blocs within the military to prevent the colonial army from galvanizing into a unified force capable of threatening the British once again. Separate Sikh regiments were subsequently instituted, and they were encouraged to observe elaborate rituals and external accoutrements of the Khalsa faith in order to highlight their regiments' distinctiveness. In the 1880s, with the "martial races" doctrine dominant, the Indian Army deliberately underscored the martial characteristics of the Sikh community, especially those associated with the militarized Khalsa. The regulation providing for the recruitment of the Sikhs stipulated that:

> The *pahul*, or religious pledge of the Sikh fraternity, should on no account be interfered with. The Sikh should be permitted to wear his beard, and the hair of his head gathered up, as enjoined by his religion. Any invasion, however slight, of these obligations would be construed into a desire to subvert his faith, lead to evil consequences, and naturally inspire distrust and alarm.

[11] Quoted in Census of India, 1881; *Report on the Census of the Punjab*, by Denzil Ibbetson, Calcutta, 1883, Vol. 1, p. 140.

> *Even those, who have assumed the outward conventional characteris-*
> *tics of Sikhs should not be permitted after entering the British army,*
> *to drop them.*[12] (author's emphasis)

To be recruited into the army, the Sikh had not only to observe the tenets of the Khalsa, but was compelled to maintain the external trappings of the faith as well. British recruiting policies served therefore, perhaps inadvertently, to contribute towards the definition of a Sikh identity. Furthermore, by encouraging the Sikhs in the army to regard themselves as a distinct and separate people, the military was in effect fostering the growth of Sikh communal consciousness.[13]

Sikh communal awareness was heightened in 1873 by the activities of the Singh Sabha, a society founded in Amritsar by the Sikh gentry aimed at spreading Sikh religion, history and culture through educational and literary efforts. By emphasizing the acquisition of knowledge as the key to religious revival, the Singh Sabha attempted to provide the religious and cultural underpinnings for Sikh identity. Despite being plagued by divisions, the activities of the first Singh Sabha proved very successful, and subsequently encouraged the mushrooming of similar societies elsewhere in the Punjab. By 1899 there were 121 Singh Sabha branches in the Punjab.[14]

The efforts of the Singh Sabhas in promoting Sikh cultural and historical awareness were spurred on by the activities of the Arya Samaj movement in the Punjab. Founded by Dayanand Saraswati, an ascetic from western India, the Arya Samaj movement sought to bring about the revival and purification of traditional Hinduism through social reform and a return to the original doctrines of the *Vedas*. In 1875 an Arya Samaj society was founded in Lahore, and before long it had found widespread support amongst the middle class, educated Hindus in the province. A primary feature of Samajist proselytizing activities was the search for new converts who, when found, would be reclaimed into the folds of Hinduism

---

[12] Quoted in Khushwant Singh, *History of the Sikhs*, Vol. 2, pp. 112–13.

[13] D. Petrie, *Developments in Sikh Politics (1900–1911): A Report*, Chief Khalsa Dewan, n.d., p. 10.

[14] The origins and activities of the Singh Sabhas, including the politicking that took place, are fully recounted in *ibid*.

through a purification ceremony known as *shuddhi*. Initially Arya Samajists and Sikh reformers shared a common concern in their efforts to reform and revitalize their respective faiths, in defence against Christian missionary influences. But before long the vexing uncertainty of the position of the Sikhs in relation to Hinduism brought about a conflict between the two. In 1900 the Arya Samaj purified a group of outcaste Sikhs, and as a part of the ceremony shaved their heads and beards, transforming them into pure caste Hindus.[15] This alarmed the traditional members of the Sikh community who began to see in the Arya Samaj a threat, perhaps as dangerous as Christianity, to the community. The direct threat posed by the Arya Samaj once again highlighted the uncertain nature of Sikh identity, especially with regard to its relation to Hinduism.

The question of what constituted traditional Sikh orthodoxy, and the nature of a true Sikh identity, soon became the main topic of debates among Sikh reformists. In 1899, a group of reformers, calling themselves Tat (True) Khalsa, began advocating Sikh separateness from Hinduism. They argued vehemently that the Sikhs were a separate nation, and not part of the greater Hindu community. In a spate of debates in newspapers, journals and a series of pamphlets, the slogan *Ham Hindu Nahin Hain* ("We are not Hindus") soon became the battle cry of the Tat Khalsa. By the early twentieth century the Tat Khalsa, which was emerging as the dominant group in the reform movement, was determined to give Sikh identity a clear definition. They insisted that *sahajdhari* Sikhs either adopt Khalsa tenets or choose to be regarded as Hindus. As far as these reformists were concerned, only the Khalsa was synonymous with Sikhism.

In the process of trying to promote a true Sikh identity, the Sikh reformers inevitably turned their attention to the question of the management of the Sikh gurdwaras. Since its inception in the sixteenth century, the Sikh gurdwara had always occupied a central position in the religious, social and cultural life of the Sikhs. The management of these gurdwaras and shrines, which involved the maintenance of the temple precincts, supervision of temple revenues and the collection of subscriptions from the congregation,

---

[15] For a narrative of the activities of the Arya Samaj in the Punjab, see Kenneth Jones, 'Communalism in the Punjab: The Arya Samaj's Contribution' in *JAS*, Vol. 28 (1), 1968, pp. 39–54.

had traditionally been entrusted to a caretaker, usually selected on an ad hoc basis from among the congregation. In the early eighteenth century, with the large-scale Muslim persecution of Sikhs, first by the Mughals and then by the Afghan invaders, taking charge of Sikh places of worship became a hazardous enterprise. As large numbers of *keshdhari* Sikhs were forced to flee into exile, the management of Sikh shrines were entrusted to the Udasis, a sect of ascetic Sikhs founded by Guru Nanak's eldest son Sri Chand. Udasi Sikhs subsequently filled the positions of *granthi* (scripture reader) and *mahant* (manager) in most of the important Sikh gurdwaras. The arrangement worked well. The Udasi Sikhs were greatly renowned and revered for their asceticism and devotion to the religious tenets of Guru Nanak, yet as *sahajdhari* Sikhs, they did not maintain the outward appearances of the Khalsa and thus were able to avoid Muslim persecution aimed at the followers of Guru Gobind Singh.

During Sikh rule in the Punjab, the Udasis continued to serve as *granthi*s and *mahant*s in Sikh gurdwaras, and since no rules had been laid down for the management of Sikh religious institutions, their positions in the gurdwaras became entrenched as they began admitting disciples and appointing successors. The post of the *mahant* soon became a hereditary one, passing on from *guru* to *chela*. During the period of Sikh political ascendancy in the Punjab, the management of gurdwaras became a profitable undertaking when Sikh patrons, most notably Maharajah Ranjit Singh, began to donate large sums of money and make generous grants of revenue-free estates to the gurdwaras. After 1849 legal ownership of these estates were conferred on the manager of the shrines, and as the value of land escalated with agricultural expansion in the province, the revenue derived from gurdwara property increased enormously. The office of the *mahant* soon became not only an influential post but an extremely lucrative one as well. Gradually, the *mahant*s gained complete control over the temples, converting gurdwara lands and revenue into their personal possessions, and leaving the congregation virtually powerless to exercise any influence on the ways they conducted the affairs of the temple. Without having to account for their conduct to the congregation, the *mahant*s turned the Sikh temples into their private properties, and in some cases, Hindu practices and idol worship soon found their way into the gurdwara.

At the turn of the century, efforts aimed at reforming the management of the Sikh gurdwaras was started by the Singh Sabha reformers, supported by several pro-Khalsa newspapers. The reformers, mostly Khalsa Sikhs, complained particularly of the abuse of the precincts of Sikh places of worship. They protested that Sikh rituals performed in the gurdwaras had been tainted by Hinduism, as many of the *mahants* being *sahajdhari* Sikhs were Hindus, and not orthodox Sikhs. Furthermore, some of the *mahants* were accused of diverting income from temple endowments into their own pockets. Reformers further alleged that, in some instances, *mahants* had allowed temple precincts to degenerate into places of vice and debauchery, frequented by "unsavoury characters and scoundrels", making it impossible for decent Sikh worshippers to visit the temples. The reformers finally demanded that the temples and attached endowments, which were the rightful properties of the Sikh community as a whole, should be administered on terms acceptable to them.[16]

Popular pressure from the reformists and the pro-Sikh newspapers was brought to bear on a number of *mahants*, but the methods employed, mainly through boycotts, had little effect on the latter. A gurdwara was traditionally dependent on donations from its congregation for its upkeep. But in the Punjab, many of the gurdwaras had become financially independent as a result of the revenue earned from the property owned by its management. Consequently attempts at boycott usually proved ineffective against the *mahants*, whose financial position was not dependent on donations from worshippers. Some of the reformers tried to seek redress in the civil courts, but such litigation was usually lengthy and extremely expensive, and this favoured the *mahants*, who usually had ample resources with which to combat and prolong such litigation effectively. Unable to bring corrupt *mahants* in line through legal means, bands of radical reformers began taking matters into their own hands by forcibly ousting corrupt *mahants* from the temples.

The first major success in the forcible occupation of Sikh shrines was achieved early in 1920 at the Golden Temple in Amritsar, the most important of all Sikh shrines. The Golden Temple, with its group of five associated shrines, had always been managed by a group of Sikhs, with a Sikh manager as its executive head. With

---

[16] C.M. King, Offg Chief Secretary to the Government, Punjab, to the Secretary to the GoI, Lahore, dated 26 March 1921. IOR: L/P&J/6/1734, fos. 343–48.

the annexation of the Punjab the provincial administration, wishing to exercise control and prevent this very important Sikh institution from being used for political purposes, had a direct hand in appointing the manager of the Golden Temple. Thus appointed, the manager was obliged to consult the deputy commissioner of Amritsar on all matters concerning the secular administration of the temple. Sikh reformers regarded official control over their premier temple as religiously improper and started agitating for its removal. In October 1920, a party of Sikhs occupied a section of the temple. The Punjab government, accepting that the upsurge in communal awareness of the Sikhs was bound, eventually, to lead to the question of control of the Golden Temple, announced in the summer of 1920 that it was planning to consult the Sikh members of the provincial legislative council, shortly to be elected, on the introduction of a reformed system of administration for the temple. Although not officially stated, this was clearly a move calculated to win Sikh opinion, especially after the massacre at Jallianwalla Bagh, during which a large number of Sikhs were killed.[17] But as the reformers had pre-empted such a move, the government announced that it would form a council, constituted of elected Sikh members, to draw up a scheme by which the management of the Golden Temple would be transferred wholly to the community.

At the beginning of November 1920, after discussions with the Maharajah of Patiala, the government announced that a provisional advisory committee of thirty-six members would be constituted to advise on the management of the Golden Temple, pending a permanent arrangement for the supervision of the temple. Members of the Sikh aristocracy and landed families were thereupon invited by the government to form such an advisory committee. The official committee, however, never met. Almost immediately after the government's announcement, the reformers, seeing in this a disguised attempt to re-impose official control over the Golden Temple, decided to form a committee of their own. Subsequently, following a huge meeting at the Golden Temple, a separate, independent committee was formed. The new committee consisted

---

[17] Similarly, under pressure from Sikh students, evidently affected by the unrest in 1919, the government decided to withdraw official control over the Khalsa College at Lahore in 1920. See 'Note on Sikh Question' by H.D. Craik, Offg Chief Secretary to the Punjab government, in GoP, Home Proceedings, May 1922. IOR: P/11277.

mainly of middle-class professionals—barristers, vakils, and college and school teachers—though as a gesture of communal solidarity, it agreed to incorporate members of the officially appointed committee into its own to constitute one unified committee. As the new committee was prepared to incorporate moderate members (Sunder Singh Majithia, a loyalist landlord, was elected as its first president) and seemed to enjoy general support from the community, the government agreed to this arrangements[18] The committee, subsequently called the Shiromani Gurdwara Parbandhak Committee (SGPC), comprising a total of 175 members, claimed as its moral right and duty the control of the Golden Temple and all Sikh shrines in the Punjab. Buoyed by the alacrity with which the government had given in to its demands, and consumed by the zeal to rid Sikh religious places of corrupt management, the SGPC announced that its aims were now to extend control over all Sikh gurdwaras and other religious institutions so that these could be managed on terms acceptable to the Sikh community.

In the meantime, parties of reformers continued the forcible seizures of shrines all over the Punjab. These were carried out by Akali *jathas*, bands of Sikh volunteers who called themselves Akalis (immortal soldiers) after the sixteenth century warrior-ascetics who regarded themselves as the self-appointed guardians of the Sikh faith. Like their sixteenth-century models, the Akalis, who first appeared in the Punjab in the autumn of 1920 to carry out reforms in the temples in their respective areas, wore dark coloured turbans and armed themselves with large kirpans (swords), axes and lathis. These Akali *jathas* first sprung up on an independent and uncoordinated basis and received no instructions on their functions and duties from any central organization. The first such *jatha* was formed early in 1920 in Amritsar district, when a local agitator gathered some seventy to eighty Sikh volunteers in Tarn Taran to prepare for the seizure of the gurdwara in Nankana. Subsequently, as the Akali cult gained popularity in other Sikh districts, Akali *jathas* began to appear all over central Punjab. The size of these *jathas* varied from twenty to a few hundred, although the average *jatha* was reported to be about fifty strong. *Jathas* usually functioned within the geographical locality from which the volunteers

[18] V.W. Smith, 'Akali Dal and SGPC'.

were drawn, and each *jatha* was headed by a jathedar, who would be in charge of all the activities of the *jatha*.[19]

Soon after its formation, the SGPC decided to bring these independent *jatha*s under its wing. In December 1920 the SGPC sanctioned the formation of the Shiromani Akali Dal, a central body to unify and coordinate the activities of the numerous *jatha*s which had sprung into existence throughout the province. The chief function of the Shiromani Akali Dal was to maintain a register of the membership of the *jatha*s which were subordinate to it, and to convey instructions from the SGPC to the *jatha*s at the local level.[20]

By the end of 1920, with the support, and under the supervision, of the SGPC, Akali *jatha*s began physically seizing disputed shrines without any regard for civil law. On 21 November 1920 a party of Akali Sikhs occupied the Panja Sahib shrine at Hasan Abdal; on 8 December 1920, the Sacha Sauda Gurdwara in Sheikhpura district was occupied by a Sikh *jatha* and the *mahant* ousted; in January 1921, a gurdwara at Chola village in Amritsar district was occupied by a party of Manjha Sikhs. Some of these forced evictions were carried out violently and often resulted in casualties. At Tarn Taran in Amritsar district, a serious confrontation occurred on 26 January 1921 between the *mahant*s and his followers and a *jatha* of Akalis. Some twenty-five persons from both parties were injured, and two Akalis were killed in the fray. The Akalis, however, succeeded in taking over the shrine, which they continued to hold.[21]

The activities of the *jatha*s, much of which veered towards violence and a total disregard for the law, began to trouble the Punjab government. The Punjab government, which usually met this sort of behaviour with a firm hand, was, however, prepared to tolerate such transgression of the law. Two reasons could be suggested to explain its conciliatory attitude. The Punjab government was prepared to regard the Akali movement, first and foremost, as having a religious rather than a political motivation. From the very outset, it had made it clear that in dealing with the Sikh question its object was to treat as sympathetically as possible all issues which were of a religious nature.[22] It refused, therefore, to regard an agitation

---

[19] V.W. Smith, 'Akali Dal and SGPC'.

[20] *Ibid.*

[21] C.M. King to the Secretary, GoI, 26 March 1921.

[22] John Maynard, 'The Sikh Problem in the Punjab, 1920–1923', p. 300.

by Sikh reformers to free Sikh places of worship from the mismanagement of corrupt managers as a political problem. The government was aware that the reformers regarded it as their legitimate right to reassert control over their places of worship. The gurdwaras, according to the reformers, were not secular properties whose ownership could be claimed by an individual; they belonged to the congregation, and *mahant*s were only attached to the gurdwaras in the service of the congregation. If the government was to intervene on the side of the incumbents, their action would be construed by the reformers as official interference in the attempts of the community to claim what was rightfully theirs.[23] The Punjab government, therefore, decided to adopt a policy of conciliatory inactivity, knowing full well that the Sikhs were a "proud nation" who could easily be mobilized into opposition against the government if they felt that an affront was being committed against their religion. As C.M. King, the officiating Chief Secretary to the Punjab government, was to note in March 1921: "this [religious] chord of the Sikh nature is easily touched and will vibrate easily .... the Sikh is intensely proud of himself, his race, and his traditions, both militarily and religious ... and is easily inflamed".[24]

Then, there was also the military factor to take into consideration. According to government reports, more than seventy per cent of Akali volunteers in the districts of central Punjab were Jat Sikhs,[25] the community which had constituted almost exclusively the Sikh element in Punjab regiments of the Indian Army since the 1860s. The government was therefore careful not to adopt any posture which would result in the alienation of this militarily important community. This was particularly critical in the unsettled conditions following the war. In 1920 a general anti-government mood had affected the country, the Punjab not excluded. Indian Muslims had been unhappy with the peace terms imposed on Turkey by Britain and her allies; and the Congress, under the leadership of Gandhi, was stirring up support for a non-cooperation campaign against the government. Amidst such conditions, the government was

[23] H.D. Craik, 'Review of action taken by the Punjab government to check the lawless activities of Akali associations in the Punjab', 6 May 1922, GoP, Home proceedings, June 1922. IOR: P/11277.

[24] C.M. King to Secretary, GoI, Home Dept., 26 March 1921.

[25] V.W. Smith, 'Akali Dal and SGPC'.

anxious not to provoke a conflict with the Sikhs, which would be a sure way of driving them into an alliance with other anti-government forces. Furthermore, in view of the uncertainty of the response of the Muslim soldiers of western Punjab to the growing influences of the Khilafat movement, the military authorities might be forced to turn to the Sikhs should the reliability of the Muslims be adversely affected. The Punjab government, therefore, judiciously decided to adopt an attitude of non-interference, "with a view to avoid any semblance of partiality towards one or the other of the religious parties, and more especially with a view of avoiding anything which might drive the Sikhs, who had as a body behaved most loyally during the war, into anything like opposition to the government".[26] It consequently made an unequivocal undertaking to the Sikhs that it had no role to play in maintaining the status quo of the gurdwara arrangements, which meant that the government would give no special protection to the *mahant*s to preserve their positions in the gurdwaras. The Punjab government hoped that by assuaging the Sikhs' religious demands, saner and more moderate counsel would eventually prevail, which could hold in check the excessive activities of the *jatha*s.

The conciliatory attitude of the Punjab government, however, whetted the appetite of the Akalis for a more confrontational approach towards gurdwara reform. Emboldened by the fact that their actions had not been checked, the Akalis began to adopt a more defiant stance, and threatened to seize and occupy disputed shrines by force, if the incumbent *mahant*s did not voluntarily surrender their shrines to the *jatha*s. With their apparent immunity from government repression, the Akali *jatha*s began attracting huge followings. According to official reports, the movement served as a convenient platform on which disaffected sections of the population, especially demobilized soldiers failing to obtain rewards, or faced with financial hardships caused by insufficient pensions, could vent their frustrations against the government.[27] The police, keeping a close watch on Akali activities, expressed concern that "many unsavoury characters, motivated more by personal gains and the intent to do mischief rather than with intentions for religious

---

[26] *Ibid.*

[27] Report of a Tour carried out by the Commandant of the Jullunder Brigade in the Malwa region of the Punjab. Home (Pol.), 1924, File no. 1/VI.

reforms, were swelling the ranks of the Akalis".[28] The superintendent of police of Hoshiarpur district, for example, reporting in January 1921 on the formation of a *jatha*, pointed out that it "had very close relations with the returned emigrants".[29] The superintendent of police of Amritsar district, where the Akalis were most active, reported that "many bad characters had entered the movement tempted by loot and mischief", and also quoted an authoritative opinion that "discharged sepoys would probably enlist [in the *jathas*] ... both because they were discontented at having to leave the army, and could obtain more creature comforts with less work in the Akali Dal".[30]

Despite this, and the problems relating to law and order in some districts caused by the periodic invasions by armed Akalis, the government continued to be convinced that the most appropriate and prudent policy to adopt for the moment was one of non-interference. It was not unaware that the religious character of the agitation had earned it a groundswell of popular support amongst the Sikh population. Accordingly, it decided against issuing special instructions to the police to prevent the occupation of shrines by the reformers in the normal course of their duty.[31] Furthermore, if the police had to be called upon to enforce the law in a gurdwara dispute, officers were instructed to be careful to abstain from any action which might suggest the existence of any hostility on the part of the government to the Sikhs; for instance, police officers were not to treat the wearing of black turbans as an emblem of hostility towards the government.[32] The government was anxious not only to preserve its religious neutrality, but, more importantly, the appearance of it.

Ironically, it was the government's anxiety to show their goodwill to the Sikhs, by adopting a strict policy of non-interference in

[28] V.W. Smith, 'Akali Dal and SGPC'.

[29] Ever since the *Ghadr* episode, returned Sikh emigrants were viewed with much distrust by the Punjab government, see *ibid.*

[30] V.W. Smith, 'Akali Dal and SGPC'.

[31] 'Resolution issued by Punjab government in regard to present Sikh religious movement in the province' April 1921, in IOR: L/P&J/6/1734, part III, fos. 325–30; John Maynard, 'The Sikh Problem in the Punjab, 1920–23', p. 300.

[32] V. Connolly, Home Secretary to the Punjab government, to all district magistrates in the Punjab, 6 September 1921, in Majithia's Papers, File no. 47. Nehru Memorial Museum and Library, New Delhi.

the dispute over the gurdwara management, that was indirectly responsible for precipitating a collision between the government and the Sikhs, and radicalizing the movement. The episode which turned the course of the movement was the massacre which occurred at the Nankana Gurdwara.

Radicalization of the Akali Agitation

Built on the reputed birthplace of Guru Nanak, the first Sikh guru, the Janam Asthan shrine at Nankana occupied a special position amongst the Sikh places of worship. The incumbent *mahant*, Narain Das, a member of the Udasis sect and a *sahajdhari* Sikh, was regarded by Sikh reformers as being more Hindu than Sikh. Narain Das was not well regarded by his congregation; he was alleged, amongst other things, to have misused gurdwara funds, estimated to amount to more than 500,000 rupees a year, for personal purposes. The notoriety of Narain Das inevitably caught the attention of the reformers, who condemned his conduct and asked for his removal as *mahant* of the gurdwara. He was warned that he would be forcibly evicted if he did not voluntarily step down. Narain Das ignored the warnings, and his intransigent attitude merely intensified the demands by the Sikh reformers for militant action. As popular pressure failed to have an effect on him, an attack by the Akali *jathas* on the Janam Asthan gurdwara seemed imminent.[33] On 27 November 1920, a party of Sikhs came to the temple armed with kirpans and axes, and was confronted by a large party of armed sadhus, similarly armed, gathered by the *mahant* for his protection. The police, however, arrived in time to disperse the party, and a collision was averted. But the danger for the *mahant* had not passed as rumours of another attack on the shrine by the Akalis persisted. The harried *mahant*, fearing for his safety, sent an urgent telegram to the police to seek their protection. Sticking to his strict instructions to be neutral in gurdwara disputes, the superintendent of police dismissed the call as "unduly alarmist". Despite the

[33] The whole account of the Nankana massacre and the events leading up to it are contained in a report of 26 March 1921 by C.M. King, who was Commissioner of Lahore at the time of the massacre, and later Offg Chief Secretary to the Punjab government to the Secretary, GoI, Home Dept.

intervention by a prominent Udasi, Kartar Singh Bedi, an influential member of the Sikh landed gentry and a prominent religious leader in western Punjab, urging the deputy commissioner of Lahore to give executive protection to the *mahant* at Janam Asthan, the authorities refused to commit themselves. C.M. King, the commissioner of Lahore, and D. Currie, the deputy commissioner of Sheikhpura district, reiterated the government's stand that they were not responsible for preserving the status quo of Sikh gurdwaras, and that without an actual act of violence being carried out on the *mahant*, the police were unable to do anything. Unable to get government protection, the *mahant* had to resort to his own devices. He began fortifying his temple precincts, employed armed mercenaries, mostly Pathans, and stockpiled arms and ammunition. The confrontation reached its explosive and tragic denouement on 20 February 1921, when a *jatha* decided to take its own initiative to seize the shrine. Moments after the *jatha* had entered the temple, they were set upon by the *mahant's* mercenaries. In the ensuing bloodbath several Akalis were killed and their bodies burnt in an apparent attempt to obliterate traces of the massacre.

Troops and police arrived at the spot after news of the massacre reached the deputy commissioner. The shrine was occupied by troops, and the *mahant* and his retinue of some twenty-six mercenary Pathans were arrested and sent off to Lahore. As news of the massacre spread, a great deal of excitement was roused among the Sikhs. Large numbers began to flock to Nankana to pay homage to the memory of the killed, and to protest against the outrage. Members of *jathas*, numbering between 500 and 1,000, began arriving armed with kirpans and axes, to take up permanent quarters in the neighbourhood of the Janam Asthan.[34] In an attempt to placate the Sikhs, and to defuse a potentially explosive situation, the commissioner of Lahore and the deputy inspector of police met with leaders of the *jathas*, and agreed to withdraw troops from the Janam Asthan, and to hand over the management of the temple to a representative committee of the Akalis. The commissioner later explained his decision:

The *jathas* were apparently in a defiant mood, and angered by the hideous crime which had been committed against the Akalis; they

[34] C.M. King to Sec., GoI, Home Dept., 26 March 1921.

were not in a mood to be stopped from entering the temple by the troops, and were apparently resolved to advance on the troops to be shot down, a catastrophe which, in the existing state of feeling, might have permanently alienated the community.[35]

The massacre at Nankana opened a rift between the government and the Sikhs. The commissioner of Lahore had acted decisively in handing over control of the Janam Asthan gurdwara to a representative committee of the SGPC to prevent an immediate confrontation with the Akalis, but it did little to temper the sense of outrage felt by the Sikhs. A tirade of allegations of official complicity in the massacre rapidly created an environment full of suspicion against the government.[36] The rumours hinted that the murderous crime would not have been perpetrated by the *mahant* if it had not been for the acquiescence of the authorities. The commissioner of Lahore and his deputy commissioner were accused of having connived with the *mahant* in the killing of the reformers, and similar allegations were levelled against the government itself. It was alleged that the Punjab government knew of the *mahant's* plans but did nothing to stop him. The comments of an Akali newspaper were typical of the mood prevalent amongst the Sikhs in the aftermath of the massacre:

> The butcherly Narain Das maintained a regular workshop for the manufacture of *chavis* (billhooks) and other arms for use against the Sikhs .... four thousand *chavis* are reported to have been found in his possession, besides sixty rifles and a large quantity of ammunition. And as is well known that his preparations were not secret ... but it is nothing short of a miracle, if not a mystery, that all this escaped the notice of the police, the magistrate of the station, and the deputy commissioner, and the commissioner ... those who know ... that the *mahant*s and his proteges have very often been going to see the officials, cannot be led but to only one conclusion that all the preparations went on progressing under official connivance.[37]

---

[35] *Ibid.*

[36] Note by C. Kaye, 2 September 1921, GoI, Home (Pol.) 'A', pros. 282–315, May 1921, NAI.

[37] Quoted in Rajiv Kapur, *Sikh Separatism*, p. 111.

The consequences of the tragic incident at Nankana were manifold. First, it generated tremendous sympathy for the Akali cause, and the popularity of the movement increased in the Sikh districts of the central Punjab. This was evident by the increase in the numbers of Akali volunteers coming forward during the SGPC recruiting campaigns in the districts. Sikhs were also reported to be contributing to a "*Shahidi* (martyrs) Fund", originally instituted with the object of assisting the relatives of those who were killed at Nankana, but subsequently used to compensate relatives of volunteers who were prepared to fight for the cause of liberating the Sikh temples.[38]

The massacre had also intensified the anti-government mood amongst the Sikhs. Sikhs saw themselves as not only having to fight the corrupt *mahant*s, but also their perceived backers, the Punjab government. This in turn strengthened the SGPC's popularity as it openly jettisoned all idea of dependence on the government for the reform of Sikh gurdwaras and assumed the mantle of Sikh leadership in the struggle to liberate the Sikh gurdwaras.

The government was alarmed by the massacre at Nankana. Its refusal in the past to interfere in what was considered a religious movement had led to a bloodbath. The authorities were concerned that if they were to persist in their policy of holding aloof in the gurdwara disputes, a series of similar tragedies might occur. The conflict between the Akalis and *mahant*s, unless quickly resolved, could throw the whole of central Punjab into turmoil. The government decided at this stage that the best approach was not inactive neutrality, but to give tacit recognition to the objectives of the Akalis, and then encourage them to realize these objectives through legal and constitutional means.

In pursuit of this course of action the Punjab government sought a legislative solution to the problem of gurdwara control. It calculated that legislation passed by the newly formed Legislative Council would be a quicker and more convenient method of dealing with the shrines than the existing method of going through the long and complicated process of civil litigation. The latter could only increase the impatience of the Sikhs, who, when prompted by the militant wing of the SGPC, would be prepared to deal with the question outside the law. It was subsequently left to the Minister of Education, Fazli Hussain, to whose portfolio the management

[38] V.W. Smith, 'Akali Dal and the SGPC'.

of religious institutions belonged, to introduce a bill to overhaul the law relating to "charitable and religious endowments of the province", and to apply it to the settlement of the disputed Sikh gurdwaras.

A draft Gurdwara Bill was submitted to the Council in July 1921. The proposed Sikh Gurdwaras and Shrines Act of 1921 envisaged the establishment of a temporary board of commissioners to enquire into cases of disputed shrines, and, if necessary, to take possession of them for a period of three years, during which it would ascertain where the actual ownership of the gurdwaras lay. Once the board was constituted, all past jurisdiction of ordinary courts regarding the ownership of the temples would be superseded by any decisions taken by the board.[39] The inquiry to be conducted by the board, and its eventual findings, were to provide the basis for an eventual piece of legislation which would determine, once and for all, in whose hands the future control of the disputed Sikh gurdwaras would be placed. The representative nature of the board,[40] with an official nominee included to balance the interests of the contending parties, would ensure that the legislation would be acceptable to all concerned; and it was hoped that the legislation, formulated in this manner, would remove all religious grievances that seemed to be the very basis of the dispute over the management of the gurdwaras. In the meantime, the board of commissioners would be given full responsibility for the management of the disputed shrines. Thus, as the Punjab government noted: "as soon as this machinery is created, this government feels that one great incentive to violence will be removed, and that if violence is still resorted to, the government will command the fuller support of the public opinion in suppressing it".[41]

When the Bill was published, the SGPC signalled its strong objections to the proposal to appoint a board of commissioners to conduct an inquiry into disputed gurdwaras. It argued that the proposal merely amounted to

[39] The provisions and clauses in the Bill are found in the Sikh Gurdwaras and Shrines Act of 1921, GoI, Public and Judicial, File no. 1220 of 1921. IOR:L/P&J/6/1734, part III, fos. 308–22.

[40] At least two-thirds of the board had to be non-official Sikhs, although the term Sikh as applied in the bill was not defined. See Sikh Gurdwaras and Shrines Act of 1921.

[41] E. Joseph, Sec., Transferred Dept., GoP to Sec., GoI, Home Dept., 24 March 1921, in GoI, Home (Pol.), pros. 276–81, May 1921. NAI.

... a veiled extension of the present defective law under which gurdwaras are being attached and which treated the whole Sikh *panth*, the rightful owners, as a mere party against its servants, the *mahant*s. The effect of such legislation will be that instead of one *sabrah* [manager], whom the Sikhs have with great difficulty ousted, there will be many *sabrahs*, and instead of one Golden Temple, the government will be controlling all Sikh temples.[42]

Intervention by the government or any non-Sikhs in the management or administration of gurdwaras would be considered an encroachment on the religious liberty of the Sikhs.[43] At a large meeting at Nankana Sahib, the SGPC announced that the proposed bill would be acceptable to the community only if all members of the proposed board of commissioners were Khalsa Sikhs, with two-thirds of these appointed by the SGPC. It further stated that it would take no part in the formulation of legislation unless all Sikh prisoners arrested in connection with gurdwara reforms were released.[44]

The *sahajdhari* Sikhs and the Hindu community were equally critical of the proposed Bill. They resented the hostile allegations of corrupt conduct directed against various *mahant*s, and claimed that the government should not attempt to interfere in the traditional custom of temple management merely as a concession to the Akali section of the Sikh community.[45]

Unable to receive support from either of the contending parties, the government's attempts to legislate its way out of the crisis was clearly failing. Within the Provincial Legislative Council, similar disagreements divided members representing the Khalsa Sikhs and those sympathetic to the *sahajdhari* Sikhs. This notwithstanding, the Bill was hurriedly pushed through two select committees. But the contention over the constitution of the board proved insurmountable. Finally, with members of the council unable to come to any agreement on the Bill, the government had no option but to postpone its adoption. The 1921 Bill was finally dropped in November 1921.

---

[42] *The Tribune*, 26 March 1921.
[43] *The Tribune*, 6 April 1921.
[44] Kapur, *Sikh Separatism*, p. 119.
[45] *Ibid.*, p. 118.

Growing Militancy and the Politicization of the Movement

So far, the Punjab government had made gestures of goodwill to the Akalis, and had asserted its desire to treat as sympathetically as possible all demands which were of a religious nature.[46] It had refrained from adopting repressive measures to curb the *jathas*, despite the fact that the latter's activities often led to disturbances in the countryside. The Nankana massacre was followed by a period of restlessness in the Sikh countryside, during which the government found it necessary to arrest a number of Sikhs for "disturbances of the peace". Sikh offenders were, however, not incarcerated for long, as the authorities decided subsequently to take the view that Sikh behaviour was a result of "pardonable excitement".[47] The conciliatory approach adopted by the government was aimed at creating an amenable environment in which it could attempt to negotiate with the Sikhs to find an acceptable solution to the gurdwara disputes. The government was anxious that unless the religious grievances of the Sikhs were allayed, they would exploited by the Congress, which would, as it had tried in the Kisan agitation in the United Provinces, use the Sikhs as a "physical brigade" to engineer civil disorder in the Punjab.[48] The government's policy of assuagement was, however, construed by the reformers as weakness, and instead had the reverse effect of strengthening the extremist elements within the SGPC and the Akali Dal. This in turn contributed to the growing militancy of the movement.

As attempts at finding a legislative solution to settle the gurdwara disputes failed, reformers grew increasingly impatient with the stalemate. Those within the SGPC who counselled a more moderate approach towards temple reforms found their positions weakened by the extremist members who favoured adopting militant methods to settle the issue. In elections carried out in August 1921 to elect a new SGPC, a majority of extremists were re-elected, giving them a dominant voice within the committee. The new committee resolved that in view of the government's failure to solve

---

[46] H.D. Craik, 'Review of the Action taken by the Punjab Government to check the lawless activities of some of the Akali associations in the Punjab', 6 May 1922.

[47] H.D. Craik, 'Note on the Sikh Question', May 1922.

[48] Hailey to O'Dwyer, 6 August 1925, Hailey Papers. IOR: MSS.EUR.E.220/7B.

the problems of the Sikh gurdwaras through legislation, it would adopt a policy of non-cooperation with the government, and would resort to passive resistance against any official opposition to the Sikhs pursuit of gurdwara reform.[49] Consequently, with the SGPC adopting such a radical posture, the rhetoric and tone of the movement took on an anti-government line; subsequent attempts by the government to check the lawless activities of some of the Akali *jathas* were portrayed as the deliberate and unjust official repression of the Sikh community, to be met with resistance and civil disobedience.

In October 1921 the executive committee of the SGPC (now dominated by the extremists) demanded that the keys to the treasury of the Golden Temple be handed over to them. The treasurer of the Golden Temple was a government appointee, and his control of the finances of the temple was seen by the extremist Sikhs as an unacceptable symbol of continued official domination of the Sikhs' holiest shrine. Alarmed by the growing audacity of the SGPC, the Punjab government immediately took possession of the keys to the treasury, as a pre-emptive move to prevent the extremists Sikhs from seizing the wealth of the temple to finance a political movement.[50] To justify its actions, the government explained that the keys to the treasury of the Golden Temple would be held in its custody while it instituted a "friendly civil suit" to determine where the legal authority to manage the Golden Temple lay. Although the government had given the SGPC tacit recognition as the guardian of the Golden Temple in 1920, it now claimed that the SGPC's authority over the temple had to be legally sanctioned by a civil court before the committee could be allowed to assume total control of the shrine.

Not unexpectedly, the government's move brought about a sharp reaction from the SGPC. It charged the government with deliberately withholding control of the Golden Temple from the Sikh community, who were its rightful owners, and urged all Sikhs to protest at what it portrayed as government repression against them. A huge protest meeting was organized in Amritsar, and Akali *jathas* from all over the Punjab began congregating in the vicinity of the Golden Temple to picket and demonstrate against the seizure of the keys

---

[49] Kapur, *Sikh Separatism*, p. 123.
[50] *Ibid.*

of the treasury. By early November of 1921, thousands of Akalis were in the city demonstrating their support for the SGPC. In an act of open contempt towards the government, the SGPC issued a call to the Sikh members of the Punjab Legislative Council to resign their seats in protest, and Sikh soldiers were asked to leave the army.[51] By the end of 1921, the relationship between the Sikhs and the Punjab authorities had deteriorated significantly.

During the agitation in Amritsar, the SGPC demonstrated its ability to mount a widespread and well-organized anti-government campaign. Through its *jathabandi* system, the SGPC had established a very effective organizational network throughout central Punjab, with a chain of command that effectively linked the president of the SGPC in Amritsar to the Akali volunteers in the villages. This system of command and control enabled the SGPC and the Akali Dal to penetrate the Sikh countryside, and to carry out propaganda and the recruitment of Sikhs in a systematic and well-coordinated manner. At the beginning of the movement recruitment to the Akali Dal had proceeded in a very haphazard way; although there was a high degree of enthusiasm among the Akali volunteers, their energies were often misdirected because of the lack of any central controlling and coordinating agency. The method of enlistment and the constitution of the rural *jatha*s varied from district to district; most of the rural *jatha*s functioned as independent units, and often in times of excitement were prone to get out of control. But as the movement gathered momentum, the SGPC strengthened its control and systematized the recruiting of Akalis carried out in rural central Punjab. Akali *jatha*s and preachers from the Akali headquarters would go to the villages and arrange politico-religious *dewan*s in which they would explain the objectives of the movement. Volunteers would then be gathered together and grouped into *jatha*s, which were usually named after the area to which they belonged or after some Sikh patron.[52]

Each *jatha* functioned as it own propaganda unit; it possessed its own *granthis, ragis* and *updeshaks*, whose duties were to tour the villages, hold *dewan*s, encourage the enlistment of Akalis and disseminate Akali propaganda. *Jatha*s were expected to meet the expenses

[51] V.W. Smith, 'Akali Dal and SGPC'.
[52] Mohinder Singh, *The Akali Movement*, p. 93.

of all local *dewan*s and local propaganda. This money was taken from the *jatha* fund, to which all members were expected to contribute. The normal subscription rate averaged four annas per month or, in some cases, ten per cent of the income of an Akali. Members performing national work, however, were paid by the Akali Dal, reported to be at the rate of twenty to twenty-five rupees a month. This money was derived from a central gurdwara fund, which was kept at the disposal of the SGPC. Communication between *jatha*s and the Akali Dal was carried out by messengers. These were employed for rapid transmission of important information which needed to be kept secret. The Akali Dal had learnt to refrain from utilizing telegraphic and postal services when important instructions had to be transmitted, knowing that these could easily be intercepted by the government.[53]

What particularly alarmed the Punjab government during the agitation was the ability of the Sikhs to organize themselves along military lines, evidently applying the knowledge and experience which the ex-soldiers amongst them had acquired in the Indian Army. Military-style campsites were established to accommodate the approximately 50,000 Akalis who had congregated in Amritsar for the agitation in 1921. The camps were laid out in a military fashion complete with proper watering and sanitary arrangements. Duties performed by the Akalis were of a semi-military nature, which consisted of protecting the temples in the vicinity at which sentries equipped with Sam Brown belts and swords of a uniform pattern were posted. Sentries were relieved at fixed hours and registers were maintained to ensure correct rotation of duty. A body of some 400 Sikh volunteers was also employed to attend to the detraining and entraining of visitors, and to conduct them to camps and serais where accommodation could be obtained. An army of hand-picked Akalis, estimated at about 5,000, and containing a large proportion of ex-soldiers, was kept in reserve to deal with any emergency that might arise. This force was kept under the command of an ex-subedar of the Indian Army and it showed that it was capable of operating in military fashion, responding to commands conveyed by whistle and hand signals. The SGPC even possessed its own intelligence unit, to keep an eye on government

---

[53] V.W. Smith, 'Akali Dal and SGPC'.

officials or those who were known or believed to be hostile to the Akali movement.[54]

In addition to the local *jathas*, a central force of Akali volunteers, known as the Akali Fauj, was created and organized under the direct supervision of the SGPC. The Criminal Intelligence Bureau described them as the Sikh reproduction of the volunteer movement of the Congress, and the military authorities saw the Fauj as the "potential rebel army of the Sikhs".[55] In 1922, the Fauj was reputed to have a strength of 30,000 men. Military intelligence reported that the Fauj was a disciplined and well-organized body; its volunteers marched in fours, wore badges, carried flags and were armed with knives, cudgels, battle-axes, and even firearms, mostly sporting guns obtained under license by retired soldiers. The Fauj was believed to have up to battalion size formations and its own "staff organization".[56] It had the organizational ability to carry out house-to-house collection of funds, payment of and rations for volunteers, and the performance of routine administrative chores in shrines under the control of local Akali *jathas*.

What all this revealed was that the SGPC had at its disposal a well-organized and coordinated semi-military force which it could use when the occasion warranted as the basis of a widespread rebellion in the province.[57] Unlike the *Ghadr* rebellion, the Akali movement did not suffer from a lack of widespread support and organization; its ability to mobilize and organize the Sikhs therefore presented a significant military threat to the authorities. As army headquarters noted,

... the situation today in the Punjab is very similar to that which pertained in 1919, before the outbreak. There is, however, one very important difference; namely, the existence of definite organization which was lacking on the former occasion.[58]

[54] Lieutenant General J.S.M. Shea, Offg Chief of General Staff, 'The Military Aspect of the Present Situation in the Punjab', Army Headquarters, 24 February 1922, GoI, Home (Pol.), pros. 459/II, 1922.

[55] *Ibid*.

[56] *Ibid*.

[57] 'Note on the present Akali situation with suggestions for future policy', by Sir Reginald Arthur Mant, Revenue and Finance Sec., Viceroy's Council, 30 October 1923, Hailey Papers. IOR: MSS.EUR.E.220/6A.

[58] Lieutenant General J.S.M. Shea, 'The Military Aspect of the Present Situation in the Punjab', 24 February 1922.

Besides the organizational strengths of the movement, the government was worried that the SGPC was enjoying popular support from the Sikh peasantry, its propaganda having escalated anti-government feelings amongst the entire Sikh rural population.[59] In January 1922 the Punjab government noted,

> The Akali movement is gaining ground in the villages, and by an organized system of propaganda the Shiromani Gurdwara Parbhandak Committee has succeeded in persuading the ordinary Sikh zamindar that it is really representative of the *panth* (community) generally and that the actions of the government are both dubious and harsh ... at the present, the rate of conversion of the average villager to this state of mind is increasing at an alarming rate and the entire rural Sikh population is within measurable distance of turning against the government and joining the propagandists in active denunciation of the government. Should this come to pass ... words will soon give way to deeds and open rebellion will begin.[60]

As the authorities saw it, the SGPC was clearly utilizing its popularity as the champion of Sikh religious aspirations to mount a challenge against the authority of the government.[61]

By the end of 1921, the government was losing considerable ground to the SGPC and the Akali Dal in the Sikh countryside over what became known as the "Keys affair". In an attempt to bring the situation under control, the government evoked the Seditious Meetings Act, and began arresting several leaders and prominent speakers in Amritsar. But these measures failed to contain the defiance of the agitators. As arrests of the leaders continued, new ones emerged to take their place. The effect created by the arrests proved detrimental for the government, as they served to fuel SGPC propaganda that the government was determined to destroy the Sikh religion.

In an attempt to put an end to Sikh intransigence, the government tried to negotiate with the SGPC to come to an agreement

[59] FR 15 January 1922, GoI, Home (Pol.), pros. 18 of January 1922. NAI.

[60] FR, 15 January 1922.

[61] 'Note on the present Akali situation...,' R.A. Mant, 30 October 1923, in Hailey Papers. IOR:MSS.EUR.E.220/6A.

over the administration of the Golden Temple. But the SGPC, sensing that it now had the upper hand, refused to negotiate with the government until all prisoners arrested during the agitation were unconditionally released. The government made a further conciliatory gesture by offering to hand over the keys to the SGPC, pending a decision by the civil courts, to enable it to proceed with the celebrations of the birthday anniversary of Guru Gobind Singh. The SGPC rejected this and reiterated its stand that no negotiations were possible until the government released all Sikh prisoners arrested in connection with the gurdwara dispute.

In early 1922, the Punjab government had become increasingly nervous regarding the political situation in the Sikh districts. The unrest over the "Keys affair" had coincided with the height of the Congress Non-cooperation movement. Congress activists in the Punjab had tried to exploit the Sikh unrest, to enlarge it into a wider nationalist struggle against the government. In January 1922, the nationalist Sikh political party, the Central Sikh League, resolved to increase Sikh participation in the non-cooperation movement, and appealed to the Sikh masses to join the Congress-led civil disobedience campaign. Party activists then went on an intensive campaign in the Sikh districts to spread the propaganda of non-cooperation. The government reported that in the second half of February 1922, the number of political meetings had increased from 100 in the previous fortnight to 350, and most of them were held in the Sikh districts.[62]

By 1922, army authorities reported that the general unrest in the Sikh villages had begun to permeate into the ranks of the Indian Army. Although numerous attempts had been made to undermine the loyalty of the Sikh soldier since the start of the movement, the army had so far withstood "the campaign of sedition". However, the army authorities were becoming increasingly concerned that with the SGPC's organizational network gathering in strength and efficiency, agitators were apparently meeting with some success in engineering agitation amongst the Sikhs in the Indian Army, and doubts were now expressed as to how long the army could remain entirely unaffected.[63] In January 1922, Lieutenant Colonel R.H. Anderson, an officer of the 45th Sikh Regiment, reported that

[62] FR, 28 February 1922.
[63] Lieutenant General J.S.M. Shea, 'The Military Aspect of the Present Situation in the Punjab', 24 February 1922.

a few of his Sikh officers were of the opinion that the unrest in the Punjab was growing to dangerous proportions, and was beginning to have an affect on the Sikh regiments in the army.[64] These fears were not unfounded. Since the Nankaná massacre, recruiting officers had reported difficulties in obtaining Sikh recruits,[65] and Sikh units were believed to be in constant touch with the SGPC, directly or indirectly, seeking its advice on all matters affecting Sikhs in the army regiments. Disaffection had been noticed in several Sikh regiments, while Sikh soldiers, in defiance of army regulations, had begun wearing black turbans and carrying kirpans while in uniform. Although the army authorities dealt firmly with Sikh soldiers who flouted army regulations, they were concerned that their behaviour was symptomatic of the general mood of defiance of authority that had began to affect the Sikh regiments.[66] Disaffection amongst the Sikhs was further fuelled by agitators spreading rumours that the government no longer trust the Sikhs, and that all Sikh units were to be disbanded.[67] The loyalty of the Sikhs had become so affected by February 1922 that the commandant of the Jullunder Brigade Area, where most of the Sikh regiments were based, reported that he could no longer send Sikh regiments out in aid of the civil power, and that his officers commanding Sikh regiments were urging that Sikhs should be removed from the disaffected areas.[68]

The campaign to win over the Sikh soldier to the Akali cause was not only conducted in the cantonments and regiments; soldiers on home leave, as well as their families, were often targets of the Akali agitators. Akalis were reported to have resorted to persecution and bullying tactics to harass soldiers and their families in the villages who refused to join their ranks. Insults, boycotts, cutting of the use of wells, of facilities and other conveniences of

[64] Report by Lieutenant Colonel R.H. Anderson, 45 Sikh Regiment, 6 February 1922, in GoI, Home (Pol.), 459/II.

[65] FR, 15 January 1922.

[66] The units affected were 13th–16th Cavalry, 14th Sikhs, 19th Punjabis and 9th Bhopal Infantry. See 'Brief Note on Trouble in four Indian Units during February 1922' in GoI, Home (Pol.), pros. 459/II, 1922.

[67] Report by Sant Singh, Criminal Intelligence Bureau, 7 March 1922, in GoI, Home (Pol.), pros. 459/II of 1922.

[68] Memo from Colonel Commandant W.F. Bainbridge, Jullunder Brigade Area, to Headquarters, Lahore District, Lahore Cantonment, 8 February, 1922 in GoI, Home (Pol.) pros. 459/II, 1922.

village life were some of the ways in which the Akalis sought to make things very difficult for the loyalists.[69] In 1922, the wives and families of the 23rd Sikh Pioneers petitioned against the despatch of the unit on field service for fear of being subjected to Akali mockery and harassment when their men went away on duty.[70]

Finding that its position on the Sikhs was becoming untenable, and not wishing to further alienate the rural Sikh population, the government decided to back down over the "Keys" issue. It withdrew the civil suit which it had taken up against the SGPC, accorded the SGPC full recognition as the body responsible for managing the Golden Temple, and handed to it the keys of the treasury. All prisoners arrested in connection with the recent agitation were moreover released. The government hoped that by conceding on the "Keys affair", it could reconcile moderate Sikh opinion and remove the basis for further Sikh agitation, which was clearly having an unfavourable effect on the Sikh military districts in central Punjab, as well as the Sikh regiments in the army. But they miscalculated on this.

The immediate impact of the concession was to boost the popularity and prestige of the SGPC, and bolster the strength of the movement. The SGPC had emerged triumphant from its first trial of strength with the government; it had not only won back the keys to the Golden Temple, but had secured the release of the Sikh prisoners as well. The commissioners of Jullunder and Lahore divisions reported that the "Keys affair" was regarded as an "unqualified triumph by the Sikh community".[71] In the immediate aftermath of the agitation in Amritsar, the Punjab authorities reported a boost in the popularity of the SGPC and the Akali Dal. It was then reported that membership to the Akali Dal had doubled in the few months following the return of the keys to the treasury of the Golden Temple, and the movement had gained strength in the Sikh countryside.[72]

[69] Recruiting Officer, Jullunder, to the Chief of the General Staff, Simla, 3 March 1922, in GoI, Home (Pol.), pro. 459/II, 1922.

[70] Report from Officer Commanding of 23 Sikh Pioneers, 2 February 1922, in GoI, Army Department, note of 1922, Home (Pol.), File no. 415.

[71] FR, 31 January 1922.

[72] 'Sikhs and the Government', pamphlet published by Punjab government, 27 November 1922, in Salmon Papers, No. 44, File no. 4, Centre for South Asian Studies (SAS), Cambridge.

The government's concession to the SGPC had backfired. Instead of improving its position in the Sikh districts, the government's standing was soon deteriorating rapidly amongst the Sikh peasantry. Intelligence reports revealed that the numbers of Akali *jathas* were increasing rapidly, and becoming more hostile to the government. Entire villages were reported to have "gone Akali", sometimes forced to do so through intimidation and force.[73] In districts controlled by the Akalis, it was reported that a general campaign of intimidation and defiance of authority was being carried out. Loyalist elements were especially targeted by the Akalis. Subordinate officials, zaildars, village headmen and others who were thought to be in sympathy with the government or had given evidence in political trials were boycotted or humiliated, and acts were openly committed to engender contempt for authority. Frequent speeches were made by Sikhs threatening to take forcible action against police stations and other government buildings, and preaching direct incitements to the public to violent defiance of the law.[74]

The position of the Akalis was so dominant in the villages that loyalist elements—the pensioners, landed gentry and so on—found themselves in a position of weakness, largely because, it was claimed, of the government's inability, or refusal, to take firm action against the Akalis. As a result, the Akalis were brave enough to openly preach anti-government propaganda, sometimes even in government and cantonment schools.[75] In the villages the militants became bolder, while the moderate loyalist Sikhs, on whose local influence the government had previously relied as a form of social and political control over the Sikh soldier population, was cowed into ineffectiveness. Sikh pensioners, sympathetic to the Akalis, organized Akali societies to rival the loyalist pensioners' clubs and DSBs in the Sikh districts. With the state's rural intermediaries being forced into retreat, the government had in effect lost control over the Akali-controlled districts. In some villages, Akalis were rapidly coming to be regarded as a privileged class, owing to the manner in which they moved about in armed bodies, terrorizing

[73] *Civil and Military Gazette*, 9 November 1922, Lahore, in Salmon Papers, No. 50A, File no. 4, SAS, Cambridge.

[74] H.D. Craik, 'Review of action taken by the Punjab government to check the lawless activities of the Akalis...', 6 May 1922, GoP, Home Proceedings. IOR:P/11277.

[75] Report from the Recruiting Officer, Jullunder, to the Chief of the General Staff, Simla, 3 March 1922, Jullunder, in GoI, Home (Pol.), pros. 459/II of 1922. NAI.

passers-by with open displays of swords and battle-axes, travelling in trains without tickets and displaying open contempt for the government. They were often a law upon themselves, setting up non-cooperation courts to carry out trials of Sikhs guilty of offences against the movement. Consequently, in many parts of central Punjab, the contempt for law was widespread.[76]

When reports of the extent of the disturbances reached the GoI and Army Headquarters in Delhi, alarm signals were soon raised. Both the central government and Army Headquarters feared that continued disturbances in the central districts of the Punjab would have a negative effect on the Indian Army, and even worse, that a Sikh mutiny might erupt. Members of the Viceroy's Council were unanimous in their belief that the movement should be quelled before it got out of hand. S.P. O'Donnel, Secretary in the GoI's Home Department, whose approach was supported by Sir William Vincent, urged that "drastic action should be taken at once against the Akalis."[77] Another member of the Council, C.A. Innes, argued in favour of "dispersing the Akalis by force and reasserting [government] authority in the Punjab".[78] The views of the Council were shared by the general staff in Army Headquarters, which suggested that the situation in the Punjab could be effectively dealt with by calling in the troops.[79]

Despite exhortations from the Delhi government and the army authorities, and clear evidence of the continued militancy of the movement, the Punjab government decided against calling in the army to deal with the militant Sikhs. It argued that army officers in the Punjab were still unsure if such a step was necessary, and indeed advisable; they would rather err on the side of caution. The Punjab government was aware that a full-scale repression of the Akalis could precipitate a terrible backlash from the Sikhs, who at this time seemed willy-nilly to be fully behind the SGPC and the Akalis. Furthermore, repressive military action on the movement would permanently alienate the Sikhs in the Punjab and lose for the army an important source of recruits from the districts of the central Punjab.

[76] V.W. Smith, 'Akali Dal and SGPC'.

[77] Note by S.P. O'Donnel, 18 February 1922, GoI, Home (Pol.), pros. 459/II. NAI.

[78] Notes by C.A. Innes, 2 February 1922, in Note by S.P. O'Donnel, 18 February 1922.

[79] Lieutenant General J.S.M. Shea, 'The Military Aspect of the Present Situation in the Punjab', 24 February 1922.

The Punjab government believed that the Sikh peasants were simply being misled, and that the extremist leadership, under the influence of the Congress, was to blame for the anti-government mood of the Sikhs. The crux of the problem, the provincial government felt, was to bring back the ordinary Sikh peasants and soldiers, "the simple minded non-political majority", to reason,[80] and to break the extremist leadership which was gaining political mileage by appearing to champion the Sikh cause in the face of government persecution. It therefore decided to persist in the strategy of divorcing the political issues from the religious. Regarding the SGPC's demands, the government explained its position in an official communiqué:

> [The] Government desire[s] to explain in deciding in January last to leave the administration of the Golden Temple in the hands of the committee, it was guided by the consideration that no opposition was made by any Sikh body to the adoption of that course and accordingly the committee might be looked on as representing a large section of Sikh religious opinion on the subject of Sikh gurdwaras. In dealing with questions connected with Sikh shrines the government is prepared to take a similar attitude so long as the committee confines itself to religious matters and does not adopt undesirable political activities. In cases where offences are committed in respect of shrines, local officers will of course be guided by the requirements of order and of the law, but in dealing with such offences and in discussing possible arrangements in connection with shrines for the prevention of the breach of peace ... the local officers are at liberty ... to consult the Shiromani Gurdwara Parbhandhak Committee or its local representatives, and to give to their views on the gurdwara questions the attention due to the representatives of a large section of Sikh religious sentiment on the subject.[81]

While the government reiterated its sympathy with the religious objectives of the Akali movement, it at the same time sought to dampen the enthusiasm of the Sikhs for the SGPC's tactics of direct political

---

[80] FR, 15 January 1922.

[81] Punjab Govt. Press communique, 10 March 1922, GoI, Home (Pol.), pros. 459/II of 1922.

action. It decided subsequently to embark on a low key operation to disband Akali *jathas* in central Punjab. On 20 March 1922, an extensive operation aimed at suppressing Sikh political activities was started simultaneously in the thirteen Sikh majority districts.[82] In carrying out these operations the government decided to use the police and not troops from the army so that there was no danger of excessive force being used against the Sikhs. However, as a precautionary measure, police action was backed in most cases by the military on stand-by.[83] In districts where there were no military cantonments, troops were called in as a backup for police action. District officers were instructed to use as little force as possible while breaking up bands marching about the country in military formation. They were only to arrest the leaders and organizers of these bands, persons guilty of intimidation and violence, and those who had taken part in meetings where seditious speeches had been delivered. District and police officers were told to be careful not to provide any pretext for representing the action taken as interference with religion; for instance shrines were not to be forcibly entered and meetings at which the Granth Sahibs were present were to be respected till the meetings dispersed.[84] Deputy commissioners were instructed to explain to Sikhs that the action taken was directed solely against the political activities of the Akali bands and not aimed at persecuting the Sikh religion.[85]

In the following weeks, the gradualist and low key approach adopted by the Punjab government seemed to bring about a decline in Akali activities. In any case, enthusiasm amongst the Sikh peasantry had waned due to the commencement of harvesting activities in March 1922. Also, the collapse of the Khilafat non-cooperation movement in February 1922 on Gandhi's orders removed the context of excitement in the Punjab, which could have had a cautionary effect on the Akalis. By the end of April, the incidence of disturbances and temple seizures in the Sikh districts had

[82] 'Operations against the Akalis', S.P. O'Donnell to Sir William Duke, Under Sec. of State, India, 20 April 1922. IORL/P&J/6/1734, part II, fos. 223–29.

[83] *Ibid.*, fo. 225.

[84] 'Instructions bearing of present political situation in the Punjab', from Chief Sec., GoP to all Deputy Commissioners of Sikh districts, 16 February 1922. IOR:L/P&J/6/1734, part II, fos. 235–38.

[85] *Ibid.*; see also Craik, 'Review of action taken against the Akalis...', 6 May 1922.

dropped dramatically. In the summer of 1922, an uneasy calm prevailed in the central Punjab. The lull, however, proved to be short-lived. In August 1922, a quarrel over access to the grounds of a Sikh gurdwara at the Guru Ka Bagh, situated about twelve miles from Amritsar city, sparked off another confrontation between the Akalis and the government, and a resurgence of the movement.

Sited at the Guru Ka Bagh were two gurdwaras, surrounded by a large piece of agricultural land belonging to the incumbent *mahant*, an Udasi Sikh. In August 1921 a party of Akalis had seized the larger of the two gurdwaras and, after some negotiations with the *mahant*, retained possession of it. The *mahant*, however, remained in control of the other gurdwara, and the land surrounding it. In August 1922, trouble started when a party of Akalis entered the *mahant*'s land to cut trees for use as fuel for a communal feast in the gurdwara controlled by them. The *mahant* complained to the district officer that the act amounted to theft as the trees were removed from his property without his prior permission. The police were called, and after some investigations, five Akalis were arrested and tried for theft. Angered by the attitude of the *mahant*, the SGPC despatched *jatha*s to cut down more trees on the land claimed by the *mahant*. To prevent the resurgence of the excesses of the Akalis, and fearful that if the *mahant* was left to his own devices another Nankana massacre might happen, the government decided to arrest the perpetrators.[86] The SGPC refused to be intimidated, and in defiance of police warnings made repeated attempts to gather wood from the land around the gurdwara. The police responded by making arrests for theft and criminal trespass. The arrests generated an excited response from the Akalis, and *jatha*s began to converge at the Guru Ka Bagh to defy government arrests; by 26 August, the Deputy Commissioner of Amritsar reported that some 1,200 Akalis had assembled at the shrine.[87] The authorities, encouraged by their recent success in restraining Akali activities in the Sikh districts, tried to contain the situation by forcibly dispersing *jatha*s before they could reach Guru Ka Bagh. Despite police beatings and arrests *jatha*s continued to pour into the disputed site from all over the Punjab.

[86] Statement by the Punjab government regarding Guru Ka Bagh, GoI, Home (Pol.), pros. 914 of 1922. NAI.
[87] 'Sikhs and the Government', 1922, p. 5.

Sensing the opportunity to revive the flagging movement, the SGPC decided to make the incident at Guru Ka Bagh the focal point of its agitation. From late August, the SGPC despatched Akali *jathas*, each comprising about fifty men, from Amritsar to Guru Ka Bagh to carry out non-violent defiance of the authorities. These persistent acts of passive resistance, with Akalis marching up to the police to be beaten and arrested, gave the SGPC and the Akalis much publicity and sympathy, and provoked widespread anti-government passions amongst the Sikhs. The march from Amritsar to Guru Ka Bagh became a rallying point for the Akalis, and again roused popular Sikh support as it soon took on the form of a holy pilgrimage.[88]

Table 5.1
Involvement of Sikh Jats and Ex-Soldiers in Akali *Jathas*
November 1921–February 1922

Region	Number of Akalis	Percentage of Jat Sikhs	Percentage of Ex-Soldiers
Doaba	1,974	85.8	15
Malwa	1,277	78.2	25.9
Manjha	3,994	66.9	8.0
Total *	**11,245**	**74.0**	**12.9**

Note: * Numbers including areas outside the above-mentioned regions.
Source: Government of India, Home/Political Proceedings, 459/11 of 1922, National Archives of India.

The government's decision to contain the situation proved unsuccessful. As in the "Keys affair", the SGPC was able to mobilize the Sikhs into a prolonged contest against the government at Guru Ka Bagh through its *jathabandi* system. The Sikh peasantry was roused into opposition against the government, and, once again, the excitement began affecting Sikh regiments in the Indian Army. Many ex-soldiers were reported to have joined the Akali Dal in large numbers in the summer of 1922. This was most noticeable in Ludhiana district, the recruiting ground of several Sikh regiments, where out of a total of 672 known Akali activists, no less than 210 were reported to be either pensioned or discharged soldiers.[89] Sikh soldiers from the Peshawar cantonment sent subscriptions to the SGPC to demonstrate their support for the Sikh struggle.[90] During

[88] FR, 15 September 1922.
[89] V.W. Smith 'Akali Dal and SGPC'; see Table 5.1.
[90] FR, 15 September 1922.

the visit of the Prince of Wales to the Punjab in 1922, Sikh soldiers and pensioners were prevented by Akali activists from attending the official reception.[91] To demonstrate its popularity in the military districts, the SGPC formed a pensioner *jatha* of about a hundred Sikh ex-officers and soldiers and sent them off to Guru Ka Bagh with much publicity. In October 1922, British commanders of Sikh regiments reported that their soldiers were more likely to obey orders from the SGPC rather than their own commanders when it came to Sikh-related matters.[92] The military concern was perhaps best summed up by the commander of the Jullunder Brigade Area Command, who noted after his tour of the district:

> I have no hesitation to say that disloyalty prevailed to an extent which has to be experienced to be believed.... The disloyalty embraces all classes and is inspired by the SGPC, which has a secret grip on all Sikhs. Its prestige is very high and very little escapes its notice; its agents are everywhere ... until the government shows its ability to control or breakup the Sikhs, it will not be able to depend on the loyalty of the Malwa Sikhs ... the damage done by the *jatha*s in the opinion of the Sikh officers is being underestimated. It is said that disorder may break out before the rains.[93]

The Punjab government was, once again, put on the defensive. The non-violent protest at the Guru Ka Bagh had strengthened the moral grounds of the movement, and SGPC propaganda against government brutality was once again stirring up popular resentment against the authorities.[94] The government felt compelled to avoid a confrontation which might yet precipitate a rebellion by the Sikhs. To defuse the tension at Guru Ka Bagh, it decided to allow *jatha*s access to the shrine at Guru Ka Bagh itself, but, not wishing to encourage a disregard for the law, which might strengthen the Akalis, insisted that trespass into the disputed piece

[91] Gwynne to O'Donnel, 20 September 1922, Home (Pol.), pros. 914, 1922.
[92] *Ibid.*
[93] 'Report of Tour of Jullunder District', in GoI, Home (Pol.), pros. 15/II, 1924.
[94] See C.F. Andrews' eyewitness account of the Guru Ka Bagh incident in Ruchi Ram Sahni (ed. Ganda Singh), *Struggle for Reforms in the Sikh Shrines*, Sikh Ithas Research Board, SGPC, Amritsar, n.d., pp. 176–83.

of property by *jathas* would not be tolerated. In the meantime, the government persisted in its arrests, particularly of Akali leaders, with the hope of weakening the movement by depriving it of its leadership. This approach was aptly summed up by one officer:

> If the [Akalis] attempt to wear down the government by some form of non-violence, we should try to deal with them as a mob of cattle driven into the city to obstruct traffic. In such cases, we should not hurt or impound the cattle but to punish the men who drove them in.[95]

At the end of 1922 the arrests of Akali leaders and volunteers turning up daily at Guru Ka Bagh had clearly not succeeded in stemming the flow of the *jathas*. The government had hoped that the Sikhs would soon tire of marching to Guru Ka Bagh, and that the autumn rainfall would encourage the Sikh peasants to return to the fields, depriving the SGPC of recruits. But the rains did not bring about the desired effect. *Jathas* continued to arrive at the disputed site, and arrests continued; by November 1922, some 4,000 Akalis had been arrested in connection with the agitation at Guru Ka Bagh.[96]

As the government reviewed the situation, it came to the conclusion that continued repression was not going to solve the problem. The very basis of the Guru Ka Bagh agitation and the "Keys affair" was the controversy surrounding the management of the Sikh temples. Unless the source of the problem was tackled Sikh unrest would persist. The government therefore decided to return to the negotiating table to try to get a piece of legislation that would settle, once and for all, the thorny issue of temple management.

The attempt in 1921 to find a legislative solution to the dispute over temple management had foundered on disagreements over the constitution of the board of commissioners. In August 1922, in the midst of the Guru Ka Bagh agitation, a new bill was drafted by the government, which sought to overcome that problem by making vital concessions to the Akalis. Under its provisions, the official representative on the board was to be omitted, and two of the

---

[95] 'Note on the present Akali situation...', A.R. Mant, 30 October 1923, in Hailey Papers, MSS.EUR.E.220/6A.
[96] FR, 31 October 1922.

remaining three members of the board were to be Akali Sikhs, each to be nominated by the SGPC and the Sikh members of the Legislative Council. To satisfy the *sahajdharis* and Hindus, the bill stipulated that the board would not be empowered to adjudicate in all Sikh gurdwaras, only in the ones which were listed as "disputed". In all other aspects, the new bill of 1922 was similar to the 1921 version.[97]

Despite these concessions, the Sikh Gurdwaras and Shrines Bill of 1922 met with objections from all concerned parties when it was published on 15 September 1922. The SGPC refused to consider the bill until all Sikh prisoners were released. With the SGPC intransigent, Sikh members of the provincial legislature found their positions undermined. The Guru Ka Bagh incident had boosted the prestige and popularity of the SGPC, which was now regarded by the majority of Sikhs as leaders of the community. If Sikh members were to accept the bill without the support of the SGPC, they would lose the support of Sikh voters, thereby jeopardizing their own political positions. The *sahajdharis* and Hindus, on the other hand, were still unhappy that the bill had not provided enough safeguards to protect their religious rights.[98]

The negative reception of the bill notwithstanding, the government decided that it would not ease up on the initiative at this stage and decided to push through the bill, even in the face of opposition from the Sikh and Hindu members of the Legislative Council. On 18 November 1922, with the support of the official and Muslim members, the bill was adopted by the Punjab Legislative Council. However, although the bill was passed, it proved to be a dead letter because the SGPC and the Sikh members refused to nominate their representatives to the board as provided by the bill.

In the meantime, while the bill was being considered in the Council, the government received a fortunate reprieve in the dispute at Guru Ka Bagh. A Hindu philanthropist, Sir Ganga Ram, offered the government a way out by agreeing to lease the disputed piece of land at Guru Ka Bagh from the *mahant*, and then permit access to the property. The government seized upon this opportunity and arranged for the land to be leased to him for a

---

[97] See 'A Bill to provide for the Administration and Management of certain Sikh gurdwaras and shrines, and for an enquiry in the matters connected therewith', *Punjab Gazette*, 17 November 1922.

[98] Kapur, *Sikh Separatism*, pp. 158–60.

year. The new tenant requested that the police deployed around the site be removed, and on 17 November 1922 the arrest of Akalis at Guru Ka Bagh ceased.

The termination of arrests at Guru Ka Bagh and the passage of the bill in the Council enabled the government to go on the offensive against the SGPC. It launched a propaganda campaign among the Sikh peasantry to emphasize the government's readiness to fulfil the religious objectives of the Sikhs, and meetings were arranged with Sikh troops to elucidate the government's position regarding the Sikh unrest.[99]

The GoI, in the meantime, urged the Punjab government to press on with the formation of the board of commissioners as provided by the 1922 Act. This was most strongly advocated by Sir Malcolm Hailey, finance member of the Viceroy's Executive Council. He argued that the bill by itself would not solve the problem relating to the dispute of the gurdwaras, but that the formation of a board to take charge of disputed gurdwaras would undermine the credibility of the SGPC as the champion of the Sikh cause, and would eventually remove the basis of its support.[100] Hailey's views were supported by the other members of the Viceroy Council, who urged the Punjab government to appoint the board of commissioners as soon as possible.[101]

The Punjab government, however, decided on another approach to the problem, one that it hoped would effect a permanent settlement of the gurdwara disputes and which would remove the source of further Sikh unrest. Reports reaching officials at Lahore had indicated that there was a divergence of opinion within the movement's leadership with regard to the course of action to pursue after the cessation of the Guru Ka Bagh agitation. The Akali Dal wanted to persist in militant action and the continued seizure of shrines, but the moderate section of the SGPC preferred at this stage to negotiate with the government. It was not difficult to see the reason behind the desire of the SGPC to adopt a more moderate stance. The SGPC was disconcerted by the 1922 Act, which now enabled the government to form a board to manage the disputed temples. Once that happened, the basis of the agitation would be removed and with that the authority of the SGPC within the Sikh community as

[99] Note by C.M.G. Ogilvie, 4 November 1922, GoI, Home (Pol.), pros. 914, 1922.
[100] Note by W.M. Hailey, 15 November 1922, in *ibid*.
[101] S.P. O'Donnel to H.D. Craik, 20 November 1922, in *ibid*.

well. It was therefore very much against its interests, at this stage, to be intransigent, and to provoke the government into constituting the board.[102] The SGPC therefore agreed to negotiate with the government for a permanent settlement of the gurdwara disputes. Negotiations were initiated, but for several months achieved no results. The major stumbling block was the question of prisoner release. The Punjab government agreed, in private discussions with members of the SGPC, to release Sikh political prisoners on the condition that the SGPC would publicly announce its disapproval of illegal seizure of shrines. The SGPC refused, and the negotiations stalled.

In the summer of 1923, confrontation flared up between the Sikhs and the government once again, this time over the abdication of the ruler of the princely state of Nabha. When the Punjab government announced that the Maharajah of Nabha had abdicated in favour of his son, the Akalis were quick to see in this a forced abdication. It was believed that the maharajah was being punished for having been a keen supporter of the Akali movement. The SGPC accordingly decided to launch an agitation to reinstate the maharajah.[103] It issued calls to Sikhs to protest against the Nabha's abdication, and proceeded through its propaganda machinery to whip up anti-government feelings once again. To prevent trouble from erupting, the Nabha authorities prohibited all political meetings from taking place in the princely state and began arresting any Akalis who gathered there. As with the "Keys" affair and the Guru Ka Bagh protests, the Akalis adopted an intransigent attitude, and in open defiance against the injunctions of the state, continued to hold public meetings in various parts of Nabha, during which virulent anti-government speeches were made. During one such meeting at Jaito, the state authorities responded by arresting the speakers involved. In an attempt to give the entire episode a religious complexion, the Akalis initiated an Akhand Path (a three day non-stop prayer) at the gurdwara at Jaito. When the police moved in to forcibly remove the participants, the SGPC were quick to accuse the government of forcible interruption of a sacred Sikh ceremony. The unaccomplished Akhand Path subsequently became the issue of

---

[102] FR, 30 November 1922.

[103] For a fuller account of the events that led to the abdication of the ruler of the Nabha, see Mohinder Singh, *The Akali Movement*, p. 180.

contention between the Sikhs and the authorities, and on the orders of the SGPC, *jathas* began to converge at Jaito in an attempt to resume the unfinished ceremony.

For the Punjab government, the SGPC's protest against the abdication was an indication that it was now getting openly involved not only in gurdwara disputes, but in political matters also. This was the clearest evidence that the movement for temple reform had developed into an outright political contest between the government and the SGPC. In October 1923, the government accordingly declared the SGPC and Akali Dal illegal and rounded up its leaders.

Attention on the Nabha agitation and the arrests were momentarily diverted by elections to the Provincial Legislative Council in December 1923. Just before the elections, the SGPC decided to field its own candidates to run for the Sikh seats, so as to extend its influence in the Provincial Legislative Council via the Sikh members. The elections turned out to be a stunning success for the SGPC candidates; they managed to secure an overwhelming majority of Sikh votes, and in only one Sikh constituency, out of eleven Sikh rural constituencies, was the SGPC candidate defeated.[104] It was mainly due to the results of the 1923 elections that the rural Sikh members of the Punjab legislatures were never fully incorporated into the Punjab National Unionist Party.

In the meantime, while arrests were carried out against militant leaders of the SGPC, the government tried to appeal to the moderate section of the SGPC leadership to accept the 1922 Act. The moderates within the SGPC for their part were becoming increasingly anxious that enthusiasm in the movement would not last unless tangible results were achieved regarding the gurdwara disputes. Already the SGPC was having difficulties finding volunteers for continued *jathas* to Nabha, a problem that was likely to worsen with the approaching harvesting season.

In 1924 Sir William Birdwood, Officer Commanding the Northern Command, was appointed by the Delhi government to conduct negotiations with the Akalis on the question of gurdwara legislation. The choice of General Birdwood, made by Sir Malcolm Hailey and the Viceroy, Lord Reading, was one that was calculated towards winning back the confidence of the Sikhs in the army and

---

[104] FR, 15 December 1923; Kripal C. Yadav, Elections in the Punjab, 1920–47 New Delhi, 1987, pp. 56–57.

the peasantry. Birdwood was a popular figure amongst the Sikhs, having had a long and intimate association with them during his military career in which he had commanded a succession of Sikh regiments. He was well versed in *gurmukhi*, the Sikh written script, and was familiar with the Sikh religion. Birdwood commanded much respect amongst the Sikh soldiery and was a military figure with whom the Sikhs, especially those who had served in the army, could identify with.[105] It was hoped that Birdwood, a military man untainted by any association with the Punjab government, would be an acceptable figure with whom the moderates amongst the Sikhs could come to an agreement.

Birdwood's attempts to reach a settlement with the SGPC, however, proved futile. The extremist members of the SGPC, still very influential within the committee, declared that it would only stop the Nabha agitation and cease sending further *jatha*s to settle gurdwara disputes if the government met the following demands: that the Sikh prisoners arrested in connection with recent agitations should be released, and that the SGPC be permitted to perform 101 continuous Akhand Paths at Jaito. The government was unwilling, however, to release the prisoners before the passage of the 1922 Bill, and Birdwood tried in vain to convince the SGPC that on the successful completion of negotiations the Nabha administration would permit free access to the shrines at Jaito for the performance of the Akhand Path, and that once the dispatch of *jatha*s to Jaito ceased the government would lift the ban on the SGPC and the Akali Dal. The SGPC remained intransigent, insisting that its demands be met first. By June 1924, unable to come to any agreement, the negotiations were abandoned.[106]

Agitation Contained

In May 1924, in the midst of the stalemate between the government and the SGPC, Sir Malcolm Hailey assumed governorship of the Punjab. The change of governorship in the Punjab was greeted

[105] Quoted in the memorandum on the Akali situation by Malcolm Hailey, 20 June 1924. MSS.EUR.E.220/6A.

[106] Based on Ganda Singh (ed.), *Some Confidential Papers of the Akali Movement*, Amritsar, 1965, pp. 69–71; The Birdwood Committee, GoI, Home (Pol.), no. 297 of 1924.

by a call from the extremists in the SGPC for the Sikhs to prepare for a "new era of tyranny".[107] Hailey took this as a sign that the SGPC "was desirous of reviving an enthusiasm which they feel to be waning at the moment".[108] Hailey was not unfamiliar with the Akali agitation; as finance member of the Governor General's council, he had kept in constant touch with the Home member, Sir William Vincent, on the Sikh question,[109] and had been actively involved in formulating various approaches towards solving the problem.[110] He knew that the movement's leadership needed an impetus, in the form of a dramatic confrontation with the government, to keep the movement going, and he was not prepared to provide it. At the very outset, he was determined not to adopt any measures that would excite or alienate the community, having been briefed by his intelligence officers that enthusiasm amongst the Sikhs for the Nabha agitation was on the wane. Reports revealed that the SGPC was experiencing considerable difficulties in finding fresh recruits for continued *jatha*s to Jaito; and district officers had reported that recently formed *jatha*s were not up to their usual strength and in many cases were made up of "a miserable band of old men and boys [marching] up to the police each day, offering itself for arrest".[111] Furthermore, the influence and effect of these *jatha*s in the Sikh districts were declining. Not long after he had assumed office in Lahore, Hailey explained to Birdwood the line that he was going to adopt in dealing with the Akalis:

> I have recently seen a considerable number of district officers and others connected with the Sikh districts. I may say that for my part I have come to the conclusion that for the moment it would be very unwise to attempt anything of a description that I may call 'dramatic' either in one direction or another—I mean

[107] Memorandum by W.M. Hailey on the Akali situation, 20 June 1924, Hailey Papers. IOR: MSS.EUR.E.220/6A.

[108] Memo by Malcolm Hailey on the Akali situation, 20 June 1924.

[109] See the correspondence between Hailey and Vincent in Hailey's collections. IOR:MSS.EUR.E.220/5D.

[110] For instance, he strongly advocated the formation of the Board of Commission in the Punjab, as provided by the 1922 Bill, as a means of removing disputes over gurdwara management, which had been the basis of continued Sikh agitation in the Punjab. See pp. 226–27, this volume.

[111] Memo by Malcolm Hailey on the Akali situation, 20 June 1924.

either in the way of conciliation or repression. They so recently showed themselves unwilling to accept reasonable conditions that I am not inclined to believe that conciliation would yield any results. As for repression, I do not think that this is the psychological moment. All their papers are advising their sympathizers to unite against a new tyrant, (my humble self), and they are certainly on the lookout for something which would put some enthusiasm into their movement.[112]

Hailey was not prepared to let government action at this stage be construed as an initial step towards a new reign of terror or as a sign of a move towards concessions. His immediate concern was to deprive the extremist section of the SGPC of any excuse to generate a revival of fervour amongst the extremists. But while Hailey recommended that nothing of a dramatic nature should be done, he was not advocating a policy of inactivity. His strategy was one of slow attrition, which he once likened to "trench warfare". He decided to persist in the policy of applying continuous pressure on the SGPC, and contemplated a series of measures which, while not arousing public interest, would erode the capacity of the SGPC to wage further campaigns against the government.

To begin with, Hailey displayed a firm hand against those who persisted in flouting the law and carrying out a campaign to subvert state authority.[113] This was clearly aimed at undermining the position of the extremists, which he believed to be an "active minority" within the leadership of the movement.[114] Thus he reported to the Government of India:

I shall press on the trial of the committee; if fresh leaders arose of the same complexion, I would prosecute them also. I would resist by all legal means any attempt to use illegal force to gain possession of more gurdwaras and their lands.... I would continue the policy of pressure by all ordinary legal means, only

[112] Hailey to Birdwood, 20 June 1924, Hailey Papers. IOR:MSS.EUR.E.220/6A.
[113] H.D. Craik, Chief Secretary to Punjab government, to Major Ogilvie, Deputy Secretary to the GoI, Foreign and Political Dept., 27 June 1924, in Hailey Papers. IOR: MSS.EUR.E.220/6A.
[114] H.D. Craik, Chief Sec. to Punjab Govt., to Major Ogilvie, Dy. Sec. to GoI, Foreign and Political Dept., 27 June 1924, Hailey Papers. IOR:MSS.EUR.E.220/6A.

avoiding any step which may once more help to bring the extremist section forward as a champion of Sikh interests.[115]

Accordingly, the Punjab government implemented measures aimed at purging the movement of its radical elements. Pro-Akali newspapers were repeatedly prosecuted for inflammatory writing and action was taken against publishers and proprietors when elusive editors proved difficult to charge. Akali public meetings were closely watched and individuals singled out for prosecution. To dampen the appeal of the Akalis among the Sikh masses, the government announced moreover that the pension and land grants of persons participating in Akali campaigns would be confiscated,[116] while the army was asked to instruct their recruiting officers not to take recruits from villages known to be sympathetic to the Akalis.[117] While the Hailey government struck hard at the extremists, it thus offered conciliation to those who were genuinely concerned with religious reforms, and were prepared to accept a constitutional solution to the problem. It proceeded to reward the efforts of loyalist Sikhs, who had assisted the government in maintaining law and order in the villages and acted as informers for the authorities, by awarding them land grants in the canal colonies.[118] To rally the moderates, Hailey stressed that the government had no intention of interfering with the religious affairs of the community, and was prepared to concede most of the Sikhs' religious demands.[119] To promote the more conservative section of Sikh opinion into a position where they could once again venture to assert their authority against the extremist members of the SGPC,[120] Hailey sponsored the creation in districts with major Sikh population of

[115] Memo by Malcolm Hailey on the Akali situation, 20 June 1924.

[116] H.D. Craik, Chief Sec., Punjab Govt., to T. Sloan, Dy. Sec. to GoI, Home Dept., 5 July 1924, GoI, Home (Pol.), 1924, File 1/VI. NAI.

[117] W.M. Hailey to G. de Montmorency, Pvt. Sec. to the Viceroy, 8 July 1924, in Hailey Papers. IOR:MSS.EUR.E.220/6A.

[118] Lists showing grants of colony land to Sikhs for loyalty to government can be found in files 301/3/25/5A-B in the Board of Revenue Department, Lahore, Pakistan.

[119] H.N. Mitra (ed.) *Indian Annual Register (IAR)*, Vol. II, Delhi, 1924, reprint 1988, pp. 199–200.

[120] W.M. Hailey to Vincent, 7 November 1923, Hailey Papers. IOR:MSS.EUR.E.220/5D.

anti-Akali associations known as *sewaks* or *sudhars*. The member-ship to these associations was drawn largely from conservative landed interests and the Sikh gentry class whose influences had been eclipsed by the political ascendency of the SGPC. In addi-tion, they included a number of retired Sikh army officers and civil pensioners. District officers were instructed to give whatever sup-port they could to these organizations with the object of turning them into bodies capable of "going into loggerheads with Akali leaders".[121] Interestingly, this tactic of Hailey's was indicative of the extent to which the government depended, in the final resort, on their local allies to re-establish control in the Sikh districts.

The government sponsored anti-Akali organizations thereupon launched a campaign to clarify the religious issues behind Sikh unrest and isolate these from the political programmes of the Akalis. Through widely distributed posters and the publication of news-papers directed at the Sikh peasantry they attacked the SGPC's tactics while urging the fulfilment of Sikh religious aspirations. Their objectives, the Punjab government reported to the GoI, "was by these ... means to create in time a body of opinion which will put pressure on the Akalis to adopt a more reasonable attitude...".[122] With quiet government support—since these associations were technically non-official organizations—the *sudhar* committees grew in strength and number, and by August 1924 the Punjab govern-ment reported that anti-Akali associations had been or were in the process of being formed in districts with a substantial Sikh popu-lation, namely, Karnal, Hoshiarpur, Ludhiana, Sialkot, Sheikhpura, Rawalpindi, Amritsar and Gujranwala. Some of these associations, particularly in Amritsar and Hoshiarpur, soon reported member-ships of well over 10,000 people.[123] By the end of 1924, with the district associations attracting such popular support, a Provincial *Sudhar* Association was formed to rival the SGPC, and to take the lead in working for a Gurdwara Bill.

By the end of 1924, the SGPC had lost the initiative to the Punjab government. The agitation had been going on for more than four

[121] W.M. Hailey to Malcolm Seton, Clerk of Council, 17 July 1924, Hailey Papers. MSS.EUR.E.220/6A.

[122] FR, 31 July and 31 August, 1924; W.M. Hailey to W. Vincent, 12 August 1924, Hailey Papers. IOR:MSS.EUR.E.220/6B.

[123] FR, 15 August 1924; see also W.M. Hailey to G. de Montmorency, 8 July 1924, Hailey Papers. IOR:MSS.EUR.E.220/6A.

years, and the Sikh masses, who had suffered considerably during this time, had become tired of it. It was also difficult for the SGPC and the Akali Dal to keep up flagging interests amongst the Sikh peasantry, especially when the movement was getting nowhere. Furthermore, the restoration of the Maharajah of Nabha had ceased to be an issue and the *jatha*s marching to Jaito were diminishing. In October 1924, the recently formed provincial Sikh *sudhar* committee sent its own *jatha*, composed of prominent members of the landed gentry and landlords drawn from the various district *sudhar* committees, to complete the interrupted Akhand Path at Jaito.

The rug had been pulled from under the feet of the SGPC, and the religious platform from which it had staged its campaign against the government had been removed. Sensing that the Punjab government had seized the advantage, and hoping to salvage its position amongst the Sikhs, the SGPC approached the government for a renewal of negotiations. Hailey, however, decided to bide his time; he realized that by negotiating with the SGPC at this stage he would be giving them the recognition they wanted—as the sole representatives of the Sikhs. He therefore made it known that if negotiations were to be started with the government, it would have to be with a body of Sikhs representing different shades of Sikh opinion, which could certainly include the extremist Sikhs.[124] Although the SGPC had been a thorn in the side of the government, and moderate Sikhs might have distrusted the political programme of the SGPC, Hailey was realistic enough to realize that the great mass of Sikhs still regarded it as representative of their religious interests; it would not be possible for the government to disregard the SGPC in any attempt at finding a solution to the religious impasse connected with the dispute over the gurdwaras. But Hailey was determined that if a fresh attempt was to be made to draft a new Gurdwara Bill, he would want a bill which would suit the intentions of the Punjab government; the provincial Sikh *sudhar* committee would therefore be required to play a major role in the formulation of a new Gurdwara Bill.[125]

In July 1925, the third attempt to legislate for a solution to the gurdwara problem finally proved successful, and with the passage

---

[124] W.M. Hailey to de Montmorency, 20 August 1924, Hailey Papers, IOR: MSS.EUR.E.220/6B.

[125] W.M. Hailey to de Montmorency, 5 August 1924, Hailey Papers, MSS.EUR.E.220/6B.

of the Sikh Gurdwaras and Shrines Bill of 1925, the government finally overcame the thrust of the Akali movement. The bill, which placed responsibility for the management of all Sikh religious institutions with the Sikh community through an elected board of management, was introduced in the Punjab Legislative Council on 7 May 1925, and after it had been referred to a select committee, was passed on 8 July 1925. The Act contained major concessions to the Sikh reformers. The term Sikh as applied in the Act referred to anyone who would declare that he was a Sikh and a believer of the Granth Sahib and the Ten Gurus. This meant that *sahajdharis* who wished to participate in the management of the temples would have to declare themselves separate from Hindus. The Act also accepted that the central body, which would manage the Golden Temple, would be called the SGPC, thus signifying the government's acceptance of the latter as representative of Sikh religious interests.[126]

Although concessions were made to placate the Sikhs, several safeguards were included in the bill to curtail the power and influence of the SGPC. The bill had after all been drafted by Sikh members of the Council in consultation with a senior government official, Herbert Emerson. One of the main safeguards built into the Act was that the SGPC could no longer use its position as a central Sikh body to mount a political challenge against the government.[127] The central committee at Amritsar was charged with general functions concerning the administration of the Golden Temple. Its power however would not be absolute, but was defined by statute. Furthermore, temple funds were to be subjected to regular examination by government appointed auditors, to prevent them from being used for political purposes. Moreover, local gurdwaras were to be managed by locally elected district committees, based on the franchise for the legislative council. These committees were to counter the overarching influence of the SGPC in the Golden Temple.[128]

The Akali episode thus ended in 1925, but its legacy remained for long after. The movement had established the SGPC and the

---

[126] See Sikh Gurdwaras and Shrines Bill of 1925, as reproduced in *Punjab Gazette*, 26 June 1925.

[127] W.M. Hailey to A. Langley, Commissioner of Lahore, 25 November 1924, Hailey Papers. MSS.EUR.E.220/6C.

[128] All these conditions were insisted upon by Hailey during the drafting of the Bill. See Hailey to Muddiman, 25 November 1924, Hailey Papers. MSS.EUR.E.220/6C.

Akali Dal as major actors in Sikh politics, with which the old landed Sikh elites had to contend for the leadership of the community. Unlike the Muslims and the Hindu Jats, the Sikhs remained politically disunited both within and outside the provincial legislature, a factor which was to account for the confused state of the community during the constitutional negotiations leading up to Independence and Partition.[129]

Conclusion

Underlying the Punjab government's policy towards the Akali movement was the endeavour to preserve the two staunch bulwarks of British administration in the Punjab—Sikh troops and the Sikh peasantry. Unlike the *Ghadr* and the 1919 disturbances, the agitation for gurdwara reform, which during its peak phases— the "Keys affair", the Guru Ka Bagh agitation and the Jaito protests—showed signs of being a popular rural movement, not only posed a problem for law and order in central Punjab, but threatened to disrupt one of the Indian Army's main recruiting districts. The military repercussions were considerable. During the movement, recruiting officers reported a drop in the enlistment of Sikhs. The usually loyal military pensioners and Sikh veterans, either motivated by purely religious sentiments or resentment against the government caused by post-war conditions, wavered in their support for the government, and most disturbing of all, Sikh regiments showed signs of restlessness, to the extent that their British commanders were not sure if they could be relied on for use in aid of the civil power. The need to prevent the possibility of a widespread rebellion in the Sikh districts and the mutiny of Sikh regiments limited the options which the British had in dealing with the agitation. The full use of troops to quell the Akalis was ruled out, despite support in this direction from the GoI and Army Headquarters. A military operation, similar to that carried out to crush the Moplah rebellion, would have had a disastrous effect on the province. It would have resulted in an outright clash between the government and the Sikhs—and the latter had shown that they

[129] For this story, see Tan Tai Yong, 'Sikh Responses to the Demand for Pakistan, 1940–47', *International Journal of Punjab Studies*, Vol. 1(2), October 1994, pp. 167–75.

were capable of organizing themselves to put up a stiff resistance. The introduction of martial law, as was implemented in five cities during the 1919 Disturbances, would have served to confirm Akali propaganda that the government was bent on the repression of the Sikh religion, and would certainly have done considerable damage to the relationship between the Sikh community and the British. The Punjab government was therefore faced with the difficult task of developing a strategy of curbing the political unrest while at the same time maintaining the allegiance of the Sikh community.

Initially, the Punjab authorities tried to assuage the Sikhs by conceding their religious demands. It handed over control of the Golden Temple to the SGPC, tried to adopt a neutral position in gurdwara disputes and demonstrated its willingness to find a permanent solution to the problem of gurdwara management through legislation. These early attempts at assuagement, however, failed to contain the movement. Instead, it gave encouragement to the reformers who favoured a more militant approach towards achieving their religious objectives. Subsequently, the SGPC and the Akalis came under the influence of the more extremist and politically-oriented Sikhs, who, drawing support from the Congress, began to transform the agitation for religious reforms into a civil disobedience movement. The government responded by arresting the Sikh militant leaders and political agitators, but was careful at the same time to emphasize that it was still sympathetic to the religious aspirations of the Sikhs.

This dual approach was given coherence with the arrival in 1924 of Sir Malcolm Hailey as Governor of the Punjab. Hailey's approach was simple: he would not feed the SGPC's propaganda machine by attempting anything dramatic. He had assessed that enthusiasm for the movement was ebbing, and was not prepared to provide the excuse for a revival by taking a repressive policy or by making a major concession. He also realized that the SGPC and the Akalis were able to dominate the Sikh countryside because there was a total absence of alternative leadership. He, therefore, created anti-Akali associations in the Sikh districts, and with tacit official support, these associations significantly undermined the SGPC's support in the Sikh districts.

By 1925 Hailey's success was complete. He had effectively stopped the Sikh political unrest, removed the grounds for further gurdwara disputes by the passing of the Sikh Gurdwara and

Shrines Act of 1925, curbed the SGPC's potential for future political intrigue and, most importantly, secured the allegiance of the Sikhs and successfully maintained the Sikh recruiting districts.

The Akali episode demonstrated that the Indian Army, composed of soldiers from a subject population, was always vulnerable to political influences from outside the barracks and cantonments. The military authorities were only too conscious that opponents of the Raj had fixed their eyes on the possibility of seducing the Indian Army from its allegiance to the government, and family, property and religion were probably matters on which any agitator wishing to arouse the feelings of the classes from which soldiers came, could most readily appeal. This meant that the crucial responsibility of maintaining the military recruiting grounds lay very much in the domain of the civil authorities in the Punjab, and this was to be a major factor affecting the orientation of the colonial state in the Punjab during the inter-war period.

SIX

Securing the Reins of Power: Politics and Punjab's Rural-Military Elites

In the preceding chapters, we have seen that both in peace and war, the administration in the Punjab had had to rely heavily on the active collaboration of the province's landed elites to maintain the loyalty and viability of the military districts. The preservation of the old aristocracy in the Punjab—the chieftain/military families of the western districts and the dominant peasant proprietors and rural notables of central and eastern Punjab—was indeed central to the imperial enterprise in the province. In addition to their critical function as the state's rural intermediaries, the landed elites had shown that they could perform the equally important role of the state's military intercessors in the recruiting grounds of the province. The military importance of these rural allies, first highlighted during the 1857 Mutiny, was once again emphasized during the First World War, when they played a major part in the mobilization and control of the greatly expanded recruiting base in the Punjab. All this was to have an important bearing on political developments in the Punjab after the war. When post-war constitutional reforms created new opportunities for political power in the provinces, the Punjab government sought to ensure that power would be devolved to their traditional rural-military allies. The landed elites, for their part, took the occasion to exert their influence as the state's military brokers to stake a claim in the newly-emerging structures of political power in the province. Consequently, political reforms in the Punjab came to be heavily biased in favour of these rural-military elites, and this was to lay the foundation of almost three decades of their dominance in the politics of colonial Punjab, and thereafter. From 1920 onwards the rural-military elites constituted a majority in successive legislative councils in the Punjab, and in 1923 they coalesced into the Punjab National Unionist Party, which dominated provincial politics until 1946. This entrenchment of the civil-military elites had repercussions for the political development of the Punjab. Once in government, the rural-military elites acted as the bond between the locality (the military districts) and the Legislative Council at Lahore, thus reinforcing the entire civil-military structure in the Punjab. In addition, by representing the interests of the enfranchised landed and soldiering classes, political reforms further entrenched the traditional rural hierarchy in the Punjab. And with the rural-military elites dominating the councils, politics in the Punjab came to be closely associated with localized rural-military interests, thereby allowing little prospects for nationalist organizations, most notably the Congress, and purely communal associations like the Muslim League, to establish any political foothold in the province. The politics of the Punjab, shaped to a large extent by military dictates, was to create a distinctly Punjabi-centred political ideology that had little room for the all-India nationalism preached by the Congress and the Muslim League.

This chapter examines the processes by which the province's rural-military elites came to dominate Punjab politics from 1920 to 1937. It analyses how political reforms, both in 1919 and 1935, established these elites as the centrepiece of provincial politics, and how their political positions were entrenched by their ability to function as a rural-military lobby in the provincial legislative arena.

The Montagu–Chelmsford Reforms

The seeds of the first substantive step of political reforms in India were sown in the midst of the First World War, when the Secretary of State for India, Edwin Montagu, announced in the House of Commons, on 20 August 1917, British intention of "increasing [the] association of Indians in every branch of administration, and the gradual development of self-governing institutions with a view to the progressive realization of responsible government in India ...

[after the War]".[1] Following the announcement, Montagu and the Viceroy, Lord Chelmsford, toured India during the winter months of 1917–18, during which they met, discussed and debated with a host of British and Indian individuals and groups about the form and content of political reforms to be introduced in India after the war.[2]

The Secretary of State's political initiative had grown out of British anxiety at political developments in India during the war. In 1915 the Congress demanded a British declaration of policy concerning the advancement of self government for India. The call struck a chord in the Indian political community, particularly at a time when India was sending men and materials to support Britain in a fight to "defend the rights of nations". Even moderate politicians, who had hitherto been prepared to work the 1909 Morley–Minto provisions, and who believed that political advancement in India could only be a gradual process under British tutelage, were becoming increasingly disappointed by the sluggishness of political advance. The Congress, reunified with the return of the extremists to its ranks, was rapidly emerging as the authoritative voice of Indian national aspirations. It had also gained the backing of the Muslim League, which, under the accord struck in the Lucknow Pact of 1916, was prepared to work with the Congress on a shared political platform. Political excitement had further been fanned by the demand for Home Rule by the Home Rule League organizations of Tilak and Annie Besant.[3] Against such a political backdrop, the

[1] For the background and political context in which the August Declaration was made, see Richard Danzig, 'The Announcement of August 20th 1917' in *JAS*, Vol. 28(1), November 1968, pp. 19–37. See also S.R. Mehrota, ' Politics behind the Montagu Declaration of 1917', in C.H. Philips (ed.), *Politics and Society in India*, London, 1963, pp. 71–96.

[2] A rather full account of the debates and attitudes of various individuals towards the reforms are recounted in Peter Robb, *Government of India and Political Reforms*, Oxford, 1976. See also Sir Algernon Rumbold, *Watershed in India, 1914–1922*, London, 1979, pp. 101–89; and E.S. Montagu (ed. Venetia Montagu), *An Indian Diary*, London, 1930.

[3] The first Home Rule Leagues in India were established in April and September of 1916 by Bal Gangadhar Tilak and Annie Besant respectively. It ushered in a period of aggressive politics, largely in response to the disappointment of the Morley–Minto reforms and the repressive policies of the government during the war. See H.P. Owen, 'Towards Nationwide Agitation and Organization: The Home Rule Leaguers, 1915–1918' in D.A. Low (ed.) *Soundings in Modern South Asian History*, London, 1968, pp. 159–95.

British considered that the time and circumstances necessitated the promise of political concessions to rally to their side "those politicians who seemed increasingly to be potentially important allies or dangerous enemies".[4] The British were certainly not contemplating any form of radical political concessions in the autumn of 1917, but the intention behind the August Declaration was clear: limited constitutional reforms would be introduced as a means to conciliate public opinion in wartime India, and to win back moderate opinion to support the Raj.[5]

The Montagu–Chelmsford Report, published in 1918, announced that the proposed political reforms would represent an "advance towards self-government by stages".[6] This contemplated a limited devolution of ministerial responsibility to Indian hands through the introduction of a system of government in the provinces known as dyarchy, or "double government". Under this system, certain departments of provincial government, considered to be looking after "nation-building subjects" such as local government, education, agriculture, health, commerce and industry, were "transferred" to the control of ministers who would be responsible to elected legislatures. Subjects related to revenue and law and order, such as land revenue administration, justice and police, were, however, to remain "reserved" in official hands.[7] Political reforms under dyarchy reflected what one of its framers, Lionel Curtis, described as the failure of the framers "to discover any less dangerous alternatives".[8] It was essentially a compromise solution— a limited degree of devolution of political power would take place as a means of providing education in self government, but the essentials of power were still to be retained in the hands of the British to enable them to safeguard their imperial interests.[9]

[4] Judith Brown, *Modern India: Origins of An Asian Democracy*, Oxford, 1985, pp. 192–94.

[5] See D.A. Low, *Congress and the Raj*, London, 1974, pp. 24–25.

[6] See *Report on Indian Constitutional Reforms (The Montford Report), 1918* in *PP*, Cmd. 9109, Vol. 8, pp. 113–421.

[7] *Ibid.*

[8] Lionel Curtis, *Dyarchy*, London, 1920, p. 25.

[9] Under the provisions of the Montford Report, provincial governors reserved the powers to take over the administration of transferred departments if they could find no ministers backed by a majority of their legislative councils. They also had the power to pass bills over the heads of the legislatures if they were certified to be

Notwithstanding these qualifications, the terms of the Montagu–Chelmsford reforms signified a big step in the political advancement of India; it marked a shift in the relationship between the British and their Indian subjects by giving the latter a greater measure of responsibility, albeit still on a limited scale, to govern themselves. The reforms led to enlarged provincial legislatures with a substantial elected majority to which local ministers of "transferred" departments were ultimately to be responsible. After 1920, although the key departments were still held by the British, British officials were no longer to have a monopoly of political power, and they would have to depend on the "goodwill and cooperation of elected politicians for the effective administration of the provinces".[10]

In the eighteen months following its publication, the Report was discussed and debated by different sections of the GoI, the British Parliament, and the Franchise and Functions Committees. The principle of reforms, espoused in the Montagu–Chelmsford Report, found general acceptance amongst members of the Indian Civil Service and heads of provinces in India[11] for, as Peter Robb explains, "without their backing, the reforms would never have been approved".[12] But there were divergent views on how the reforms were to be actually implemented in the provinces.[13] The more liberal among the British administrators, including James Meston, Lieutenant Governor of the United Provinces, George Lloyd, head of the Bombay Presidency, and William Vincent, Home Member in the Viceroy's Council, agreed on the need for reforms, but even among them, there was little consensus on the most efficient way of enfranchising Indians.[14] Despite the general endorsement for

---

necessary for the safety and tranquillity of India. This was known as the power of certification, and was later incorporated into the Government of India Act of 1919. See 'Montford Report', Cmd. 9109, pp. 327–30.

[10] David Page, *Prelude to Partition: The Imperial System of Control*, New Delhi, 1982, p. 30.

[11] After the publication of the Montford Report the Government of India sent a despatch conveying "its cordial support to the general policy which the Report embodies". See *Views of the Government of India on the Report of Lord Southborough's Committee, 1919*, Cmd. 176, Vol. 16.

[12] Robb, *Political Reforms*, p. 106.

[13] The details of the responses and reactions to the reforms proposals need not concern us here. They have, however, been examined in some detail in *ibid.*, pp. 102–16.

[14] *Ibid.*

reforms from a wide range of political opinions in Britain and India, there were still a number of influential individuals in India who were fundamentally at odds with the very idea of political reforms in India, and perhaps the most ardent of these dissenting voices came from the Lieutenant Governor of the Punjab, Michael O'Dwyer.[15]

O'Dwyer's Responses to the Reforms

Michael O'Dwyer's opposition to constitutional progress stemmed from his basic belief that political reforms were not necessary for India, nor were they wanted by its general masses. A committed paternalist, O'Dwyer believed that the vast majority of Indians were incapable of political judgement on their own and that the British government knew what was best for the people and must remain "the trustee of their interests". This belief convinced O'Dwyer that there was no need at the moment for any immediate transfer of real political power to Indians.[16] Political reforms, he believed, would only threaten the interests of those whom Montagu claimed to be helping. The Montagu–Chelmsford Report had stated that "the placid, pathetic, contentment of the masses is not the soil on which ... nationhood will grow, and that in deliberately disturbing it ... [the British] are working for her highest good".[17] But O'Dwyer believed that this "placid contentment" was not due to dull apathy, but to a consciousness that they (the Indian masses) were being fairly dealt with by the British government.[18] As far as he was concerned only strong and autocratic government could provide what the rural masses of India were interested in: peace, order, impartial government, light taxation and proper administration.[19]

[15] The other ardent opposition to reforms came from the conservative Pentland, the Governor of Madras, whose attitude together with O'Dwyer proved a great source of annoyance to the Viceroy and the Secretary of State. *Ibid.*

[16] For his reactions to political reforms, see Memorandum by O'Dwyer on Constitutional Reforms, 10 January 1918, in *Annexure to Enclosure 22 of letter from Government of India, 5 March 1919 and Enclosures of the Question Raised in the Report on Indian Constitutional Reforms* in *PP*, 1919, Vol. 37, p. 825. See also O'Dwyer's autobiography, *India As I Knew It* (London, 1930).

[17] See *Montford Report,* Cmd. 9109, Vol. 8, p. 242.

[18] O'Dwyer, *India As I Knew It,* p. 56.

[19] *Ibid.*

O'Dwyer's dislike for any form of devolution of power to Indian hands also sprung from his deep-seated distrust of Indian politicians. He believed that the people who had been clamouring for reforms were essentially self-serving politicians who had little in common with the people they claimed to represent. He felt these politicians were interested only in making irresponsible demands on government, but would "disregard the views and needs of the solid masses" once political power was put in their hands.[20] Citing the example of his province, he insisted that the politicians in the Punjab, the mainly English-educated and urban professionals, were useless for the real tasks involved in running the province. He warned that they would not know how to organize recruitment to the army, prevent religious riots and manage sectional tensions. By yielding to political pressure and conceding reforms, O'Dwyer felt that the British government would only end up creating an "Indian oligarchy, lacking in efficiency, integrity, and impartiality... [which] being unrepresentative and out of touch with the masses, and inexperienced in the conduct of administration, will, even with the best intentions, eventually blunder, [and] possibly give rise to a sense of injustice amongst the masses...."[21]

O'Dwyer's inherent distrust in the politicized urban trading and professional classes was compounded by his personal experience as Lieutenant Governor of the Punjab during the First World War. His government had relied mainly on the rural classes for recruitment during the war, and those who had done most to assist his administration were the rural-military elites. The urban classes, on the other hand, not only responded poorly to the government's call for recruits, but, by calling for political reforms in the midst of war, had preached conditional loyalty at a time when the Empire was engaged in a desperate struggle. O'Dwyer also believed these urban politicians were primarily responsible for inciting the anti-government sentiments which had resulted in the political disturbances of 1919. What was perhaps most galling to him was that these politicians, who had done nothing to assist the government during the war, now stood to benefit from the political and administrative reforms promised by the British government while the

---

[20] Robb, *Political Reforms*, p. 13.

[21] Memo by O'Dwyer on the Question of Constitutional Reforms, 10 January 1918, in *Report on the Indian Constitutional Reforms*, Cmd. 123, Vol. 37, p. 825.

province's landed aristocracy and the mass of peasant-proprietors, who had solidly supported the British war effort, but who had no interests in reforms whatsoever, would eventually be left out in the cold.[22] O'Dwyer was convinced that in whatever form political reforms were introduced, it was unlikely that the rural classes would be adequately represented,[23] and by catering to urban politicians instead of the peasants, the government would have "disregarded the men who had fought and can fight, and considered only the men who can talk".[24]

To O'Dwyer and other conservative members of his government, to have future legislative bodies in the Punjab dominated by the urban classes was militarily unacceptable too. Punjab's military districts would be ill-served if future provincial legislative councils were to be dominated by urban politicians who had little empathy with the agricultural and military classes. Successive Punjab governments in the past had carefully nurtured the military districts, on whose active cooperation the reliability of the army, and ultimately the security of India, depended. Policies had been adopted that not only aimed at shielding the military districts from external political influences, but also protecting the economic, social and religious interests of the military classes, thus keeping them contented. But Punjab's role as the military bulwark of the Raj could be seriously jeopardized if urban politicians were to be elected and were to become uncooperative partners in government, especially in protecting the interests of the rural-military classes. This concern was felt most strongly by O'Dwyer; to him, it was a matter of utmost importance that a province as militarily important as the Punjab was spared the fate of being run by an "elected majority of .... irresponsible politicians .... in the legislature".[25] Consequently, while the Secretary of State and the GoI were prepared to carry out the promise made in the August Declaration, O'Dwyer was intent on preventing the introduction of reforms in his province, prompting Motilal Nehru to accuse him of turning "the Punjab into a kind of Ulster in relation to the rest of India, a bulwark of reaction against

---

[22] Michael O'Dwyer, in a speech in the Imperial Legislative Council Debates, September 1917, as quoted by David Page, *Prelude to Partition*, p. 58.

[23] *Ibid.*

[24] O'Dwyer, *India As I Knew It*, p. 407.

[25] Robb, *Political Reforms*, pp. 12–13.

all reforms".[26] In a sense, one could see O'Dwyer attempting here to save the military districts of the Punjab from the urban politicians, just as Ibbetson had earlier saved the Punjab peasantry from the Hindu urban moneylenders.

Despite his strong objections, O'Dwyer was never in a position to stop the momentum of political change that had already been set in motion. Realizing that he could not prevent the devolution of power to Indian hands, O'Dwyer decided that if political changes had to be brought about, he would bring in the "Old World to redress the balance of the New".[27] If actual political power was to be devolved to Indian hands, and if his government had to work with local politicians, it would be in his interest to ensure that such power devolved to the government's allies in the province, the rural-military elites.

The proposals submitted by the Punjab government to the Franchise Committee in 1918 clearly showed its intention to "fix" the terms of the reforms, so as to marginalize the urban politician and ensure the entrenchment of the rural-military elites. The government proposed the creation of a relatively small provincial Legislative Council of fifty-one members, of whom seventeen, or one-third of the council, would be nominated, and the remainder elected. Of the proposed thirty-four elected seats in the council, twenty-five were to be allocated to the rural areas, while only six were to be designated as urban seats. Two seats were to be allocated to represent the interests of trade and industries, and one for a representative of Punjab University.[28] The twenty-five elected rural seats would consist of sixteen seats from rural constituencies and nine special seats. Four of these special seats were to be reserved for the landed gentry, "in recognition of their importance to the military and the administration of the province", and in the belief that these "representatives will form a valuable steadying influence in the

[26] Motilal Nehru, *The Voice of Freedom: Selected Speeches of Motilal Nehru*, Bombay, 1961, p. 22.

[27] Page, *Prelude to Partition*, p. 47.

[28] Of the twenty-five rural elected seats, ten were Muslim seats, six Hindu, four were for large landowners, and five for Sikhs. In the urban seats, three were designated for Muslims and three for Hindus. Three seats were allocated to Industry and Trades and the Punjab University. Proposals of Punjab Government, enclosed in letter from Offg Addl Sec., Punjab Government to Government of India, 23 November 1918, in *Franchise Committee Report* (Southborough) in *PP*, 1919, Cmd. 141, Vol. 16, pp. 661–82.

Council chamber where their practical experience and conservative tendencies should prove a healthy check on the impatient idealism of the middle class politicians".[29] Five special seats were to be allocated to the Sikh community who, according to the Government's proposals, in spite of their minority status deserved a greater degree of representation in the Legislative Council on the ground of their large share of landholdings and military importance.[30] According to the Punjab government's recommendations, of the six elected urban seats for the proposed council, two were to go to Lahore division, and one each to the other four divisions.[31]

The Punjab government's proposals regarding the franchise were designed to establish a small and overwhelmingly rural and conservative electorate in the Punjab. Its calculations about these suggested that the provincial electorate would consist of approximately 230,000 votes, of which 161,000 would be rural votes and only 70,000 urban. At the same time, the Punjab government tried to ensure that only the rural notables, landlords and dominant zamindars were eligible to vote. To achieve this, it first proposed that only landowners and crown tenants paying land revenue of at least fifty rupees would be enfranchised; this qualification was twice as high as that proposed by the other provincial governments, and would only enfranchise about 85,000 amongst the landowning classes. In addition, the government proposed that every village lambardar, usually the most influential member of the proprietary body in the villages and an officially recognized agent of government, should be given the vote. According to the government's calculations, this proposal would make the 65,327 lambardars in the province the second most substantial component in the total rural electorate, next to the landowning classes. Other rural notables who held official appointments, such as

---

[29] *Ibid.*, p. 665.

[30] *Ibid.*, p. 662.

[31] According to the Punjab government's proposals, Lahore division, comprising two of the largest cities in the province (Lahore and Amritsar) would be given one Muslim and one Hindu seat; the Hindus or Ambala and Jullunder divisions would return one member, and the Muslims of the two divisions would also return one member, with a similar arrangement for Rawalpindi and Multan divisions. In this manner, there would be three Hindu and three Muslim urban seats. The Sikhs in the urban areas would vote not in the urban constituencies, but in special Sikh constituencies. See *ibid.*, p. 665.

zaildars, sufed poshes and inamdars, honorary magistrates and sub-registrars were to be given the vote too, but as many of them would have already qualified as landowners the number of voters projected under these categories was not expected to be large, estimated indeed to be only about 200. Jagirdars, assignees of land revenue who constituted an important rural class and who enjoyed their present position as a result of supporting the state, were to be enfranchised too, but of the thousands of such people in the province, ranging from those who enjoyed jagirs worth thousands of rupees to small muafis whose grants amounted to no more than a few rupees a year, the Lieutenant Governor proposed to give the vote only to those who enjoyed land assignments worth at least 500 rupees a year. Once again this would not constitute a large group by itself, as many would have already been enfranchised as landowners. Other categories to be enfranchised included retired military officers of the rank of jamedar and above (as a provision for those who were military officers but did not qualify to vote in any of the above categories); presidents of agricultural societies, all persons residing in rural areas who paid a tax on incomes of at least 2,000 rupees per year (estimated tax amount around fifty-five rupees), non-official members of district boards living in rural areas, and retired graduates.[32] Under the Punjab government's proposals, rural tenants-at-will would not be given the vote.

The urban franchise proposed by the Punjab government was weighted, moreover, in favour of the urban bourgeosie and minor officialdom. It was proposed that the vote should be given to those who belonged to the various categories of individuals who paid an annual income tax (no minimum income qualification); registered graduates of Indian universities; retired military officers residing in urban areas; non-official members of municipal and area committees; honorary magistrates and sub-registrars; presidents of urban cooperative societies; owners of immoveable property with a value of not less than 4,000 rupees; and owners of agricultural land residing in urban areas.[33]

The franchise proposals of the Punjab government were thus clearly aimed at creating a conservative electorate with a strong

---

[32] For all the above details, see *Proposals of the Punjab Government*, PP, Cmd. 141, Vol. 16, pp. 668–69.

[33] *Ibid.*, p. 670.

rural-military bias. The rural classes which the government intended to enfranchise were mostly beneficiaries of state patronage, whose interests were closely connected to the status quo. Most importantly, in a predominantly rural electorate, those to be enfranchised were the very elements that were the mainstay of the Indian Army, had supported the government during the war, and were in a position to maintain the military machinery of the province in its aftermath. According to the calculations of the Punjab government, out of a projected total of about 161,000 rural votes, more than 150,000 would come from government officials, the military and rich landholders and peasant proprietors.[34]

In November 1918, in an interview with the Franchise Committee, O'Dwyer explained the rationale behind the proposals of his government. He stressed that conditions in the Punjab were such that, in formulating a scheme for the reforms, "local conditions rather than logical precision or theoretical completeness" were of primary importance.[35] He pointed out that the rural-urban dichotomy was a central feature of the Punjab, and that it was the rural population

Table 6.1
Estimate of Total Number of Rural Voters in the Punjab Government's
Franchise Proposals of 1918

Categories	Estimated Numbers
Lambardars	65,000
Landowners and Crown Tenants with property qualifications of fifty rupees	85,000
Zaildars, Sufed Poshes and Inamdars	100
Assignees of land revenue	900
Members of District Boards	200
Honorary Magistrates and Sub-Registrars	60
Pensioned Military Officers	2,000
Civil Pensioners	500
Presidents of Cooperative Societies	2,000
Registered Graduates	600
Total	**161,610**

Source: Franchise Proposals of Punjab Government, November 1918, in *PP*, 1919, Cmd. 141, Vol. 16, p. 671.

[34] *Ibid.*, p. 671. For the above calculations, see Tables 6.1, and 6.2 (overleaf).
[35] Note of discussion with the Lieutenant Governor of the Punjab, 7 December 1918, in *PP*, 1919, Cmd. 141, Vol. 16, p. 677.

Table 6.2
Estimated Number of Urban Voters

Categories	Estimated Numbers
Income-tax payers	21,000
Graduates	2,000
Retired Military and Civil Pensioners	1,000
Non-official members of Local Bodies	800
Honorary Magistrates and Sub-Registrars	200
Presidents of Co-operative Societies	60
Owners of immoveable property to a gross value of not less than 10,000 rupees	20,000
Owners of agricultural land	5,000
Persons paying municipal taxes amounting to not less than 20,000 rupees and persons occupying premises valued at not less than 20,000 rupees	20,000
Total	**70,060**

Source: Franchise Proposals of the Punjab Government, November 1918, in *PP*, Cmd. 141, Vol. 16, p. 672.

which was predominantly important in terms of their numbers, the amount of revenue they paid, as well as their prominence in the Indian Army. According to O'Dwyer, the unique position of the Punjab as the major recruiting ground for the Indian Army, as well as the crucial military base for operations across the north-west frontier, made it imperative for the government to ensure that political power be devolved to its rural-military allies.[36]

Responses of the Rural-Military Elites

As O'Dwyer had anticipated, the rural-military elites of the Punjab regarded the promise of constitutional reforms in post-war India with a fair amount of trepidation. Prior to 1919, in return for their support of the civil-military structure in the Punjab, their positions of dominance in the province had been assured. But political reforms could signal an end to all that, especially if the urban politicians were to come to dominate the political arena. Unless political power was heavily biased towards the countryside, representative politics would not favour the old rural aristocracy. These rural elites knew

[36] *Ibid.*

that as things stood they were in no position to successfully wage an electoral contest against the western educated and organized urban politicians. Their influence as rural notables was essentially dependent upon the patronage of the state. Each of them exercised influence only over his immediate caste, tribe or locality, and most of this influence revolved around economic dominance and kin-ship ties which were extremely localized. As a collective class of agriculturists they lacked an effective organizational structure with which they could mobilize support in a general election. During the preliminaries to the reforms, therefore, fearing that their posi-tion in the provincial state structure would be usurped by the "ad-vanced urban politicians", the rural-military elites decided to make a collective effort to influence reforms in their favour. They realized that the only way in which the reforms could be made to work to their advantage was to use their influence in the administration, especially in the military, to pressurize the British into acquiescing to their political demands for special provisions that would safe-guard their interests. What emerged from the fears and anxieties of this period was a loosely constituted rural-military lobby within the Punjab which was able to use its importance in the rural ad-ministration and in the military as leverage with which to stake a claim in the newly emerging reformed political structures.

During the Secretary of State's tour of India in the winter of 1917–18, representatives of the rural-military elites of the Punjab, represented by two organizations—the Punjab Muslim Associa-tion and the Punjab Zamindar Central Association—submitted proposals on how they felt reforms should be implemented in the Punjab. Although organized on a communal basis, both associa-tions shared a common concern; their objectives, like those of the Punjab government, were to secure special representation for land-holders and to obtain a predominant share of political power for the rural-military classes. Although they were supposed to repre-sent the agricultural population, irrespective of class, these organizations were clearly acting in the interests of the dominant landed-military classes of the province. The proposals of the rural-military elites were very similar to those of O'Dwyer's, indicating the extent to which the interests of the state and its rural-military allies had become integrated.

The Punjab Muslim Association, the older of the two bodies, was established in 1916 to represent the interests of the Muslim

zamindars and the "military races" of the Punjab.[37] The associa-
tion had a pronounced military flavour—almost all members were
heads of military families and many of them were retired officers
who held honorary British ranks. The deputation which met the
Secretary of State in Delhi in 1918 included, amongst others, Nawab
Sir Behram Khan, Khan Bahadur Syed Mehdi Shah, Khan Bahadur
Malik Muhammud Ali Amin, Makhdum Syed Rajan Shah, Mirza
Ikram Ullah, Raja Muhammud Akbar, Khan Bahadur Sardar Abdur
Rahman, Nawab Fateh Ali Khan, Honorary Captain Ajab Khan,
Honorary Captain Ahmad Yar, Nawab Malik Mubariz Khan,
Nawab Ibrahim Ali Khan, Sultan Muhhamud Khan, Muhhamud
Hayat Qureshi, Raja Muhammud Akbar of Jhelum, Honorary Cap-
tain Ghulam Muhammud, Honorary Captain Muhammud Hayat,
Malik Khan Muhammud, Malik Khan Reza Ali and Ali Mardan
Qureshi, all leading members of prominent landed-military fami-
lies of western Punjab, with intimate connections with the Indian
Army.[38] Captain Ajab Khan, for instance, was typical of the rural-
military lobby in the Punjab. He was nominated to the Viceroy's
Legislative Assembly from 1918–19 as a representative of the military classes of the Punjab, during which he constantly raised his
concerns for commissions, rewards and after care for the soldiers
of the Punjab.[39] In its representation to the Secretary of State in
Delhi, the association emphasized the contribution made by Punjabi
Muslims to the military, especially during the war, and argued that
political reforms should not be allowed to affect the special relationship between Muslim rural classes and the state adversely.[40]

The Association's views and concerns regarding reforms were
elaborated by Honorary Lieutenant Colonel Malik Umar Hayat Khan
Tiwana, a leading member of the association and an influential
spokesman for the military classes in the province.[41] In a personal

---

[37] Address presented by the Punjab Muslim Association to the Viceroy and
Secretary of State, 1918, Cmd. 9178, Vol. 18, pp. 478–79.

[38] Representation from the Punjab Muslim Association received by Montagu in
Delhi, Montagu Collections. IOR: MSS.EUR.D.523/35.

[39] See for example Captain Ajab Khan to Viceroy, 11 January 1918, in Chelmsford
Papers, Vol. 2. IOR:MSS.EUR.E.264/20.

[40] *Ibid.*

[41] For a brief history of his involvement with the state, see the earlier chapters.
In the immediate aftermath of the war, Umar Hayat served in the Punjab Soldiers'
Board, where he strongly advocated increased rewards and welfare benefits for
soldiers who had fought in the war.

memorandum to the Secretary of State in 1918, Umar Hayat pointed out that the rural-military classes of the Punjab were not only responsible for paying ninety per cent of the province's revenue, but also supplied nearly two-thirds of the Indian Army. But the mutually dependent relationship between them and the government, he said, was now being threatened by political reforms.[42] He was fearful that political reforms, which he thought to be inherently biased against the agriculturists, would only benefit the "small classes of traders who had been clamouring for them" and not the zamindar class which had all along provided soldiers and revenue to the government.[43] He explained that unlike the urban trading classes, the zamindars of the Punjab did not have the advantage of better education and organization and were in no position to lobby the GoI and the British government for their interests.[44] He warned that, unless adequate steps were taken to ensure that the rural-military classes had a satisfactory share of political power, the government would undo all that it had achieved in the past. He pointed out that the smooth running of government machinery would be difficult if the urban trader class, who had never really been loyal to the British, came to dominate the Punjab Legislative Council. There would always be the danger of legislation and of resolutions being passed that could work against the interests of the government, and if the latter tried to use its special powers to prevent it, agitation would be the inevitable result.[45] If political reforms were to replace British rule with a "Bania Oligarchy" the outcome would be one of potential danger for the Punjab as a whole. Umar Hayat warned that:

> ... the continuance of such distressing conditions among the peasantry may also have the result of alienating the sympathies of those representatives of the leading zamindar families who have hitherto shown conspicuous and steadfast loyalty and have stood by the government through thick and thin.... when the zaminders will find their interests endangered by this class

---

[42] Memorandum on Indian Constitutional Reforms by Major Sir Umar Hayat Khan Tiwana of Shahpur district, Punjab, July 1918. IOR:L/P&J/9/9.

[43] *Ibid.*

[44] *Ibid.*

[45] *Ibid.*

[the urban trading classes] and see that they fared badly in courts and government offices and are not adequately represented according to their numerical strength and their services and sacrifices this will lead to a general discontent among the millions, which will be more dangerous than the discontent among the small minority of the educated classes.[46]

To ensure that the rural-military classes of the Punjab would not be left out in the cold by political reforms, Umar Hayat proposed that certain constitutional provisions be adopted as part of the reforms to ensure the protection of the landed and military interests. To this end, he suggested that a second chamber be created in the provincial legislature specifically for representatives of soldiers and landholders. He also wanted the franchise to be extended to include all discharged and pensioned soldiers so that they could use their vote to send one of them into the Legislative Council. He further suggested that only hereditary zamindars should be allowed to stand in rural seats so as to prevent urban politicians from securing rural seats in the council.[47]

The Punjab Zamindar Central Association, originally known as the Jat Sikh Association, was also representative of the rural-military interests of the province. About one-third of its members consisted of retired soldiers—many of whom had long connections with the military and had assisted in recruitment during the war.[48] Members included prominent Jat leaders like Chaudhari Lal Chand and Chhottu Ram, both of Rohtak district, who had received titles and land grants for their work during the war, Honorary Captain Sardar Janmeja Singh, a retired Risaldar Major who was given honorary rank in recognition of his recruiting work in his district during the war, Honorary Captain Sardar Bishan Singh, aide-de-camp to the Viceroy, Honorary Captain Hanwant Singh, an honorary magistrate in Rohtak district, and Honorary Captain Sardar Gurdit Singh, an assistant recruiting officer in Ferozepur district during the war.[49]

[46] *Ibid.*

[47] *Ibid.*

[48] Presentation by the Punjab Zamindar Central Association, and accompanying note by W.S. Marris, 20 November 1917, in Montagu Collections. IOR:MSS.EUR.D.523/35.

[49] *Ibid.*

Like their Muslim counterparts, leaders of the Punjab Zamindar Central Association were concerned that constitutional changes should be made in such a way as to ensure that "town bred educated people" did not monopolize the councils in the Punjab.[50] In a memorandum to the Joint Parliamentary Committee, the vice-president of the Association, Chaudhari Lal Chand, proposed that the rural classes be given ninety per cent of the seats in the provincial council.[51] Echoing the arguments made by Umar Hayat Khan Tiwana, he emphasized that the interests of the zamindars and peasant-proprietors who had consistently supplied combatants to the Indian Army must be safeguarded, especially against the urban classes. He felt that if the politics were left to chance, the urban classes would dominate government departments, at the expense of the rural classes.[52]

The rural-military elites' fears regarding a possible urban dominated political arena in the Punjab had been aroused by the political activities of the main urban political associations in the province, the Provincial Congress Committee, the Hindu Sabha[53] and the two branches of the Muslim League,[54] especially by their demands for the wider enfranchisement of the urban areas. In its memorandum to the Franchise Committee, the Punjab Congress Committee demanded that thirty per cent of elected seats should be given to urban areas.[55] The Punjab Hindu Sabha, representing non-Congress Hindus in the Punjab, called for the abolition of reserved seats for communal

[50] *Ibid.*

[51] Rao Bahadur Chaudhari Lal Chand, a jagirdar and landholder, who was a member of the Punjab Legislative Council, and who had served during the war in the Punjab Recruiting Board, was an honorary assistant recruiting officer in Rohtak, president of the All-India Jat Association. See his memorandum to the Joint Parliamentary Committee, n.d. IOR:L/P&J/9/9.

[52] *Ibid.*

[53] The Hindu Sabha was established in Lahore in 1907 with the objective of promoting the welfare of the Hindu community in the Punjab. Most of its members were leading Hindus of the province, and the Sabha claimed to be loyalist, but its members took part in 'advanced politics'. See note by Sir William Marris, 21 November 1917, in Montagu Collection. MSS/EUR/D/523/35.

[54] A breakaway Punjab Provincial Muslim League was constituted when the old Muslim League organization in the Punjab, under the leadership of Muhammud Shafi, refused to allow in 1916 the lead of the All India Muslim League in adopting a joint political programme with the Congress.

[55] Cited in Page, *Prelude to Partition*, p. 57.

representatives; it wanted half the seats of any future Legislative Council to go to Hindus, with an eighteen per cent share for urban members.[56] The Provincial Muslim League proposed the establishment of a council of 125 members, of whom eighty per cent were to be elected, with six urban seats being created for every ten rural seats in the Council.[57]

The Government of India Act, 1919

The terms of the Government of India Act of 1919 for the Punjab eventually incorporated much that had been proposed by the Punjab government and the province's rural-military lobby, while rejecting those of the urban parties, indicating, perhaps, the extent to which urban considerations had become marginal to the politics of the Punjab. Although the Punjab government's proposals were not accepted in toto (the recommendations they forwarded being modified by the Franchise Committee)[58] the gist of its original suggestions remained largely intact. The reformed provincial Legislative Council would be expanded to comprise seventy-one elected and twenty-three official members. Of the elected members, sixty-four were to be elected from territorial constituencies and seven more from special constituencies. Of the sixty-four territorial seats, fifty-one were rural and thirteen urban. They were divided into twenty non-Muslim (seven urban and thirteen rural), thirty-two Muslim (five urban and twenty-seven rural) and twelve Sikhs (one urban and eleven rural).[59]

The rural franchise for the Punjab was to be based on payment of land revenue of at least twenty-five rupees (half the amount proposed by O'Dwyer) or holdings as tenants of more than twenty-four acres of irrigated or forty-eight acres of un-irrigated land, while

---

[56] See Address presented to the Viceroy and Secretary of State, 1918, *PP*, Cmd. 9178, Vol. 18, p. 480.

[57] Reforms Committee (Franchise), p. 226. IOR:L/PARL/409B.

[58] The original proposals of the Punjab government were slightly altered by the Reforms Committee. For instance, the thirty-four elected seats proposed by the Punjab government was increased to forty. But the Committee reported that in its proposals regarding the franchise, it adhered faithfully to the general lines of the schemes submitted by the provincial governments. See *Report of Franchise Committee* (Southborough), in *PP*, 1919, Cmd. 141, p. 459.

[59] *Punjab Electoral Statistics and Maps*, Lahore, 1921. IOR:POS 5546.

the urban vote was based on the obligation to pay income tax or the possession of immoveable property worth at least 4,000 rupees. These qualifications consequently created a small and restricted electorate in the Punjab; only 500,789 people, or 3.1 per cent of the province's total population, were actually given the vote. More significantly, the electorate was heavily tilted towards the countryside; of the total enfranchised, rural voters accounted for 423,192, and urban voters for 77,597. The figures indicate, however, that there was, despite the resistance to urban demands, a larger percentage of urbanites (7.5 per cent) who were given the vote as opposed to only 2.8 per cent of the rural population,[60] indicative of the exclusiveness of the rural-military lobby and the elitist nature of political power in rural Punjab.

One of the most important features of the 1919 constitution related to the provision for the military vote. In its original proposals, the Punjab government had recommended that only retired and pensioned Indian officers with the rank of jemadar and above should be enfranchised, while the rural-military representatives had demanded that the vote should be given to all ex-soldiers. The Franchise Committee, after considering these proposals, decided to recommend the enfranchisement of all retired and pensioned Indian officers.[61] It worried about the politicizing of the army if serving soldiers were given the vote.[62] However, these proved to be inconsequential as many of the serving soldiers secured the right to vote by being landowners. The recommendations of the committee were incorporated in the draft provincial electoral rules, but when these were presented to the House of Commons, an amendment was moved (possibly influenced by the representation of the rural-military elite) suggesting the enfranchisement for provincial legislatures of "all retired, pensioned, and discharged officers, non-commissioned officers, and soldiers of His Majesty's Forces".[63] This was accepted and in the final constitution, all ex-soldiers, irrespective of rank, were given the right to vote.

[60] *Ibid.*

[61] *Franchise Committee Report*, 1919, Cmd. 141, Vol. 16, p. 460.

[62] Views of GoI on Report of Southborough Committee, in *PP*, 1919, Cmd. 176, Vol. 16, p. 868.

[63] 'The Military Service Qualification For Franchise' in *Report of the Indian Franchise Committee (Lothian), 1932*, in *PP*, Cmd. 4086, Vol. 8, p. 641.

Although the military vote generally formed a quite negligible portion of the electorate in the other provinces, it constituted a very substantial element in the Punjab electorate. In the upshot, the military vote in the Punjab was estimated to be 190,000, or 31.6 per cent of the entire provincial electorate.[64] The significance of the military vote in the traditional military districts of the Punjab, such as Jhelum, Rawalpindi, Attock, Shahpur, Amritsar and Rohtak, was even more pronounced. It is difficult to calculate with any accuracy the percentage of the military vote in any particular constituency in any year, given the lack of definite figures of retired military personnel in the districts, but if we assume that one-third of those who had been recruited during the First World War were demobilized, the proportion of voters who had military connections in such districts would still average over seventy per cent of their respective district electorates.[65]

The real substance of the Punjab government's proposals, and which had also been the main demands of the rural-military lobby, that power be devolved to the traditional allies to the exclusion of urban politicians, were thus embodied in the Government of India Act of 1919. The terms and provisions of the act were consequently skewed very much in favour of the rural-military elites of the province. The electorate was overwhelmingly rural and conservative—more than seventy per cent of the rural voters in the Punjab (299,461 of 423,192) were landlords, dominant zemindars, rural notables, minor officials and ex-soldiers—and their interests dominated the council.[66] The old aristocracy in the Punjab had been returned to power. The significance of this first constitutional reform for the subsequent political development of the Punjab cannot be underestimated. By providing for the overwhelming dominance of the

[64] Report of Indian Franchise Committee, 1932, Cmd. 4086.

[65] Roughly, in Rohtak, the proportion would be approximately 12,000 out of 18,000 (sixty per cent); in Jhelum, Rawalpindi and Attock, almost 100 per cent; in Shahpur, 9,000 out of 17,000 (fifty-three per cent); in Amritsar, 9,000 out of 18,000 (fifty per cent). For figures see M.S Leigh, *Punjab and the War*, pp. 59–60, and *Punjab Electoral Statistics, 1920*.

[66] The electoral statistics of 1920 did not provide a separate count of the ex-soldiers vote in the districts. However, it can be assumed that the bulk of Punjab's ex-soldiers would already have qualified for the vote under the property or title qualifications. The numbers who actually only qualified under the military vote would thus be a small one. *Punjab Electoral Statistics, 1920*.

landed and military vote in the Punjab electorate, the act set the stage for the political domination of the very classes whose coop- eration was always crucial for the preservation of Punjab's posi- tion as the military bulwark of the Raj.

The Rural-Military Elites and Legislative Politics

The first provincial elections under the Government of India Act of 1919 were carried out in the Punjab in December 1920. Of the seventy-one elected seats only fifty-nine were contested; the rest of the seats were returned unopposed.[67] The Khilafat non-cooperation movement, coupled with the unsettled conditions in many parts of the province following the end of the First World War in 1920, had dampened enthusiasm for the province's first ever general elec- tions.[68] In the fifty-nine contested constituencies, only 32.2 per cent of the electorate—130,152 out of 404,371—voted.[69] As part of its non-cooperation movement, the All India Congress Committee had issued a call for all Congress candidates to boycott the elections and for the population not to participate in the elections. In the Punjab, Congress candidates withdrew their candidature from the council elections. As a result, voter turnout was particularly low in urban areas (only 8.5 per cent of urban votes were cast), especially in places where Congress propaganda to boycott the elections had been effective.[70] In the urban non-Muslim seat of Lahore city, for example, only 269 out of an electorate of 7,637 voted, while in the Muslim urban seat of Amritsar city, only 75 votes (out of 3,718) were cast.[71] The rural constituencies, however, were less affected by the boycott propaganda and recorded the considerably higher polling percentage of 33.2 per cent.[72]

Elections in the Punjab had not been fought on party lines and the success of the candidates was largely determined by personal

---

[67] *Returns Showing Results of Election in India, 1921: Punjab Legislative Council*, in *PP*, Cmd. 1261, 1921, Vol. 26, p. 11.

[68] See Satya M. Rai, *Legislative Politics and the Freedom Struggle in the Punjab, 1897– 1947*, Delhi, 1984, p. 98.

[69] *Returns Showing Results of Elections in India, 1923: Results in the Punjab, PP*, Cmd. 2154, 1923, Vol. 18, p. 497.

[70] Weekly Reports, Punjab, 7 January 1921. IOR:L/P&J/6/1726.

[71] *Election Returns, 1921, Punjab.* Cmd.1261. p. 12.

[72] *Ibid.*

and kinship factors, religious ties, factional interests, and influence and patronage. No party creeds informed the choice of voters, and political issues meant little to a predominantly rural electorate, ninety per cent of whom were reported to be illiterate.[73] It was observed that rural voters tended to exercise their franchise along personal lines and were inclined to judge the personality, rather than the programme, of the candidate. This sort of voter behaviour in rural Punjab was best summed up by Firoze Khan Noon, a long-standing member of the Provincial Councils. He explained

> The voters were not able to judge the quality of the candidates. They were influenced by feelings of tribes, caste, friendship or by the ability of the candidates and relations to influence officials in various directions in favour of the voters.[74]

Such voting behaviour and the restricted nature of the franchise favoured candidates who were from rural-military elites at the expense of urban politicians. The former consisted of individuals who were landlords, pirs, local officials and kinship and factional leaders; in other words, men of considerable standing in their localities and who had extensive patronage at their disposal. Their command of economic resources and local networks of influence enabled them to secure the votes of an electorate whose interests were very closely tied to theirs.

These candidates were also able to benefit from the military vote which was substantial in the key military districts of the province. As these elites were often representatives of the military classes in their districts, they were able to secure the electoral support of ex-soldiers who chose to place their faith (and therefore their votes) on the person most likely to protect their interests in the council. It was this view that led the Indian Soldiers' Association in Jullunder doab to define as one of its objectives "the support of suitable candidates at elections for the benefits of [its] serving, pensioned and discharged soldiers and officers".[75]

---

[73] Satya M. Rai, *Legislative Politics*, p. 100.

[74] Firoze Khan Noon, *From Memory*, Lahore, 1969, p. 93.

[75] 'Note on formation of Indian Officers' Association', PHP(M) 'B', pros. 85, January 1922.

The 1920 provincial elections thus returned, as the provincial government had hoped, a Legislative Council dominated by the "Old World". The first expanded council inaugurated in 1921 comprised mainly "landlords, peasant-proprietors, ex-army officers, and a sprinkling of traders and lawyers". The Punjab government reported that "a large number of members of the council were landed proprietors .... typically representative of the province .... and the council as a whole represented a moderate current of political opinion".[76]

This first expanded Legislative Council in the Punjab contained thirty-eight members who belonged to the landed/military families of the Punjab, or were rural notables, ex-soldiers and minor officials who had functioned as the state's military intermediaries during the war. Notable members of this group of rural-military elites included: Syed Mehdi Shah of Gojra, a leading Muslim from Lyallpur who was actively involved in recruiting during the war, elected from his rural Muslim seat in Lyallpur; Raja Mahommed Akbar of Jhelum, chief of the heavily recruited Chib Rajputs of Jhelum, elected from the west Punjab towns; Honourary Lieutenant Sikander Hayat Khan, a member of the militarily prominent Wah family from Attock district.[77] Others in the list of rural-military elites elected to the provincial council in 1920 included men like Syed Muhammud Reza Shah, a prominent landlord from Multan, Khan Bahadur Malik Muhammud Amin, Captain Ahmad Yar Khan Daultana, an influential landed/military gentry from Multan, Malik Khan Muhammud, Zaildar Chaudhary Ali Akbar, Honorary Lieutenent Chaudhary Lal Chand from Rohtak, Sardar Kharak Singh, Sardar Dasaundha Singh (both members of the rural/military Central Zamindar Association), Honourary Lieutenant S. Rajbhir Singh, Sardar Harnam Singh, Sardar Sahib Risaldar Dilbagh Singh, Sikh landlords like Hara Singh Bedi, Sunder Singh Majithia and Jogendra Singh; Mian Muhammud Shah Nawaz of the Arain Mians of Baghbanpura, Allan Khan of the influential Drishak family of Dera Ghazi Khan, Chaudhari Fazli Ali, a leading landowner from Gujrat district, Firoze Khan Noon, from the Noon family of Mitha Tiwana, a related branch to Umar Hayat Khan Tiwana, Muhammad

---

[76] *Punjab Administrative Reports (PAR), 1923–24*, Lahore, 1925, pp. 1–2.

[77] Sikander played a prominent role in the recruitment campaign during the war and held the British honourary rank of lieutenant. He later became the first Premier of the Punjab under provincial autonomy.

Saifullah Khan of the Isakhel family, Muhammud Khan of Muzzafargarh, Pir Makhdum Reza Shah of Gilani, the Pir of Makhad, the Pir Sayyad Hussein Shah of Rajoa, Pir Ali Hyder Shah of Rawalpindi, Malik Amir Muhhamud Khan of Kalabagh, Attock, Pir Sayyad Ghulam Muhammud of Shahpur, Malik Muhamud Ali Khan of Shamasabad, Karimullah Khan, a leading member of the militarily prominent Darapur branch of the Janjuas of Jhelum and Khan Bahadur Muhammud Jamal Khan Leghari, a Baluch tumandar chief from Dera Ghazi Khan.[78]

The election of 1920 had, therefore, returned to the council a majority of individuals who not only had close connections with the military classes in the province, but who were intimately involved in the workings of local institutions of civil-military cooperation at the district level, more particularly the Soldiers' Boards. By being elevated to the status of "partners in government" at Lahore, they were, in effect, reinforcing the civil-military regime in the province. It is relevant to note that several members of the council, most notably Sikander Hayat Khan, Mehdi Shah of Gojra, Sardar Ragbhir Singh Sindhanwalia and Chaudhry Chhottu Ram,[79] had all been involved in the first few years after the war in the Punjab Soldiers' Board.[80]

As legislators these elite figures were now able to influence government decisions directly for the benefit of their constituents, on which they, in turn, were dependent for their position in the council. At the very outset of their involvement in legislative politics, therefore, these men preoccupied themselves with promoting the interests of the landlords and landholding peasantry (the classes from which recruitment in the Punjab was mostly done), the very stratum of agrarian society which had constituted the overwhelming bulk of Punjab's restricted electorate. They were not concerned

[78] For the list of members returned to the first provincial council, see Kripal C. Yadav, *Elections in the Punjab, 1920–1947* (New Delhi, 1987), pp. 45–50. The most prominent spokesman for the military classes in the Punjab, Malik Umar Hayat Khan Tiwana, was elected by an overwhelming majority from the western Punjab constituency to a seat in the Council of State, the upper house of the Central Legislative Assembly in Delhi.

[79] Chhottu Ram was defeated in his first election attempt in 1920, but was later elected in a by-election from East Rohtak in 1923. Yadav, *Elections in the Punjab*, p. 52.

[80] Proceedings of Punjab Soldiers' Board meeting, 7 May 1925 in PHP(M) 'C', File 418, 1925.

with the lower strata of Punjab's agrarian society, namely landless tenants and rural labourers, which while contributing vital manpower to the countryside, were not regarded as sufficiently politically significant by the British to be enfranchised. To maximize their influence in the council, these elite representatives decided to act collectively as a rural-military lobby, and soon after the first Legislative Council was constituted coalesced into a solid rural voting bloc.[81] Muslim rural members, almost without exception, belonged to this bloc, which was also supported by Hindu Jat and Sikh members on issues affecting the interests of the landed class. The pirs amongst them, who, as landlords, had already established close social and economic ties with the tribal leaders of western Punjab, were able to fit easily into this political grouping. With this bloc dominating the council, the chief legislative agenda was centred on the containment of land revenue demand and taxation—the very matters which concerned the landowning and military classes directly. Ex-soldiers who were landowners constantly complained that the land revenue demand on their land took up almost all of their agricultural earnings and pensions during years of poor harvests.[82] The rural-military lobby, therefore, put considerable pressure on the government to place the procedure of assessment for land revenue on a statutory basis[83]—the amounts of payment to be decided by the Legislative Council and not by settlement officers—in the hope that they could exert a direct influence in the Council on the revenue administration of the province, particularly in the fixing of land revenue. Under pressure from this lobby, the government framed a Land Revenue Bill in 1922 aimed at placing a statutory regulation on land revenue. The Bill was, however, later dropped as the GoI was unwilling to endorse its proposal, suggesting that the collection of land revenue remained central to the

---

[81] It is not known if these elites still retained any affiliation with the Punjab Muslim Association and the Central Zemindar Association, of which many of them had been members. With the exception of their representations to the Secretary of State and Viceroy in 1918, there was no mention of either association in subsequent government reports.

[82] Proceedings of Punjab Soldiers' Board's meeting, 21 February 1921, in PHP(M) 'C', File 67, 1922.

[83] Memorandum on the Working of Reforms in the Punjab by H.D. Craik, Chief Sec. to GoP, 13 August 1924, in *Views of Local Governments on Working of Reforms, 1924–25, PP,* Cmd. 2362, Vol. 10, p. 672.

imperial enterprise and could not be compromised.[84] In 1923, during a budget debate in the council, the government proposed an increase in the canal land occupiers' rates in an attempt to raise provincial revenue. The British administrators defended this increase on the grounds that the prices of agricultural produce had generally risen, and that profits from irrigated lands had accordingly escalated. Not surprisingly, the government's proposal met with stiff resistance from the rural lobby, which complained that the proposed enhancement of water rates would have to be borne entirely by their community, which constituted the bulk of occupiers of canal-irrigated land. The rural members warned the government that the increase would alienate the sympathies of its rural supporters,[85] and recommended instead the imposition of a salt tax as this would be spread more evenly across the province, affecting the urban as well as the rural population of the Punjab.[86] The rural-military lobby did not always get what it wanted. Despite its opposition, the unpopular canal occupiers' rates were eventually raised by an executive order, and it was reported that the effects of this, plus the inability of the Punjab government to put forward a Land Revenue Bill, generated much disaffection amongst the rural members of the council.

In 1923, towards the end of the term of the first Legislative Council, the rural-military lobby constituted itself into a political party, the Punjab National Unionist Party. The main mover behind the formation of this party was Fazli Husain, a Muslim member of strictly urban origins.[87] Although elected into the Council in 1920

[84] *Ibid.*

[85] *PAR, 1923–24*, p. 3.; *PAR, 1924–25*, p. 85.

[86] *Ibid.*

[87] Although a landlord—he possessed a small estate in Gurdaspur district—Fazli Husain was essentially from a service family. Fazli's grandfather had served in the Sikh armies, and his father served as a district judge. Fazli received his legal training at Cambridge University and started his political career as a member of the Punjab Muslim League. Before 1920 he was elected to the Morley–Minto Council from the Punjab University, and following the Montagu–Chelmsford reforms, he was elected in 1920 to the Muslim landlord seat. Under dyarchy, he served as one of the two ministers chosen by the Governor, the other one being a Hindu, Lala Harkishen Lal. He remained a minister until he was appointed to the Executive Council in 1926. In 1930 he was appointed to the Viceroy's Executive Council in New Delhi where he remained till 1935. See Azim Husain, *Mian Fazl-I-Husain: A Political Biography* (London, 1966).

from the landholders seat, Fazli did not belong to any prominent landed/military family. Like most other politicians without a strong rural support base in the Punjab, Fazli would have gradually faded into political oblivion had it not been for his fortuitous appointment as a minister in the first Council. His appointment as a minister was a gesture by the Governor Edward Maclagan to win over moderate politicians from the influence of the Congress. In contrast to his predecessor, Maclagan was more readily prepared to appoint a minister representing moderate opinion in the council, but whose political credibility was not tainted by being too closely associated with the Raj. Fazli Husain fitted the bill perfectly.[88] He had begun his political career in the Punjab Muslim League, and in 1919 had openly protested against the Rowlatt Act and the Jallianwala Bagh massacre. The following year, however, he decided against participating in the non-cooperation movement, and chose not to boycott the elections.[89]

After his appointment as Minister, Fazli sought to create a bloc of supporters in the council to enhance his political influence. As a Muslim minister, Fazli could have easily enjoyed the allegiance of Muslim legislators, but he realized that an exclusively Muslim communal party would not constitute a sufficiently potent and effective bloc within the council, half of which was composed of Hindu and Sikh members. He understood very well that the real basis of power in the council lay not with any exclusive communal grouping, but in the rural-military lobby, whose command over the rural electorate in the Punjab ensured their majority in the Legislative Council. In 1923 Fazli thus sought an alliance with the Hindu Jat members by successfully lobbying for the appointment of Chaudhary Lal Chand, a leading Jat member, as Minister for Agriculture. The latter, however, lost his seat in the council following a successful election petition against him and his place was taken over by Chaudhary Chhottu Ram, who consequently emerged as the leading Jat member in the council and eventually became a co-founder of the Unionist Party. Chhottu Ram had chosen to align himself with the Muslim rural bloc because he understood that the social and economic advancement of the Jat community could best be served by a rural-

[88] Satya M. Rai, *Legislative Politics and the Freedom Movement in the Punjab, 1897–1947*, p. 150.
[89] Azim Husain, *Fazl-i-Husain*, p. 123.

military grouping in the Legislative Council. Despite the communal differences, Chhottu Ram was aware that an alliance between the Hindu Jats and Muslim and Sikh landowners would secure a safe majority in the Council for policies favouring the agricultural classes. The rural-military interests of the Hindu Jats provided them with a common ground on which to work with the Muslim landowners, who were also closely tied to the military.

At the same time Chhottu Ram was aware that his own political survival depended upon his championing the economic interest of the Hindu Jats from the Ambala division.[90] His political influence in south-eastern Punjab was owed mainly to the support of the peasant proprietors and the military classes. In his constituency of East Rohtak, more than sixty per cent of those enfranchised had been or still were soldiers and a majority of them were rich Jat peasants.[91] It would thus be politically detrimental for him to associate too closely with urban Hindu politicians who had little in common with the interests of the rural Hindu Jats. This explains his decision to resign from the Congress in November 1920. He had justified his resignation on the grounds that non-cooperation was unconstitutional and that it would lead the masses to violence.[92] A pragmatic politician, he was aware that the Congress' proposed land revenue strike and call to boycott the army would adversely affect the economic interests of the very social groups upon whom he had to rely for political support, as he made clear when he observed:

> We the Jats are being invited to leave the army and not to take to education and remain illiterate. We are asked not to give them land revenue so that government would confiscate our land. Is this policy going to benefit us? We must look at the non-cooperation movement from the point of view of what is beneficial to our caste.[93]

[90] For a political biography of Chhottu Ram, see Prem Chowdhury, *Punjab Politics: The Role of Chhottu Ram*, New Delhi, 1984.

[91] *Ibid.*, p. 144. Although serving soldiers had not been given the franchise as such, many serving soldiers had qualified for the vote as landowners, title holders or as jagirdars.

[92] *Ibid.*, p. 162.

[93] *Jat Gazette*, 23 February 1921, cited in *ibid.*, p. 145.

The Sikh members in the council did not enter into any formal alliance with the Unionist Party. Members of the loyalist Sikh political party, the Chief Khalsa Diwan, led by Sunder Singh Majithia,[94] collaborated, however, with the Unionists on rural matters, but chose to retain their separate organization. With the Akali movement gaining ascendancy in the Punjab in 1922–23, most of the Sikh members chose indeed to keep a cautious distance from the pro-government Unionist Party.

The Unionist Party was, therefore, more a caucus of landowning rural-military elites in the Legislative Council than an actual political party with an ideology, wide organizational grassroots support or an effective local hierarchy. It did not formally contest the subsequent 1923 elections as a political party. However, the elections of that year returned thirty-three members belonging to the Unionist Party,[95] reaffirming the dominance of the rural-military elites in provincial politics.

The Punjab government was initially pleased with the formation and success of the Unionist Party, claiming that "it was the best instance of the right kind of provincial government, based broadly on the landlords, peasants and soldiers".[96] The desirability, and indeed need, to have a party of rural and military representatives dominating the ministries had been realized by the British at the very outset of political reforms in the Punjab.[97] Just before the provincial elections in 1920, J.P. Thompson, Chief Secretary to the Punjab Government, suggested to some candidates the desirability of forming a conservative political party, and prompted them to prepare a manifesto for the election campaign.[98] Thompson and

---

[94] Sardar Sir Sunder Singh Majithia (1872–41) was a member of a prominent landed family from Amritsar. He was nominated to the Punjab Legislative Council in 1909, where he served until 1915. He was a member of Punjab's executive council from 1921–26, and later served as a minister in the Unionist government under provincial autonomy from 1937–41.

[95] Yadav, *Elections in the Punjab*, p. 133.

[96] Note by F.L. Brayne, Deputy Commissioner, Gurgaon district, 1920 to 1927, Financial Commissioner and Secretary to Revenue Department, Punjab Government, 1939–40, n.d. in Brayne Collections. IOR:MSS.EUR.F.152/69.

[97] Here developments in the Punjab resembled those in the United Provinces. For the latter, see P.D. Reeves, *Landlords and Governments in Uttar Pradesh: A Study of their Relations until Zamindari Abolition*, Bombay, 1991.

[98] Thompson Diaries, 8 November 1919, in Thompson Papers. IOR:MSS.EUR. F.137/13.

other seasoned British administrators recognized that British rule in India depended in the final resort on the continued reliability of the Indian Army, and that in turn was contingent on a loyal and contented peasantry in the Punjab.[99] It was, therefore, crucial that the Punjab government must be perceived to be in close touch with, and sympathetic to, issues affecting the interests of the two bulwarks of the Raj in Punjab: the dominant zamindars and the soldiers. Working hand-in-hand with a Legislative Council dominated by a rural-military party was thus thought to be the best possible guarantee of the continued contentment of the rural-military classes.

Yet if the British had encouraged the formation of the Unionist Party to facilitate control of the rural-military districts, they soon realized that there was a price they had to pay. From 1923 onwards, and in the subsequent Unionist-dominated councils elected in 1926 and 1930,[100] attempts by the Unionist Party to further the economic interests of the military classes, the landlords and the dominant peasantry frequently resulted in its colliding head-on with the government. In a memorandum submitted to the Muddiman Reforms Enquiry Committee in 1924, the Punjab government reported that the Unionist dominated "Councils showed general antipathy to supporting, or indeed considering any project of fresh taxation .... however embarrassing it may prove to the government".[101] It further complained that the Council was unable to "convince itself of the necessity of balancing provincial budgets" despite the drain on provincial resources caused by a series of crop failures in the early 1920s.[102] The demand by council members for powers to influence directly the land revenue administration in the province was another source of contention between the government and the rural-military lobby. Despite the failure of its earlier attempt to introduce statutory regulations relating to revenue administration in the province in 1922, the rural-military lobby did not give up and its persistent

---

[99] Malcolm Hailey, quoted by H.D. Craik, Governor of Punjab, in Craik to Brabourne, 10 September 1938, in Linlithgow Papers. IOR:MSS.EUR.F.125/87.

[100] In the 1926 elections, thirty-one Unionist members were returned to the council, and in 1930 (the last elections under the 1919 Act), thirty-seven Unionist members were returned. See Yadav, *Elections in the Punjab*, pp. 133–34.

[101] Memorandum on the Working of Reforms in the Punjab, from H.D. Craik, 13 August 1924, in *Views of Local Governments on Working of Reforms*, 1924, *PP*, Cmd. 2362, 1924, Vol. 10, p. 672.

[102] *Ibid.*, p. 676.

demands finally bore fruit when the government decided to introduce the Punjab Land Revenue (Amendment) Bill in 1926. The bill was referred to a select committee which recommended, under the provisions for land revenue assessments, a reduction in the standard of assessment from half to one-third of net assets; a prolongation of the period of assessment from thirty to fourty years; and the limitation of enhancement to thirty-three per cent of the existing rate of assessment. However, when it was presented to the Council in 1928, members of the rural-military lobby found that the provisions suggested by the selected committee were inadequate, and proceeded to make substantial modifications to the bill, which included inter alia a fixed reduction of assessment at one-quarter of the net assets, and the lowering of the limitation of enhancement to twenty-five per cent of the existing assessment. The government was greatly concerned that the bill in this form would result in a significant loss of revenue for the province. Geoffrey de Montmorency, the Financial Commissioner, pointed out the Punjab had owed it present prosperity to the careful building up of land revenue, and that the measures contemplated by the Bill would affect that source of revenue.[103] Such official interjections notwithstanding, the bill was passed in May 1928 by the solid vote of the rural members of the council. In December 1930, as the province was suffering the effects of the Depression, the rural-military lobby pressured the government once more to grant at least a fifty per cent remission of land revenue on all spring crops of 1931 throughout the province. They warned that unless the government took this measure, the agriculturists, suffering severe financial difficulties, would join the Congress civil disobedience movement. The government finally conceded and approved of remissions which cost the provincial revenue more than a hundred million rupees.[104]

The performance of the elites in the council demonstrated a paradoxical relationship between the government and its allies in the council. Prior to 1920, the old aristocratic landlords and rural notables had been entirely dependent upon the government's goodwill for

---

[103] Punjab Legislative Council Debates, 1927 as recorded in *Indian Annual Register*, 1928, Vol. 2, pp. 244–45.

[104] Punjab Legislative Council Debates, 27 November–3 December 1930, as recorded in M.N. Mitra (ed.), *Indian Annual Register*, 1931, Vol. 2, p. 207.

the continued enjoyment of their special status. They had to show active loyalty, as they had during the First World War, to earn the state's patronage. Although successive Punjab governments had been careful not to alienate them and so lose their active support, these elites had seldom been in a position to dictate terms to the government, and had virtually no direct influence in government policies. But changes introduced by post-war political reforms brought about, perhaps inevitably, a shift in this relationship. These elites were no longer entirely dependent on the state for their political position, but on the support of their electoral base. This meant that they had to cultivate the support of their constituencies by championing their interests in the Legislative Council, sometimes at the expense of official interests. Yet, despite their constant jockeying against the government for advantages in terms of land revenue and taxation, these elites realized that, in the last resort, their interests were still mainly predicated upon British rule, which they could not afford to challenge or jeopardize. Consequently political affairs were therefore kept to a minimum in council debates,[105] and the Punjab government was able to report that "the executive ... have been supported by a party which has not attempted to force [the government] into an extreme position".[106] The reforms had, therefore, brought about a new breed of collaborators who, although they emphasized their continued loyalty to the Raj, were able to use their newly found leverage to assert greater control over affairs affecting them and their constituents. It is perhaps a reflection of this paradoxical relationship that in the early 1930s the Unionist Party was regarded by the British as an official opposition within the Legislative Council, frequently voting against the government. In the 1931–32 sessions the party accounted for 200 out of 345 votes against the government.[107]

Despite the sometimes uneasy relationship between the government and its allies in the council, the Montagu–Chelmsford reforms had established a political arrangement in the Punjab that generally satisfied both the Punjab government and its friends. The state was happy with the arrangement, as the men who came

[105] *PAR, 1923–24*, p. 7.
[106] H.D. Craik, Memorandum on the Working of Reforms in the Punjab, 13 August 1924, Cmd. 2362, Vol. 10, p. 671.
[107] *PAR, 1932–33*, p. 7.

to control the levers of power in the province after 1920 were those who were heavily committed to the maintenance of the Punjab military machine. It was the classes recruited to the army that derived most benefit from the power which had been devolved.[108] For the rural-military elites, their position in the province was reinforced by their dominance in the political arena. Their traditional antagonists, the urban politicians, had been severely handicapped by the distribution of seats and the franchise provisions of the reforms. But this arrangement, predicated upon the restrictive terms of the 1919 Act in the Punjab, were then brought into question by the constitutional changes brought about by the Government Act of 1935.

Dyarchy to Provincial Autonomy

The Constitution of 1919 was finally replaced by the Government of India Act of 1935. The latter introduced a constitution that provided for a political structure in which autonomous units, consisting of governor's provinces, chief commissioner's provinces and the acceding princely states, would be united in a federal framework. At the all-India centre, considerable powers would be kept in British hands and the governor general would retain discretionary powers in matters concerning defence and external affairs. He would not be responsible to the elected legislature, but only to the Secretary of State for India and through him, to the British Parliament. The central executive was to operate on a dyarchic basis, and only "transferred" departments were to be responsible to the federal legislature.[109]

In six "Governor's provinces", including the Punjab, the system of "dual government" was replaced by full provincial autonomy. In these provinces, dyarchy was abolished and full powers were now vested in Councils of Ministers responsible to legislatures elected from a wider franchise, constituted by at least ten per cent of the province's population. The Governor remained the titular head of the province and retained certain safeguards to protect minority interests and, should the need arise, to maintain law and order in

[108] David Page, *Prelude to Partition*, p. 59.
[109] For details and a discussion of the Act, see Reginald Coupland, *The Indian Problem, 1833–1935*, Oxford, 1968, pp. 134–35.

the province. Beyond this, however, the Council of Ministers was in full control of provincial affairs.[110]

Following the 1935 Act the Punjab Legislative Council was replaced by an expanded Legislative Assembly. The new Assembly contained 175 seats, including special seats reserved for women, landholders and the scheduled castes. Of the 175 seats, eighty-four were Muslim seats, forty-two general, and thirty-one were reserved for Sikhs. Eighteen seats were also reserved for special groups, such as women, landowners, small communal groups like Europeans, Anglo-Indians and Indian Christians, and other functional groups, such as commerce, labour and university graduates.[111]

The first elections under the 1935 Act were held in 1937. Out of the 175 seats in the Punjab Legislative Assembly, the Unionist Party won a comfortable majority of ninety-five seats. Unionist candidates took seventy-three of the seventy-five rural Muslim seats, and all but one of the Hindu rural seats in the Hindu Jat heartland of Ambala division.[112] After the elections, it formed the government in coalition with the Sikh Khalsa Nationalist Party (fourteen seats), a party representing the conservative landed Sikh gentry, and the Hindu National Progressive Party (eleven seats)[113]. The Council of Ministers formed in the Punjab in 1937 was essentially a Unionist Ministry, comprising Sikander Hayat Khan as the premier, Khizr Hayat Khan Tiwana (son of Umar Hayat Khan Tiwana and leader of the Mitha Tiwana family in Shahpur), Chhottu Ram, Sunder Singh Majithia, representing the Sikhs, Abdul Haye (Unionist) and Manohar Lal, an independent Hindu member.

The Unionist victory in the Punjab was especially remarkable in view of the electoral success of the Congress in other provinces. In 1937 the Congress swept the provincial elections, winning 716 out of 1,585 "open" constituencies. It had a clear majority in five

[110] *Ibid.*

[111] Yadav, *Elections in the Punjab*, p. 17.

[112] Stephen Oren, 'The Sikhs, Congress, and the Unionists in British Punjab, 1937–45' in *MAS*, Vol. 8(3), 1974, pp. 397–99; see also Ian Talbot, *Provincial Politics and the Pakistan Movement: The Growth of the Muslim League in North-west and North-east India, 1937–47*, Karachi, 1988, p. 87.

[113] The Hindu National Progressive Party was a loyalist Hindu organization comprising mainly of non-Congress Hindu landed interests. It was noted that seven of the eleven elected members belonging to this party were title-holders. See Satya Rai, *Legislative Politics and the Freedom Struggle in the Punjab*, p. 223.

provinces (Madras, Bihar, Orissa, Central Province and the United Provinces), and emerged as the single largest party in three others (Bombay, Assam and the North-Western Frontier Province). In some provinces Congress victories had been achieved at the expense of erstwhile politically powerful landlord parties, most notably the National Agriculturist Parties of the United Provinces[114] and the Justice Party of Madras.[115] Yet in the Punjab the Congress was trounced at the polls by the Unionist Party, and managed to win only ten per cent of the seats in the Assembly (eighteen seats). Why had the Unionists thrived when the other pro-government landlord parties had fallen to the Congress? To understand the basis of the continued Unionist dominance under provincial autonomy, it is necessary to examine the franchise provisions of the 1935 Act for the Punjab and to ask to what extent the 1919 electoral system in the Punjab, which had favoured the rural-military elites, had been altered by the 1935 Act.

Under the Montagu-Chelmsford reforms, the Punjab rural-military lobby's dominance of successive provincial legislative councils had been facilitated by a restricted franchise. In the Punjab, the allegiance of the bulk of the electorate had been secured by the rural-military elites, first through their personal standing in the constituencies, and then by their ability to collectively champion the interests of their electoral base in the councils. This gave the Unionists a solid base, which the Congress, with its image as the political vehicle of urban Hindu political interests, was unable to erode. The Congress' only hope of electoral success in the Punjab thus depended on a provincial franchise that would be extended to significant numbers of non-agriculturists (as statutorily defined by the Land Alienation Act) and the landless, namely the urban classes, rural tenants, farm labourers and scheduled castes—the very classes which were beyond the canvassing power of the Unionist Party.

[114] For an analysis of the declining fortunes of the landlord politicians in the United Provinces in the 1930s, see P.D. Reeves, 'Landlords and Party Politics in the United Provinces, 1934-37' in D.A. Low (ed.), *Soundings in Modern South Asian Studies*, London, 1968, pp. 261–82.

[115] The full story of the rise, decline and eventual eclipse of the Madras Justice Party is recounted in C.J. Baker, *Politics of South India, 1920–37*, Cambridge, 1976. See also David Arnold, 'The Politics of Coalescence: the Congress in Tamilnad, 1930–1937' in D.A Low (ed.), *Congress and the Raj*, pp. 259–88.

The 1935 Act provided for a significantly extended franchise in the Punjab, from 745,000 in 1930 to 2.75 million in 1935 (from 3.1 per cent to 11.7 per cent of the provincial population). But, as in 1919, under the influence of the Punjab government, and the rural-military lobby in the council, the rural character of the Legislative Assembly and the provincial electorate was preserved. Of the 175 seats in the Punjab Legislative Assembly, 143 were rural.[116] The qualifications for enfranchisement, although lowered in most cases, were not, however, radically altered. With the exception of special constituencies, the qualifications for the vote were still based on land and property ownership, land revenue or income payment, official appointments and titles.[117] Seventy-five per cent of the extended franchise provided by the 1935 Act was constituted by members of the agricultural classes, as defined by the 1900 Land Alienation Act.[118] Only seventeen per cent of landholders and fifty per cent of tenants to be enfranchised (238,000 out of 1,398,000, and 200,000 out of 407,000 respectively) in 1935 in the Punjab belonged to non-agriculturist classes.[119]

On the advice of the provincial government and the Army Department, the military vote was retained.[120] This, as we have seen, had formed a significant bloc in a number of constituencies, and

[116] The territorial constituencies were divided communally, based on the Communal Award of 1932. The Muslims had eighty-four seats (nine urban and seventy-five rural), the Hindus, under General Constituencies, had forty-two seats (eight urban and thirty-four rural), and the Sikhs were given thirty-one seats (two urban and twenty-nine rural). In addition, there were five special seats for the landlords. Yadav, *Elections in the Punjab*, p. 17.

[117] Property and status qualifications of voters in the Punjab from 1937 included persons having passed primary school or any other higher examinations; women who were literate, widows or mothers of soldiers who had died in the war, wives of voters; owner/assignee/lessee/tenant of land/Crown land with land revenue assessed at twenty-five rupees per annum; Title holder; retired military personnel; and government officials. For the urban vote, the qualifications were similar to the above except that in the place of land revenue and ownership of land, the voter had be paying an annual income tax of sixty rupees per annum or be in the possession of immoveable property worth at least 4,000 rupees. *Ibid.*, p. 18.

[118] See *Report of Indian Franchise Committee (Lothian), 1931–32*, in *PP*, Cmd. 4086, 1931–32, Vol. 8, pp. 505–6.

[119] *Ibid.*

[120] 'The Military Service Qualification for Franchise' in *Report of the Indian Franchise Committee, 1932*, in *PP*. Cmd. 4086, Vol. 8.

its proportion was a continually growing one, as soldiers who were pensioned or discharged from the Indian Army were automatically given the vote. By 1930 the military vote was significant enough for the Punjab government to propose to the Indian Statutory Commission to create a non-communal constituency to represent military interests in the provincial and central legislatures. They suggested that five special military seats should be allotted to the provincial Assembly (one for each division), and two in each house of the Central Assembly.[121] The proposal was, however, rejected by the Franchise Committee on the grounds that the military interests were already recognized in the electorate and that there were no reasons for the creation of separate seats.

The provincial electorate eventually approved for the Punjab, consisting of 263,000 urban voters and 2,482,000 rural voters, was therefore still predominantly rural, with a strong conservative element, and dominated by the agricultural classes whose interests were closely tied to the state.[122] What all this implied was that the electoral base, on which continued Unionist domination in the provincial legislatures was predicated prior to 1935, had remained essentially unchanged. By giving the agricultural classes, whose support had been firmly secured by the Unionist Party, seventy-five per cent of the electorate, the terms of the 1935 Act assured the Unionist Party of its majority. The eighteen seats won by the Congress, most of them from the reserved seats for the scheduled castes and Sikh communists, indicated that the Congress' support base in the Punjab had been limited to the marginal voters in the province, among the untouchables and agricultural labourers.[123]

Another factor which had ensured that the Unionist Party was not swept aside, as was the fate of other provincial landlord parties in 1937, was its unique character as a party of landlords and rich peasants. This unity was personified in its two most important leaders, Sikander Hayat Khan, a Muslim tribal chief and landlord

---

[121] See *Report of Punjab Reforms Committee, 1929* in *Reports of Committees appointed by the Provincial Legislative Councils to cooperate with the Indian Statutory Commission, 1929–30,* in *PP,* Cmd. 3572, Vol. 12, pp. 419–20. The Punjab Committee comprised Sikander Hayat Khan, Chhottu Ram, Zafarullah Khan, Narendra Nath, Gokal Chand Narang and Owen Roberts.

[122] *Report of Punjab Government Committee, 1929,* p. 403.

[123] See Prem Chowdhry, 'Social Support Base and Electoral Politics: The Congress in Colonial Southeast Punjab' in *MAS,* Vol. 25(4), 1991, pp. 811–31.

from Attock, who succeeded to the leadership of the party after the death of Fazli Husain in 1936, and Chhottu Ram, a rich Hindu Jat peasant from eastern Punjab. The landlord-peasant cleavage in the Unionist Party had been submerged by the collective concern among its members to protect the agricultural and military interests of their constituencies against the common enemy, the urban commercial and professional classes. And while these political leaders claimed to represent their rural constituencies, regardless of the economic class division within it, their social mobilization was often limited to the enfranchised classes—the landowners and military personnel in the districts.[124]

After the 1937 elections, the Unionist Party, with its commanding majority in the Legislative Assembly, seemed to have reached the height of its power in the Punjab. It had effectively shut out its political adversaries in the province, namely the Congress and the Muslim League, and had enhanced its popularity—and at the same time tightened its leadership—among the enfranchised landed-military classes. In 1937 the Unionist Ministry passed in quick succession a series of bills aimed at perpetuating the protection of agricultural classes through the Land Alienation Act, and to weaken the grip of the urban moneylenders on the agriculturists. One of the bills aimed to liquidate all mortgages made before 1901 whose interests paid over the years had exceeded the principal sum of the loan. Another bill aimed to nullify all land transactions involving the use of "dummy buyers" by non-agriculturist classes, while a third bill required all urban moneylenders to register themselves. The bills, known as "Golden Bills" by the agriculturists, were vehemently opposed by urban legislators, who argued that these bills were aimed at eliminating the moneylending classes. But this was of little avail as the Unionists, with their strong majority in the Assembly, were able to push the bills through without much difficulty.[125]

Conclusion

One of the most distinctive features of politics in the Punjab from 1923 till the eve of Independence was the continued political dominance

---

[124] *Ibid.*

[125] Satya M. Rai, *Legislative Politics and the Freedom Movement in the Punjab, 1897–1947*, pp. 248–55.

of the Unionist Party. Formed from the rural Muslim and Hindu members elected to the Council in 1920, the Party came to dominate constitutional politics in the Punjab for nearly a quarter of a century, until its final defeat in the elections of 1946. This chapter has argued that the Unionist Party was essentially a rural-military lobby, whose dominance of provincial politics had been facilitated by the provisions of the 1919 Government of India Act. On the eve of those reforms, the Punjab government, concerned about the possible alienation of the rural-military population, and therefore the debilitation of the military machinery of the province should a "bania oligarchy" be imposed in the post-reform Punjab, sought to influence the terms of the reforms to work in favour of its rural-military allies. Its proposals concerning the franchise and the distribution of seats in the Punjab, reinforced by representations from the province's rural-military elites, provided the framework within which the final 1919 Reforms were settled in the Punjab and laid the foundation for the political domination of the rural-military elites in the Punjab. The reformed Provincial Councils in the Punjab consequently came to be dominated by the same classes that were militarily and political important to the state in the countryside. Once in the Council the rural-military lobby formed the backbone of a potent rural bloc, determined to use its influence to protect the rural and military interests of the constituents. This bloc was then institutionalized as the Punjab Nationalist Unionist Party. Thereafter the Unionist Party dominated Punjab politics for more than two decades, during which it promoted the interests of the very classes on which its political power was based—the military classes, the richer strata of landowners, rural notables and government officials. That, coupled with an electorate which was only marginally changed by the Government of India Act of 1935, enabled the Unionists not only to survive the transition from dyarchy to provincial autonomy, but also re-confirmed its dominance in Punjab politics.

The nature of Punjab's political experience from 1920 to 1937 left an indelible mark on the political landscape of the province. First, politics in the Punjab were dominated by the very classes whose interests were intimately tied to the British. As rural-military elites, the position of these classes was predicated upon the Punjab's continued position as the "sword arm" of the Raj, and ultimately on British rules itself. Politicians of these rural-military classes were thus cautious to preserve the status quo, and to operate locally in the Punjab within the broad framework of British rule. By securing the reins of power in the province, the rural-military elites thus constituted the conservative bulwark against nationalist agitation in the Punjab and secured for the colonial government a province that would otherwise have been potentially troublesome because of its garrison character. This helps explains why the Punjab not only remained a backwater for the nationalist movement, but also lagged behind in the Muslim League's campaign for Pakistan.[126]

The terms of the reforms, both in 1919 and in 1935, fixed the political focus firmly in the countryside, strengthening the hands of the landed rural-military elites at the expense of the urban politician. What emerged out of the political development of colonial Punjab during the inter-war years was thus the political entrenchment of landlord politicians who were not only able to operate comfortably in a civil-military regime, but very much held it together. This political configuration was to provide the basis for the powerful and deeply entrenched landlord lobby in the post-colonial state of Pakistan.[127]

---

[126] For this story, see Imran Ali, 'The Punjab and the Retardation of Nationalism' in D.A. Low (ed.), *The Political Inheritance of Pakistan*, pp. 29–52.

[127] See Hamza Alavi, 'Authoritarianism and Legitimation of State Power in Pakistan' in Subrata Kumar Mitra (ed.), *The Post Colonial State in Asia*, New York, 1990, p. 27.

SEVEN

The Garrison State Cracks: Punjab and the Second World War

Between 1939 and 1945, when the Second World War took place, Punjab was at war again. The garrison province was once again mobilized in support of Britain's war effort against the Axis powers. As the primary recruiting ground of the Indian Army, Punjab bore the main burden of providing cannon fodder for the various theatres of war, supplying more than one-third of all military manpower raised in India during the war.[1] The efficiency with which the province had been mobilized was indicative of the efficacy of the civil-military nexus that had been established and perfected over the past two decades. Throughout the war, the civil bureaucracy operated seamlessly with the military establishment, squeezing every village for manpower for the war, while, at the same time, maintaining a stabilizing presence in an atmosphere strained by war anxiety, economic difficulties, political uncertainties and communal tensions. Although Punjab survived the war, cracks had appeared in the garrison province. The reliability of one of the mainstays of the martial classes—the Sikhs—was brought into question during the war, and the collaborative mechanism that had been carefully cultivated between the colonial state and its rural-military elites came under strain as the British struggled

---

[1] The Punjab contributed 36.67 per cent of the total number of combatants and non-combatants recruited from India during the war. 'Recruiting in India'. L/WS/ 1/136.

to steer a careful balance between provincial interests and all-India needs.

This chapter examines the impact of the Second World War on the Punjab, and argues that mobilization and militarization did not reinforce the garrison province as it had in the previous war. Instead, wartime economic conditions, compounded by political uncertainties, created conditions that eventually led to the unravelling of the collaborationist regime in the Punjab. The crumbling of the Unionist Party towards the end of the war did not, however, lead to the collapse of the rural-military formation in the Punjab. The old order remained intact despite the changing political context and provided continuities, particularly into the post-colonial state of Pakistan.

Garrison State in Action

As in the previous war, initial responses in the Punjab were enthusiastic. British officials from the military districts reported strong support from the local population for the war, not least for service in the army.[2] In the heavily recruited Attock district of western Punjab, the deputy commissioner reported:

> Everybody is keenly interested in the possibility of recruitment and there seems little doubt that if it becomes necessary, we should be able to obtain large numbers of recruits in this district.... Would be (sic) recruits have appeared ... asking to be enrolled...[3]

The landlords and the peasantry in rural Punjab saw the war as an opportunity to increase rural employment and raise prices of agricultural products. The rise in prices would provide the much-needed economic lift for a province still feeling the effects of the agricultural depression of the 1930s.[4] Remembering how they had been amply rewarded for their services in the last war, the soldiering community in the military districts saw this as yet another unique occasion for acquiring cash, titles and generous allotment

---

[2] FR, 30 September 1939.
[3] Craik to Linlithgow, 16 September 1939, in 'Recruitment in India'. L/WS/1/136.
[4] Ian Talbot, *Punjab and the Raj, 1849–1947*, New Delhi, 1988, p. 143.

of land in the canal colonies. Among the landowning and cultivating classes, news of India's imminent involvement in the Second World War was, therefore, warmly received, and the rural/military-dominated Punjab Assembly lost no time in passing resolutions in support of the British effort. Not surprisingly, recruiting officers reported no difficulties in acquiring recruits for the army during the early months of 1940.[5]

The task of mobilization was made easier by the open and active support given by the Unionist government. Chief Minister Sikander Hayat Khan of the Punjab, the "soldier premier", confidently assured Governor Henry Craik that his province could supply half a million recruits for the Indian Army within weeks, if needed.[6] Indeed, he urged the Governor to fully exploit the readiness of the Punjab to help in the war, and not to "miss out on the psychological moment" when the enthusiasm among the local population was high.[7] Sikander's assurance was soon matched by a series of open demonstrations of loyalty in the villages; rural notables and their supporters personally toured villages to drum up enthusiasm among prospective recruits for the army and to raise funds to fill the war coffers.[8] These tour parties, which on occasions comprised students, university professors and local officials, carried out activities that included pro-war propaganda and war service exhibitions to generate recruitment and to counter anti-war activities.[9] It was evident that the civil-military edifice that had been set up during the Great War more than two decades earlier was functioning once again, and with great enthusiasm and efficacy. Propaganda, publicity, fundraising, recruitment, and maintenance of law and order proceeded without much difficulty simply because the structures that enabled recruiting officers, deputy commissioners and local notables to act rapidly and with minimum friction were already in place.

[5] *Report on the Situation in the Punjab*, 30 September 1939, by the Chief Sec. to the Govt. of the Punjab, in L/P&J/5/242, Oriental and India Office Colls., British Library, London.

[6] FR, 31 August 1939.

[7] Linlithgow to Zetland, 25 September 1939, in 'Recruitment in India', L/WS/1/136.

[8] Craik to Linlithgow, 2 April 1941, Governor's Report, L/P&J/5/244.

[9] Notice from Sec. to Punjab Govt. to all Deputy Commissioners, 14 February 1940, File U (IX), Deputy Commissioner's Record Office, Rawalpindi Division, Pakistan.

On this occasion the Punjab seemed better prepared, and in the first two years of the war, mobilization and militarization were effected with impressive results. By June 1940 a provincial civil guard of some 300,000 men, ostensibly formed by the Unionist government in anticipation of mass mobilization and as a demonstrable force for maintaining law and order in the province, was already in place.[10] The recruitment net was cast beyond the traditional military districts and communities. Communities that had hitherto been excluded from military service because they were deemed unsuitable for military service, including members of the province's "criminal tribes", were recruited in large numbers, their willingness to enlist motivated in no small measure by promises of land allotments as rewards for loyal service.[11] Within two years of the start of the war, the Indian Army had quadrupled in size—from about 200,000 men in late 1939 to 865,200 by the end of 1941—with the bulk of the new recruits coming from the Punjab.[12] Equally impressive was the amount of money collected for the war chests from within the province. By the end of 1941 a total of fifty-five million rupees had already been collected, the amount surpassing the total donated for the entire duration of the previous war.[13]

Yet while official reports emerging from the Punjab suggested that the province was flush with enthusiasm during the early years of the war, there were indications, as the months wore on, of cracks emerging in the mobilization machinery. First, public confidence started to slip as news of German military successes began spreading among the local population. Signs of uncertainty in the province were evident from reports of increasing amounts of savings being withdrawn from banks and the increase in demand for rupees rather than currency notes (bank credit notes).[14] The situation was duly exploited by opponents of the war, and in several key recruiting districts, anti-war campaigns, waged mainly by the communists and radical nationalists, contested with government

---

[10] Craik to Linlithgow, Governor's Report, 14 June 1940. L/P&J/5/243.

[11] Home Sec. to Punjab Govt. to Deputy Commissioners in the province, 25 June 1941, File U (IX), No. 396, Rawalpindi Division, Pakistan.

[12] Sri Nandan Prasad, 'Expansion of the Armed Forces and Defence Organization, 1939–45' in Bisheshwar Prasad (ed.), *Official History of the Indian Armed Forces in the Second World War*, Calcutta, 1956, pp. 400–07.

[13] Craik to Linlithgow, Governor's Report, 2 April 1941.

[14] FR, 31 May 1940.

propaganda for public attention.[15] Communist cells incited labour unrest, exploited local grievances and spread alarmist rumours in their attempt to disrupt the government's mobilization efforts,[16] while the "Forward Bloc" of the Punjab Congress Party and the Congress Socialists called for non-cooperation in the war effort, arguing that India needed to be free first before it could successfully resist Axis aggression on its soil.[17] The grassroots grew increasingly susceptible to such propaganda. The much anticipated war-generated boom did not materialize, and the local population began instead to feel the strain of wartime economic disruptions. Owing to shortages caused by the diversion to war needs, the prices of essential commodities, especially clothing and wheat, had, by the end of 1941, gone up by almost 300 per cent.[18] The disruption in imports led to an acute shortage of consumer goods and other daily necessities in the towns as well as the countryside of the Punjab.[19]

These problems notwithstanding, the civil-military infrastructure seemed to have coped with what were still regarded as minor irritations and distractions in the province's mobilization process. Intelligence reports on the activities of the Kirti Kisan suggested that these communist-inspired organizations were being closely monitored by the state. Likewise, anti-recruitment meetings organized by the Congress and other political parties rarely escaped the notice of the police and their informers, and their speakers were usually promptly arrested and convicted whenever they threatened to infect the local population.[20] Intelligence reports also suggested that while the provincial Congress organization was active in its anti-war campaigns—fourty-two anti-recruitment campaigns in the last three months of 1941—its influence in the military districts was weak and its propaganda had little direct effect on recruitment.[21] Congress activities, it seemed, were having little influence on Punjab's recruiting efforts; army recruiters had observed that the ebb and flow of recruits from the villages were determined more

---

[15] Intelligence Bureau Report, December 1939. L/P&J/12/431.

[16] Bhagwan Josh, *Communist Movement in the Punjab, 1926–47*, New Delhi, 1979, p. 148.

[17] FR, 28 February 1942.

[18] Talbot, *Punjab and the Raj*, p. 175.

[19] FR, 30 November 1941.

[20] Intelligence Report on the Punjab, No. 15, 13 February 1942, L/WS/1/1433.

[21] *Ibid.*

by local conditions such as floods, diseases, availability of man-power and harvesting seasons than by the political exhortations of the Congress party.[22]

The Sikh Question

Paradoxically, one of the first significant recruiting problems in the Punjab did not stem from disruptions caused by anti-British elements, but from the ranks of one of Punjab's favoured "martial classes"—the Sikhs. Although the Sikh community, particularly Jat Sikhs from the central districts, had featured very prominently in the Indian Army since the 1857 Revolt, their relationship with the colonial state, strained by the Akali-led Gurdwara movement in the 1920s, never truly recovered, despite major concessions to the community in the wake of the unrest.[23] Throughout the 1920s and 1930s, the special relationship between the Sikh community and the British was further undermined when the Sikhs attempted to institutionalize a political identity in the midst of constitutional and political changes and challenges in India. The Muslim League's Lahore Resolution of 1940 had heightened fears in the community that a Muslim state of Pakistan might be imposed on Punjab—a Muslim majority province—should the Muslim separatists have their way. By 1940 British–Sikh relations could best be described as ambivalent: could the Sikhs continue to trust the British to protect Sikh culture and identity, as they had done in the past? Or would the community have to make contingency plans should the British decide to allow the Muslim League to ride roughshod over the Sikh and Hindu communities in the Punjab? This ambivalence was reflected in the community's responses to the war.

The Shiromani Akali Dal, which dominated Sikh politics through its control of the gurdwaras and their considerable resources, was sharply divided on the subject of recruitment. The more nationalistic elements in the Shiromani Akali Dal opposed support on the grounds that it was unacceptable for them to support an imperialist war. An opposing faction, however, championed increasing Sikh representation in the military, arguing that such show of support for the

[22] Intelligence Report on the Punjab, No. 60, 24 December 1942. L/WS/1/1433.

[23] Tan Tai Yong, 'Assuaging the Sikhs: Government Responses to the Akali Movement, 1920–1925', in *MAS*, Vol. 29(3), 1995, pp. 655–703.

British would generate goodwill on the part of the latter when it came to political devolution after the war. Aware that the communist Kirti Kisans were especially active in the Sikh districts of central Punjab and had already infiltrated a number of Sikh regiments, members of this faction urged closer links with the British and cautioned against displays of disloyalty or opposition to the war. Such behaviour, they argued, would be seen as subversion and would prejudice hopes of being recognized as an important, independent minority in post-war constitutional reforms.[24] In matters of Sikh participation in the war, this faction allied itself closely with the loyalist Sikh party, the Khalsa National Party, a coalition partner in the Unionist government.[25] The dissension within the Shiromani Akali Dal reflected the community's fundamental dilemma in 1940. While it could not openly preach cooperation in the war effort without exposing itself to attacks by rival political parties such as the Congress, the Sikh political party was fully aware of the long-term advantages that would accrue from representation in the armed forces in the event of a communal crisis resulting from the devolution of political power. Despite the efforts of the loyalist Sikhs to promote Sikh recruitment—such as the establishment of a Khalsa Defence of India League to encourage and coordinate Sikh enlistment into the Indian Army—the internal division within the Sikh community and the deepening political distrust of the Muslims eventually took its toll on the recruitment of Jat Sikhs. By late 1941, of the traditional groups that the Indian Army could turn to for recruitment, Jat Sikhs registered the lowest growth.[26]

From the British point of view, the Sikh situation had been a major cause of concern among the military authorities in the Punjab since the late 1930s. Military intelligence had reported that there was "an undercurrent of restlessness" among the Sikh soldiers, and attributed this to the activities of the Kirti Kisan organization in the Punjab.[27] The Kirtis were communist-influenced revolutionaries who had reorganized themselves following the failure of the *Ghadr*

---

[24] FR, 30 November 1943.

[25] See, for instance, resolution of total Sikh support for the British war effort by Sardar Gurcharan Singh of the Khalsa National Party on 3 November 1939, in *Punjab Legislative Assembly Debates*, Vol. 10(7), pp. 471–523.

[26] Johannes Voigt, *India in the Second World War*, New Delhi, 1987, p. 66.

[27] 'A survey of the Sikh situation as it affects the Army', n.d., Home (Pol.) File no. 232/40, Pol. (I), 1940. NAI.

movement. The party went underground after it was proscribed by the authorities in 1934, but the movement had been kept alive by returning Sikh emigrants and funds from overseas Sikhs.[28] By 1938 military intelligence had discovered the Kirti agitators had identified the Sikh regiments as one of the prime targets of the revolutionary activities, and had established extensive contacts with Sikh soldiers.[29] Evidence of sustained Kirti influence among Sikh troops during the first two years of the war, leading to an increased incidence of desertions by Sikh soldiers, was regarded as an unhealthy sign that "all was not well in the Sikh community".[30] The British perception of the steadfast and loyal Sikhs was further dented by a series of mutinies among Sikh units stationed in India and abroad. In Egypt, a mutiny instigated by Sikh communists broke out in the motorized transport company in December 1939, and in June 1940, more than sixty per cent of the Sikh squadron of the Central Indian Horse refused to be transported overseas.[31] Although military officers routinely maintained that "the vast majority of the serving Sikhs in the army are believed to be perfectly loyal", confidence in the reliability of the Sikhs was badly shaken, leading to a temporary suspension of recruitment of Sikhs in the Punjab in 1940.[32] In 1941, the enrolment of Jat Sikhs into the army began to slip further, and by the end of the year the number of Jat Sikhs recruited had dropped to half the number recruited in the previous year.[33]

The strained relationship between the British and the Sikhs was dealt a further blow by announcements in 1942 that self-government was likely to be granted to India after the war. As in the previous war, political concessions were necessitated by war conditions. Until December 1941, the Second World War for India was but a distant reality. However, when war broke out in the Pacific and

[28] 'A note outlining "kirti" agitation in the Punjab', n.d., Home (Pol.) File no. 216/40, Pol. (I), 1940. NAI.

[29] *Ibid.*

[30] 'A survey of the Sikh situation as it affects the Army', n.d., Home (Pol.) File no. 232/40, Pol. (I), 1940. NAI.

[31] Voigt, *India in the Second World War*, p. 65.

[32] Memorandum by General R.C. Wilson, Adj. Gen., India, 9 October 1940, in 'A survey of the Sikh situation as it affects the Army', Home (Pol.) File no. 232/40, Pol. (I). NAI.

[33] Intelligence Report on the Punjab, No. 19, 13 March 1942. L/WS/1/1433.

south-east Asia, India suddenly found itself on the frontline: by early 1942 an invasion from the north-east, through Burma, by the Japanese Imperial Army had become a distinct possibility. Faced with a state of emergency, the British decided to act quickly to prevent any further deterioration in public morale by promising to take specific steps after the war for the earliest possible realization of self-government for India. This led to the Cripps Mission, and the subsequent promulgation of a constitutional plan for post-war India.[34] Among other things, the Cripps Plan of 1942 offered provinces the right to opt out of the Indian Union if they did not wish to be part of a unitary India. This alternative was factored in as an apparent concession to Muslim demands for a separate state after Independence. The Sikhs believed it was a sure step towards surrendering the Punjab to the Muslim League, thereby subjecting their community to Muslim rule.[35] Accordingly, Sikh leaders exhorted their followers to boycott recruitment to the army, urging them instead to form volunteer brigades to safeguard their community's interests.[36] Indeed, soon after the Cripps report was published, the Sikh community began to form a Sikh Volunteer Corps in their majority districts. This pre-emptive move was taken in anticipation of trouble from the Muslims should there be a breakdown of law and order in the Punjab.[37] Soon these reactions on the part of the Sikhs began to have an impact on military recruitment.[38]

The rupture in the relationship between the British and the Sikhs would have been inconsequential had the Sikhs been marginal to the colonial state in the Punjab. However, for decades the British had carefully cultivated the loyalty of the Sikhs, securing their allegiance through special considerations as a "martial race", and maintaining the military districts by keeping the Jat peasantry contented

[34] 'Draft declaration for discussion with Indian leaders', 30 March 1942, in N. Mansergh and E.W.R. Lumby (eds.), *Constitutional Relations between Britain and India: The Transfer of Power, 1942–47* (henceforth *TP*), Vol. 1, London, 1970, p. 65. Specifically, the Cripps Mission and Plan arose out of an imperial desire to garner political support in India for the war, and, to a certain extent, ensure continued enlistment of Muslim soldiers in the army.

[35] For the story of Sikh reactions to Pakistan, see Tan Tai Yong, 'Sikh Responses to the Demand for Pakistan 1940–1947', in the *International Journal of Punjab Studies*, Vol. 1(2), 1994.

[36] FR, 15 April 1942.

[37] Ogilvie to Pinnell, 30 March 1942, *TP*, Vol. 1, p. 564.

[38] FR, 15 April 1942.

through land grants and friendly agricultural policies. With the political future of the Sikh community at stake, and with the British dithering on the nature of political safeguards that the Sikhs could expect in the future, a major crack had developed in one of the main pillars of British rule in the Punjab.

The fracture in Indo–Sikh relations was not simply an upshot of the stresses caused by the war, the political activism of the Kirti Kisan, or the Congress, although the latter political groups did contribute to undermining the loyalty of some of the Sikhs serving in the military. Although there was a period of tension with the Akali Dal in the 1920s, Sikh sensitivities were assuaged whenever their material and religious demands were carefully managed by the British. From the 1930s the Sikhs were no longer content to be treated as a special minority whose interests were maintained by the imperial state, and they began asserting a form of territorial nationalism based on an ethno-religious identity. Communal politics certainly played its part. With the Muslim League becoming more strident in its demand for a separate state for the Muslims of India, the Sikhs inclined towards the Congress and other communist groups as "an assurance against Pakistan becoming a reality".[39] The political structure of the province, premised upon a form of inter-communal agrarian communitarianism, had come under the threat of the deepening communal politics of the 1940s.

With reliance on the Sikhs becoming increasingly questionable, the weight of recruitment shifted to other martial classes, particularly the Punjabi Muslims from the Salt Range Tract of north-western Punjab. Muslims in the districts of western Punjab showed a marked readiness to enlist and had been largely uninfluenced by any form of anti-war activities.[40] Between 1940 and 1942, the number of Muslims recruited from the Punjab quadrupled.[41] The extent to which the army had come to rely on the Punjabi Muslims struck the then governor, Sir Bertrand Glancy, during a personal tour of the districts in late 1942; there was a dearth of young men in the area, he observed, as most of them had gone off to the army.[42]

[39] 'Note on Sikhs', n.d. Army General Headquarters. L/WS/2/44.
[40] Intelligence Report on the Punjab, No. 15, 13 February 1942. L/WS/1/1433.
[41] In 1940, 43,291 Muslims were recruited from the Punjab. By 1942 the number had risen to 165,497. Figures from Voigt, *India in the Second World War*, p. 65.
[42] Glancy to Linlithgow, Governor's Report, 13 November 1942. L/P&J/5/245.

In the three most heavily recruited districts in western Punjab—Rawalpindi, Jhelum and Attock—the percentage of total male population who were enrolled into the army reached fifteen per cent.[43] Although the British tried turning to other sources—for example, the semi-nomadic tribes of western Punjab, which proved resistant to recruitment—British recruiters failed to attain much success in this category.

The shift in recruiting was significant. While the Punjab continued to be the main supplier of soldiers throughout the war, accounting for about thirty-six per cent of all soldiers recruited from India during that period, the respective balance of communal representation in the military tilted significantly in favour of the Punjabi Muslims, and the regional emphasis of recruitment took on a pronounced western province flavour. By 1943, Punjabi Muslims and Pathans accounted for twenty-five per cent of the annual intake into the army, while the Sikhs and Hindu Jats accounted for roughly seven and five per cent respectively.[44] In the upshot, the military establishment in western Punjab assumed greater significance, and this was to provide the basis for the entrenchment of the rural-military elites who would later dominate the post-Independence state of Pakistan.

The Food Crisis

In the midst of the war another challenge, quite unrelated to recruiting and military manpower, struck at the core of the collaborationist regime in the Punjab. This was the food crisis that culminated in the devastating Bengal Famine of 1943–44, which claimed an estimated three-and-a-half million lives. While India was a primary food producer, wartime exigencies and the central government's lack of preparedness in dealing with a major food emergency resulted in a situation that quickly reached crisis proportions.[45] By the end of 1941 the supply of food was running desperately low in India.

[43] 'Cash rewards to villages for outstanding recruitment services', 23 January 1945, File U (IX), No. 42, Rawalpindi Division, Pakistan.

[44] 'Recruitment in India', 15 September 1943. L/WS/1/136.

[45] These issues are incisively discussed in Vanaja Dharmalingam's 'The Politics of Food: Punjab and the British Raj, 1939–45', (Unpublished BA Honours thesis, submitted in 1992 to the History Department, National University of Singapore).

The shortage of the dominant staple, rice, had exceeded 2.8 million tons in 1941, and this shortfall could not be met by imports.[46] The situation worsened with the loss of the Burmese rice supplies in 1942, estimated at about 1.5 million tons annually for India.[47] In an attempt to avert a potential food crisis, the GoI asked for an import of foodgrains into India, only to have London reject the request because of strategic concerns that a diversion of shipping services for the purpose of sending food imports to India would affect Allied naval operations.[48] All that London could promise was 100,000 tons for a couple of months by early 1944, with no assurance that this supply would continue.[49] Unfortunately for India, London was clearly not prepared to compromise its naval operations for the transportation of food. Indeed, both Amery and Linlithgow conceded that London had planned its war without India in mind.[50] Left to its own devices, the GoI had little option but to look internally to solve these food problems; and the most obvious solution was to transfer food grains from surplus provinces to deficit ones by forced requisitioning and price controls.

The issue of food requisitioning created immediate tensions between the central government and the Punjab administration on the one hand, and the British administration and the Unionist government on the other. As a surplus province with a series of fine harvests in its favour, the Punjab was expected to play its part in helping the deficit provinces. Punjab farmers were concerned that their needs had to be satisfied first; only after they had fed their deficit towns and districts would they agree to export their surpluses.[51] The agriculturists were also determined to benefit from the high demand for foodgrains, and resisted all attempts at price control which would have lowered the profits accruing from the sale of their huge surplus of food stocks. An early move in December 1941 by the GoI to introduce statutory price control for wheat proved extremely unpopular with cultivators in the Punjab and

[46] Famine Inquiry Commission, *Report on Bengal*, Delhi, 1945, Appendix 1.

[47] Andrew Grajdanzev, 'India's Wartime Economic Difficulties', in *Pacific Affairs*, Vol. 16(3), June 1943, p. 199.

[48] Report by Shipping Committee on India's food requirement of imported grains, 30 July 1943, *TP*, Vol. 4, pp. 133–39.

[49] War Cabinet Minute, *TP*, 10 November 1943, Vol. 4, p. 301.

[50] Amery to Linlithgow, 5 August 1943, *TP*, Vol. 3, p. 158.

[51] Knight, *Food Administration*, p. 156.

immediately placed a strain on the relationship between the government and its rural intermediaries. As expected, the Punjab Legislative Assembly registered an unequivocal opposition to the central government's decision to impose price control for the province's wheat supply.[52] No sooner had price controls been imposed than Punjabi cultivators began retaliating. They hid their supplies, causing stocks to disappear from the market.[53] The province was soon declaring that it too was facing a famine![54] Realizing that price controls were meaningless without the support of the provinces, the GoI relented and agreed to buy wheat through a central purchasing agency appointed in every province. This was clearly perceived as an admission that price controls had failed.[55]

Faced with an intransigent Punjab—with the Hindu Jat leader, Chhottu Ram, who was also Minister of Revenue in the Unionist government, openly calling for cultivators to hoard their wheat until they could secure a higher price for their products[56]—the central government tried, but without success, on a couple of subsequent occasions to impose price controls in the Punjab. Forced requisition would have been the simple answer, but the repercussions of such a move on the Punjab—particularly on recruitment—troubled the administration. Linlithgow had little doubt that should the government decide on a policy of forced requisition and price control, there would be "something of an agrarian revolution in the province",[57] and he knew that this would have an unsettling effect on the military districts. Already, when the government issued an order in January 1942 to all farmers to declare stocks of wheat exceeding 20 *maunds* (a maund is roughly equivalent to 80 pounds), rumours of official intentions to requisition stocks without payment began circulating, and started to unsettle soldiers who had been concerned about economic conditions in their villages.[58] Concerned

---

[52] *Punjab Legislative Assembly Debates*, Vol. 18(11), pp. 257–305.

[53] FR, 15 July 1942.

[54] *The Tribune*, 11 December 1942.

[55] FR, 31 December 1942.

[56] FR, 15 June 1943.

[57] Linlithgow to Amery, 20 September 1943, *TP*, Vol. 4, p. 301.

[58] Regimental intelligence officers reported that the economic conditions in the villages—particularly the prices of wheat and *atta*—featured largely in the concerns of the soldiers. Intelligence Report on the Punjab, No. 71, 12 March 1943. L/WS/1/1433.

about the detrimental effects of these rumours on the morale of
the soldiering population, the government undertook a series of
counter-propaganda campaigns through the soldiers' boards and
other official channels.[59] The Viceroy was especially mindful of the
disastrous consequences that an unhappy Punjab would have on
the government and on the war effort itself; if the Unionist government should fall, there would not be an alternative party capable of mobilizing the province for the war effort. For their part,
the Unionists knew that policies which went against the interests
of their landed support base would be politically untenable. The
Unionists were, therefore, unequivocally opposed to food controls
of any form, and while they pledged continued loyalty and commitment to the war effort, they took every opportunity to attack
the government's food policies at the national level. For a while,
their efforts to stave off price controls proved successful.[60] Indeed
the Punjab government was able, until 1943, not only to resist the
imposition of price controls, but prevent the central government
from acquiring all surpluses from the province for the deficit provinces. When the Punjab Assembly warned that price control "would
result in very keen resentment and discontent among agricultural
classes [sic]",[61] this was taken as a veiled threat that support for the
British war effort might be jeopardized by unsympathetic policies
imposed on Punjab's food producers. Eventually, however, the GoI
had to act. With the deepening crisis caused by the Bengal famine,
forced food requisitioning was finally imposed in the Punjab in
the summer of 1943.[62]

For the Unionists, 1943 proved to be a bad year. In September of
that year, very much against the wishes of the Unionists, the GoI
imposed rationing as well as requisitioning upon the Punjab.
To make matters worse, the United Provinces were excluded
from this plan, and a further defeat followed when price control
was re-imposed in November. The Unionists were deeply disappointed. They had hoped that their loyal commitment and contribution to the war would strengthen the collaborative mechanism
which had served them so well in the past and that, despite the

[59] Intelligence Report on the Punjab, No. 17, 27 February 1942. L/WS/1/1433.
[60] Gov. Gen. (Food Department) to Amery, 11 January 1944, *TP*, Vol. 4, pp. 623–26.
[61] *Punjab Assembly Debates*, 4 November 1943, Vol. 22(3), pp. 80–119.
[62] War Cabinet Paper (44), 27 June 1944, *TP*, Vol. 4, p. 1,049.

difficulties facing the British elsewhere, the agricultural classes would continue to enjoy the profits of patronage on account of their support for the Raj. Members of the Punjab ministry felt that provincial autonomy had been flouted by a "dictatorial centre" and many representing the rural-military classes made no secret of their intentions to defend the interests of the zaminders.[63] But unfortunately for the Unionists and their supporters, the advantages accruing from the province's bumper harvests and handsome profits proved to be illusory. By the end of 1943 the validity of the collaborative relationship between the rural elites and the state that underpinned the civil-military edifice had been severely eroded. Both parties were beginning to abandon their partnership in the aftermath of the food crisis.

The food crisis drove a wedge into the system of patronage that the British had built in the Punjab. The British had nourished their rural intermediaries with benevolent paternalism, and in return these elites, using their local powers of patronage, popular religious leadership and biradari networks, had served as mediators between rural and military Punjab on the one hand and the British rulers on the other. As long as their interests and those of their constituents were aligned with that of the colonial state, the collaborative structure would remain intact and work well. Up to the 1940s, the Unionists were bound by a special political and military bond to the British, and this was the basis of their political power and authority in the Punjab. However, the food crisis in the midst of war had ruptured that special relationship. The rural-military elites that formed the Unionist party had publicly and wholeheartedly supported the war effort despite a general lack of enthusiasm, and in some cases, open opposition, from the rest of the country. Yet, this commitment to the war also meant supporting policies that might be unpopular in the province, such as requisitioning and price controls. Here, all-India imperatives and provincial interests collided. The provincial logic was compelling: had not the British kept at arm's length when the province needed official help to recover from the slump triggered by the Great Depression? And now, when profits could be made from bumper harvests, were the British now denying them their due?[64] Punjab's cultivators deemed it

[63] Intelligence Report on the Punjab, No. 103, 22 October 1943. L/WS/1/1433.
[64] See *Punjab Assembly Debates*, Vol. 22, November 1943, p. 98.

grossly unfair that they were now prevented from enjoying legitimate profits from rising grain prices because of state procurement
and price-control policies.[65] Did their loyalty to the British—in the
form of a million recruits for the war and the growing of wheat on
land set aside for Punjab's two other chief exports, sugar and cotton—not count for anything now? Why should the agriculturists
be punished in spite of their commitment to the war? The Hindu
Jat leader, Chhottu Ram, who at the beginning of the war had taken
the lead in setting up a loyalist "Union of Martial Races" in support
of the war, was sufficiently embittered by the GoI's policy on food
requisition and price control to complain in 1944 that the GoI had
"never paid any heed to the legitimate claims of the martial and
agricultural classes [of the Punjab]".[66] Clearly, the interests of rural
Punjab and the colonial state had diverged on the food issue. On
the part of the colonial state, reliance on the "selfish" Unionists had
clearly caused major embarrassment to the central government.
But the Unionists were equally dissatisfied that their support for
the Raj turned out to be a major liability to their interests as well as
those of their constituents. Not only had the war caused an increase in food prices, but financial stringency had led to the aban-
doning of rural improvement programmes and the failure of the
Unionist government to reduce water rates in the canal colonies[67].
To the rural-military elites, it seemed increasing obvious as the
war wore on that the loyalty of the rural population would not
been met with commensurate returns and rewards from the state.

The Unionists Crumble

In the midst of all this, the Unionists were dealt a double blow by
the deaths of two of its stalwarts within two years of each other.
Sikander Hayat Khan, whose unwavering support for the war effort
had been crucial to the British cause, died suddenly in December
1942, at the age of 55. His death not only robbed the rural-military

[65] Sugata Bose and Ayesha Jalal, *Modern South Asia: History, Culture and Political Economy*, Delhi, 1999, p. 159.

[66] Chottu Ram to Brayne, 2 January 1944, Brayne Papers. F.152/69, IOLR.

[67] Talbot, 'Deserted Collaborators: The Political Background of the Rise and Fall of the Punjab Unionist Party, 1923–1947', *The Journal of Imperial and Commonwealth History*, Vol. 11(1), 1982, p. 512.

lobby of one of its most influential members, but triggered the unravelling of the cross-communal rural alliance that he had secured during his term as premier. In addition to his alliances with the Hindu Jats, epitomized by his strong political ties with Chhottu Ram, Sikander had attempted to assuage the Sikhs by entering into a pact with the Sikh leader Baldev Singh, acknowledging Sikh rights in social and religious issues as well as the community's representation in government departments.[68] All this, however, was soon attacked by the Muslim League as being a sell-out of Muslim interests in the Punjab. During the troubled months of 1942, the Muslim League's propaganda was particularly lethal as Muslim landlords were worried that their communal and urban rivals— Hindu and Sikh businessmen—were profiting from a new and lucrative form of government patronage, namely civil supply contracts for grains.[69] The increasing association of the Unionists with these urban non-Muslim castes, of which Sikander Hayat's pact with the Sikh industrialist Baldev Singh was seen as a prime example, raised strong suspicions, especially in the Muslim-majority districts of western Punjab where the strong rural-urban divide had always assumed a communal character. Although Sikander had been able to fend off Jinnah's overtures in the Punjab in the months following the League's Lahore Resolution in 1941, the growing stature of Jinnah as the undisputed Muslim leader in the whole of India was beginning to put the Unionists on the defensive. With the economic impact of the war, unpopular food measures and forced recruiting in some districts further undermining its popularity, the government that Sikander's successor, Khizr Hayat Khan Tiwana, scion of the famed Tiwana "martial tribe" of Shahpur, inherited was a weakened one.[70] The Punjab Governor admitted that Khizr was indeed in a much "weaker position than his predecessor", and this was in part the result of Sikander's "sometimes unnecessary surrenders" to Jinnah.[71] With the politically weaker and inexperienced

---

[68] The Sikander–Baldev Pact of 1942 acknowledged Sikh religious rights by granting, inter alia, *jhatka* meat the same status as *halal* meat. It also provided for an increase in Sikh representation in government departments where the communal proportion for Sikhs had fallen to below the statutory twenty per cent.

[69] Talbot, *Punjab and the Raj*, p. 151.

[70] Ian Talbot, *Khizr Tiwana, the Punjab Unionist Party and the Partition of India*, Surrey, 1996, pp. 85–87.

[71] Glancy to Linlithgow, 20 July 1943, *TP*, Vol. 4, p. 110.

Khizr at the helm, the Unionist edifice began to crumble when the Muslim League, sensing that Khizr was a political lightweight, increased its political onslaught. Khizr's position was certainly not helped by the death in 1944 of the Unionists' key Hindu Jat pillar, Chottu Ram, who succumbed to a heart attack.

It was at this stage that the Unionist government became especially vulnerable to the political challenges mounted by the Muslim League. The League had been unable to gain political ground in the Punjab in the 1930s simply because its all-India communal political concerns had little appeal to the localized landed and peasant interests in the Punjab. This time around, the Punjab Muslim League organization made a tactical switch and decided to portray themselves as champions of the Muslim agriculturists in the province. The Nawab of Mamdot, a rural notable and leader of the provincial Muslim League, readily offered to form the next Muslim League ministry if the Unionists carried out their threat to resign over the issue of food controls.[72] Given its commitment to the famine-stricken Muslim-majority province of Bengal, the Muslim League was careful not to oppose the central government's food control policies. At the same time, however, the requisition of grain supplies imposed by the Central Food Department offered the League a tactical opportunity to embarrass the Unionist Party, which was seen to condone profiteering by Hindu and Sikh supply officers at the expense of the Muslim producers.[73] Clearly, the Muslim League had decided, as a political gambit, not to openly support food controls there in order to win the agriculturists over to their side. That the Punjab Muslim League leader the Nawab of Mamdot had decided to place himself and his followers behind Punjab's agricultural interests, and had chosen to ignore the fact that the Muslim League ministries in Assam, Bengal, Sind and the Frontier Provinces all stood for the fixing of wheat prices, suggests the triumph of political expediency over principles and ideology.[74]

The Muslim League dug deeper into the Unionist base by playing the communal card. Aware that its early attempts to mobilize through the name of Islam and that the idea of Pakistan had made

[72] *Punjab Assembly Debates*, Vol. 23, no. 2, p. 106.

[73] Ian Talbot, *Provincial Politics and the Pakistan Movement: The Growth of the Muslim League in North-West and North-East India, 1937–47*, Karachi, 1988, p. 94.

[74] *The Tribune*, 6 November 1943.

little impact on the mass of rural population, the League attempted to gain political ground among Punjab's Muslim population by suggesting that the Unionists were selling out Muslim agricultural interests to the Akali Sikhs (in a bid to woo more Jat Sikhs into the army) as well as to the pro-Ambala and pro-Hindu, Chhottu Ram. As suggested by the Muslim League, what were at stake were no longer Punjabi agricultural interests, but specific Muslim agricultural interests. When the All-India Jat Mahasabha held a meeting in Lahore in 1943, during which Christian, Sikh, Hindu and Muslim Jats shared the platform to profess the common economic interests and "martial" identity of the Jat community, the Muslim press roundly condemned the meeting "as a tool of colonial interests which ignored the religious differences between the Hindus, Muslims and Sikhs".[75] The Muslim League had chosen not to attack the pro-zamindar policies of the Unionists; it chose instead to "communalize" them, to differentiate between Muslim and non-Muslim agrarian interests and by so doing to remove the ground from under the Unionists' feet. In short, the Muslim League had sought first of all to win over the rural elites so that it could use their patronage to reach the grassroots, and the most effective tactic was to appeal to the material interests of these people.

The tussle for political supremacy in the Punjab led inevitably to a fight for the hearts and minds of the crucial military constituency in the province. Just as the Punjab Muslim League had positioned itself as the champion of Muslim agrarian interests in the province, it now challenged the Unionists' qualifications to represent the interests of the "martial castes", particularly in the heavily recruited districts of western Punjab. While Khizr struggled to generate continuous support for the war effort among an increasingly exhausted population, promising that the contributions and "sacrifices of the martial castes" would earn them their "due place[s] in the future of India", he was, by 1943, no longer the sole spokesman for the soldiering classes in the Punjab. Members of the rural-military elites who had crossed over to the Punjab Muslim League, most notably, Shaukat Hayat Khan, eldest son of the late Sikander Hayat, began declaring that the Unionists had not done enough

[75] Ian Talbot, *Khizr Tiwana, the Punjab Unionist Party and the Partition of India,* Surrey, 1996, p. 94.

for the martial communities of the Punjab.[76] Hailing from a traditional military family as famous as Khizr's, Shaukat was no outsider to the military community, and his promise that the Muslim League would give "whole-hearted support in all matters relating to post-war resettlement and welfare", represented an attempt to strike at the heart of the Unionist power base in the Punjab.[77]

The political inroads achieved by the League at the expense of the Unionists did not, therefore, mean an unravelling of the traditional power structure of western Punjab. While the Muslim League's victory in the 1946 elections signalled the end of the Unionist party in the Punjab, it did not alter the power configuration that had long been in existence there. Rather, the electoral success of the Muslim League was simply a case of the landlords and sufipirs moving en-bloc from one party to the other. In other words, the traditional civil-military and landed oligarchy in western Punjab remained very much intact despite the disruptions caused by war-time dislocations in the Punjab.[78] This swing, according to Imran Ali, "provided the basis for maintaining major continuities [for] the Muslim landed elite chose to use the League as its vehicle for carrying over its authority into the post-colonial period".[79] The political defeat of the Unionists in 1946 signalled but a change in political labelling. The Muslim League may have been in the ascendant during the tumultuous period leading to Independence and Partition, but the rural-military formation that had all along been the basis of power and authority in the Muslim-dominant western Punjab region remained intact. Even with the bifurcation of the province, the Muslim rural-military elites maintained their control of their power bases in western Punjab, as nearly all Muslim-majority districts, including Lahore, were allocated to Pakistan under the Radcliffe Award. The valuable agricultural tracts in the canal colonies were now claimed solely by the Muslim landlords as the entire Jat and Sikh population of the colonies emigrated in the wake of Partition.

[76] *Ibid.*, p. 89.

[77] *Dawn* (Delhi), 8 October 1945, as quoted in *ibid.*, p. 104.

[78] Ronald J. Herring, 'Zulfikar Ali Bhutto and Eradication of Feudalism in Pakistan', in *Economic and Political Weekly*, Vol. 15(12), 22 March 1980, pp. 599–614.

[79] Imran Ali, 'The Punjab and the Retardation of Nationalism', in D.A. Low (ed.), *The Political Inheritance of Pakistan*, London, 1981, p. 47.

Conclusion

From 1939 to 1945 the Punjab was mobilized once again to support Britain in a major world conflagration. This time, however, the initiative for mobilization was spearheaded largely by the local Unionist government. Almost immediately after the British Government declared war on Germany, Punjab premier and provincial Muslim leader, Sikander Hayat Khan, issued a statement calling on the people of the Punjab to "maintain their splendid traditions as the sword arm of India" by supporting the imperial war effort. In a manner reminiscent of Sir Michael O'Dwyer and his government during the First World War, Sikander and the Unionist Ministry committed themselves to gearing up the province for a massive contribution to the British cause. At the outbreak of the war, Sikander and his ministers toured the districts to drum up enthusiasm for enlistment to the Indian Army, and at the same time warn their detractors against any opposition to the government's policy of cooperation. Until 1945 (even though Sikander was to die suddenly of a heart attack in December 1942), the Unionist government fully backed the mobilization process, by which some 800,000 combatants were recruited from the Punjab and 250,000,000 rupees gathered through war loans. This experience was not a new one for the Punjab. During the First World War, the province was turned into a veritable "home front" through an intensive mobilization process that had been co coordinated by an integrated civil-military bureaucracy and assisted by its rural-military elites.[80] In the early 1940s, the mobilization process was orchestrated by the conjoining of the bureaucratic edifice and a local political structure which was dominated by the rural military elites. Potential recruits were urged to fill the ranks of the Indian Army and civilians were mobilized to support the war industries. At the same time, the rural population was rallied to intensify the areas under cultivation through a "Grow More Food" campaign.[81]

---

[80] For the story of Punjab's involvement in the First World War, see T.Y. Tan, 'An Imperial Home-Front: Punjab and the First World War' in *The Journal of Military History*, Vol. 64, April 2000, pp. 371–410.

[81] This campaign was aimed at increasing the acreage of land under foodgrain cultivation. See the Famine Inquiry Commission, *Final Report*, New Delhi, 1945, part 1, chapter 2.

The apparent success of the mobilization process in the Punjab between 1939 and 1945 concealed, however, far-reaching changes that would shake the relationship between the province and its imperial overlords to its core. Wartime discontent and wartime political developments, particularly the Pakistan movement and Sikh political concerns, undermined the special Anglo–Sikh association that dated back to the Revolt of 1857. And these were but the first of many cracks to appear during 1939–45 in the civil-military structure that had formed the bedrock of colonial Punjab. The collaborative mechanism was further weakened by a divergence of interests between the state and its intermediaries. Through its policies of food requisition, rationing and price controls that were driven by the pressing needs of war, the Raj, in effect, compromised its cardinal principle of maintaining rural stability. As that special bond that had held the Punjab together since 1849 started to unravel, it set off a series of ramifications that would fundamentally alter the political face of the province.

Conclusion

When the Punjab was annexed in 1849, the British, fired by "imperial confidence ... and an Evangelical-Utilitarian zeal for reform", and eager to start on a clean slate with their latest acquisition, decided to establish a "non-regulation" system of colonial administration that would rapidly transform the hitherto volatile frontier region into a stable, model province. This system of government was initially premised on the break-up of the local hierarchy of the old Punjab through administrative reforms. However, the decision to diminish the local hierarchy had to be reversed by the upheaval of 1857 when the British had to turn to the old ruling classes for support in their armed struggle against the rebels and mutineers. As it turned out, the vital intervention of the Punjabis on the side of the British during the 1857 Revolt revived the fortunes of Punjab's old elites and chieftain classes, who thereafter played a significant role in the entrenchment of British rule in the province.[1] By the 1880s, with the opening of the province as the main recruiting base of the army, the authoritarian and paternalistic "Punjab School" of administration, whose non-regulatory system allowed for the unusual combination of judicial, administrative and revenue powers in their district officers, and buttressed after 1857 by local elite groups "acting as intermediaries between state and people", developed into a unique "garrison state", with military requirements writ large in the character of its social, economic and political structures during the colonial period.

---

[1] For this story, see Andrew J. Major, *Return to Empire*, New Delhi, 1996.

This study has attempted to establish the processes by which the colonial state in the Punjab was modified into a unique civil-military regime during the first half of the twentieth century. It has argued that this was the outcome of the state's increasing need, from the beginning of the twentieth century, to involve itself in the management of the army's main recruiting ground in the Punjab. The civil and military structures in the province were first integrated during the First World War to facilitate the mobilization and control of a greatly expanded recruiting base in the province. A distinct nexus between the state and the military was maintained during the inter-war period to insulate the military districts from external political influences. This nexus was then reinforced by the establishment of a local political structure dominated by rural-military elites, following constitutional reforms in 1920 and 1937. This civil-military regime, particularly it's western half, remained essentially intact despite the major political developments, and upheaval, in the mid-1940s, and was inherited thereafter by state of Pakistan.

When the Punjab was annexed to the British Empire in 1849, there were few indications, if any, that by the end of the century this region would come to constitute the principal recruiting ground for the Indian Army. British priority immediately after annexation was to pacify their newly-acquired territory, which had been in a state of anarchy for the past two decades, and to lay the foundations of a stable civil government. The province was accordingly demilitarized, and strict orders were laid down to exclude Punjabis, who had hitherto constituted the mainstay of the Sikh armies, from the ranks of the Indian Army, except for service with the Punjab Frontier Force, which was raised to police the newly formed north-western frontier. The first few years of British rule in the Punjab thus seemed to signal an end to the region's long association with the military.

Yet, within a decade, all this had changed. Portions of the Bengal Army rebelled in 1857, and in desperation, Punjabis were recalled to arms to bolster the forces required to put down the mutineers. Their intervention on the side of the British brought about their return to the army. In the wake of the 1857 rebellion, with internal security and the "safety" of the army dominating military thinking in India, distinct Punjabi regiments were raised to balance and counterpoise the *purbiyas* within the Bengal Army. This did not entail the wholesale recruitment of Punjabis by the British, but it did signal the beginning of the reopening of the Punjab for recruitment by the army.

By the 1880s, the military thinking of the British in India underwent a change. The main function of the colonial army shifted from internal security of the Raj to its protection against external attack. Military officials thus began placing efficiency above security, and recruitment came to be concentrated on a few select groups, believed to be better equipped for fighting an enemy across the frontier. By the end of the century these groups, then regarded by the British as "martial races", came to dominate the ranks of the Indian Army, and as most of these were recruited from the Punjab, the latter came to constitute the principal recruiting ground for the Indian Army.

Although recruiting came to be concentrated in the Punjab, the actual military labour market in the province was extremely restricted, and only selected groups within certain localities, which I have termed "military districts", had access to military service. This restricted market was well provided for, by pay and pensions and other "prizes", most notably grants of land in the newly-opened canal colonies in the province. The state also took special care to ensure that this market was constantly kept pacified. The passing of the Land Alienation Act of 1900 was intended to safeguard the "martial peasantry" from rural indebtedness, while the repeal of the Canal Colonies Bill seven years later was clearly an attempt to placate the excited military classes in central Punjab.

The First World War intensified the state's involvement with the military in the province. During the war the Indian Army was substantially expanded to meet the demands of operations in various war theatres. As most of the recruiting for the Indian Army had, by the turn of the century, come to concentrate mainly in the Punjab, the province came to bear the brunt of raising the necessary manpower needed to meet this expansion. The requirements of rapid mobilization demanded by the war, however, showed the inadequacies of the peacetime recruiting arrangements. Consequently, during the war, the entire bureaucratic structure in the province was militarized, as nearly all aspects of its activities were geared towards the provision of men and material for the war effort. To meet the crisis of manpower, and to stimulate and facilitate recruiting in areas hitherto untouched by the recruiting officer, the civil and military structures in the province, which had hitherto functioned quite independently of each other, coalesced into a formidable machinery, dedicated to generating canon fodder for the war. This civil-military integration entailed not just the interlinking of the provincial civil structure with the military command, but very importantly, involved the full support of the rural-military elites as well. The process of mobilization during the War thus laid the foundations of a militarized bureaucracy in the Punjab, whose administrative/military tentacles were able to reach into every level of society and the economy.

This integrated civil-military bureaucratic structure, particularly as institutionalized in the form of the District Soldiers' Boards (DSBs), remained very much intact in post-war Punjab, as the state sought to tackle the problems associated with demobilization, and later to secure the military districts against internal disturbances and external political influences. These unique civil-military institutions functioned as welfare organizations, mechanisms of state control, communications channels between the state and the soldiers and served collectively as important ring fences around the military districts, keeping out external influences from tampering with the "loyalty" of the soldier population. These boards were to remain a vital part of the bureaucratic edifice of rural Punjab till the end of the Raj, and their existence and operations provide the best evidence of the functioning of a quasi-military colonial state in the Punjab.

The political and military ramifications of disturbances in the military districts, and the extent to which military considerations governed the behaviour of the colonial state in the Punjab were shown during the Sikh agitation that took place between 1920 and 1925. At the height of the movement, Sikh unrest disrupted the recruiting activities, upset the stability of Sikh regiments and threatened a rebellion in the Sikh districts. The state's response to the agitation, which centred on the general assuagement of the Akali Sikhs, reflected its underlying concern of preventing a military backlash in the Sikh military districts of central Punjab.

The civil-military regime that had emerged out of the First World War in the Punjab was reinforced by the political entrenchment of the rural-military elites in the provincial legislatures created by political reforms following the war. Their importance in propping up the military regime in the Punjab prompted the government to influence the reforms to work in their favour. These elites were consequently able to dominate the councils by functioning as a rural-military lobby, which was eventually constituted into the Punjab National Unionist Party. The Unionist Party dominated Punjab politics throughout dyarchy and was able to survive the transition into provincial autonomy, largely through its ability to champion the interests of its electoral base, which remained only marginally changed by the Government of India Act of 1935.

The establishment of a civil-military regime in the Punjab was not only instrumental in maintaining the military districts in the Punjab, but had wider consequences for the province as well. The province as a whole was relatively well-insulated from major communal disturbances and nationalist or anti-government agitations. The Khilafat non-cooperation movement and the Civil Disobedience movement never really took off in the Punjab. The Congress was never able to establish a political foothold in the province, as politics came to be dominated by the rural-military elites. The relative stability of the Punjab under British rule could largely be attributed to the close contact between the government and the people, a hallmark of the paternalistic ethos of the "Punjab School" of administration of the nineteenth century. This distinctive feature of the administration in the Punjab was perpetuated in the first half of the twentieth century through the civil-military regime, as the government continued to function, through the DSBs for example, as the *mai-bap* to the military districts. It could plausibly be argued that this was more easily carried out in the Punjab than elsewhere, as the civil officers in the Punjab, used to combining judicial, administrative and revenue powers in a non-regulation province, were, by training and instinct, more adept at incorporating the additional military function in their execution of duties once military requirements became paramount.

Until the late 1930s, the civil-military state in the Punjab served its purpose well. Communal unrest, communist disruptions and nationalist agitation were kept well at bay, and stability was carefully maintained in the key military districts of the province. But the relationship between the colonial state and its rural base (and military constituencies) had always hinged on a precarious balance of vested interests on either side. Loyalty and support were secured in return for patronage and special treatment. If that equation was disrupted, the relationship suffered. The special bond between the rural-military elites and the colonial state in the Punjab was severely tested during the Second World War.

Between 1939 and 1945 the civil-military regime in the Punjab managed a successful mobilization process, despite the political uncertainties within the province, especially amongst the Sikhs, generated by the Muslim League's demand for Pakistan. It held the province intact throughout the early 1940s, although cracks were beginning to form in the garrison state. By the mid-1940s, larger all-India issues—the Muslim League's campaign for Pakistan, increasingly strident communal politics and impending self-government—"quite suddenly and traumatically broke the Punjab into two distinct parts upon Independence in 1947".[2] At Partition in 1947, the garrison province, by now militarized through its long association with the military, fell apart, and anarchy was unleashed upon the Punjab. It has been shown that nature of violence that accompanied the partition of the Punjab had a distinct "military quality",[3] and active as well as demobilized soldiers, skilled in the planning and execution of military operations, "were a conspicuous presence in the violence".[4]

The violence and anarchy notwithstanding, the rump of the civil-military regime, especially in western Punjab, was quickly restored to constitute the mainstay of the new state of Pakistan. In explicating the political inheritance of Pakistan, D.A. Low suggested that it is now necessary "to steer away from the more conventional approaches, via the history of the Pakistan movement, and move into territory ... whose full significance has yet to be appreciated".[5] The story of the militarization of colonial Punjab can therefore be crucial in explaining the character of the post-colonial state of Pakistan. While the "interplay of domestic, regional and international factors" in the post-1947 period may have facilitated the dominance of the bureaucracy and the military in the evolving structure of

[2] See D.A. Low, 'Introduction: Provincial Histories and the History of Pakistan', in D.A. Low (ed.), *The Political Inheritance of Pakistan*, London, 1991, p. 25.

[3] See, for example, Indivar Kamtekar, 'The End of the Colonial State in India, 1942–47', Ph.D. dissertation, University of Cambridge; and Swarna Aiyar, '"August Anarchy": The Partition Massacres in Punjab, 1947', in D.A Low and Howard Brasted (eds.), *Freedom, Trauma and Continuities: Northern India and Independence*, New Delhi, 1998, pp. 15–38.

[4] Aiyar, '"August Anarchy"', p. 25.

[5] D.A. Low (ed.), *The Political Inheritance of Pakistan*, p. 24.

the Pakistani state,[6] it can be suggested that the rise of a Punjabi controlled military-bureaucratic oligarchy which was organized and powerful enough to wrest control of, and dominate, the post-Independence state of Pakistan stemmed from developments in colonial Punjab during the first half of the twentieth century. First, in the post-1947 political adjustments, Punjab completely overshadowed the other constituent units of Pakistan, not only by the size of its population and economic potential, but mainly by its preponderance in the military and bureaucracy. Punjabis accounted for two-thirds of the Pakistani Army's rank and file and overwhelmingly dominated its officer corps. The province's landed aristocracy, with its close collaboration with the military and civil service, also remained among the most powerful elements in post-Partition Punjab. This civil-military regime, based on the "organic collaboration" between a Punjabi-dominated bureaucracy and army on the one hand, and the Punjabi landed families on the other, in turn provided the mainstay of the fragile Pakistani state and prevented it from collapse and disintegration, when the governors and bureaucrats, in managing the state and ensuring its very survival, were solidly backed by the military elite in Pakistan. The conjoining of the country's civil-military authorities was an outcome as much of tradition as of necessity. Indeed, as this study has shown, the alliance among the three most powerful groups in Pakistan— the military, bureaucracy and landlords—was an arrangement that had been worked out and perfected in the past, in colonial pre-Partition Punjab. The militarization of state and society therefore constituted the dominant theme that linked the pre-independence history of Punjab to the post-independence history of Pakistan.

---

[6] See Ayesha Jalal, *The State of Martial Rule. The Origins of Pakistan's Political Economy of Defence*, Cambridge, 1990.

Glossary

Akali	warrior ascetic; member of organization of Sikh zealots
Akhand Path	Uninterrupted reading of the Adi Granth, the Sikh holy scriptures, by a team of readers
Bagh	A garden
Bania	Hindu trader and moneylender
Biraderi	Kinship clan
Chaprassi	An orderly or messenger
Chowkidar	Watchman; guard over property
Crore	Ten million
Darbar	Ceremonial assembly
Doab	Tract between two rivers
Gurdwara	Sikh temple
Gurumukhi	Written script of the Sikhs
Jagir	Assignment of land revenue
Jagirdar	Holder of a jagir
Jangi Inams	Cash allowances for services rendered during war
Jatha	A band of Sikh volunteers
Jathedar	Leader of a jatha
Kamin	Artisan or village menial
Kesh	Uncut hair
Keshdhari	Sikh follower of the Khalsa order
Khalsa	Lit. "Pure". Religio-military fraternity instituted by Guru Gobind Singh in 1699; also used to refer to the orthodox Sikh community
Kirpan	A sword
Kisan	Cultivator
Lakh	One hundred thousand

Lambardar	Village headman
Mahant	Manager or caretaker of a Sikh temple (before the Gurdwara Act of 1925)
Manjha	Central Punjab tract, between Beas and Ravi Rivers
Maund	A unit of weight, approximately 80 pounds
Muafis	A small assignment of land revenue
Panchayat	Lit. "Council of Five", but generally refers to Council of Elders, heads of families; or applied to a committee of arbitrators
Pir	Sufi saint; a holy man
Purbiya	An "easterner"
Risaldar	A Viceroy Commissioned Officer in the cavalry
Sahajdhari	Lit. "slow converter"; refers to a Sikh who has not been initiated into the Khalsa order
Sajjada nashin	Shrine keeper
Sarwan	Camel attendant
Shahidi jatha	Lit. "Army of Martyrs"; Sikh militia
Shuddhi	"purification" ceremony conducted by Arya Samaj
Singh Sabha	Sikh Society; a movement of several such societies dedicated to the religious reform and revival of Sikhism
Sircar	Referring to the state or the government
Subedar	Infantry Viceroy Commissioned Officer in the Indian Army
Jemadar	Infantry Viceroy Commissioned Officer below the rank of *subedar*
Sufed posh	A yeoman grantee
Tehsil	Administrative unit below district, usually comprising a few hundred villages
Tehsildar	Officer in charge of tehsil
Udasi	Sikh order tracing its origin to the son of Guru Nanak, Sri Chand
Zail	Administrative unit; referring to a group of villages amalgamated for revenue purposes
Zamindar	Peasant proprietor; refers to landholder who pays revenue to the government directly

Bibliography

Primary Sources

Unpublished Sources

(i) Private Papers

India Office Library, London
Brayne Collections. MSS.EUR.F.152.
Chelmsford Papers. MSS.EUR.E.264.
Hailey Papers. MSS.EUR.E.220.
Linlithgow's Papers. MSS.EUR.F.125.
Montagu Collections. MSS.EUR.D.523.
Thompson Papers. MSS.EUR.F.137.

Centre for South Asian Studies, Cambridge
Rule Papers.
Salmon (W.H.B.) Papers.

National Army Museum, London
Papers of Field Marshall Lord Roberts.

Nehru Memorial Museum and Library, New Delhi, India
Sunder Singh Majithia's Papers.

(ii) Government Records

India Office Library, London
L/MIL series (Military Department Files).
L/P&J series (Public and Judicial Department Files).
L/WS (War Files).
P/series (Punjab Government Proceedings).
Home/Miscellaneous Records.

National Archives of India, New Delhi
Government of India, Home (Political) Department Files.

Civil Secretariat Archives, Lahore, Pakistan
Punjab Government, Home (Military) Department Files.

Deputy Commissioner's Record Office, Jhelum District;
Deputy Commissioner's Record Office, Rawalpindi District;
Deputy Commissioner's Record Office, Shahpur District, Pakistan
General/Political Files.

Published Sources

(i) Parliamentary Papers

Addresses Presented in India to the Viceroy and the Secretary of State for India,
1918, Cmd. 9178, Vol. 18.
Correspondences on the Organization of the Army, 1870, 1877, Vol. 62.
General Report of the Administration of the Punjab, 1856–1858, 1859, Vol. 18.
General Report of the Administration of the Punjab for the Years 1849–1850 and
1850–1851, 1854, Misc., Vol. 69.
Letter from the Government of India, dated 5 March 1919, and Enclosures on the
Question Raised in the Report on Indian Constitutional Reforms, 1919, Cmd.
1923, Vol. 27.
Papers Relating to Punjab, 1847–1849, 1849, Cmd. 1071, Vol. 41.
Report of Indian Constitutional Reforms (Montagu–Chelmsford Reforms), 1918,
1918, Cmd. 9109, Vol. 8.
Report of the Committee Appointed by Secretary of State for India to Inquire into
Question Connected with the Franchise and Other Matters Relating to Con-
stitutional Reforms, 1919, 1919, Cmd. 141, Vol. 16.
Report of the Indian Franchise Committee (Lothian) 1932, 1932, Cmd. 4086,
Vol. 8.
Report of the Commissioners Appointed to Inquire into the Organization of the
Indian Army, together with Minutes of Evidence and Appendix, 1859, Cmd.
2515, Vol. 5.
Report of Committee Appointed to Investigate the Disturbances in the Punjab,
1920, Cmd. 681, Vol. 14.
Report of Committee Appointed by the Secretary of State to Enquire into the Ad-
ministration and Organization of the Army in India (Esher Committee), 1919–
20, Cmd. 943, Vol. 14.
Reports of the Local Governments on the Working of the Reformed Constitution,
1923, 1924–1925, Cmd. 2361, Vol. 10.
Returns of Actual Strength of Queen's and East India Company's Forces in the
Three Presidencies and the Punjab, 1859, Session 2, Vol. 23.

Returns Showing Results of Election in India, 1921, Punjab Legislative Command, 1921, 1921 Cmd. 1261, Vol. 26.

Returns Showing Results of Elections in India, 1923, Results in the Punjab, 1923, Cmd. 2154, Vol. 18.

Views of Government upon Reports of Lord Southborough's Committee, 1919, 1919, Cmd. 176, Vol. 16.

(ii) Punjab Land Settlement Literature

Punjab District Gazetteers

Craik, H.D., *Land Settlement Report, Amritsar District, 1910–1914* (Lahore, 1914), IOR: V/2/27/314/451.

Joseph, E., *Land Settlement Report, 1905–1910* (Lahore, 1910), IOR: V/27/314/618.

Leigh, M.S., *Land Settlement Report, Shahpur District, 1911–1917* (Lahore, 1918), IOR: V/27/314/621.

Purser, W. C., and **Fanshawe, A. C.,** *Land Settlement Report, Rohtak District, 1873–1877* (Lahore, 1880), IOR: V/27/314/6167.

Talbot, W. S., *Land Settlement Report, Jhelum, 1895–1901* (Lahore 1902), IOR: V/27/314/544.

Thompson, R. G., *Land Settlement Report, Jhelum District, 1874–1880* (Lahore, 1883), IOR: V/27/314/542–43.

(iii) Other Government Publications

Government of India, Census of India, 1901, Vol. 17, *The Punjab, its Feudatories and the Northwest Frontier Province, Report by Rose, H.A.* (Simla, 1902).

Government of India, Census of India, 1921, Vol. 15, *Punjab and Delhi, Report by Middleton, L.* (Lahore, 1923).

Government of India, Census of India, 1881, *Report on the Census of the Punjab, Report by Ibbetson, Denzil Charles Jeffrf* (Calcutta, 1883).

India's Contribution to the War. IOR: V/27/281/32.

Punjab Electoral Statistics and Maps (Lahore, 1921). IOR: Pos. 5546.

Punjab Administrative Report, 1851, 1915–1935. (Lahore, 1851, 1915–1935).

Punjab Government Records, Vol. 7 and 8 (Lahore, 1911).

War Histories of the Punjab Districts. Pos. 5540, 5545 and 5547.

Punjab Legislative Assembly Proceedings.

(iv) Newspapers

The Tribune (Lahore).

Secondary Sources

Books and Articles

'Army Review' in *Calcutta Review*, Vol. 26 (June–December, 1956).

Alam, Muzaffar, *Crisis of Empire in Mughal North India: Awadh and the Punjab, 1707–48*, Delhi, 1986.

Alavi, Seema, *The Sepoys and the Company. Tradition and Transition in Northern India, 1770–1830*, Delhi, 1995.

Ali, Imran, *The Punjab Under Imperialism: 1885–1947*, Delhi, 1989.

Anderson, M. S., *Britain's Discovery of Russia, 1553–1815*, London, 1958.

Andrzejewski, Stanislaw, *Military Organization and Society*, London, 1954.

Baird, J. G. A., (ed.), *Private Letters of the Marquess of Dalhousie*, Edinburgh, 1911.

Bajwa, Fauja Singh, *The Military System of the Sikhs*, Delhi, 1964.

Baker, C. J., *The Politics of South India, 1920–1937*, Cambridge, 1976.

Barrier, N. G., *The Punjab Land Alienation Bill of 1900*, Durham, 1966.

————, 'Punjab Disturbances of 1907: Government Reponses', in *Modern Asian Studies*, Vol. 1(1), 1967.

Barstow, A. E., *Recruiting Handbooks for the Indian Army: Sikhs*, Calcutta, 1898.

Bayly, C. A., *Indian Society and the Making of the British Empire*, Cambridge, 1988.

Benians, E. A. et al., *The Cambridge History of the British Empire*, Vol. 3, Cambridge, 1959.

Bingley, A.H., *Handbook on the Sikhs*, Simla, 1899.

Bond, Brian, *War and Society in Europe, 1870–1970*, London, 1983.

Bose, Sugata, and Jalal, Ayesha, *Modern South Asia: History, Culture and Political Economy*, Delhi, 1999.

Bosworth-Smith, R., *Life of John Lawrence*, Vol. 2, London, 1883.

Brown, Judith M., *Gandhi and Civil Disobedience*, Cambridge, 1977.

————, *Modern India: The Origins of an Asian Democracy*, Delhi, 1985.

Chowdhry, Prem, 'Social Support Base and Electoral Politics: The Congress in Colonial Southeast Punjab', in *Modern Asian Studies*, Vol. 25(4), 1991.

————, *Punjab Sikhs and the Role of Chhottu Ram*, New Delhi, 1984.

Clayton, Anthony, *The British Empire as Superpower*, London, 1986.

Coupland, Reginald, *The Indian Problem, 1833–1935*, Oxford, 1968.

Curtis, Lionel, *Dyarchy*, London, 1920.

Danzig, Richard, 'The Announcement of August 20th 1917', in *Journal of Asian Studies*, Vol. 27(1), 1986.

Darling, Malcolm, *Rusticus Loquitur, or The Old Light and The New in The Punjab Villages*, London, 1930.

————, *Wisdom and Waste*, London, 1934.

Darling, Malcolm, *The Punjab Peasant in Prosperity and Debt,* London, 1936.
Datta, V. N., *1919 Disturbances,* Ludhiana, 1969.
————— (ed.), *New Light on the Punjab Disturbances in 1919,* (Vols. 6 and 7 of Disorders Inquiry Committee Evidence), Simla, 1975.
Dewey, Clive J. (ed.), *Arrested Development in India,* Delhi, 1988.
—————, *The Settlement Literature of the Greater Punjab,* New Delhi, 1991.
Dodwell, H. H., *The Cambridge History of India,* Vol. 6, Cambridge, 1932.
Ellinwood, Dewitt C. and **Pradhan, S. D.** (eds.), *India and World War One,* Delhi, 1978.
Falcon, L. W., *Handbook on Sikhs for Use of Regimental Officers,* Allahabad, 1896.
Farwell, Byron, *Armies of the Raj: From the Mutiny to Independence, 1858–1947,* London, 1986.
Fox, Richard, *Lions of the Punjab: Culture in the Making,* New Delhi, 1987.
French, David, 'The Dardanelles, Mecca, Kut: Prestige as a Factor in the British Eastern Strategy, 1914–1916', in *War and Society,* Vol. 5, 1987.
Gilmartin, David, *Islam and Empire: Punjab and the Making of Pakistan,* Berkeley, 1988.
Gleason, J. H., *The Genesis of Russophobia in Great Britain,* Cambridge, 1950.
Government of India, *Army in India and Its Evolution,* Calcutta, 1924.
Griffin, Lepel, et. al., *Chiefs and Families of Note in the Punjab* (Rev. Edn.), Lahore, 1910.
Grajdansev, Andrew, 'India's Wartime Economic Difficulties', *Pacific Affairs,* Vol. 16(3), June 1983.
Grover, D. R., *Civil Disobedience in the Punjab,* Delhi, 1987.
Gulati, K.L., *Akalis Past and Present,* New Delhi, 1974.
Gwynn, C., *Imperial Policing,* London, 1939.
Habib, Irfan, *The Agrarian System of Mughal India,* Delhi, 1963.
Heathcote, T. A., *The Indian Army: The Garrison of British Imperial India, 1822–1922,* London, 1974.
Heeger, G. A., 'Growth of the Congress Movement in the Punjab, 1920–40', in *Journal of Asian Studies,* Vol. 32(1), (1972)
Hussain, Azim, *Mian Fazl-i-Hussain: A Political Biography,* London, 1966.
Ingram, E., *The Beginning of the Great Game in Asia, 1838–1834,* Oxford, 1979.
Isemonger, F. C., and **Slattery, J. S.,** *An Account of the Ghadr Conspiracy, 1913–1915,* Lahore, 1919.
Jones, Kenneth, 'Communalism in the Punjab: The Arya Samaj's Contribution', in *Journal of Asian Studies,* Vol. 28(1), 1968.
Josh, Bhagwan, *Communist Movement in the Punjab, 1926–1947,* Delhi, 1979.
Josh, Sohan Singh, *Tragedy of Komagata Maru,* New Delhi, 1975.
Juergensmeyer, Mark (ed.), *Sikh Studies: Comparative Perspectives on a Changing Tradition,* Berkeley and New Delhi, 1979.
Kapur, Rajiv, *Sikh Separatism: The Politics of Faith,* London, 1987.
Kaye, J. W., *History of the Sepoy War in India,* Vol. 2, London, 1867.

Kolff, Dirk H.A., *Naukar, Rajput, Sepoy: An Ethno-History of the Military Market in North India,* Cambridge, 1990.

Kumar, R. (ed.), *Essays on Gandhian Politics: The Rowlatt Satyagraha of 1919,* Oxford, 1971.

Lary, Diana, *Warlord Soldiers: Chinese Common Soldiers, 1911–1937,* Cambridge, 1985.

Leigh, M. S., *Punjab and the War,* Lahore, 1922.

Low, D. A. (ed.), *Soundings in Modern South Asian History,* London, 1968.

_____, 'The Government of India and the First Non-Cooperation Movement, 1920–1922', in *Journal of Asian Studies,* Vol. 25(2), 1966.

_____ (ed.), *Congress and the Raj: Facets of the Indian Struggle, 1917–47,* London, 1971.

_____ (ed.), *The Political Inheritance of Pakistan,* London, 1991.

_____, 'Pakistan and India: Political Legacies from the Colonial Past' in *South Asia, Special Issue,* Vol. 25(2), 2002.

Major, Andrew J., *Return to Empire. Punjab under the Sikhs and British in the mid-Nineteenth Century,* New Delhi, 1996.

Mansergh, N. and **Lumby, E.W.R.** (eds.), *Constitutional Relations between Great Britain and India: The Transfer of Power, 1942–47,* Vols 1–12, London, 1970–83.

Marwick, A., *War and Social Change in the Twentieth Century,* London, 1977.

Mason, Philip, *A Shaft of Sunlight: Memories of a Varied Life,* London, 1978.

_____, *A Matter of Honour: An Account of the Indian Army, Its Officers and Men,* London, 1974.

Maynard, John, 'The Sikh Problem in the Punjab, 1920–23', in *The Contemporary Review,* Vol. 124, July-December, 1923.

Mustapha Kamal Pasha, *Colonial Political Economy: Recruitment and Underdevelopment in the Punjab,* Karachi, 1998.

McCleod, W. H., *The Sikhs: History, Religion and Society,* New York, 1989.

_____, *Evolution of the Sikh Community: Five Essays,* Delhi, 1975.

McInnes, Colin, and **Sheffield, G. D.,** *Warfare in the Twentieth Century: Theory and Practice,* London, 1988.

McMunn, G. A., *Armies in India,* London, 1911.

_____, *The Martial Races of India,* London, 1933.

McNeill, W. H., *The Pursuit of Power: Technology, Armed Forces and Society since A.D. 1000,* Oxford, 1983.

Minault, Gail, *The Khalifat Movement: Religious Symbolism and Political Mobilization in India,* Delhi, 1982.

Mitra, H. N., (ed.), *Indian Annual Register, 1924,* Vol. 2 (reprinted), Delhi, 1988.

Mitra, Subrata Kumar (ed.), *The Post-Colonial State in Asia,* New York, 1990.

Mollo, Boris, *The Indian Army,* Poole, 1986.

Montagu, E. S. (ed. Venetia Montagu), *An Indian Diary,* London, 1930.

Narain, Brij, *India in Crisis,* Allahabad, 1934.

Nehru, Motilal, *The Voice of Freedom: Selected Speeches of Motilal Nehru,* Bombay, 1961.

Noon, Firoz Khan, *From Memory,* Lahore, 1969.

O'Dwyer, Michael, *India as I Knew It,* London, 1925.

Omissi, David, '"Martial Races": Ethnicity and Security in Colonial India 1858–1939', in *War and Society,* Vol. 9, 1991.

Omissi, David, *The Sepoy and the Raj: The Indian Army, 1860–1940,* London, 1995.

Oren, S., 'The Sikhs, Congress and the Unionists in British Punjab, 1937–1945', in *Modern Asian Studies,* Vol. 8(3), Cambridge, 1974.

Page, D., *Prelude to Partition: The Indian Muslims and the Imperial System of Control, 1920–1932,* Delhi, 1932.

Peers, Douglas, *Between Mars and Mammon: Colonial Armies and the Garrison State in Early Nineteenth Century India,* London, 1995.

Petrie, D., *Developments in Sikh Politics, 1900–1911,* Chief Khalsa Dewan, Lahore, n.d..

Philips, C. H. (ed.), *Politics and Society in India,* London, 1963.

Prasad, Bishewar (ed.), *Official History of the Indian Armed Forces in the Second World War,* Calcutta, 1956.

Puri, Harish K., *The Ghadr Movement: Ideology, Organization and Strategy,* Amritsar, 1983.

Rai, Satya M., *Legislative Politics and the Freedom Struggle in the Punjab, 1897–1947,* Delhi, 1984.

Ram, Sita (ed. James Lunt), *From Sepoy to Subedar,* London, 1988.

Reeves, P. D., *Landlords and Government in Uttar Pradesh: A Study in the Relations until Zamindari Abolition,* Bombay, 1991.

Robb, Peter, *Government of India and Political Reforms,* Oxford, 1976.

Roberts, F., *Forty One Years in India: From Subaltern to Commander-in-Chief,* London, 1897.

Sahni, Ruchi Ram (ed. Ganda Singh), *Struggle for Reforms in the Sikh Shrines,* Sikh Itihas Research Board, SGPC, Amritsar, n.d..

Sandhu, K. S., *Indians in Malaya: Immigration and Settlement, 1786–1957,* Cambridge, 1969.

Singh, Harbans, and **Barrier, N. G.** (eds.), *Punjab Past and Present: Essays in Honour of Ganda Singh,* Patiala, 1976.

Singh, Mohinder, *The Akali Movement,* Delhi, 1974.

Singh, Madan Paul, *Indian Army Under the East India Company,* Delhi, 1976.

Singh, Khushwant, *History of the Sikhs,* Vols. 1 and 2, Delhi, 1986.

Spate, O. H. K. et al. *India, Pakistan and Ceylon: The Regions,* London (reprint), 1960.

Stokes, Eric (ed. C.A. Bayly), *The Peasants Armed: The Indian Rebellion of 1857,* Oxford, 1986.

Talbot, Ian, 'Deserted Collaborators: The Political Background of the Rise and Fall of the Punjab Unionist Party, 1923–47', in *International Journal of Commonwealth History*, Vol. 11(1), 1982.

_____, *Provincial Politics and the Pakistan Movement: The Growth of the Muslim League in North-West and North-East India, 1937–47*, Karachi, 1988.

_____, *The British and the Punjab*, Oxford, 1986.

_____, *Khizr Tiwana, the Punjab Unionist Party and the Partition of India*, Surrey, 1996.

Tan, Tai Yong, 'Maintaining the Military Districts: Civil–Military Integration and District Soldiers' Boards in the Punjab, 1919–1939', in *Modern Asian Studies* Vol. 28(4), 1994.

_____, 'Sikh Responses to the Demand of Pakistan, 1940–47', in *International Journal of Punjab Studies*, Vol. 1(2), 1994.

_____, 'Assuaging the Sikhs: Government Response to the Akali Movement, 1920–1925, in *Modern Asian Studies*, Vol. 29(3), 1995.

_____, 'An Imperial Home-Front: Punjab and the First World War', in *The Journal of Military History*, Vol. 64, April 2000.

Thackwell, E. J., *Narrative of the Second Sikh War, 1848–1849*, London, 1851.

Trench, Charles Chenevix, *The Indian Army and the King's Enemies, 1901–1947*, London, 1988.

Trevaskis, Hugh Kennedy, *Land of the Five Rivers: From Earliest Times to 1890*, Oxford, 1890.

Turner, John (ed.), *Britain and the First World War*, London, 1988.

Van den Dungen, P. H. M., *The Punjab Tradition: Influence and Authority in Nineteenth-Century India*, London, 1972.

Voigt, Johannes, *India in the Second World War*, New Delhi, 1987.

Wace, F. C., *Punjab Colonization Manual*, Lahore, 1936.

Washbrook, D.A., 'India, 18180–1860: Two Faces of Colonialism', in Andrew Porter (ed.), *The Oxford History of the British Empire: Vol. III: The Nineteenth-Century*, Oxford, 1999.

Wikeley, J.M., *Punajb Mussalmans*, Calcutta, 1915.

Willcocks, James, *With the Indians in France*, London, 1920.

Yadav, Kripal Chand, *Elections in the Punjab, 1920–47*, New Delhi, 1987.

Yang, Anand, 'An Institutional Shelter: The Courts of Wards in late 19th Century Bihar', in *Modern Asian Studies*, Vol. 13(2), 1974.

Yapp, Malcolm, *Strategies of British India, Iran and Afghanistan*, Oxford, 1970.

Unpublished Dissertations/Theses

Brief, David, 'The Punjab and Recruitment to the Indian Army, 1846–1918', unpublished M. Litt. dissertation, Oxford University, 1978.

Burns, J.M., 'Sir Michael O'Dwyer and the Polarization of Punjab Politics', unpublished thesis for Diploma in History, Cambridge University.

Cheema, Amrita, 'Punjab Politics, 1919–1923', unpublished D. Phil. dissertation, Oxford University, 1987.

Dewey, Clive, 'The Army as Safety Net: Military Service and Peasant Stratification in British Punjab'; 'The Rise of the Martial Caste: Changes in the Composition of the Indian Army, 1878–1914', unpublished seminar and conference papers.

Dewey Clive, 'The Official Mind and the Problem of Agrarian Indebtedness, 1870–1910', unpublished Ph.D dissertation, Cambridge University, 1973.

Dharmalingam, Vanaja, 'The Politics of Food and the British Raj, 1939–45', unpublished BA Honours thesis, National University of Singapore, 1992.

Harcourt, Max, 'Revolutionary Networks in Northern Indian Politics 1907–1935: A Case Study of the Terrorist Movement in Delhi, Punjab, the UP and the Adjacent Princely States', unpublished Ph.D. dissertation, Sussex University, 1972.

Index

About the Author

Tan Tai Yong is Associate Professor of History and Dean, Faculty of Arts and Social Sciences, National University of Singapore (NUS). He has written extensively on Sikh and Punjabi history, as well as on Southeast Asia and Singapore. His recent publications include *The Aftermath of Partition in South Asia* (co-authored, 2000) and *The Transformation of Southeast Asia: International Perspectives on De-colonisation* (co-edited, 2003). He was Head of the History Department at the NUS from 2000 to 2003, and is currently serving as Acting Director of the newly established Institute of South Asian Studies at the NUS.